A

. . .

B O O K

ıne Philip E. Lilienthal imprint
honors special books
in commemoration of a man whose work
at the University of California Press
from 1954 to 1979
was marked by dedication to young authors
and to high standards in the field of Asian Studies.
Friends, family, authors, and foundations have together
endowed the Lilienthal Fund, which enables the Press
to publish under this imprint selected books
in a way that reflects the taste and judgment
of a great and beloved editor.

The publisher gratefully acknowledges the generous support
of the Philip E. Lilienthal Asian Studies Endowment Fund
of the University of California Press Foundation, which
was established by a major gift from Sally Lilienthal.

# Ancestral Leaves

# Ancestral Leaves

*A Family Journey through Chinese History*

Joseph W. Esherick

UNIVERSITY OF CALIFORNIA PRESS
*Berkeley   Los Angeles   London*

University of California Press, one of the most distinguished university
presses in the United States, enriches lives around the world by advancing
scholarship in the humanities, social sciences, and natural sciences. Its
activities are supported by the UC Press Foundation and by philanthropic
contributions from individuals and institutions. For more information,
visit www.ucpress.edu.

University of California Press
Berkeley and Los Angeles, California

University of California Press, Ltd.
London, England

Library of Congress Cataloging-in-Publication Data

Esherick, Joseph.
    Ancestral leaves : a family journey through Chinese history / Joseph W.
Esherick.
        p.   cm.
    Includes bibliographical references and index.
    ISBN 978-0-520-26699-5 (cloth : alk. paper)
    ISBN 978-0-520-26700-8 (pbk. : alk. paper)
    1. Ye family.   2. China—Biography.   3. China—Genealogy.
4. China—History.   I. Title.
    CS1169.Y42   2011
    929'.20951—dc22                                        2010024831

Manufactured in the United States of America

19   18   17   16   15   14   13   12   11
10   9   8   7   6   5   4   3   2   1

This book is printed on Cascades Enviro 100, a 100% postconsumer waste,
recycled, de-inked fiber. FSC recycled certified and processed chlorine free.
It is acid free, Ecologo certified, and manufactured by BioGas energy.

*In memory of Ye Duzhuang*

# CONTENTS

# ILLUSTRATIONS

## FIGURES

MAPS

TABLES

PREFACE

The Ye family from the Yangzi riverside city of Anqing—later of Kaifeng, Tianjin, and Beijing—was neither a great lineage of China's highest elite nor an ordinary Chinese family. It was an elite family of a middling sort. It rose to prominence in the nineteenth century, fighting floods and rebels in Henan, but Ye family service in the Anhui Army received little mention in histories of that famous force. Two generations later, a Ye served briefly as police commissioner in Tianjin, and the family had close enough relations to President Yuan Shikai of the early republic that one of Yuan's grandsons was adopted into the Ye family; but the Tianjin newspapers rarely mention the family. In the twentieth century, the sons of the former police commissioner attended the prestigious Nankai Middle School in Tianjin, and most went on to elite universities in the 1930s, until war with Japan interrupted their education. In the postwar period, two became prominent in the Democratic League (a party of intellectuals seeking a liberal middle course between Communists and Nationalists), so that the name Ye Duyi is recognizable to many Chinese. Another brother, Ye Duzheng, is a leading atmospheric scientist in China's Academy of Sciences who also served in the People's Congress. Two others reached "high cadre" status with party secretary positions at the New China News Agency and the Central Party School. Yet none were decision makers in the political leadership of the People's Republic of China (PRC). The family managed to maintain elite status in the latter part of the Qing dynasty (1644–1911), under the Republic of China (1912–49), and in the People's Republic (1949– ), never rising to the top, but never falling to the level of the general population.

The Chinese character for the surname Ye (pronounced "yeah") also means "leaf," and that alternate meaning seems particularly appropriate for this family. On the one hand, the many generations of the Ye lineage were attached to different branches of one tree, and the family genealogy traces them to a common root. On the other hand, at critical points in the family history, these "leaves" blew about in the turbulent winds of China's modern history. The account here follows the lives of these Ye descendants over the past two centuries, seeking, through their lives, to humanize the vast processes of rebellion, invasion, war, and revolution that shaped modern China.

In studies of Europe and America, there has been no shortage of family histories and histories of the family, and many of these have explored the changes we associate with the modern transition: the weakening of patriarchal authority, the gradual disappearance of large elite households, the rise of the nuclear family, the increasing emphasis on love and mutual affection between spouses, attention to the nurturing and education of children. European and American family histories have also permitted an exploration of private life, with letters and diaries providing windows into the realm of emotions and intimate interpersonal relations. Through such histories, we have learned much about the intersection of private and public realms— the interaction of large-scale economic, cultural, social, and political transformation on the one hand and changes within individual families on the other.[1]

Despite the well-attested importance of the family in Chinese society, and although some of these same processes have affected the Chinese family (the decline of patriarchy, the rise of the nuclear family, the growing importance of the spousal bond), the literature on Chinese family history is far less extensive.[2] The scarcity of personal correspondence before the twentieth century and the lack of introspection in Chinese diaries make it extremely difficult to write the same sort of intimate history of family life that one sees in the West. China, of course, has a long tradition of compiling genealogies of prominent lineages. The Ye family genealogy has been an invaluable source for this study, allowing me to trace the lineage back to the fourteenth century and probe the ethical principles embedded in its family instructions, and providing important biographical material from the nineteenth century. But such genealogies have their limitations as historical sources: their focus is entirely on the male patriline; their purpose is to glorify the family name, which leads to selective coverage; and their attention to interpersonal family dynamics is largely confined to virtuous displays of filial piety or paternalistic generosity. To get beyond these limitations, I have relied on a large collection of poems from the nineteenth century and conducted extensive interviews of the surviving members of the generation born in the early twentieth century.

This book traces the history of the Ye family from its founding in the fourteenth century to the present, but it focuses especially on the nineteenth and twentieth centuries, for which reliable historical documentation is most plentiful. My goal is to put a human face on this turbulent period of Chinese history, to capture the lived experience of one Chinese family during a critical epoch of social and political change. The story begins with the vast destructive rebellions of the nineteenth century, examining the private and public lives of men who rose to prominence in the imperial bureaucracy through their success in suppressing rebels and contending with natural disasters. The next generations witnessed the aggressive assault of Western and Japanese imperialism, the collapse of empire, and the travails of the new republic. By the early twentieth century, the key branch of the family had moved from the agricultural heartland in Anhui and Henan provinces to the north China treaty port of Tianjin. There it experienced the turmoil of the warlord era and the advance of Japanese imperialism. When war with Japan broke out in 1937, the family scattered, and the young men followed separate paths through the period of war and revolution. The founding of the People's Republic of China brought new opportunities and new challenges, with ceaseless political campaigns culminating in the persecutions of the Cultural Revolution. Too often, histories treat this long and troubled period of rebellion, invasion, war, and revolution as the product of large impersonal social and political processes or the result of political machinations by a small group of national leaders. This book aims to humanize that history, to explore how individuals and families experienced this momentous era of historical change.

I have also sought to show that the story of the Ye family is more than a tale of personal victimization. Many books (mostly by émigré authors) already recount the suffering that so many endured under Mao's regime.[3] The members of the Ye family certainly suffered as well, but they were not simply passive victims; they were also active participants in the making of history. The long sweep of this book's coverage permits a broader perspective on the changes that swept the family and the nation, and the mutually constitutive relationship between family and sociopolitical change.

The first five chapters of this book describe the Ye family in the late imperial (Ming-Qing) period. The closest focus is on a father-son pair of officials, who rose during the mid-nineteenth-century rebellions and their massively destructive suppression. These were conservative Confucian literati, for whom the most important and always-linked virtues were filial piety toward one's ancestors and loyalty to one's ruler. The same ethical principles applied in the public and private realms: "Governing the people is like governing a family," wrote the elder of these two gentlemen.[4] His son was tutored at home by uncles and then mentored by his father while assisting with the latter's official duties. Family obligations and official responsibilities were joined, and in these men's rise through the imperial bureaucracy, each profited from the merit of his kin.

Conservative though the values of the late Qing Ye generation might have been, the men's official careers reflected important changes in imperial governance. Though all were well educated in the Confucian classics and spent years of their youth preparing for the examinations that would qualify them for office, they never passed beyond the lowest-level exams. Their official appointments came more from demonstrated competence as local administrators. In this career path, they reflected the breakdown of the long-established system of examination-based recruitment, which would end with the abolition of the exams in 1905. By that time, the dynasty was tottering on its last legs, and the Ye family had moved from the interior to the coastal treaty port of Tianjin, where the tides of change would utterly transform the twentieth-century family and twentieth-century China.

The middle chapters (7–10) of this book treat the republican era (1912–49). This chaotic period began with an unruly decade of warlord rule, then saw a semblance of order under the Nationalist Party, followed by all-out war with Japan from 1937 to 1945, and ended with a quick but bloody civil war from which Mao Zedong and the Chinese Communist Party emerged victorious in 1949. For the Ye family, the most significant aspect of this era was the new set of influences that shaped the lives of the young men once they left the family compound and its home schooling. The younger brothers who boarded at school achieved a new level of personal independence that manifested itself in every aspect of their lives, from the rejection of family-arranged marriages to involvement in sports and drama groups and the embrace of patriotic radicalism and revolutionary politics. The war years further weakened family bonds as the Ye brothers scattered to pursue a variety of political, academic and career paths, their lives shaped more by their peers, their personalities, and their social environment than by their place in the family structure.

The PRC years (chapters 11–13) saw the reconstitution of the family in a new form: as a nuclear family with a husband-wife pair and their children. The spousal bond became more important than ever, though it was often tested in the turmoil of political campaigns. The new more powerful party-state expanded its role in the education of children, most of whom attended nursery school from an early age. Especially during the Cultural Revolution, the Communist Party often challenged the family, urging children to "draw a clear line" between themselves and parents accused of counter-revolutionary crimes. The contrast between this period and the imperial era, when the family and the dynasty were governed by a parallel set of rules, is most stark. But by the end of the Cultural Revolution, the family, ironically, emerged stronger than ever. In the bitter political and factional struggles of that era, people learned that family ties were the most reliable. The family had a new form, to be sure, but it promised a degree of emotional comfort and private personal space that was quite unprecedented in Chinese history.

This book is founded on the proposition (borrowed shamelessly from feminist theory) that "the personal is political." We cannot fully understand large historical processes unless we appreciate their impact on individual human lives. Conversely, the small habits of personal and daily life help shape the larger society in which people live and determine the course of history. For this reason, I have sought to bring major historical events and transitions down to the level of individual lives.

I have been able to do so only because a unique set of circumstances provided access to an extraordinary body of documentation on the Ye family. Almost twenty years ago, my father-in-law, Ye Duzhuang, started composing a record of his life for his two granddaughters. These handwritten memoirs inspired several of his brothers to recall their pasts, and in 1994–95, my wife and I began collecting many hours of oral histories from these brothers and their children, as well as documentary records from the schools they attended in the 1930s. After Duzhuang's death, his daughter was allowed to copy his personnel dossier from the agriculture academy where he worked, and this file included vital confidential information on the political campaigns of the 1950s. In addition, fragments of his and his wife's diaries survive. The project achieved significant historical depth when we discovered a manuscript autobiography *(nianpu)* of the most prominent nineteenth-century scion of the family in the rare books section of the Beijing Library and were able to copy memorials of this official from the First Historical Archives. In the spring of 1995, we returned to the ancestral home in Anqing, where distant family members generously allowed us to copy a well-preserved 1944 edition of the Ye family genealogy. The Ye brothers in Beijing had not seen such a genealogy since their childhood. The decades of war and revolution had destroyed this key link to their family's past, but in the countryside outside Anqing, the record had been preserved. Finally, Mi Chu Wiens of the Library of Congress located a massive twenty-volume collection of poems from a nineteenth-century ancestor of the family. These poems provided invaluable insight into the personal and political lives of the late imperial family.

These memoirs, oral histories, school records, dossier, diaries, genealogy, biographies, memorials, essays, and poems of the Ye family members have permitted a reasonably detailed account of family life from the early nineteenth century to the present, with context provided by local gazetteers, newspapers, student publications, and secondary works on the various places and periods in which the family lived and worked. My wife and I could not have collected these materials and I could not have written this book without the assistance of a number of people and institutions throughout the world. I received generous financial support from a University of California Presidential Fellowship in the Humanities and the Hsiu Endowment for Chinese Studies at the University of California, San Diego. The First Historical Archives in Beijing, the Beijing Library, Peking University Library, Tsinghua University Library, the library of the Institute of Modern History at the Chinese Academy of Sciences, the Tianjin Municipal Archives, the Tianjin Municipal Library, the library of the Tianjin Academy of Social Sciences, Nankai University Library, the Sophia University Library, Toyo Bunko, the Stanford University Library, the Library of Congress, the Center for Chinese Studies Library at the University of California, Berkeley, the library at the University of California, San Diego, and the professional staff at all of these institutions have been most helpful in locating and providing access to key materials.

Students in my Chinese family history course and colleagues and friends offered many useful comments on the manuscript. I am indebted to William Rowe and Elizabeth Perry, readers for the University of California Press, and Linda Grove for many helpful suggestions, and to my colleagues Paul Pickowicz and especially Sarah Schneewind. Hardly a paragraph of the early chapters escaped without revision after Sarah's rigorous scrutiny. Ch'en Yung-fa read the manuscript with meticulous care and saved me from several embarrassing errors. Ye Baomin provided invaluable expert assistance in interpreting the poetry. Over the years, my graduate students at UCSD have influenced my thinking on this era of Chinese history in ways large and small. Michael Chang, Susan Fernsebner, and Charles Musgrove offered useful and perceptive comments on early drafts of several chapters; and Zheng Xiaowei helped as a research assistant. Wilson Kwan drafted the timelines, Steven Nakamura helped in the reproduction of many of the illustrations, and Bill Nelson drew the maps. At the University of California Press, Reed Malcolm expertly guided the manuscript through the review process, and Suzanne Knott and Adrienne Harris were particularly efficient, talented, and sensitive copyeditors. All of these people improved this book in more ways than I can count, and such shortcomings as remain are entirely the result as my own limitations as an author and scholar.

Above all, thanks go to the members of the Ye family who have contributed so much to this project over the years. My wife, Ye Wa, was an indispensable collaborator throughout the project, doing many of the early interviews, locating sources, helping with translations, and correcting many details of the narrative. My greatest regret is that I was unable to complete this book before many of those who contributed so much to this project had passed away. In the years since Ye Duzhuang drafted his first memoir, he and three of his brothers have departed this life. Because these brothers' lives spanned most of the twentieth century and form the heart of the recent story, I have made only a minimal attempt to extend the account into the generation of their children—most of whom are still in the midst of busy careers of such diversity that any coherent narrative would be next to impossible. For this reason, I end this tale at the close of the twentieth century and dedicate it to the memory of the man who inspired me to write, the late beloved Ye Duzhuang.

# PART I

# The Imperial Era

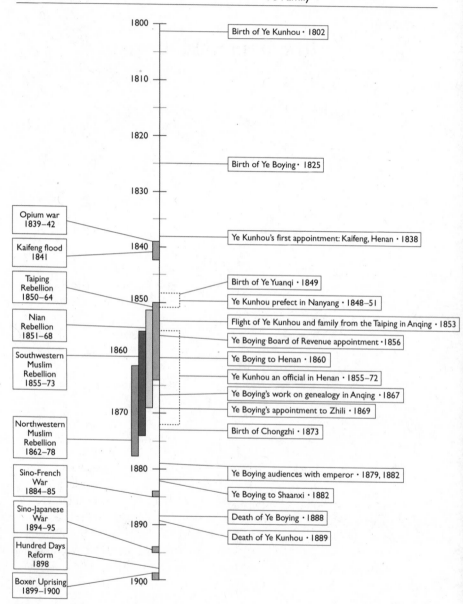

FIGURE 1. Nineteenth-century timeline.

# 1

## Fleeing the Long Hairs

In 1852, Ye Kunhou went home to bury his mother. The filial son, then fifty years old, was at the prime of his career as a local official in the north China province of Henan, along the Yellow River. He had distinguished himself by fighting floods and then pursuing bandits and rebels. At a recent awe-inspiring audience in the capital, the emperor had commended him for diligent service.[1] But the Confucian precepts of the imperial code required that an official resign his post for three years of mourning on the death of a parent. Together with his brother, he fulfilled his filial obligations by retiring to his home in the walled city of Anqing, to give his mother a proper burial.

Anqing, on the north bank of the Yangzi River, lies about six hundred kilometers upstream from Shanghai at the river's mouth. In the mid-nineteenth century, it was the provincial capital of Anhui. A fairly new province, Anhui had been split off from the large lower Yangzi province of Jiangnan only in 1662 and given a name that derived from its two largest prefectures, Anqing and Huizhou—the latter lying south of the Yangzi and renowned as a homeland of Chinese merchants.[2] Like other Chinese capital cities, Anqing was surrounded by a sturdy brick-faced wall, but the area within the wall measured only one square mile (2.5 square kilometers). With a population of perhaps seventy thousand, it was one of China's smallest provincial capitals. Commerce along this stretch of the Yangzi centered downstream at the port of Wuhu, and Anqing was primarily a political center—which was one reason scholar-officials like Ye Kunhou and his brothers moved there from the nearby village of their ancestors. Here they were close to official power and could enjoy the amenities of urban life: bookstores, teahouses, antique shops, picturesque temples and pavilions, and the company of their peers. A missionary in the early

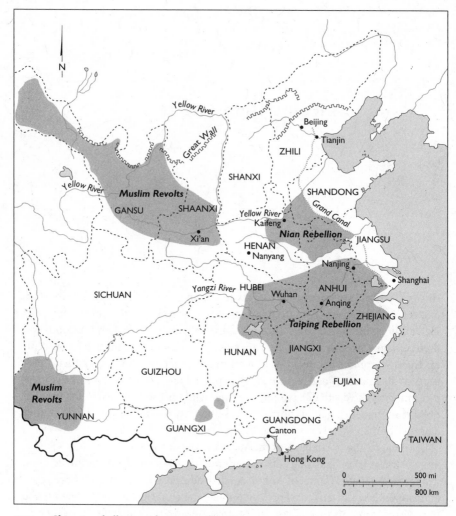

MAP 1. China in rebellion, mid–nineteenth century.

twentieth century reported that roughly one-fourth of the area within the walls was occupied by public buildings: the officials' *yamen* (as their combined office and living quarters were called), schools, jails, and temples. Anqing, in his words, was "a rather sleepy, conservative, comfortable place."[3]

In normal times, Anqing might have been sleepy and comfortable, but the mid-nineteenth century was not normal times. Indeed, no sooner had Ye Kunhou moved back to Anqing than the city found itself threatened by a massive rebel armada sailing down the Yangzi River. The rebels, known as the Taiping, were inspired by a quasi-Christian religious fervor (their leader conceived himself to be Jesus's younger brother) and an intense hatred of the China's Manchu ruling elite. The rebellion would wrack central China for over a decade, killing tens of millions and bringing unprecedented devastation. It was a watershed in China's modern history, but a cataclysm long in the making.

The Manchu dynasty, called the Qing (pronounced "ching"), had been ruling China since 1644. During the first two centuries, the country had enjoyed unprecedented prosperity. Long years of domestic peace, the spread of new subsistence crops from the New World (especially corn and sweet potatoes), commercial crops (cotton, peanuts, rapeseed, sesame), the handicraft production of silk and cotton textiles, an efficient market in grain, and a state-supported safety net of granaries provided the foundations for this prosperity. Famine relief in bad years meant that most people had enough to eat, clothing was relatively cheap and widely available, and young men could afford to marry and raise families. As a result, China's population tripled, approaching 450 million: growth that was initially a sign of prosperity but ultimately a demographic burden. The Qing state did not keep up with this economic and population growth, its revenues limited by a 1712 edict freezing the all-important land tax. Corruption spread, and officials covered up problems they were ill equipped to solve. When dikes and waterworks were not well maintained, floods became more serious. By the nineteenth century, the granary system was plagued by leaky warehouses, rotting rice, and false reporting: an efficient state response to famine was no longer possible.[4] Not long before he returned home, Ye Kunhou wrote a sad poem describing repeated floods in Anhui that left nine in ten people destitute: beggars filled the roads, people ate bark and weeds, and parents sold their children.[5]

The Qing state faced another problem—one scarcely mentioned in official documents. The Manchus were an ethnically alien conquest dynasty. From their homeland in the Northeast, they had conquered China in the seventeenth century. In some places, the conquest was extremely brutal, especially when Chinese men resisted the imposition of the Manchu hairstyle, which required them to shave their foreheads and keep a long braided queue. The conquering armies, organized in banners and including Mongols and ethnic Chinese (Han) from the Northeast, garrisoned key points throughout the empire, living in separate walled compounds. In the central government, every board (ministry) had two presidents: one Manchu and one Chinese. In provincial posts, Manchus and Han bannermen, descendants of the original allies, predominated.

Over time, the cultural differences between Manchus and Han gradually faded. Despite vigorous imperial efforts to define and maintain a distinct Manchu identity, the bannermen acculturated to the Chinese environment. By the nineteenth century, Manchus wrote and spoke in Chinese, educated their children in the Confucian classics, composed poetry, and absorbed the cultural norms of the Chinese literati. Their skills as horsemen and archers, which the Qing emperors promoted to preserve Manchu identity, declined markedly. Still, they were a separate and privileged elite, and resentment of their political dominance was natural.[6]

In the mid-nineteenth century, these domestic problems were exacerbated by European imperialism. Westerners had traded directly with China since the sixteenth century, buying silk, tea, and porcelain (known in Europe as "china"). In the late eighteenth century, the pace of trade picked up, especially as the English developed a taste for tea. Tea became Britain's prime Asian import. Heavily taxed (causing well-known problems in the American colonies), tea also provided invaluable revenues for the crown. But the British were unable to identify an export product to balance their imports of tea, silk, and china—until they began cultivating opium in India. The trade was illegal, but the Qing state, whose navy was inadequate to patrol its long coastline, proved powerless to stop it. In the nineteenth century, and especially in the 1830s, opium sales increased dramatically until silver—which had long flowed into China to pay for Europe's purchases—began to flow out. This brought a shortage of silver, a fall in prices, and a significant economic downturn. In addition, as is always the case with illegal drugs, the profits from opium sales were sufficient to corrupt the Chinese armed forces and officials in the coastal regions.

In 1839, the crisis came to a head. Determined to stop the opium flow, the emperor sent an imperial commissioner to Canton (or Guangzhou), the exclusive southern port for trade with the West. The commissioner closed opium dens, confiscated opium pipes, and punished addicts, and then sought to sanction the Western opium merchants. The British merchants persuaded their government to use the dispute as an opportunity to forcibly "open" China to trade. Soon the Opium War broke out. China's armies, neglected during long years of peace, were utterly unfit to confront this new challenge. In Ye Kunhou's words, "Half the soldiers on the registers are phony names [a padding of the rolls to enrich the officers]. / The old and the weak inherit their positions. / Men are drafted from the riff-raff of the towns and worthless rascals join the ranks."[7] The superior discipline, training, tactics, and military technology of the British Navy and its marines won a quick victory, sealed in the 1842 Treaty of Nanjing. Hong Kong was ceded to the British; several ports, including Shanghai, were opened to trade and Christian proselytizing; and the Qing suffered a humiliating defeat at the hands of the Western barbarians.[8]

In one of the world-shaping tragedies of modern history, China and the West confronted each other politically and militarily just at the point when the Qing empire was growing corrupt and entering a period of decline while the West, bursting with confidence from the advances of the scientific and industrial revolutions, was more convinced than ever of the superiority of its civilization. The Opium War that resulted from this fateful confrontation exacerbated the decline of Manchu rule. Unrest had been spreading for some time, in the form of banditry, secret societies, and small-scale rebellions by religious sectarians, ethnic minorities in mountain enclaves, and underemployed, unmarried, and rootless young men drawn to gambling and criminal activity. Opium smuggling provided new opportunities for secret societies, and British efforts to suppress piracy along the southern coast drove many brigands into inland waterways.

Amid this growing unrest, a frustrated scholar from the Canton region, who had repeatedly failed the civil service examinations, came to believe—after reading a Christian pamphlet—that he was the son of God and the younger brother of Jesus Christ. In the 1840s, Hong Xiuquan and a small band of devoted followers formed the God Worshippers Society in the ill-governed hill country of Guangxi province in southwestern China. Leaders of the God Worshippers, claiming to be possessed by the spirit of Jesus Christ or the Heavenly Father, offered prophecies, denounced immoral practices, cured sickness, succored the needy, and promised salvation for the faithful. The gentry elite in nearby towns became suspicious of this heterodox faith, reporting the group to the local authorities and harassing it with militia forces raised from their tenants and neighbors. But the God Worshippers attracted more and more followers, especially among the Hakka minority to which Hong belonged, poor charcoal burners and unemployed miners, other vulnerable groups seeking protection and support, and secret-society members willing to offer their fighting skills. By 1850, the government had grown sufficiently suspicious to move against this new religion, which reorganized itself as the Taiping ("Great Peace") Heavenly Kingdom and rose in open rebellion. The Taiping added a clear anti-Manchu message to its religious millenarianism. The Manchus were decried as alien "imps," and the Taiping displayed their anti-Manchu mission by abandoning the Qing-mandated hairstyle and marching forth with unshaved foreheads and loose tresses, which earned them the name "Long Hairs."[9]

For two years, the rebels fought and gathered strength in their southwestern hill-country base. Then in 1852 they broke out of government encirclement and headed north into central China, where the size of their army increased exponentially. By the end of the Chinese lunar year, the Taiping had captured the strategic cities of central China, and their vast fleet lay poised to move down the Yangzi toward Anqing and China's economic heartland in the lower Yangzi valley—down toward the ancestral home of the Ye family.

Back in Anqing, Ye Kunhou and his family mourned his departed mother. Neighbors came to console him, but after a while, the number of visitors declined, and he regretted his loss of official status: "When one's time comes, guests are plentiful; / When one's influence wanes, even relatives are distant."[10] He attended to family affairs—notably plans to build a proper lineage hall and compile a new edition of the genealogy. As the family's first official in many years, he was eager to establish the written record and ritual institutions that would preserve his family's place in local society.[11] He also relished the opportunity to relax, away from the cares of office. He had returned from Henan with an enormous collection of some 460 antiques; old friends still came to chat over wine and poetry, an important form of socializing among the literati; and he had a substantial library where he spent a good deal of time reading history, turning often to accounts of earlier dynasties in crisis.[12] The rebel advance was never far from his mind, and the city's lack of preparation distressed him. "From the walls, the sound of war drums; / Within the city, they are singing and dancing."[13] When disaster struck, it seemed appropriate and inevitable retribution: "The prosperity of Jiangnan [the lower Yangzi region] has reached the level of arrogant extravagance. / Out of such peace and happiness comes sudden change. / The flames of war foretell a disastrous punishment."[14]

The advance of the Taiping armada along the river toward Anqing sent the city into an uproar.[15] Strange omens foretold trouble: clouds without rain on a particular day, pear trees bearing melons, bamboo flowering across the city, rats fleeing, a falling meteorite.[16] Such portents suggested that the dynasty had failed to maintain cosmic harmony and was losing the Mandate of Heaven. The populace was growing uneasy. After the fall tax collection, the city's granaries were filled with rice, which the governor feared would be an attractive target for the rebels. Additional troops were requested to defend the city, but when two thousand soldiers arrived from neighboring Zhejiang province, Ye Kunhou's son Boying was not impressed: they were "short, small, timid and weak—most unreliable."[17] The governor sought help from the gentry—the local elite of former officials like Ye Kunhou, scholars who had passed the civil service examinations but never taken office, and other gentlemen whose wealth and status made them leaders of their communities. Ye Kunhou was asked to apply his experience fighting rebels in Henan to organize a local militia to defend the city. He responded by forming a gentry-led militia bureau, which first sought to identify Taiping spies who had infiltrated the city. He had little confidence in the governor, whom he found hopelessly weak: real power lay in the hands of the lieutenant governor, who in turn relied on an aide whose arrogance was unconstrained by moral principles. Ye Kunhou had good relations with another local official, the son of a colleague he had known in Henan, but this lower-ranking official could offer little help.[18] With the official establishment in disarray, no one thought the city could be defended, and residents prepared to flee. One commander, fearing that Taiping soldiers might use the dwellings along the outside of Anqing's walls to scale the walls or to protect sappers digging tunnels to blow up the city's defenses, ordered the houses destroyed—a desperate (though prudent) move that both angered and frightened the residents. Officials and gentry retreated to the relative safety of the countryside. The young Ye Boying took his large extended family by boat some fifty kilometers north to the hills of neighboring Tongcheng county, where a former official and colleague of his father offered refuge.[19] Back in the city, Chinese New Year came without celebration. Snow covered the ground. The markets were still. Most of the people had fled.[20]

Some four hundred kilometers upriver, on the first day of the Chinese New Year (February 8, 1853), the Taiping set forth from the central China city of Wuchang. A large ground force on both sides of the river protected a flotilla of some twenty thousand commandeered junks. In the middle of the fleet, the Taiping Heavenly King Hong Xiuquan rode in a majestic dragon boat, testifying to the imperial ambitions now added to his religious mission. The rebel army was virtually a nation on the move—perhaps five hundred thousand people in all, males and females in carefully segregated camps. Many were conscripts from the towns and cities the Taiping had already conquered, and not all would prove loyal to the cause. The immediate effect, however, was to produce such a massive force moving relentlessly down the Yangzi that resistance crumbled in city after city.[21]

Two weeks after the Taiping departed Wuchang, boats filled with refugees appeared on the river beyond Anqing's walls. Rumors flew that rebels were hidden in their midst. At dawn on the twenty-fourth, hundreds of rebel boats assembled on the south bank, opposite the city. The Qing defenders bombarded them with 189 antiquated cannons until the guns became too hot to take powder without exploding. Then the Taiping crossed the river and massed under the walls. The soldiers on the ramparts lowered themselves down ropes on the inside of the walls and fled. In the afternoon, the rebels scaled the walls, their war cries scattering the remaining defenders in chaotic retreat. The governor, hearing that the defenses had been breached, sent a final urgent report to the throne, then went to meet the enemy, who cut him down on the spot. The lieutenant governor took responsibility for safeguarding the tax revenues and grain, but as the rebels advanced, he fled for his life, abandoning the grain and treasure, which immediately fell into Taiping hands.[22]

The Ye men and other members of the gentry who had remained in the city first sought refuge in their homes. Late in the evening, a family servant reported that Anqing's north gate was open and still without rebel guards. Ye Kunhou fled the city with his son and brother, resting briefly at the home of a relative in a nearby village. Then the men struggled on through the night, crossing new snow and muddy fields, until they reached the rest of the family at dawn. The larger family, including wives, children, concubines, and servants, numbered forty people, and it took days to determine that all were safe. The joy of their eventual reunion was mixed with deep anxiety about the future. The countryside was full of soldiers who had fled the rebels. At first the villagers treated them as bandits and drove them off. Their will to fight utterly broken, the soldiers begged for mercy, and the peasants gave them pan bread and a little money to send them on their way.

For the next couple days, rumors flew that the rebels were moving out to control the countryside. The gentry organized militia to defend their own villages. Then four days later, the Taiping simply abandoned Anqing and moved on downstream toward Nanjing, which they quickly captured and made their capital for the next decade. Ye Boying and his uncle returned to Anqing, where they found their home and its contents undisturbed. The market had been destroyed, and a few nearby homes were still smoldering; the treasury and granary were bare; temples that offended the Taiping's new god had been ransacked, their monks and priests slaughtered.[23] Otherwise, the city looked much as it had before. The gentry organized men to dispose of corpses and put out fires. Once the rebels were gone, a new batch of officials and troops arrived, bringing relief grain for the poor, and a hurried attempt to restore order ensued. The respite would not last long.

In June, the rebels returned. As usual, rumors preceded their advance. Roving bands of defeated soldiers disturbed the villages and towns along the river. Finally, a rising cadence of cannon fire (at first mistaken for thunder) announced the Taiping arrival. Again the Qing forces put up no defense, their officers retreating and soldiers melting away. The city residents fled in panic, but the gates had been partially blocked as part of the defensive preparations. As the fleeing mob pushed through, the old and weak and women and children fell and were trampled to death. Bodies piled up, belongings were abandoned in the road, and those behind simply climbed over the piles of death and debris. The Ye family members who had returned to the city joined in the flight. Ye Kunhou's feet were hurting, and when he was unable to continue, his son carried him on his back. They fled again to their relatives in the suburbs; then, as a storm broke out, they struggled through the rain— the women weeping and children crying—to seek refuge with friends farther out in the countryside. Looking back, they saw flames rise above the city.

Once again, the Taiping left soon after taking the city. Two days later, Ye Boying was back in Anqing with an uncle and a reliable servant to check their home. They arrived just in time to scare off looters taking advantage of the disorder. This time the city had been thoroughly plundered, the city gates and official *yamen* had been burned, and bodies lay everywhere. Victims of battle and those trampled in flight lay rotting in the streets; those (mostly women) who chose suicide over capture by the rebels were found at the bottom of wells. With officials and army gone, bandits and rebels moved freely along the river, but few paid much attention to the city. It had been picked clean. "Who would have thought," asked Kunhou, "that this prosperous place would suddenly become a war zone? . . . The destruction of war darkens the deserted city."[24] Ye Kunhou decided that his family too must abandon the city that had been its home for generations. He ordered his son to salvage their valuable possessions, including a library of some ten thousand volumes and hundreds of antiques.[25] For the next few weeks, Ye Boying traveled back and forth between the city and friends' homes in the countryside, moving clothes, books, and artwork to safety. None knew at the time, but this would be the final departure from Anqing for this branch of the family. During the summer, Anqing sat in limbo between the imperial and rebel forces. Local gentry appeals for the return of the provincial government and imperial troops were unavailing. The Qing armies remained in the central part of the province, between another group of rebels, the Nian, in the north and the Taiping in the south. The Yangzi River was essentially controlled by the Taiping, and their boats often stopped at the city. In October, the dashing young Taiping commander Shi Dakai arrived to establish his headquarters in Anqing. Only twenty-three years old, Shi Dakai was the scion of a wealthy family of early Taiping supporters in the southwest. One of the rebels' ablest generals and a capable administrator, he organized a stable regime in the region around Anqing. The Taiping had earlier promulgated regulations calling for the equal distribution of land rights, an egalitarianism inspired both by Chinese classical models and the Christian notion that all are equally the children of God. But this sort of revolutionary program apparently was never carried out, and Shi Dakai went out of his way to work with local landowners, protecting their property in exchange for ready payment of taxes.[26]

The relatively pragmatic policies of Shi Dakai affected the situation in the countryside where Ye Kunhou and his family were hiding. On the national level, the Taiping Rebellion represented a fundamental challenge to both Confucian orthodoxy and alien Manchu rule; but on the local level, two regimes competed for legitimacy and resources while the rural population maneuvered to minimize its losses from the struggle. With its own army in utter disarray, the Qing relied increasingly on gentry-organized militia to support its rule. The Taiping regime, in contrast to the "peasant rebellion" of conventional accounts, was based in the cities.[27] When Taiping functionaries moved into the countryside to collect taxes, they pursued the gentry or militia-organizing households with particular ferocity. Because the Ye family included both former officials and militia organizers, the locals generally avoided any contact that might implicate them in anti-Taiping activities. But some local dissidents (the family termed them "bandits") saw opportunities to lead Taiping forces to gentry families in hiding and then rob them of their possessions. Ye Kunhou was surprised that these "short-sighted people" would "willingly become rebels."[28] The family was forced to move to ever more isolated villages, until finally it sought refuge in a small hut that barely kept the rain out, deep in a gully below the cliffs of Sleeping Dragon Mountain some fifty kilometers north of Anqing. The rebels controlled the main thoroughfares, but none ventured near this refuge in the mountains. Indeed, the hills became the gentry's main redoubt, and the hideout was safe enough that dozens of relatives sought shelter with the family, and Kunhou's wife welcomed and cared for them all.[29]

Ye Kunhou spent many months hiding in the hills, and the experience gave him plenty of time to think—and to record his thoughts in hundreds of poems. At first he was discouraged by his fate. Describing himself wearing "an old hat and a tattered shirt," he asked, "How can a titled man come to be so desolate and alone?" At the same time, he clearly hoped for a chance to prove himself: "A real man certainly is not ashamed to be poor and humble. / Extraordinary heroes are often forced to live off fishing and hunting."[30] He was convinced that scholars like him, especially those with experience in local government, could be of service in troubled times:

> The calamities brought by Heaven must be resolved by men.
> It is not possible that there is no one up to the task.
> Heroes are hidden in the dust,
> Frustrated by their lack of credentials.
> Why can special talent not be found among scholars?
> It was Wang Yangming [a famous Ming dynasty philosopher]
>     who pacified the Yao rebels.[31]

The reference to Wang Yangming is particularly interesting, for Wang was an idealist philosopher whose critique of some of the more rigid and conservative tenets of Confucian philosophy was often blamed for the decline and fall of the Ming dynasty. On this occasion, Ye Kunhou chose to remember his service as a successful provincial official who had quelled ethnic rebellion in southwest China.[32]

Before long, Kunhou adjusted to rural life and even began to enjoy it. One poem compares the family's isolated redoubt to the idyllic Taoyuan (Peach Blossom Spring) of early poetry: "When you meet people, you are treated with respect. / The cultured and simple are the same. / Seeking food and drink together."[33] His poems are full of references to peasants rising early to till the fields as their wives spin and weave at home. Herding boys sleep under trees, and casual encounters on rustic paths lead to close friendships. He follows a firewood collector into the hills, and the two men drink together at an inn. Neighbors visit to share a cup of wine; people trust each other and do not lock their gates at night.[34] Buddhist monks were prominent among his acquaintances, and at one point he wrote, "I would like to leave this world in a Zen escape," stopping short of such a move only because of his obligations to family.[35] His thinking took on increasingly Daoist tones of skepticism toward the role of government, revealing a conviction that people were quite capable of managing their own affairs:

> Resolve disputes and bring benefit to the entire lineage.
> Dispel troubles and bring harmony to your in-laws.
> Why do we need active government
> If we truly devote ourselves to serving the people? . . .
> In flight from rebellion, we deepen our relationships.
> In the barren hills we bond with our neighbors.[36]

Much of the time, as he wrote pastoral poems of peaceful rural life, Ye Kunhou seemed to accept his fate and embrace life as a scholarly hermit in the mountains:

> I have left the city behind to enter this rural hamlet.
> The forest is so thick, what need is there to lock the door?
> The mountain water has the taste of licorice and sugar.
> My ambition for fame and fortune is now cut at the root.
> When poor I wish to sell my books by the thousand.
> When happy I down wine by the bucket.[37]

Though he probably did sell many books and antiques to support his large family, he kept enough books to read and enjoyed discussing them with his brothers.[38] Other literati in the area, gentry members and former officials, visited to share news and concerns and to cultivate companionship.[39] On his wife's birthday, he borrowed wine from a neighbor to celebrate.[40]

In the end, however, Ye Kunhou's Confucian sense of duty precluded a life of Daoist escape or bucolic exile in the hills. Early hopes that imperial resolve would produce a quick victory gave way to anger at successive military failures.[41]

> In battle, the officers are in the rear.
> As soldiers advance, who is to lead them?
> In flight, the officers are in front.
> When the ranks collapse, who is to restrain them?
> Far from stopping them, [the officers] lead them in flight.
> The officials do not defend the cities—the rebels do.[42]

Ye's previous experience fighting bandits in Henan had convinced him of the efficacy of militia systems built on the classical model in which soldiers lived among the people. In antiquity, he wrote, everyone knew how to fight, and people fought for their country as for their family. With soldier and peasant roles now separated, ordinary people had become afraid of battle and viewed defense against disorder as a responsibility of soldiers that had nothing to do with them. The army, for its part, was filled with unfit soldiers and worthless rascals who never attacked the enemy but only harmed the people.[43] The appeal of local militia was founded on their capacity to harness peasants' natural desire to protect their homes and families to the security interests of the state. At the time of the Opium War, exaggerated stories of militia victories over the British in the villages around Canton renewed people's interest in militia organizing in the 1840s, and gentry-led militia became critical to Qing efforts to combat the Taiping and other rebellions.[44] Ye Kunhou's commitment to militia organizing was enhanced by the sense of community that he imagined linking literati like himself to the peasants in the Anhui hills. His experience in this rural exile had convinced him that literati could and should lead a response to rebellion that rested on different principles from the estrangement he perceived between the regular army and the people. He committed himself to organizing resistance to the rebels.

In the winter of 1853, with a cold wind blowing through ice-covered trees, Ye Kunhou and a single servant left his family to head toward the Qing lines to the north. Armed only with a wooden staff and wearing a short jacket instead of the long gown of a scholar, he traveled through mountains and across icy streams to reach the camp of Yuan Jiasan, the imperial officer commanding the effort to recover Anhui. Though himself a former official, Kunhou had to plead outside Yuan's gate for three days before receiving permission to organize a force to retake the area around Anqing.[45] His younger brother, Ye Lian, headed west at the same time to persuade another official that the people of Anqing were not, as many believed, obedient subjects of their Taiping rulers. Taiping taxes were heavy and much resented, he argued, but the people feared the rebels' overwhelming power. If an army could be raised to challenge the insurgents, the people would rally to its support. So Ye Lian was sent back with authority to organize a militia force. With another brother, Ye Yun, he visited relatives and friends to rally resistance to the Taiping.

One day, as the two brothers emerged from a gentryman's home, they encountered two mounted Taiping soldiers coming from Anqing. The brothers' shaved foreheads and queues aroused suspicion, for in rebel-occupied territories, most peasants now wore their hair long in the Taiping style. The brothers claimed to be visiting from outside the province, but the soldiers did not believe them. A search of Ye Lian's gown uncovered the letter authorizing militia organizing. Fortunately, the rebel soldiers were illiterate, but they took the letter and left Lian in the hands of a local Taiping official, promising to take him to the Taiping capital for trial on their return.

The Taiping official was a local man, clearly distinguished from the main rebel force in Anqing. His ambivalence about his position was palpable. He collected taxes and managed local affairs for the Taiping, yet feared them as a powerful outside force with strange customs and heterodox beliefs. Perhaps he sympathized with the gentry militia but worried that it would only bring trouble to his neighborhood. So he temporized, unwilling either to release Ye Lian or turn him over to the rebels for almost certain execution. Ye Lian's friends visited him in confinement, some of them counseling suicide as preferable to a dismal fate in Taiping hands.

Meanwhile, the young Ye Boying pressed on with the militia organizing, giving a dramatic speech to a gathering of rural gentry leaders. He noted the brave sacrifice of his family. His uncle had been captured, and the secret of their militia organizing was out. "In the effort to save many, he has brought disaster on himself. You should be moved." He vowed to continue resisting the rebels. His father had gone seeking assistance from the Qing armies in the north. "Fathers and sons, uncles and nephews should devote their lives to the cause. Now I intend to move my family to safety in order to preserve our bloodline. I will stay behind, and if the rebels come looking for me, please turn me over to appease them and you can avoid implication." But he coupled this bold self-sacrifice with a stern warning: "If out of fear of the rebels you should bring harm to my family, when the great Qing army arrives and learns that you have killed others to curry favor with the enemy, your entire families risk execution and it will be too late to repent."[46]

Ye Yun, brother of the captive Ye Lian, took another tack. Scrambling through brush in the middle of the night, he visited a wealthy and talented local notable who had been pressed into service as a Taiping officer. The man said he could do nothing to help but in fact devised a plan to accomplish the rescue. He secretly passed word to the ambivalent functionary holding Ye Lian, suggesting that he send Lian to Anqing before the Taiping soldiers returned with the incriminating document. The official did so, and in Anqing, Ye Lian's captors informed the Taiping authorities that they had captured a man with shaven hair and a queue who appeared to be a merchant returning home. They guaranteed that Ye Lian was sincere and without Qing contacts, and he was released.

Ye Boying gives a more dramatic, but less plausible, version of his uncle's release. He has Ye Lian bravely scorning any threat to his life and proudly announcing that his family had been gentry and officials for generations and knew the meaning of loyalty. "The slice of a knife or a boiling cauldron would be like a tasty meal to me." A Taiping soldier immediately advanced to cut him down, but the officer in charge stepped forward to say, "What's the use in killing this stupid scholar?" and Ye Lian's life was saved.[47]

Ye Boying's account of his time hiding from the Taiping is presumably more reliable. In 1854, he was twenty-nine years old. He had married at nineteen, the same year he passed the examination for the lowest (shengyuan) degree.[48] He had one five-year-old son and had spent much of his adult life supporting his father's official career. When Ye Kunhou left to join the Qing military, he instructed his son to look after the family and his collected poems. This instruction was probably a fair indication of Ye Kunhou's priorities, and for several years, Ye Boying moved his family from one hilly hiding place to another, paying particular attention to his father's poems and his mother's health.

Following the detention of Ye Lian, the family felt more endangered than ever. The Taiping were aggressively scouring the countryside for gentrymen organizing opposition to their rebel regime. As Ye Boying moved his family from place to place, he was convinced that local rascals who had heard of his uncle's capture were watching family members' every move and plotting to turn them in. To ensure that some members would survive discovery, the family split up. Following his release, Ye Lian returned to western Anhui. His brother, Ye Yun, and his immediate family were in one village; Ye Boying lived alone in a second; and his mother lived in a third. Boying's account is notably silent on where his wife and child stayed, but they were presumably with his mother.

Following the Confucian obligation to bid a parent goodnight, Ye Boying traveled after dark to his mother's hiding place, stumbling along by moonlight on clear nights and carrying a lantern when skies were overcast. Servants accompanied him, carrying food and provisions. When the dogs barked on their approach, his mother would come anxiously to the window to greet him. Entering the house, Boying would bow reverently to the old lady, then chat deep into the night, returning to his own village only after she had fallen asleep and arriving barely before dawn. Even if his account of this nightly ritual appears self-serving, it shows a close bond to his mother.

One snowy night in the winter of 1854–55, Ye Boying answered a knock on his door. His father's personal servant came in, bearing a message that Ye Kunhou was second-in-command of a major force seeking to retake Tongcheng, the county just north of Anqing. Soon the family learned that the Qing army had laid siege to the city. From their hiding place in the mountains, Ye Boying and the others could hear the distant rumble of cannon. There were rumors of a great Qing victory, but a low-ranking Anqing gentryman who had joined the Taiping cause managed to ambush the Qing force from the rear; then Shi Dakai, the Taiping leader in Anqing, brought reinforcements to break the siege, killing the Qing commander and routing his forces. Anxious about his father's fate, Ye Boying set forth by back roads and mountain trails until he heard his father was safe. Eager to join the campaign and advance his own career, he sent a message to his father. Two days later came the response: Kunhou had reassembled half of the defeated army and was heading north to regroup. Boying was to look after the family and wait on his mother. "I must fulfill my obligation of loyalty [to the dynasty]; you must fulfill your filial duty."[49] Boying was now almost thirty years old, but in this family's Confucian division of labor, the father assumed responsibility for public service while the son stayed home and cared for the family.

In the spring of 1855, after two years hiding in rebel territory and holding little hope that the Qing would soon reconquer the area, the family decided to flee to Shaanxi province in the northwest, where Boying's brother held an official position. Though the brother's appointment was only as county magistrate in a poor province, the post represented a critical Ye family foothold in officialdom. His father had made every effort to stay in contact, with one letter taking a year to reach the family in the Anhui hills, but Ye Kunhou's message to this son was clear: "The whole family is hungry. / This [your] small office is very precious."[50] Whether his son in Shaanxi offered financial assistance to the family in Anhui is unclear, but he was able to provide refuge from rebellion, and by 1855, the family was ready to move. The first part of the journey was entirely through rebel territory. The group traveled by back roads, and as there were no inns, sent servants ahead to prepare resting places. The family was too large to travel together without arousing suspicion, so it divided into three groups. Boying's mother was ill and coughing blood, but she insisted on leaving. After ten days, the family reached the Qing lines, and the old lady told her son, "Since leaving rebel territory, a thousand-ton weight has been lifted from my body. Finally I am able to eat and sleep normally."[51] But when Boying looked back to the south, the smoke of signal fires filled the sky, and he worried about friends and relatives still hiding behind rebel lines.

Once safely out of Taiping territory, the family again split up. Uncle Ye Yun headed for Beijing, planning to take a special examination that might bring an official posting. The others traveled by boat and cart, first west and then north, through Henan, where they rested in the *yamen* where Ye Kunhou had once served. At another stop, they stayed with an in-law who was also an official. Finally they moved west up the Yellow River valley and through a pass into the valley of the Wei River to Xi'an, site of China's ancient and medieval capitals. Boying's brother greeted them, and the family was briefly reunited before the provincial governor sent the brother off to assume his magistrate position in northern Shaanxi.

The family members had survived the Taiping Rebellion, but not without considerable trauma. Their home in Anqing lay in ruins, and most of their possessions had been lost. Hiding in the hills for two years brought hardships that this elite family had never before experienced. Anqing would remain in Taiping hands for eight years and become the strategic point for which the armies fought to control access to the Taiping capital in Nanjing. In the final battle of 1861, sixteen thousand people were killed in the Qing assault, many if not most of them civilians. From Anqing, the Qing forces methodically mopped up the remaining rebel forces in Anhui.[52] Three years later, the Taiping capital would fall, and China's bloodiest civil war would end.

When one Ye descendant returned to Anqing after the rebellion, he found only scattered thatch huts among the desolation. "Only one in a hundred survives from the older generation," he was told. "The able-bodied adults have all fled, we know not where. The young who are left do not even know their own names."[53] With the family's most eminent members elsewhere, the Anqing Ye had lost their prominence. Those who remained were mostly ordinary peasants, struggling to survive in the wreckage of rebellion. Ye Kunhou and his descendants never returned. Although his line was driven from the Ye ancestral home, its members fled as well-connected players in the official elite. For them, and especially for Ye Kunhou and Ye Boying, the rebellion provided an opportunity for distinguished official service, which was the road to wealth and power in late imperial China. We shall turn to their official careers shortly, but first we must examine the roots that had nourished the Ye family's rise.

2

# Family Roots

Five hundred years before the tumultuous nineteenth century, the ancestors of the Ye family moved to Anqing during another age of war and rebellion. This too was a period of alien rule. The Yuan dynasty, founded by the Mongols under Khubilai Khan, was coming to an end. Since the 1350s, Anhui had been wracked by rebellion. Rival armies passed back and forth, seizing Anqing from the Mongols and from each other. Nearby areas in the Yangzi valley suffered even greater destruction, and in the late fourteenth century, most of the countryside around Anqing was repopulated by refugees from the hard-hit region around Boyang Lake in neighboring Jiangxi province.[1] Among these refugees was the founder of the Ye lineage, Ye Sheng'er.

Ye Sheng'er was a degree holder and Yuan dynasty education official in the southeastern coastal province of Zhejiang. When the province was consumed by the rebellions that finally drove China's Mongol rulers back to the central Asian steppe, he returned to his home in Jiangxi. When that province too became engulfed in war, he moved with his brothers to Anhui. The brothers sought refuge on Yellow Mud Hill, surrounded by water in this still-marshy floodplain of the Yangzi. The population was then so sparse that he was able to claim land for some three kilometers around the hill. Over time, this land was brought under cultivation and became the rich agricultural patrimony of the Ye lineage—the male line descended from Ye Sheng'er.

The fourteenth-century rise of the Ye family was typical for the Yangzi elites of late imperial China, and other families' genealogies reflect similar narratives. The chaotic transition from the Yuan to Ming dynasties depleted the population and left plenty of rich agricultural land available for the officials, former officials, or military men who rose with the Ming state. Families with financial or political resources carved out spaces for themselves and established lines whose local prominence endured for centuries. These families provided the local elite of late imperial China, gentry members if the family included degree holders, men whose status and influence in their home counties made them indispensable guardians of the social order.[2]

We know very little about Ye Sheng'er. Living from 1302 to 1388, he was a distant memory when a great-great-grandson composed his ancestor's biography for the first family genealogy in 1488. The description there lists the conventional virtues: Sheng'er was firm and clearheaded, proper and direct, warm and good-natured. As an education official, he trained and tested young men in the Confucian classics. A strict and formal teacher, he insisted on a fixed daily and monthly curriculum. Even in the heat of summer, he always wore his official robes. This official formality made his persistent teaching that moral principles were the heart of learning, that true scholars did not study just to pass the examinations and gain office, seem a trifle disingenuous.[3]

Of this patriarch's immediate descendants we know even less. They were evidently scholars, teachers, poets, and bibliophiles. One was wealthy enough to become the target of a petty thief, who, when caught by the family servants, aroused pity in the mistress of the household. She offered five ounces of silver to relieve his poverty, urged him to reform, and sent him on his way. This amount of silver would have purchased several hundred pounds of grain at the time, so the gift was remarkably generous. The story survives in the family genealogy, passed down through the generations as an example of ancestral beneficence—but the size of the gift reveals the substantial wealth that the family had accumulated.[4]

The Ye family attained political prominence when, in 1457, Ye Hua, a fourth-generation descendant of Sheng'er, earned a *jinshi* degree—the highest degree in the imperial examination system. Students qualified for this high honor by demonstrating mastery of the Confucian classics and dynastic histories in a sequence of examinations held in their home county, prefecture, province, and finally in the imperial capital. The exams at the local, provincial, and national levels were held in a three-year cycle, with great ceremony and much attention from officials and the social elite. Ye Kunhou presided over several such exams and left poems describing the ritual calling of names, the locking of the gates to the examination hall, and the illumination of exam cubicles by candles at night.[5] Competition was intense and failure the norm. The lowest examination degree, the *shengyuan,* was granted at the prefectural level only to the top 1 or 2 percent of the candidates, and only 2.6 percent of the *shengyuan* received the provincial *juren* degree in each three-year cycle. Candidates were allowed to retake the exams as often as they wished, but statistics show that only a select few ever passed. In the nineteenth century, Ye Kunhou's brothers, sons, and nephews traveled repeatedly to take the exams and almost always returned disappointed.[6] The highest (*jinshi*) degree was awarded to the top candidates after an examination in the capital and a palace exam with questions from the emperor himself. Fewer than one in ten passed at this level. Men who succeeded at any level in this intensely competitive examination regime gained status as members of the gentry, which exempted them from corvée labor required as part of taxation (because physical labor was inappropriate for the literati elite) and from corporal punishment (or torture) in court, and allowed them to meet as social equals with the officials governing their home areas. Holders of the provincial and metropolitan degrees qualified for official appointment, the ultimate source of status and personal wealth in the Chinese empire.[7]

Ye Hua left a record of the questions he was asked on the examinations, and all of them related to conventional Confucian virtues and well-known passages from the classics. The provincial exam required him to discuss the passage "The way of father and son is loyalty and reciprocity" and to write about the civil and military virtues of the ancient statesman the Duke of Zhou. The metropolitan exam prompted him to write on the injunction in Confucius's *Analects* to "control oneself and restore the rites" and the proposition that the classic virtues of benevolence, righteousness, propriety, and wisdom must come from within.[8]

Original answers on these hoary themes were unlikely, but the examinations were not looking for originality. By focusing on a standard set of classical texts, which students had memorized and studied alongside erudite commentaries by centuries of Confucian scholars, the exams identified, with reasonable objectivity, those with superior command of a well-defined body of moral and historical knowledge and the ability to articulate that knowledge in elegant essays. More importantly, all students—even those who did not advance—emerged with a shared set of values and cultural suppositions and a common understanding of the Chinese past. The examinations played a critical role in maintaining the cultural unity and integrity of the Chinese empire.[9]

Ye Hua's essays earned him the highest metropolitan degree by age thirty and an official appointment as a prefect in the northern province of Shandong, followed by a promotion to chief civil administrator of Zhejiang province. He was apparently an active and popular official, reforming taxes to reduce the burden on the people, establishing a local academy, and building up stores in the official granary. In Zhejiang, he initiated a twelve-point reform program that included impeaching and removing corrupt officials and crafty clerks, eliminating violent bullies, arresting thieves, punishing those who pressed lawsuits for profit, suppressing gambling, and burying rotting corpses. His monthly lectures on the law drew large audiences of gentrymen, and he vigorously protected law and order—personally putting a stop to illegal mining activities and leading troops to capture pirates raiding along the coast. On one such occasion, he found himself in an inn, surrounded by a gang supporting the unruly miners. The protesters set fire to the inn, and Ye Hua was saved only because a loyal family servant pulled him from the flames and carried him to safety—though the servant died of exhaustion after a long flight through the woods. Five years of this strenuous official life left Ye Hua tired and sick. He retired to Anqing, where he wrote essays, taught his grandchildren, and gathered with other local gentry to bemoan the growing corruption of official life.[10]

As a former official of some prominence, Ye Hua had considerable status in the local community. With each promotion, he obtained imperial patents granting flowery titles to his parents and grandparents: Grand Master for Forthright Service and Grand Master for Palace Counsel for the men; Lady of Suitability and Respectful Lady for their wives. His mother was praised for instructing her son in her chambers, lending imperial validation to a gentry wife's proper role in the education of the next generation. Hua's wife was granted similar titles, with the patent praising her role in ordering the female realm of the inner chambers and keeping peace in the family.[11] In 1497, two years after his death, Ye Hua was memorialized with a massive ornate archway, or *pailou*, which spanned the street in front of his home. Authorized by imperial decree, such arches carried the posthumous title of the person honored, in this case Ye Hua's highest title: Master of Court Discussion.[12]

None of these titles was hereditary. Late imperial China was a highly stratified society, but its elite was not a hereditary aristocracy. Examination degrees and bureaucratic office were the surest route to status and wealth, but each generation had to earn degrees in its own right. Status was not automatically transferred to one's sons, and wealth was divided equally among the male descendants at each generation, with some provision for unmarried daughters' dowries. Elite families tended to have several sons, so the family patrimony was threatened by repeated division among the brothers, eventually leaving descendants with no more than the small plots of land held by ordinary peasants. The institutional solution to this problem was the lineage. Elite families who had acquired some prominence and hoped to perpetuate their privileged status organized themselves in corporate lineages.[13]

Lineages took a variety of forms in different areas of China, but the central organizing principle was to identify a single founding ancestor and then endow some property for the benefit of all recognized descendants of that ancestor. Ye Hua followed this course. Land was granted to the entire lineage, never to be alienated (though in fact some was apparently later sold). Rental income from this land supported the annual rituals of ancestor worship that helped maintain family solidarity. Ideally, the property would generate enough income to support a lineage school to educate talented young men to pass the examinations and bring further glory to the extended kinship group. In 1475, a distant cousin of Ye Hua, also descended from Ye Sheng'er, established such a school.[14]

The composition of a lineage genealogy was a critical part of this process. Families had to identify the legitimate descendants of the original patriarch in order to ensure proper worship of their ancestors and to determine who was eligible for subsidized education. This was the fundamental purpose of a genealogy, and it is no accident that Ye Hua, who endowed the initial lineage estate, also compiled the first genealogy, in 1488. The record was a fairly simple hand-copied document. After a perfunctory claim of descent from a noble family of the Ye surname in ancient China, it admitted that records before Ye Sheng'er were lost and that tracing descent from these ancient worthies was impossible. Thus Ye Sheng'er was identified as the founding ancestor, and the lineage was confined to Ye family members who could trace their descent from him.[15]

Ye Hua's original genealogy was updated, revised, and reprinted in 1700, 1808, 1867, 1906, 1944, and 2001. Only the 1944 and 2001 versions survive, but they incorporate prefaces and other material from each previous edition. The genealogy provides ample evidence that preserving unity among the descendants of Ye Sheng'er was no easy matter. The preface to the third edition notes that an abortive effort to compile a new edition had begun more than fifty years earlier, and the 1808 version took more than ten years to complete because of unspecified disputes within the lineage.[16] The divisions among Sheng'er's descendants are quite evident in the genealogical charts. Sheng'er had four sons, but one left the area, and none of his descendants were included in the genealogy. At the time of the first genealogy, there were eighteen family members in the generation of the compiler, Ye Hua, but only five have any descendants listed. Each of these five was a natural brother of Ye Hua, though one had been given as an heir to a paternal uncle.[17] The branches that descended from the other thirteen cousins apparently fell away between the compilation of the first and second editions, reducing the lineage to the descendants of Ye Hua's father. Another large group disappeared between the second and third editions, presumably because of the family discord mentioned in the 1808 preface.

The precise cause of this discord is unknown, but not long afterward, a Ye Kunhou poem reflected on the inevitability of such dissension:

> Brothers are born of the same parents.
> As children they are always together.
> But as their appetites gradually develop,
> Their love and friendship diverge.
> Each establishes his own household
> And competes for land and housing.
> Over time they become like strangers on the road,
> Never sharing each other's hardship.
> Just as a stream divides,
> Never to rejoin at its source.[18]

The competition among brothers for resources and the emotional attachment each had to his wife and children posed a constant threat to lineage solidarity, and once a brother broke away, the breach was irreparable. After noting these divisions of the eighteenth century, the genealogy documents three lines, each descended from

Ye Hua or one of his brothers, into the twentieth century. The enduring ritual unity of these lines is impressive. For the most part, through twenty generations, males of the same generation shared one character in their names—a character that the genealogy had specified years in advance.[19]

If a lineage wished to preserve its reputation along with its unity, it had to ensure that its members behaved properly. The family regulations recorded in the third (1807) edition of the genealogy detail the moral standards that the lineage leaders sought to preserve and the cultural conceptions that lay behind them.[20]

"Be filial to your parents." This primal principle of Confucian values was inevitably first in the family regulations, and it was based on a logic of simple reciprocity. Family members should return the love and care they received from their parents as children, remembering the elders' worries each time their child cried and their lost sleep and missed meals when children were sick. The genealogy frankly admitted that when sons married and brought their wives into the household, new sources of conflict arose. As a young man, Ye Kunhou wrote a delightful poem on the process. After describing the parents' warm care and constant anxiety as they raised their sons, he continued:

> But when [sons] grow to be adults
> Their parents are already old.
> The sons marry and look forward to forming their own families,
> And from this suspicions arise.
> The son is proud of his work in the fields,
> While the wife is criticized for her housework.
> In their bedroom the pleasure is boundless,
> While outside their parents are scowling.[21]

To contain the inevitable intergenerational conflicts, married sons were constantly reminded where their loyalties should lie: their affection for their spouses should not deflect them from obligations to their parents.

The suspicion of scheming wives is evident in the discussion of the genealogy's second principle: "Keep harmony among brothers." Although, as we shall see, Ye Kunhou had unusually close relations with his own brothers, his poems (especially from his early years) discuss the natural fraternal competition for resources, as well as the young men's sexual and affective bonds to their spouses. But the patriline's genealogy confidently stated that discord among brothers invariably came from "bringing wives into the family, so different surnames live together competing for advantage." In the normal marriage, brides joined the family of their husband and in-laws, so they were initially outsiders in the household. Their natural allies and only source of support in family conflicts were their husband and children, who therefore became the focus of their attention.[22] When divisions among brothers or uncles arose, their wives were often blamed for looking after the narrow interest of their own small section of the family. The Chinese ideal (though rarely the practice) was that brothers continue to live together as adults. In the view of the genealogy, family divisions "are all the work of women." It cited an ancient parable of a man whose family had lived together for nine generations. Asked how this was accomplished, he replied, "It is all a matter of not heeding the words of one's wife."[23]

If the family was to avoid these problems with women, it had to arrange proper marriages, and the third regulation focused on matrimony. Wives should be carefully chosen from good families, but one should avoid selecting a wife on the basis of wealth, for she would likely be discontented with her lot. The conventional reasons for divorce (or, more precisely, for sending a wife back to her family) were listed: if she was disobedient to her husband's parents; if she was childless, adulterous, or sickly; or if she gossiped too much or stole things. Few families resorted to the extreme sanction of divorce (beating or ostracism were more common), but these regulations sought to subordinate women clearly to the authority of their husbands' families.

The correct behavior of women was a central concern in ensuring the proper order of the family. Under the heading "Preserving decorum in the women's quarters," the genealogy compilers stated unequivocally, "The proper place for men is in public; the proper place for women is at home." They admitted that complete seclusion of women was impractical. Females must go out to help in the fields, pick mulberry leaves for silkworms, or draw water from the well. If they had been properly instructed, no ill should come of this. The danger the male authors saw was the recent evil custom wherein groups of twenty or thirty women gathered to read Buddhist scriptures or went on pilgrimages to the sea or mountains hundred of miles away. Even visits to nearby temples to burn incense or an excursion to the Lantern Festival to see the sights and join the festivities was condemned. Such practices had become quite common in the eighteenth century, but elite households were clearly uncomfortable with such public activities of women. To them, the only proper role was the "three followings." Girls should follow the dictates of their parents, married women should follow their husbands, and widows should follow their sons.[24]

A series of regulations discussed lineage organization and practices. Lineage members should recompense their ancestors at the annual sacrifices, build an ancestral hall for the tablets of the deceased, and respect other lineage members, celebrating the success of the fortunate without envy. At the same time, they should establish an ancestral estate to assist the poorer members of the lineage, especially to help with the substantial ritual expenses of weddings and funerals. Behind these injunctions was a clear recognition that any large lineage included both rich and poor, and maintaining harmony among them was not easy. The solution that the elite authors of the genealogy offered was a Qing dynasty version of compassionate conservatism: the wealthy should offer charity to the poor, and the poor should respect and not begrudge the good fortune of the rich. The warnings accompanying the regulations reflect the reality behind these noble sentiments: "Nowadays within a lineage, the wealthy have all lost the virtue of offering food and clothing to the poor; while the poor show an aggressive and grasping temperament. The noble oppress people with their status, while the lowly presume upon their indigent condition. People compete with each other over common property and contrary opinions arise. Women's talk poisons and misleads; slander and treachery give rise to conflicts."[25]

Complaints that selfishness and greed were undermining ancient virtues were common in late imperial China, reflecting in part the spread of a commercial economy and the values of the marketplace.[26] The Confucian critique of profit seeking was particularly common in local literati and official circles. Ye Kunhou certainly reflected this view in his poems: "Now people value money as much as their lives, . . . know only profit and not loyalty or trust."[27] When a grand-nephew went to join his father in the central China metropolis of Wuhan, Kunhou warned against the influence of the market's noisy commercialism.[28] He bemoaned the fact that cleverness and a heartless cruelty were replacing the ancient virtues of righteousness and honesty.[29] Where people used to share personal feelings in intimate bonds of friendship, now money was required to cement relationships in lavish banquets and expensive entertainment.[30] Complaints against the corrupting influence of money were conventional rhetoric, but they also reflected deeply held Confucian values that were endlessly repeated and passed down through the generations.

Several of the family regulations reveal important characteristics of Chinese society at this time. Like other countries before the industrial revolution, China based its economy on agriculture, and the genealogy urged Ye family members to pay particular attention to agriculture and sericulture (making silk). People were reminded of the emperor's ritual plowing in the spring; but the authors admitted that people commonly despised the sweaty, mud-covered peasant carrying his hoe. Another section urged people to be content with their lot. Scholars should study hard; peasants should work diligently, guard against natural disasters, and pay their taxes on time; artisans should practice their craft; merchants should be fair in their dealings. Despite predictable Confucian injunctions against profit seeking, the genealogy compilers were practical men, and the poor were encouraged to go into commerce or learn a trade if that was the only road out of poverty.

The genealogy consistently warned against involvement with the local *yamen*. The *yamen* was the home and office of the local official, whether he was a county magistrate (governing a population of some three hundred thousand), a prefect (supervising several counties), or provincial governor (presiding over one of the eighteen provinces within the Great Wall). Such official positions were the ambition of any gentry member and the reason for taking the examinations. But for a gentry member to visit a *yamen* on private business, to press a case for a friend or relative, was improper and certain to arouse resentment and loss of respect. Other people with basic literacy might seek jobs at the *yamen* as clerks or runners, menial functionaries who carried out the routine business of the *yamen*—handling law cases, collecting taxes, transmitting instructions to village leaders, arresting miscreants. The attraction of these occupations, with their fancy clothes and considerable powers (to say nothing of the opportunities for graft), was acknowledged; but clerks and runners were consistently reviled in official discourse, and this calling would surely bring discredit to the lineage.[31]

The genealogy urged family members to be amicable toward their neighbors and respectful of friends. With the growth of population, it noted, families were living much closer together. As a result, little disputes between neighbors were common, and these disagreements should not be allowed to develop into lasting feuds. A common saying warned, "Close neighbors are more important than distant relatives." If harmony was to be preserved, people needed to avoid "coveting wealth or being ashamed of poverty; grasping wealth or abusing the poor." The clever and powerful should not "use their wits to cheat the simple, or their strength to take advantage of the weak." The need for such injunctions reminds us that the Ye family lived in a very contentious society.

The lineage regulations urged family members to be honest and trustworthy, for others would then lend them money. In this highly commercialized society, good credit was essential to family well-being. The social order also included a complex network of specialists, as the reasons for "respecting friends" reveal. Only if one offered proper respect could one secure the services of a teacher for one's children, a doctor if a family member became ill, or geomancer (*fengshui* master) to select a grave site for the dead.[32] Beneath the clichés of Confucian morality lay practical attention to the behavioral norms necessary to get along in late imperial times and acknowledgment of the important role of educational, medical, and ritual specialists.

The genealogy's family instructions were designed to preserve the Ye patriline's reputation in local society. In Ye Hua's time, the family certainly enjoyed considerable prominence, but preserving this status proved difficult. We get some sense of the ups and downs of the Ye lineage from table 1, which records the number of degree holders and minor officials in each of the first nineteen generations, stretching across the entire Ming and Qing dynasties. Although the lineage was small, it was exceptionally successful in the examinations from the middle of the fifteenth through the early sixteenth century, beginning with Ye Hua at generation 5. Ye Hua's prominence as an official and holder of the highest degree was no doubt critical to the family's

TABLE 1   Ye Family Degree Holders and Minor Officials

| Generation | Rough Dates[1] | Number of Males | Higher Degree | gong-sheng | sheng-yuan | jian-sheng | Minor Officials[2] | % with Degree/Office |
|---|---|---|---|---|---|---|---|---|
| 1 | 1302–1388 | 1 | | 1 | | | | 100 |
| 2 | 1333–1393 | 4 | | | | | | 0 |
| 3 | 1363–1423 | 8 | | | | | | 0 |
| 4 | 1394–1455 | 14 | | 2 | | | | 14 |
| 5 | 1427–1495 | 19 | 1 | | 6 | 3 | | 53 |
| 6 | 1467–1527 | 21 | | 1 | 8 | 2 | | 53 |
| 7 | 1507–1567 | 36 | 1 | 1 | 6 | 1 | | 25 |
| 8 | 1547–1607 | 47 | | 2 | 7 | 2 | | 23 |
| 9 | 1591–1645 | 49 | | | 3 | 1 | 1 | 10 |
| 10 | 1620–1678 | 64 | | | | 1 | | 2 |
| 11 | 1654–1709 | 40 | | | 3 | 1 | | 10 |
| 12 | 1683–1748 | 56 | | | 2 | | | 4 |
| 13 | 1718–1787 | 98 | | | 1 | 3 | | 4 |
| 14 | 1747–1819 | 102 | | 1 | 6 | 1 | 1 | 9 |
| 15 | 1774–1864 | 111 | | | | 4 | 3 | 6 |
| 16 | 1802–1889 | 150 | | 1 | 2 | | 9 | 8 |
| 17 | 1825–1888 | 134 | | | 1 | 1 | 6 | 6 |
| 18 | 1849–1902 | 125 | | | 3 | | 4 | 6 |
| 19 | 1873–1930 | 143 | | | 1 | | | 1 |

SOURCE: Ye-shi zupu [Ye family genealogy] (n.p.: 1944), juan 3.

Notes:

[1] The dates in this column are either the actual dates of a prominent degree holder in the generation whose birth and death dates are known or, for generations for which no such dates are available, interpolations (assuming sixty-year life spans). Clearly, many members of a given generation might live outside these dates, but they provide a rough guide to the time when a generation lived.

[2] "Higher degrees" are the provincial (juren) and metropolitan (jinshi) degrees; gongsheng was the lowest degree qualifying one for office by the examination route; shengyuan and jiansheng were lower degrees, with the latter usually a purchased title. The "minor officials" are all held extremely low-ranking positions, below the rank of magistrate, many identified only as "lower ninth rank," which was the bottom of the official hierarchy. Still, even these petty officials brought status (and presumably income) to the lineage.

success. The ancestral estate and lineage school established at this time served to cultivate new talent, and Ye Hua was surely wealthy enough to provide the library and talented tutors needed to train the family's young men for the exams. The entire lineage benefited from the reflected glory of its degree holders and could be considered an extended family of literati.

In the mid-seventeenth century, the family suffered as warfare, rebellion, and famine accompanied the fall of the Ming dynasty, the Manchu invasion, and the establishment of Qing rule. Many family members fled, and the lineage as a whole declined in status.[33] The lineage hall (then only a small hut near the founder's grave site) and some family graves were destroyed in the rebellions, and estate lands were apparently sold off.[34] The arch that celebrated Ye Hua and reminded the community of the Ye family's illustrious past collapsed in 1731 and was never rebuilt.[35] The 1807 genealogy called for the establishment of an ancestral estate but noted that this was usually possible only with a prominent official in the family, and no Ye men had achieved that status.[36] Degree holders numbered less than one-tenth of the lineage males, and none earned more than the lowest degrees or held anything greater than the pettiest office before the mid-nineteenth century. Indeed, the number of degree holders declined as the number of families in the lineage increased. Even after the rise to prominence of Ye Kunhou and Ye Boying in the mid-nineteenth century, the number of degree holders and especially of petty officials did not keep up with the expansion of the lineage.

We know distressingly little about the ordinary peasants who constituted the vast majority of the lineage. Their lives were no doubt dominated by hard work in the fields, and many of them (perhaps most) lacked education and were illiterate.[37] Rice was their primary crop, but their village was close to Anqing, so some may have engaged in truck farming, selling vegetables to the city. The poorer members were no doubt tenants cultivating the land of wealthy landlords, usually for rents that came to one-half of the main crop. Small landholders bore the burden of paying taxes to the government. These taxes were onerous enough that many hard-pressed households resisted payments or sought delays, a practice that the comfortable authors of the genealogy deplored as bringing dishonor to the family.[38] The genealogical evidence on life expectancy suggests that most lineage members were relatively well off. In the late eighteenth century, when the genealogy's record keeping was most systematic, the average lifespan of males who lived to adulthood was forty-nine years. This age is quite high for a premodern society, though infant and child mortality certainly lowered the average overall life expectancy considerably. The 1807 genealogy attempted to record early deaths, and entries for the years before that date suggest that at least one in three children died before adulthood. Even this number surely understates early mortality, as girls were undercounted. The same years record an average of only 1.1 daughters per family, just half of the 2.2 sons. Determining the social reality underlying such figures is always difficult. Were more girls dying in infancy, or were they simply ignored by the male authors of the genealogy? Both explanations are plausible. Because sons carried on the family line, the authors had a natural incentive to record their lives more completely than those of daughters. By the same token, girls, who would marry out of the family, were less valued and less likely to survive to adulthood. They were the usual victims of infanticide, when families had to limit family size; and girls probably received less medical attention when threatened by childhood diseases that could end a young life.[39]

A telling example of this logic appears in the laudatory biography of one of the women who married into the family. Her son and daughter were struck by smallpox, and she insisted on caring for them herself. It was a fatal decision, for she contracted the disease herself, dying at thirty-three. Her seven-year-old son recovered before she died, and once he was out of danger, she exclaimed, "My son's crisis has passed. He really is my son! As for this little crying girl, of what importance is she? When I die, I'll take her with me. I can't let her burden my husband and son." Sure enough, ten days after she died, her daughter succumbed.[40]

The continuous records of the Ye family over hundreds of years are an important testament to the stability of rural society in the late imperial period. The nearby graves of ancestors, the lineage hall, the fields and dwellings passed down through the generations gave a sense of permanence and rootedness to the lineage. But the stability was not absolute. Occasionally family members moved away, and despite the genealogy's injunction against allowing sons and daughters to go off as monks or nuns, a few did. The pilgrimages that were so roundly condemned were another critical form of moving about, especially for women. More locally, there were opera performances and fortune tellers in the marketplace—both of which the elite denounced for their vulgar superstition and dangerous mixing of the sexes—which attracted lively audiences, and broke the monotony of village life.[41]

As is common in piecing together the histories of distant eras, the lives of the elite are easier to trace than those of the poor. This is fortunate for our effort to chart the ancestors of Ye Kunhou and Ye Boying. It is remarkable and certainly not accidental that the direct line of ancestors of these two is an unbroken succession of degree holders and members of the elite. Figure 2 shows the descent line from Ye Sheng'er to Ye Boying and his brothers. This branch was unquestionably a line of literati. It may be significant that through the first six generations, as the family was establishing itself, first sons were the ones to achieve prominence—including the most famous of them all, Ye Hua. But the line to Ye Boying does not descend from Ye Hua but from his younger brother, and from that time on (until Kunhou and Boying, both first sons), the line of scholars was a series of second sons. By this time, examination success, not family rank, had clearly become the path to status, and from the sixteenth century on, success in the examinations was concentrated in this line to an extraordinary degree. Between Ye Hua and Ye Boying were thirteen generations with 927 adult males, among whom 93 were degree holders or minor officials. In the lineage as a whole, 1 in 10 was a member of the scholar-official elite. However, in the ancestral line of Ye Boying and his brothers, including their direct ancestors and the brothers of each generation's father, there were 32 adult males, of whom 22 (69 percent) held an examination degree or official position.

This was a family line of local gentry, whose elite status stretched back hundreds of years. The family regulations in the genealogy tell much about how they were supposed to live. But what can we say about their actual lives? Though the laudatory biographies in the genealogy conform closely to the literati ideal, they contain clues to the activities of this local elite family. Especially in the early years of living in Anqing, the Ye were intent on bringing their land under cultivation, organizing

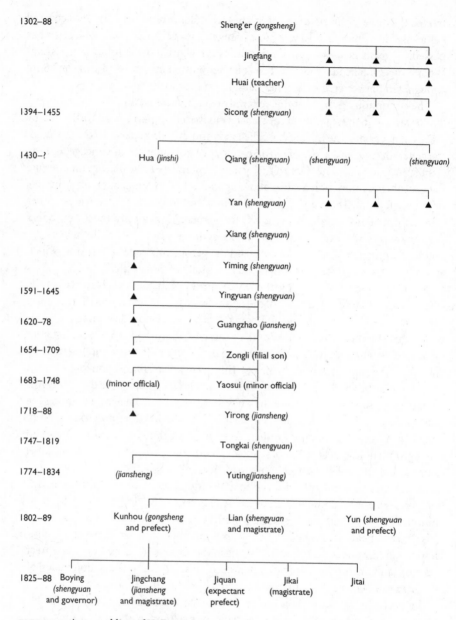

| 1302–88 | Sheng'er (*gongsheng*) | | | |
|---|---|---|---|---|
| | Jingfang | ▲ | ▲ | ▲ |
| | Huai (teacher) | ▲ | ▲ | ▲ |
| 1394–1455 | Sicong (*shengyuan*) | ▲ | ▲ | ▲ |

1430–?  Hua (*jinshi*)   Qiang (*shengyuan*)   (*shengyuan*)   (*shengyuan*)

| | Yan (*shengyuan*) | ▲ | ▲ | ▲ |
|---|---|---|---|---|

Xiang (*shengyuan*)

▲   Yiming (*shengyuan*)

1591–1645   ▲   Yingyuan (*shengyuan*)

1620–78   ▲   Guangzhao (*jiansheng*)

1654–1709   ▲   Zongli (filial son)

1683–1748   (minor official)   Yaosui (minor official)

1718–88   ▲   Yirong (*jiansheng*)

1747–1819   Tongkai (*shengyuan*)

1774–1834   (*jiansheng*)   Yuting(*jiansheng*)

1802–89   Kunhou (*gongsheng* and prefect)   Lian (*shengyuan* and magistrate)   Yun (*shengyuan* and prefect)

1825–88   Boying (*shengyuan* and governor)   Jingchang (*jiansheng* and magistrate)   Jiquan (expectant prefect)   Jikai (magistrate)   Jitai

FIGURE 2. Ancestral line of Ye Boying.

networks of dikes and ditches to control flooding and irrigate the fields. Biographies of later family members indicate that they continued to manage local water control and worked to keep granaries full to protect against bad harvests. As community leaders, they were called upon to mediate quarrels, since both officials and common people preferred to settle civil disputes outside the overburdened court system. As wealthy members of a prominent family, they were often obliged to assist their poorer kin and neighbors with the expense of weddings and burials.[42] As part of the local gentry, they were community leaders with customary responsibilities for the well-being of their neighbors.

Since Ye Hua's generation in the late fifteenth century, elite members of the family had established residence in the city of Anqing. They seem to have maintained a rural home as well, but repeated references to homes on the streets near the *yamen* indicate that degree holders in the family had moved closer to the seat of power.[43] Sharing the education, culture, and values of the numerous officials in this administrative city (and provincial capital by the early Qing period), they no doubt interacted with officials in a number of ways. In times of famine, they would be called upon to help organize relief, and they probably became involved as advisors, or plaint writers in lawsuits, despite the genealogy's warnings against inappropriate involvement in litigation. When one Ming-dynasty Ye scholar refused the resident prefect's personal request to teach his sons, his deliberate effort to distance himself from the local authorities was preserved in the genealogy section on "extraordinary behavior."[44]

From the age of about six, the young men of the family were consumed by education in preparation for the examinations. References to the hum of young men reciting their lessons into the wee hours of the morning are a conventional trope of elite biographies, but they reflect the reality of a life cramming for the all-important exams. One precocious lad who had mastered the ancient classics and twenty-one of the dynastic histories by the age of twelve reduced himself to exhaustion and died at sixteen.[45] Another young man was apparently driven mad by his studies: after a visit by a spirit, he went to the family cemetery, bade farewell to his parents, sat in meditation, and died.[46] For most, exam preparations were presumably less traumatic, but they could last for much of one's life. One persistent scholar failed the provincial examination twelve times, another ten—either of which would have consumed thirty years of preparations, given the three-year cycle of the exams.[47]

Girls were not eligible for the exams, so their education received less attention. Daughters of elite families were expected to achieve sufficient literacy to master the classic texts on female virtue, and the more talented wrote poetry. Their most important study was of the female arts of embroidery, sewing, shoemaking, and household management. Much of their needlework was devoted to quilts and clothing that would constitute their dowry in marriage, and to the tiny shoes for their bound feet. Footbinding, supervised by mothers and starting at about the same age young boys entered school, was the classic female form of painful discipline and preparation for adult life—which for young women meant marriage into another family of comparable status.[48]

Most young men and women had their marriages arranged by their parents while they were teenagers (if not before) and were married by their early twenties. Marriage partners were carefully selected from other members of the elite. Marital bonds were important means of cementing ties between two families, and it was not unusual for two elite lineages to exchange spouses repeatedly. Marital alliances were always among social equals, and the genealogy reports many daughters marrying the sons of local gentry or brides chosen from the daughters of degree holders. Many of the brides came from families who lived in the city, which no doubt reflected the regular social intercourse among the Anqing elite.[49] If a wife was childless, a well-off gentry member would usually take a concubine. Such polygamy was common in gentry families and considered both necessary and proper for the all-important purpose of ensuring a family heir. Not all concubines were taken out of obligation to the family line. An equally common pattern saw successful, middle-aged members of the elite taking one or more young concubines after their wives had already borne heirs. In these cases, the concubine replaced the wife as the husband's primary source of sexual and personal companionship.[50] Genealogical sources are generally silent on affairs of the heart, but one of the conventions of Chinese poetry was for men to write in the voice of their consorts. Ye Kunhou wrote dozens of poems in this form, and one of the most common tropes was the concubine's fear of losing favor as she aged. Was her beauty fading like a wilting flower? Was her makeup in the latest fashion? The status of these concubines was always precarious, and one can imagine the anxiety of Ye Kunhou's concubines when, late in life, a colleague presented him with a "singing girl" (geji) for companionship in his old age.[51]

The life of a woman marrying into such a family could be difficult. In most cases, the young bride had not met her husband before their wedding day, though the fact that the Ye chose brides from other Anqing elite families raises the likelihood that young women had an opportunity to steal a glimpse of their future mates. The new wife would enter her husband's household as an outsider, anxious to please but uncertain of the ways of her new home. When the bride came from a family with which the Ye had previously intermarried, she was less isolated. The established bond between the two families provided a degree of familiarity and protection, and she might well find aunts or cousins from her natal family among the in-laws of her new home. Nonetheless, the suspicion that greeted young wives was a potential source of divisive quarrels. A young bride needed to prove herself a loyal member of her new family, and especially had to please her mother-in-law. The mother-in-law instructed her on her chores and duties, for women were responsible for the smooth ordering of the domestic realm. These responsibilities mostly involved training and carefully monitoring servants, for an elite household such as these would have cooks, cleaning servants, nursemaids, and porters to do most of the work. One particularly meticulous mistress of the house was praised for carefully inspecting the house cleaning, seeing that firewood was not left near the stove, and making sure that the water cisterns were full as a precaution against the fires that threatened the closely packed wooden houses of the city.[52]

We should not overestimate the subservience of these women. The genealogy's injunctions against seeking brides from wealthy families, lest they think their husband's family too humble and become haughty and stubborn, is a reminder that even young brides found ways to work their will in a new home. They maintained contacts with their natal family, beginning with a ceremonial return visit three days after the wedding. Any complaints about the treatment they were receiving would cause a great loss of face for the husband's family. Needless to say, the Ye genealogy contains no such stories, instead describing the positive ways in which women established their place in the family.

The care and nurture of sons and parents-in-law were unquestionably a wife's most important duties. Looking after aging in-laws and accompanying their sons as they studied late at night are recurrent themes in the genealogy's brief eulogies of women. A proper wife would endure poverty without complaint, economize on food, sew and patch clothes while her son studied, all with an eye to the future prosperity of the family.[53] In these ways, a woman established her place in the family, which was likely to entail significant control of domestic life, an area in which husbands typically did not intervene.[54] As she gained position and power in family life, intimate relations with her husband might well diminish, especially if he was off traveling on official duties and her place in the bedroom was usurped by younger concubines. For such middle-aged and older wives, other diversions became important. One biography describes a family matron's fondness for the tales of blind female storytellers, who would visit the women's apartments to spin melodramatic tales of loyalty and filial piety, righteousness and good faith.[55] Despite the warnings of the regulations, many women no doubt participated in pilgrimages to local temples or visits to temple fairs, with their popular open-air operas.

For the males of the family, after their exam preparations—or even while they continued, for those who kept trying into adulthood—their family roles revolved around filial piety. Even discounting to a certain degree the genealogy's emphasis on this classic Confucian virtue, care for one's parents was unquestionably an important organizing principle of daily life. Especially as their parents aged, sons were expected to see them to bed and accompany them, perhaps reading silently, until they fell asleep. When away at school, one son sent his servant to perform this nightly ritual. Another forsook an official career to be with his sick mother. The ultimate ritual act of filial piety, recorded for several in the family, was to cut a piece of one's own flesh and cook it with medicine for an ailing parent. In almost all cases, these acts of filial piety were directed toward mothers, and the emotional bond between mother and son was certainly far stronger than the often stern authoritarian relations that prevailed between fathers and sons.[56]

Fathers, especially if they were busy officials, were unlikely to pay close attention to everyday household affairs. On one occasion, Ye Kunhou praised a letter from his wife for avoiding any bothersome mention of family matters.[57] With their children, fathers were expected to be stolid authority figures, but there is plenty of evidence for strong affective bonds with children and especially for fathers' love for their daughters. When his daughter went off to join her husband's family, Ye Kunhou wrote to remind her to be properly obedient: her in-laws would not spoil her as he had. The affection was surely reciprocated, for this daughter returned repeatedly to her natal family to care for her parents in their old age.[58] With sons, the emotional bond was more subdued, but a young boy's attachment to his father occasionally shows through Kunhou's poems. When he first leaves for office, "My little boy grabs my gown and asks, 'Where are you going? After you go, who will look after me? Who will I turn to when I'm hungry?'"[59] His brother's son longs for his father away at office and asks to join him.[60] Another poem imagines the family's distress about a son who is away from home: the mother frets over who will care for him when he is hungry or sick; the brother asks who will help him if he is in need; but the father's concern is more selfish: "Who will bring my food and drink? Who will fetch my staff and shoes?"[61] As we shall see presently, the tight bond between Ye Kunhou and his son Boying evolved into a lifelong mentorship in the duties of officialdom and the moral principles of a virtuous life.

Ye family elites presented themselves as scholars and literati. Land provided much of their income, but after they moved to the city, they were absentee landlords, and there is no evidence that they did anything more than send agents to collect rent from their properties. Some were active in community service, managing water control and famine relief; and they would certainly be consulted by local officials about pressing public affairs. All these activities were important, and essential to the family's economic well-being, but they receive only passing mention in the sources. Economic matters involved profit making and were not the sort of thing that genealogies dwelt on. The public face that the family presented was that of the scholar.

Many Ye men were teachers and earned important income from that calling. A few knew some medicine from the ancient medical texts and served as local doctors—one of the few practical specialties deemed consistent with literati status.[62] All wrote poetry, and especially in the Ming dynasty, they were noted for their ability to express sentiment in their poems, for that was required by the standards of the time. Strong and elegant calligraphy was important, and many were known for the beauty of their brushwork. Like scholars everywhere, they collected books, many hand copies of rare volumes borrowed from friends. In addition to their poetry, many wrote essays, which they distributed and discussed with friends. One of the main pleasures of their lives seemed to be gathering with friends, over a flask of rice wine, to exchange and discuss poetry, or ancient texts, or essays on current themes. These gatherings gave meaning to their lives, and such discussions were the proper avocation of scholars. This was the sort of family into which Ye Kunhou and Ye Boying were born.[63]

# 3

# Father, Son, and Family

Early one afternoon in the spring of 1802, in the old family home west of the county *yamen* in Anqing, Ye Kunhou was born. His twenty-seven-year-old mother, a devout woman who prayed frequently at the nearby temple to the bodhisattva Guanyin, had been rewarded with her first son. (She would eventually have six children, five sons and a daughter, though the daughter and two sons would die young.) On the day before Kunhou's birth, his mother had been visited in a dream by a white-gowned woman promising that the family's record of good works would be rewarded with a son. His mother's belief in the bodhisattva's loving concern was subsequently conveyed to her son, for throughout his childhood, Kunhou had a recurring dream of Guanyin coming to comb his hair, a well-known symbol of female affection.[1]

Kunhou's father, Ye Yuting, was a failed scholar remembered for filial piety and unrestrained generosity. Despite long hours of study under the supervision of his own strict father, Yuting failed repeatedly at the exams and ended up purchasing a lowly *jiansheng* degree. He lived in an extended family with his parents and an older brother, who was clearly the less conventional of the siblings. Despite a precocious start as a student, the brother espoused unusual interpretations of classical texts and wrote essays that diverged from the officially prescribed style. Ignoring an uncle's advice that he follow the rules in order to pass the exams, he persisted in his ways, with the predicted result. Thereafter, he led the relaxed life of a local literatus—writing poetry, drinking with friends, listening to music, collecting paintings and antiques.[2]

When his elder brother died in 1813 at the age of forty-seven, Yuting assumed responsibility for the household, providing fine food and beautiful clothes for his brother's children. One of these children displayed a practical streak not seen (or not recorded) in the rest of the family and abandoned his studies for the more profitable life of a merchant. Yuting himself was proverbially impractical about material things. He had inherited from his father several hundred *mu* of good farmland. Although a *mu* is only one-sixth of an acre, and these farms probably totaled less than one hundred acres—small by American or European standards—in China they were substantial holdings, and high yields of irrigated rice and rents of around 50 percent of the harvest brought the family a comfortable living. Yuting's generosity gradually changed this life. When the peasants who leased his land pleaded poverty, Yuting reduced their rents, often collecting only 20 to 30 percent of the normal amount. Friends and relatives came often to borrow money, and Yuting always obliged and rarely pressed them to repay. He was known as such an easy mark that other members of the local elite sent their relatives to him rather than offering loans themselves. Sometimes Yuting sold or mortgaged land to make loans that quickly went into default. When borrowers could not repay, he simply burned the loan documents; then on his deathbed, rather than burden his debtors and their heirs, he destroyed the records of all those who still owed him money. Yuting's sons and heirs carefully recorded these conventional acts of largesse in the family genealogy, but their accounts betray a certain bitterness that their father's generosity had left their own childhood substantially less comfortable than it might have been.[3]

What was lost materially by such munificence was rewarded in popular esteem. Friends often visited the Ye family in the comfortable house near the river, with its large garden full of flowers, where they could relax and exchange poems.[4] Neighbors often asked Yuting to settle disputes, trusting his judgment to be fair and principled. He never spoke harshly of anyone, and if others were rude, he simply walked away. In the genealogy account, he is, of course, a proper filial son. His father lived into his seventies and his mother to her eighties, with Yuting already sixty by the time of her death. In one of the proverbial marks of filial behavior, he is said to have played before his parents like a young child, helping them forget their advancing years.[5]

During Kunhou's youth, while his grandfather was still alive, an extended family with father, uncle, and cousins all lived together. The cohesiveness of this household unit is indicated in the way the boys of Kunhou's generation were counted. In Kunhou's poems and Boying's autobiography, the eleven male cousins, six of whom survived childhood, were counted in a single sequence, so that Kunhou's two younger siblings were always referred to as sixth and ninth brother (or uncle). These three brothers and the youngest surviving cousin (number three in the sequence) were particularly close, and their affectionate fraternity extended throughout their lifetimes.[6] At age four, Kunhou entered the family school, taught by a local degree holder. As custom required, he composed a poem to present on his first day of school. The lineage head was much impressed, and Kunhou never forgot the praise he received for his precocity.[7] He proved an able student, finishing (which meant memorizing) the Four Books, the core of Neo-Confucian learning, at age six and the Five Classics three years later. Kunhou's photographic memory amazed his teachers and earned him a local reputation as a prodigy—in Chinese, a divinely gifted child *(shentong)*. His grandfather occasionally tested him on his lessons, once rewarding him with a brush and ink for flawlessly reciting a complex passage from the *Book of Changes (Yijing,* or *I Ching* in the old spelling). Usually his grandfather expressed his approbation more indirectly, telling his wife that he admired the boy's talent, knowing that she would pass the word on to Kunhou.[8] The old man thus maintained an aura of patriarchal reserve and allowed the women of the household to provide soothing encouragement—and to bear the responsibility if such praise should give rise to excessive pride. Kunhou's uncle was less circumspect; he invited the boy to join his literary gatherings, showing off the lad's impressive poetic skills before his friends.[9]

Kunhou's mother played a typically prominent role in his childhood. In her sons' idealized account, she was the diligent matron whose hard work and self-sacrifice kept the family going as her husband's profligate generosity slowly depleted its re- sources. As a young bride, she dressed simply in cloth skirts, rising early to grind grain for the morning meal or draw water from the well, even before the maids started work. She skimped on food and clothing, mending clothes to keep the family budget in balance and help conceal the family's increasingly straitened circumstances. Nothing was more important than the education of Kunhou and his brothers. To ensure their proper instruction, she urged their teacher to be strict, saw to it that their meals were proper and plentiful, and when money was short for tuition, pawned jewelry from her dowry to pay it. In the evening, after the boys had reported on their lessons to their father, she took her needlework and accompanied them as they recited classical texts around the dim oil lamp in the study or practiced cal- ligraphy by tracing characters in ash sprinkled on the floor.[10] The youngest son was her favorite, and because Kunhou was nine years older, he often tutored this young brother, helping him with passages he had studied years before.[11] When the boys took a break, their mother earnestly reminded them that hard study was the route to fame and fortune. Because their house was next to the county *yamen,* she watched the commotion in the streets every time the examinations were held, anxiously ask- ing her boys when they would be ready to join the young candidates.

When the time finally came for the boys to take the examinations, their mother could hardly contain her excitement. She personally prepared their brushes and ink- stones, then sent the boys to bed early for a good night's sleep. After repairing to the kitchen to prepare breakfast, she lay awake most of the night listening to the watchman call the hour. When dawn finally came, she hesitated to awake her sons, wishing them to get every last minute of sleep but also worrying that they might be late. This anxious ritual continued for many long years before the brothers finally earned the lowest examination degree.[12] Then they headed off to higher exams down- river in Nanjing, and their mother waited fretfully for their return.[13]

Kunhou began taking the exams at age twelve, and they dominate his autobiographical account of the next twenty-five years. On his first attempt, the examiner, a member of the prestigious Hanlin Academy in the capital—perhaps impressed by a strong written paper from such a young boy—called him to the front for oral questioning; but in the end he did not pass. At age sixteen, he moved with his teacher to live with an aunt, whose husband was a local degree holder. Educational opportunity was more important than living with one's own family. The next year, his grandfather died and the family divided, his cousins (including the practical-minded merchant) perhaps wishing to protect their share of the inheritance from his father's generous ways.

In 1820, when Kunhou was eighteen, his parents found him a bride. Repeated failure in the examinations was making him nervous and sickly, and marriage was the family's solution. Regrettably, the logic behind this decision is unrecorded, but a poem Kunhou wrote about a maidservant, which seems to date from this time, suggests that he was ready for female companionship:

> Tiny body and narrow shoulders,
> Gentle temperament and graceful movement.
> When she sees I'm preparing to write, she grinds the ink.
> If I am composing poems, she spreads the paper.
> If I'm sleepy after drinking, she sweetly retires.
> After I have been sick, she still looks on me with pity.
> Her simple cotton clothes follow the current fashion,
> A delightful person, so neat and beautiful.[14]

A playful intimacy prevailed between Kunhou and this young servant, and she sometimes made fun of his struggle to compose a proper verse: "my maid turns and laughs to herself; / On the other side of the curtain, she imitates my hunched shoulders."[15] We do not know whether Kunhou's interest in this young maid played a part in his parents' decision, but they clearly saw his marriage as serving the preeminent goal of passing the examinations.[16] Years later, when Kunhou was a father, he followed the same formula, arranging his sons' weddings for the year in which they began taking the exams.[17]

Kunhou's wife was the daughter of a local *shengyuan* of the Zhao family, which had long intermarried with the Ye lineage and whose home Kunhou's mother often visited. The two young people were the same age, and a poem written by Kunhou in his wife's voice (a common genre of Chinese poetry) has her saying that "from childhood we cared for each other / Our affection has never ceased," which suggests that the couple had known each other from an early age.[18] The bride was both beautiful and literate, having read the appropriate texts for young ladies: the *Classic of Filial Piety*, the women's classic, and biographies of virtuous women. This basic level of women's culture made her a valuable companion to her husband in his studies, and like a dutiful wife, she kept him company at night, sewing as he pored over his lessons until the cock crowed at dawn.[19] Kunhou's poems suggest a real affection between the two. He writes a letter home for her when she misses her sister; she teases his efforts to rhyme a poem. When he leaves home to assume office in the north, she carefully measures his waist so that she can make and send him winter clothes. While they were apart, he wrote many poems in his wife's voice and his own, lamenting their separation.[20] One year after their marriage, she bore him a son, but the child died in infancy.

Kunhou returned to his exam preparations under a new teacher, holder of the prestigious metropolitan degree. His study became increasingly frantic when he learned that a friend had passed the provincial examination, while he had yet to gain even the county degree. Finally, in 1823, Ye Kunhou earned the initial *shengyuan* degree, and he was praised and encouraged by the governor, Tao Zhu, who would soon become one of the most prominent officials of the era. The following year, Kunhou was awarded the *gongsheng* degree in the provincial examinations— not quite equivalent to passing (which would have made him a *juren*) but adequate to qualify for office. The new governor of Anhui recognized his promise and invited him to join his own son and other talented youths in private sessions in the *yamen*. There a distinguished scholar on the governor's staff (who also presided over the local academy) and the governor himself led wide-ranging discussions of poetry, essays, and policy issues, all of which were covered in the exams. This arrangement continued for several years and illustrated the favored access to invaluable tutoring that came to those from good families, well situated in a provincial capital, who had demonstrated their basic competence in the local and provincial exams.[21]

For the next fifteen years, Ye Kunhou continued his studies, traveling repeatedly to Nanjing for the provincial-level *juren* examinations, where he failed again and again.[22] Several examiners praised his essays, encouraging him to carry on, but he always seemed to fall short. Another prominent official, a former president of the Board of Civil Appointments, took him into a select group for private tutoring in 1830, but his luck in the examinations did not change. In 1834, his father died, and Kunhou's salary from private tutoring and teaching at a local academy became the family's main source of financial support. Most of the family land had been sold or mortgaged to others, and a later Kunhou poem, envying a colleague who retired to live off two hundred *mu* (about thirty-five acres) of good farmland, makes it clear that his family had no similar landholdings.[23] Burdened by the cost of three brothers still in school studying for the exams, plus two young sons of his own, Ye Kunhou was obviously living in straitened circumstances. Poor harvests drove up the price of rice, and the family's financial position became even more precarious. They had little to add flavor to their simple meals of rice; eating meat was unthinkable; fish and shrimp were reserved for important holidays. Only when entertaining guests would they include chicken or pork to keep up appearances.[24] Unable to afford servants, Kunhou's wife personally attended to the household chores, sweating through the hot summers, her hands cracked from washing clothes in winter. This was a tough life for the educated daughter of a local degree holder, but she is said to have borne the hardship without complaint.

The preferred escape from such genteel poverty was an official appointment, and examinations were the route to office. Ye Kunhou wrote many poems about taking up office to escape poverty: "Hunger forces me to leave home; / Not a pint [sheng] of rice remains in the barrel. / My wife sells the clothes off her back to prepare a farewell feast."[25] In 1838, Kunhou traveled to Beijing for the metropolitan and palace examinations for which his gongsheng rank qualified him. His essays placed fourth in the first stage of the examination, but after entering the awesome precincts of the Forbidden City for the palace exam, he faced sixteen examiners, including six grand secretaries from the top of the metropolitan bureaucracy, who posed questions on behalf of the emperor. Kunhou was overwhelmed by the impressive palace ritual, felt terribly inadequate, and was unable to provide proper answers. He failed to win the metropolitan degree, but he did well enough to earn magistrate rank in Henan province. This was not yet a regular appointment, and he hesitated to accept it until persuaded by a prominent metropolitan official from Anqing. He later wrote to a colleague in similar circumstances, "You did not decline a petty appointment. / We are officials only because our families are poor . . . / Even a small county post provides enough to support our parents."[26]

A ceremonial audience with the emperor affirmed the Son of Heaven's direct involvement in the appointment process. The opportunity to approach the emperor's person and gaze upon the royal countenance was an unforgettable experience for a man of Kunhou's relatively modest circumstances. As he left the impressive court ceremony, with courtiers arrayed along the approaches to the throne room, he savored the scent of the palace's special incense on his clothes.[27] The Qing audience rituals were an important means by which the dynasty fostered among its officials a sense of personal obligation to the emperor. When Ye Kunhou listed the ways in which the Qing surpassed all previous dynasties, the emperor's diligent attention to these ceremonies was the first item. The other items on his list also related to the imperial institution: the emperor's personal reading of memorials (reports) from officials far away, the attention to educating the heir to the throne, and strict measures to limit the influence of consort families and eunuchs. He had no doubt that the Qing had led China to the height of its power, and he was proud to be one of its public servants.[28] From the capital he proceeded to Henan, where, as a magistrate in training, he was given responsibility for processing legal appeals in a board of judicial review. At age thirty-six, after twenty-four years of examination life, he at last entered the ranks of the imperial bureaucracy.[29]

As an expectant official, Ye Kunhou was deputized by the governor of Henan to carry out special tasks. Such assignments were a standard means to test the admin-

FIGURE 3. Ye Kunhou. Drawn
for the 1906 edition of the Ye
genealogy. At the top are
his title, Grand Master for
Assisting Governance, and his
courtesy name, Xiangjun.

istrative skills of men who had qualified for office by writing learned essays on ancient classics, and Kunhou seemed to distinguish himself. On several occasions, he was sent for short-term duty as an acting magistrate, filling in while the official appointed from Beijing was proceeding to his post. In 1839, he was given responsibility for opium suppression in the province, a reflection far in the interior of the nationwide campaign that would soon spark the outbreak of the Opium War in Canton.

These first years in office were not particularly happy. Kunhou's family remained in Anqing, and he missed his wife, his brothers, and his children.[30] All his years of studying had done little to prepare him for official life. Though his superiors forgave his mistakes, he felt that despite his best efforts, he was constantly failing in his responsibilities. He compared official life to swimming against a swift current, and the many tricks played by well-entrenched clerks and petty functionaries in the bureaucracy were particularly frustrating.[31] He wrote to his brother, "When you look from the sidelines, [governing] appears easy. / When you are responsible for [public] affairs, you realize how difficult it is."[32] As he traveled about the province, he saw peasants impoverished by successive poor harvests and in arrears on their taxes. They were often taken into custody, beaten, and tortured by tax collectors making their rounds. He pressed the country folk for details of such abuse, but they were afraid to speak out.[33]

> Officials are like tigers, lictors like foxes.
> People are seized day and night and dare not cry out.
> Iron chains and metal clasps cut their flesh to the bone.
> The pitiful souls! Nowhere is their skin unbroken;
> Then think of their state of mind.
> With no money to buy their freedom,
> They will be forced to sell their children.[34]

As Kunhou considered his position, he recalled that as a young man he had been ashamed to associate with profit-seeking merchants. Now as an official he was forced to collect taxes even in bad times, "acting like a tiger," or like a merchant collecting overdue debts.[35]

After several years of routine duty as a local official on trial, Ye Kunhou attracted favorable attention from his superiors when a major flood threatened Kaifeng, Henan's capital, in 1841.[36] Kaifeng lies on the south bank of the Yellow River, which derives its name from the heavy silt content eroded from the barren hills of northwest China. When the river reaches the broad flat north China plain and the current slows, silt is deposited on the riverbed so that over the centuries, the bed has been raised to such a height that only massive earthen dikes can keep the current within the river's banks. If the dikes cannot withstand the sudden surges of water that follow heavy summer rains, the Yellow River breaks its banks and floods over the plain in the deadly disasters that have earned it the nickname "China's Sorrow." An elaborate bureaucracy was responsible for maintaining the Yellow River dikes, but Kunhou observed that many officials enriched themselves off flood-control funds and carried out only emergency repairs.[37] The 1841 floods followed a long drought. Indeed, accounts of the disaster note that officials appealed to the Dragon God for rain, only to have their prayers answered in excess. With the dikes failing, Ye Kunhou accompanied the governor to inspect the floodwaters. Soon Kaifeng itself was threatened. As panic engulfed the city, a messenger swam to the governor on the dikes, urging his urgent return. The governor and Kunhou returned to the city by boat. With the gates closed against the flood, they had to go over the walls, lowering themselves into the city by rope. Kunhou left this poetic description of the scene within the city:

> Donkeys and horses run about; chickens cry and dogs howl.
> On the streets and alleys, people lift up their clothes and wade
>     against the current.
> [In the city there are] a myriad officials, gentry and common people,
> And also key offices, granaries and treasuries.
> The cries of the inhabitants are like thunder.

For miles about, people are in panic.
The common folk regard the water as an advancing army:
Their mouths open, eyes wide, standing like statues.
They believe that most will not survive.
The sound of wailing lasts from dawn to dusk.
On the streets is tragedy, while above the sun disappears in the darkened sky.
All is chaos and no one knows what to do.[38]

Kunhou was appointed acting magistrate of the county that included Kaifeng and given responsibility for defending the flood-encircled city, but he needed material to reinforce the walls. The Yellow River commissioner, responsible for flood control and in charge of supplies to strengthen the dikes, was involved in a dispute with the governor and secretly ordered his staff not to assist the city. Under a strong and vigorous emperor such bureaucratic infighting might have been controlled, but in these times the court was weak, divided, and preoccupied with the Opium War. No central authority brought efficient discipline to competing bureaucratic interests. Left to his own devices, Ye Kunhou collected and bought any wood, brick, tiles, or debris he could find in the city, dug up old stonework from the time when Kaifeng was capital of the Northern Song dynasty (960–1126), and had it all thrown into the advancing waters to deflect the current from the city walls. The water got through anyway, rising as high as several meters in some places, and the residents took refuge in reed sheds atop the walls or on the roofs of larger houses and temples. With food running short, the officials hired boats to bring relief from the surrounding counties and bought up grain supplies to resell to the residents at controlled prices. For twenty days, the city was cut off by the flood, and it was eighty days before the waters receded completely and recovery work could begin.

The surrounding countryside was devastated. The young and the weak were swept away by the raging waters; stronger peasants clung to trees until they toppled, or climbed on roofs until the stamped earth and wattle houses dissolved into mud and joined the torrent. Most of those who survived the flood were destined to perish in the famine that followed, many too old and weak to reach the government's soup kitchens.[39] Two years later, another flood struck the same area, and Ye Kunhou described the devastation in its wake:

Nothing grows in the barren countryside.
Vast emptiness with no spring growth,
Bare earth for a thousand *li*,
The floods have erased neighbors on all sides.
Dust and sand obscure the road.
Wind and rain block all travelers.[40]

In one probably exaggerated poem, Kunhou wrote that only three to five of a hundred people survived.[41] Casualties certainly numbered in the tens of thousands.

While Henan was wracked by flood and famine and Kunhou was performing his official duties, he could not escape obligations to his extended family. Since his father's death, Ye Kunhou had been the family's main provider. His official position now solved many of the family's financial problems. Although the nominal salaries of imperial bureaucrats were notoriously low, any official position gave access to "customary fees" and to gifts from other officials or people seeking favor or influence.[42] As a result, office was one of the most reliable routes to comfortable wealth, and this was the case with the Ye family. During his first year in office, Ye Kunhou left his family behind in Anqing, and his poetry was filled with conventional tropes of separation. He thinks of his young son grabbing his robe and recalls his wife measuring his waist so that she can prepare proper winter clothes.[43] By 1839 (his second year in office), Kunhou was able to bring his mother to Kaifeng in the comfort of a sedan chair. She was accompanied by Kunhou's wife and son and by his two brothers and their families. Kunhou's wife recognized the extent to which the family's fortunes had now turned, telling her husband with filial solicitude, "I am not so much happy at your getting an official post as I am for your mother being comfortably supported in her old age, as some compensation for the past years of hardship."[44] His mother was not sure that the family could afford so much comfort, warning that in good times frugality easily gives way to extravagance but extravagant habits are more difficult to break to return to frugality.[45]

Kunhou's mother, Lady Zhao, was the matriarch of the family and the hub of its domestic activities. Sixty-four years old when she arrived in Henan, she had been widowed for five years and now wished more than anything for her sons to be successful in their official careers. In her old age, a fairly devout Buddhism entered her routine. Every evening she burned incense to the Buddha, and she fasted several days each month.[46] One of the few pleasures she allowed herself was listening to the tales of blind female storytellers invited to the family compound, or eavesdropping when they visited the family next door.[47] As she became engrossed in their stories, she would angrily curse the villains and urge those around her to emulate the heroes' ways.[48] When the stories involved historical events or allusions with which she was unfamiliar, she asked her younger son to explain them later in the evening.[49]

From this combination of Buddhist scripture and popular literature, Lady Zhao derived a clear if conventional moral sense centered on the Confucian virtues of loyalty, filial piety, faithfulness, and righteousness. Coming from an Anqing gentry family, she was familiar with tales of official corruption and abuse of power. When she joined her son at his first official post in Henan, she was quick to offer maternal advice and warnings. "You have achieved office," she told her son, "because of the accumulated merit of your ancestors. For generations your family has been poor and humble, honest and generous, living simply from the income of its rice fields and never abusing the peasants. Now you have an opportunity to serve the court and work on behalf of the people, restraining yourself and serving the public." She had seen many families grow rich and powerful from official service. Their prosperity could not be maintained, for the gods became jealous of their high-handed ways. As a result, either they died young, or they had no heirs and their family line was cut off, leaving them the laughing stock of their neighbors. This sort of heavenly retribution, so common in the stories of which she was fond, seemed natural, even inevitable, to her. The sorry fate of previously great families was a consequence of their abuse of power in exploiting the people. She urged her son to heed this lesson.[50]

Ye Kunhou was too much the Confucian agnostic to believe in this sort of divine intervention in the affairs of men.

> I suppose I might pray to Buddha,
> But I am certainly not a disciple of Buddhism.
> I might also pray to the gods,
> But the gods may not even exist.
> So I will just cling to learning and speak from the heart,
> Earnestly and honestly behaving like a true Confucian scholar [ru].[51]

He openly disdained those who prayed to the gods for personal benefit: "Disaster or good fortune come from oneself; / The gods are without effect."[52] He shared his mother's concerns about extremes of wealth and poverty and the dangers of family extravagance. But he treated the issue in practical and purely secular terms. His explanation, in a simple rhyme probably intended for public edification, pointed to the important role of ancestors, but he turned the logic into an argument for thrift on behalf of one's children.

> Rich folks feast with wine;
> The poor have only a half year of grain.
> Though these words are very common,
> Their meaning is quite profound.
> The rich are idle all year;
> The poor are busy year 'round.
> The rich enjoy plentiful surplus;
> The poor have nothing stored.
> But if we consider the ancestors of the wealthy,
> They too were busy as they established themselves.
> In order to leave something to their descendants,
> They did not consider their own difficulties.
> Who can say whether the descendants of the poor
> Might also enjoy bountiful harvests?
> We should be sorry for the ancestors;
> They are the ones who had a bitter life.[53]

Here is how a Confucian official justified the inequities of human circumstances, supported proper respect for parents and ancestors, and also held out hope to the less fortunate that diligence and thrift would be rewarded in future generations.

In addition to Lady Zhao, other women in Kunhou's household offered advice on official matters, and their moral compass was equally Confucian. His wife reminded him of his family's good reputation and the need to protect it: "Poverty is no cause for concern. Integrity is the crux of life and one must not stray from that in the slightest." Later, as Kunhou rose to more substantive positions and eventually became a prefect, responsible for maintaining order and adjudicating legal matters, he often worked late into the night, poring over his documents and agonizing over the proper course to take. On these occasions, his wife could see his concern and urged the course of lenience and generosity, in keeping with her moral aversion to cruel and harsh governance.[54] Such counsels of benevolent governance are of course conventional, but they reveal that the women of the family were important bearers of this political morality and did not hesitate to use their domestic access to official kin to proffer advice on public affairs—an important role that is perhaps too little noted.[55]

Women, of course, were not the only voices in Ye Kunhou's household. Kunhou's brothers left their homes in Anqing to accompany him to Henan and played a significant role in his life. Despite all the rhetoric about keeping many generations of a family together, the normal pattern saw brothers establishing their own households and dividing the family property either upon marriage or upon the death of their father.[56] The Ye family did not splinter in this way, nor did either of Kunhou's younger brothers stay behind in Anqing to look after the family home and property. Though the two brothers were married and the older already had two sons, they both followed Kunhou to Kaifeng, helping to care for their mother and tutoring Kunhou's sons. They also advised and assisted their brother in his work, just as years earlier Ye Hua's brother had accompanied him to his post and helped him deal with legal cases.[57] The imperial bureaucracy was suspicious of nepotism. The "law of avoidance," which prohibited officials from serving in their home province and did not allow close relatives to hold office in the same province, was a deliberate effort to prevent family ties from interfering with officials' obligation to the emperor. But nothing prevented family members from serving on the personal staff of an official, and for Ye Kunhou (as for many other Qing officials), this was the norm. His brothers assisted him in Henan before they received appointments of their own, and later their sons and Kunhou's sons, as well as several other in-laws and nephews, served on Kunhou's staff.[58]

The bonds between Kunhou and his brothers were notably strong, and Kunhou constantly exchanged poems with them, lamenting their separation, celebrating the arrival of letters, recalling their happy times together.[59] Periodically, they returned to Anqing or Nanjing to take the examinations, and soon both brothers passed the lowest level exams and received posts of their own. Ye Lian became a magistrate in Shandong, after distinguishing himself in temporary assignments on flood control and bandit suppression. Ye Yun was posted to Anhui as an education official, but he took sick leave after a few months and returned to Kunhou's household, where he cared for their mother.[60]

At the time of the Kaifeng flood, the entire family was together in the city. The threat was sufficient that on two occasions, Ye Kunhou urged his kinsmen to flee. The first time, they were unable to get away. Later, when Kunhou was back at the office to manage the crisis, he sent a second urgent message telling the family to flee at once. Though the rates were exorbitant, the family could afford to hire boats to get away. Kunhou's mother insisted that each brother leave separately and that each take one grandson as an heir. The servants strenuously objected to the threatened breakup of the family (for their status was tied to the large extended-family household of a local official), but the mother's first concern was the survival of the family line.[61] In time, of course, the family was reunited, having survived the worst crisis of its time in Henan.

The best years came near the end of this era, after Ye Kunhou was appointed prefect of Nanyang, a rich prefecture in the southwest of the province, in 1848. This was Kunhou's first major regular appointment, and great crowds lined the roads to observe the arrival of the new prefect.[62] The family had occasion to celebrate its legendary roots when Kunhou discovered and restored a memorial hall to the duke of Ye, who was supposed to have ruled the area in ancient times.[63] He staged a major reception for his mother's arrival, with drums and music and the crowds that they attracted. With guards and banners and her son, the prefect, riding ahead of her procession, Lady Zhao was delighted by the good fortune that now blessed her progeny.[64] The family had come a long way since Ye Kunhou took office to escape poverty, and indeed it seems to have traced the proverbial route of those who would "get rich through official promotion." Soon Ye Boying's first son was born, and the family had four generations under one roof.[65] The previous incumbent had expanded the prefectural *yamen*, so it had plenty of room. Ye Kunhou constructed a large garden for his mother in open land near the *yamen*, and the servants often carried her outside in a sedan chair to enjoy the flowers and birds. The garden occupied some thirty acres, with a pond filled by a stream and a small hill to view the city wall and the surrounding mountains. Over time, Kunhou supervised the planting of hundreds of bamboo, plum trees, and a vegetable patch. The garden contained over three hundred varieties of flowers, with peonies in profusion in the spring and chrysanthemums in the fall. In addition to Lady Zhao's favorite storytellers, opera troupes were invited to entertain the elderly matriarch in the garden. In the evening, her grandchildren gathered in her chamber to keep her company. Her normal habit was to nap after dinner, then rise after midnight to change for bed; and her youngest son (who seems the most devoted) would sleep in a cot by her bedside to make sure that she was all right. Surrounded by her sons, grandchildren, and great-grandchildren, the matriarch, despite her failing health, enjoyed the happiest years of her life.[66]

The young Ye Boying seemed less content. Like all scions of the scholar-official elite, his life was dominated by preparations for the exams. At home, he was tutored by his uncles, and he studied with degree holders from Henan. By this time, he had already failed several times. Then in 1843, his father purchased for him a *jiansheng* degree, which allowed him to take the provincial examinations in Nanjing. But (according to Boying's account) the examiner disapproved of those who qualified by this purchased route, so Boying failed at this level as well. The following year, floods blocked the most direct route to Nanjing, but he traveled, probably by cart and accompanied by a servant, by a circuitous detour, only to fail again.[67] Convinced that the *jiansheng* degree was doing him no good, he returned to Anqing for the local *shengyuan* examinations, and after several days in a freezing examination cubicle, he passed. He was just twenty years old, and his father was delighted: "Today your career begins," but, he cautioned, "establishing yourself still involves many big steps."[68]

Of course, this degree alone did not qualify Boying for office, so his examination life was by no means over. In 1847, Boying left his wife in Henan and returned with his brother to Anqing to attend an academy there. His autobiography describes the pleasures of debating literary and scholarly issues with friends. This theme recurs in his account of an 1849 trip to Nanjing for another attempt at the exams. There too he gathered with his contemporaries from school, relaxed and drank rice wine, and talked about literature. These journeys to school or the exams were for the young Ye Boying something of an escape from life in a large family, a chance to be among young men his own age, to relax and enjoy himself and talk about personal and intellectual matters of common concern. In the cities of the lower Yangzi, teahouses, wine shops, and brothels were as likely places for young men to gather as bookstores or academic halls. Surely the good times that Boying enjoyed were not all derived from the scholarly discussions he records in his autobiography. His father, during one of his many visits to Nanjing, had written of a visit to the floating brothels on the river: "By chance, I thought of inviting friends to enjoy the famous 'flowers' . . . / I don't know at whose place I will spend the night."[69] Boying left no similar record, and these trips provided only a temporary escape, for soon he was back serving his father and grandmother in Henan.[70]

Ye Boying traveled twice to Nanjing in the years immediately following the treaty named for that city, which China had signed following defeat by Great Britain in the Opium War, but his autobiography makes no mention of this event. The Opium War and the onslaught of Western imperialism would change the course of China's modern history; but for this young scholar of China's interior, the new threat of the

West hardly registered on his consciousness. His father wrote a number of poems on the "English barbarians," lamenting China's military weakness after long years of peace, but he always presented the threat in terms of China's long history of nomadic attacks on the northern frontier. There was no recognition that Western imperialism represented a military, economic, and cultural threat of an entirely new order. Kunhou looked for the appearance of a brave general on the model of ancient military heroes and condemned those who sought a peaceful resolution of the crisis. Most remarkably, when peace came with the Treaty of Nanjing, he wrote of the exhaustion of the invaders who "surrendered and asked for the opening of trade."[71] Here was a classic example of what the famous twentieth-century writer Lu Xun satirized as the "Ah Q" syndrome in modern China—the proud refusal to admit defeat and confront one's failings.[72] Ye Kunhou could be quite humble and self-critical about his personal accomplishments, but he was not prepared to admit that China had been defeated or that the Western threat required a response any different from that which had subdued previous barbarian invaders.

As Boying grew older, his father began grooming him for an official career. As time permitted, Kunhou supervised his son's studies and offered advice on ethics. He warned against following the conventional opinions of common people or merely adhering to book learning—just the sort of practical advice that one might expect of a man whose administrative accomplishments were more impressive than his record in the examinations.[73] He also offered advice on proper behavior. Success in life required a certain attention to etiquette: "In clothes and food, casualness is common and should be avoided."[74] Above all, Kunhou counseled diligence, modesty, and patience. He seemed to find his son lacking in these virtues. The young man was too eager to move ahead, and his father warned, "If the tiger is not drawn properly, it will look like a dog." The remedy was to learn the modesty of the supple bamboo and the sturdiness of the windblown pine.[75]

In addition to offering hortatory poems to his son, Kunhou brought Boying along as he performed his official duties. A prefect was responsible for a substantial territory (twelve counties in the case of Nanyang), and Kunhou spent much of his time on the road. He also made periodic trips to the provincial capital, and on one occasion, the roads were so muddy that the trip took half a month.[76] Sometimes the two went sightseeing together, with Kunhou explaining historical sites. On other occasions, Kunhou probed the challenges of his jurisdiction, observing the violent temperament of the people in the unruly hill country.[77] The trips served as a kind of unpaid family internship for Boying, who had to act as his father's loyal aide in a complex social and bureaucratic environment. The extent to which the two worked as a father-son pair was most evident soon after Kunhou's arrival at Nanyang, when they had to deal with bandit gangs that would later grow into the Nian Rebellion and rage over much of north China.

The problems in Nanyang arose because the previous prefect had neglected military preparations, allowing banditry to get out of hand. As the bandits grew stronger, the military became indecisive, following the outlaws at a safe distance and avoiding any contact that might lead to casualties. The local gentry, seeing the weak government response and fearing reprisals, saw to its own defenses and lodged no official complaints that might trigger bandit retaliation. Ye Kunhou from the beginning took a more activist approach, at least according to his (and his son's) no doubt self-serving accounts.[78] He spent as much time moving about the prefecture investigating complaints as he did in the office. Traveling with only two horses, a cart, and a small guard of five or six soldiers, he brought his own food and stayed in temples rather than relying on the county offices. He heard cases in person, and managed to establish enough reputation for fairness that people began coming to him for settlement of their disputes and accepting his decisions. The approach reflected his consistent suspicion of corruption and abuse among the clerks who controlled access to the court in the official *yamen:* "When people come in they are beaten, / When they leave they are fleeced of their money." As a result, "People want to see an official, not a clerk. / When they see an official, they are not afraid. / When they see a clerk, they are pathetic."[79] In this area, where people had long regarded officials as ineffectual and were accustomed to solving problems on their own, Kunhou's direct methods reestablished public trust in the government.

After about a year as prefect, Ye Kunhou proceeded to Beijing in July 1849 for the imperial audience that would normally have occurred at the time of appointment. This time the audience was conducted at the Yuanmingyuan Summer Palace. Because Kunhou was coming directly from the provinces, the emperor used the occasion to learn about conditions in his jurisdiction. After asking where Kunhou was from and what his past appointments had been (items on which the court staff would already have provided a briefing memorandum), and several routine questions about the harvest in the prefecture, the emperor turned to the problems with the local bandits and urged vigorous efforts to control them.

Most of the imperial directives seem quite conventional—work hard, avoid indolence among subordinates, pay strict attention to military training and patrols—but several of the emperor's injunctions are notable. One cited the critical importance of personal integrity (*caoshou*) in an official, a Confucian conviction that virtuous officials (not strict adherence to regulations or new and creative policies) were the key to effective governance. He also urged Kunhou to carefully supervise the conduct of his private staff and household servants. In the Qing bureaucracy, each official hired his own private secretaries, who were specialists on such matters as legal affairs and public finance. He also hired servants and retainers attached to his household, paying out of his own pocket. They were his men, needed to oversee and control the locally recruited clerks, constables, and tax collectors.[80] The emperor worried that such retainers could abuse their authority and oppress the people.[81] Ye Kunhou's reliance on family members was one way to guarantee that his assistants would be absolutely loyal and serve his interests rather than some private agenda of their own.

After a stay of about two months in the capital, eight days of which were spent within the privileged precincts of the scenic summer palace, Kunhou returned to Nanyang.[82] The next year was relatively uneventful, but 1851 proved to be a time of troubles. Coping with the rising tide of banditry was the underlying issue, but the effort was complicated by a conflict with the neighboring district's prefect. Unfortunately, we can see only one side of the controversy, but the problem apparently rose from Kunhou's aggressive effort to get into the field and mediate disputes. Apparently his reputation was such that even residents of neighboring jurisdictions came to him, and he would handle their cases. A veteran clerk advised against this practice, warning that it would lead to trouble with his fellow officials. Not only was Kunhou interfering in the governance of other districts, he was making the officials look bad by his activism. Late in life, Kunhou would recognize the dangers of rash action in his early career,[83] but at the time he failed to heed the warning. Soon an imperial commissioner arrived to inspect the area. The neighboring prefect, eager to prove that his jurisdiction was free of bandits but that Ye Kunhou had been derelict in duty, presented a list of outlaw leaders that he claimed were based in Nanyang.

These bandits were essentially roving gangs that generally avoided victimizing peasants in their home villages, so the claim that bands from Nanyang were raiding in the neighboring jurisdiction is plausible. Local officials were also prone to deny problems in their own jurisdictions and attribute them to outside troublemakers. The only solution to this dilemma was for local officials to work together to suppress bandits and keep them from fleeing into the next district. Such cooperation was clearly absent in this case, and when the governor received the report of bandits in Nanyang, his immediate fear was that lax measures by local officials might lead to the rise of a rebel movement comparable to the Taiping Rebellion then gathering momentum in the south. To nip the problem in the bud, he ordered the immediate arrest of the outlaw leaders and, as was standard bureaucratic practice, gave Ye Kunhou a two-month deadline to accomplish the task.

Kunhou's career and the family's fortune now hung in the balance, and Boying quickly emerged as his father's chief advisor and deputy. His initial inclination was to hasten to the provincial capital to present his father's side of the story, but his father vetoed any such move. Instead he posted large rewards for the capture of the bandit leaders. Each county under his jurisdiction was ordered to select its ablest constables, and the Nanyang garrison sent out its best officers. These men scoured the countryside, paid informants for leads, and published a graduated reward schedule for the various levels of the outlaw leadership. The result was fairly predictable:

hundreds of people (undoubtedly including some who were innocent) were turned in for rewards, but after a month, not a single bandit chieftain had been captured.

With the deadline approaching, Ye Kunhou fell ill from "moist humors," and Boying spent his days leading patrols in search of bandits in the hills and his evenings preparing medicine for his dad. The governor pressed for arrests, and Boying continued scouring hideouts in Nanyang and neighboring areas, eventually seizing all but the top leader in the area, who had fled to the coast. Boying wanted to go after him, but an old family servant dissuaded him from such a long and risky expedition and went himself. Several days later, word came from informants in the bandit camp that the chieftain was conducting business in a county some three hundred kilometers east of Nanyang. Perhaps he was fencing stolen goods, perhaps he was engaged in legitimate commerce. But he was certainly avoiding the area where the officials were seeking to arrest him. Now Ye Kunhou had to act far outside his jurisdiction (or fail to meet the deadline for arrest). He sent agents to surround the rebel chief. When at last they captured him, Kunhou could report complete success in his bandit-quelling mission.

While Ye Boying was searching the hills for bandits, his wife was back in Nanyang pregnant with their second child. Soon his father was summoned to the provincial capital to consult on the prosecution of the captured bandit leaders, and Boying followed along. One can only imagine what Boying's wife thought of her husband's priorities, but they remained clear. Assisting his father and protecting his official position were more important than a wife's pregnancy. A son was born while Boying was away and died before he could return. Kunhou himself felt torn about leaving Nanyang, for his aging mother was growing steadily weaker. His youngest brother, Ye Yun, tended to her loyally, even performing the consummate filial act of cutting off some of his own flesh to boil with her medicine. While Boying and Kunhou were attending to bandit cases in the capital, word came that Lady Zhao's condition was perilous. They hastened home but heard on the way that she had passed away. The family's happy years in Nanyang had come to an abrupt end.

With his mother's death, Kunhou was required to resign his positions and return home in mourning. (His brother in Shandong had already taken sick leave from his post.) Although dynastic regulations interrupted Kunhou's official career (and the important income it provided), his bandit-fighting merit was sufficient to permit the purchase of office for his son. Court policy seemed to recognize that in resigning his position to go into mourning, a loyal official lost his most critical source of income. The state compensated for this change in fortune by providing a post for his son. Both Boying and his younger brother headed for Beijing, and the initial plan was for Boying to get the job. But Boying preferred to stay with old friends and schoolmates in Beijing. The position went to his younger brother, who was posted to Shaanxi, where he would provide refuge for his mother and others when the family fled the Taiping a few years later.

Boying stayed in the capital, studying for the exams and enjoying the sights: another happy time away from home. But when he took the exams in the fall of 1852, he failed again. Soon alarming news arrived of the Taiping rebels' advance into the Yangzi valley. With his family imperiled, Ye Boying hastened home, arriving just in time for the dramatic events described in chapter 1.[84]

# 4

# Rebellion

For many years, the history of modern China has been told as the story of "China's Response to the West." In the long run, the military and economic impact of Western imperialism in the period following the Opium War threatened the stability and even the survival of the Qing empire. Most histories of this period pay substantial attention to a few reformers who promoted the study of Western science and mathematics, urging the adoption of modern industrial technology to build arsenals and shipyards to strengthen the army and navy.[1] However this "self-strengthening" did little to address what most officials—and certainly Ye Kunhou and his kinsmen—saw as the greatest threat to their security: not Europeans along the coast but the vast rebellions ravaging the heartland. As we have seen, Ye Kunhou and his son Boying showed little interest in the new challenge from the West. The rebellions, by contrast, uprooted their family and disrupted their lives. At the same time, rebellion gave the Ye officeholders an opportunity to prove their usefulness to the dynasty and to rise within the bureaucracy, and also provoked serious thinking about the principles of effective Confucian governance.

In the mid-nineteenth century, rebels challenged the Qing on all sides. From 1853 to 1864, the Taiping occupied Nanjing and dominated the surrounding economic heartland, the source of much of the Qing's tax revenues. To the north, in Anhui and Henan, were the Nian rebels, who had their roots in the bandit gangs that Ye Kunhou and his son had fought in 1851. Their mobile armies, eventually numbering in the thousands, raided across much of north China from their impoverished base area between the Yangzi and Yellow rivers. Not until 1868 were they finally subdued. To the west, Muslim rebellions challenged Qing rule and brought great ethnic slaughter. The southwestern rebellion in Yunnan lasted from

1855 to 1873 and reduced the province's population by some 50 percent. In the northwest, ethnic conflict between Muslims and Han Chinese sparked pogroms targeting Muslim communities in Shaanxi province in 1862, which then helped to provoke a regional Islamic rebellion in far western Xinjiang that lasted until 1877.[2] No region of China was unaffected by these massive rebellions, which were a far greater threat to the Qing dynasty than the trade-seeking "barbarians" from Europe and America.

In the end, the Qing met the challenge, though not without changes. At all levels of government, officials of a new type emerged: practical men who had proved themselves on the battlefield as much as in the examination hall. Ye Kunhou, his brothers, and his son Boying were such officials at the local level. Others like them, of greater influence, rose through the regional armies of Hunan under Zeng Guofan (1811–72) or of Anhui under Li Hongzhang (1823–1901). Although Zeng and Li both held the highest examination degree, the officers of their armies were promoted for their effectiveness in fighting rebels, and some had no examination degrees at all.[3] Liu Mingquan (1836–96) was a militia leader from a peasant family with no scholarly credentials who joined the Anhui Army to fight the Nian Rebellion, rose through the ranks, and became the first governor of Taiwan when it became a province in 1885. Others, like Ye Boying, held only the lowest examination degree yet attained the highest provincial offices: Liu Kunyi (1830–1902) fought the Taiping in the Hunan Army and rose by the turn of the century to the powerful governor-general position in Nanjing; Ding Richang (1823–82) ascended by the same route to the governorship of Jiangsu; and Cen Yuying (1829–89) led the suppression of the Muslim rebellion in Yunnan and became one of the most powerful officials in the southwest.[4]

These were the sort of men who determined how China would be ruled at the local level in the latter half of the nineteenth century. Their concern was not modernization, a concept they would hardly have understood. They were focused on restoring and maintaining order. They thought a lot about the roots of rebellion and the measures necessary to combat it, because that was the activity that consumed their energy and dominated their lives for so many critical years. The poems of Ye Kunhou and private writings of Ye Boying provide an insight into these midcentury officials' thinking that is not always available in the bureaucratic record. So we return to our opening chapter's tale of the Ye family in a time of rebellion, resuming the narrative after Ye Kunhou had sent his family to Shaanxi and gone off to join the Anhui Army fighting the Taiping and Nian rebels.

As Ye Kunhou worked with the Qing officials organizing local militia to fight the insurgents in northern Anhui, fund-raising soon emerged as his greatest strength. In the mid-1850s, he devoted himself to collecting contributions from wealthy gentry, who received official titles in exchange for their support the imperial armies. After one notable victory, he persuaded the local gentry to donate one hundred thousand taels to the cause. By the end of 1855, he had moved to Henan (where he had previously held office), and the governor assigned him to the military headquarters in Guide, near Henan's borders with Anhui, Jiangsu, and Shandong, a classically difficult-to-govern area where bandits easily escaped into adjacent jurisdictions. Here Kunhou led troops in the field, eating and sleeping with them in the open and gaining their confidence. This experience was nothing like the comfortable life he had spent as Nanyang prefect with his large family and luxuriant garden. Though much of his work was administrative—writing reports, handling logistics, raising money, and commissioning agents to supply the army—he was often on the road, living in the field, and away from his family. Once he barely survived a sneak rebel attack that caught him at work in his tent; on another occasion his unit was besieged in southern Henan for half a month before relief finally arrived. The duty was physically trying and he lost weight, but years later, when he looked back on the experience, he thought of the ancient military heroes who had inspired him as a boy and concluded, "A young man beginning his career must be sharpened like a knife. / Without thorough sharpening you cannot make a great weapon. / Warfare and natural disasters must be experienced in person / In order to produce steely heroes capable of upholding heaven and earth."[5]

He was successful enough in clearing Nian rebels from the area that in the fall of 1856, on the governor's recommendation, he proceeded to the capital for an audience with the emperor. As we have seen, an imperial audience was a moment of glory in any official's career, and Ye Kunhou left a detailed account of the colloquy with his sovereign. In addition to the obvious celebrity that one gained by meeting the Son of Heaven, an audience presented a rare opportunity to display one's character, knowledge, and ability to the one person who could make or break any official career. On October 23, 1856, Ye Kunhou was ushered into the audience chamber. As before, he was moved by the size of the palace, the elegance of the courtiers' dress, and the pervasive smell of incense. He prostrated himself before the twenty-five-year-old Xianfeng Emperor (less than half his own age) to await his questions. Xianfeng seemed thin from the strains of rule yet gentle and compassionate. Virtually his entire reign was marked by rebellion and foreign invasion, and he never exercised effective command of his realm. He came across as engaged, if not always well informed. Kunhou nonetheless remembered him fondly.[6]

The emperor, following a briefing memo on Ye Kunhou's background, began with conventional inquiries into Ye's hometown, previous official positions, the route he had followed to Beijing, and harvest conditions along the way. He noted Kunhou's successes against the Nian rebels while prefect in Nanyang and his achievements in militia organizing in Anhui, and then asked why he had not been recommended for office. Kunhou modestly replied that militia organizing was the gentry's duty on behalf of their home villages, and he would not dare to request appointment for that. The emperor asked if he could ride a horse—a good Manchu standard for military prowess—and Kunhou confessed that he could ride if he had to, but he was not very good at it. After a few perfunctory questions about the commanders Kunhou had served under, he was dismissed with instructions to return the next day.

The following day, the emperor focused on strategic issues on the Anhui-Henan front. He asked about Tongcheng, the county to the north of Anqing, which Kunhou's forces had failed to capture two years earlier. Not surprisingly, Kunhou responded that Tongcheng could not be captured and held without first retaking Anqing, and he stated that Anqing, once retaken, should again be made the provincial capital. He was, if nothing else, a steadfast advocate for his hometown. If this exchange betrayed a certain imperial fuzziness on strategic issues in the Yangzi valley campaign, the next question was even more disturbing. Where, the emperor wanted to know, was Zhoujiakou, where the Henan governor was now concentrating his forces? Kunhou had to explain that this town was a key river port in eastern Henan, the point at which cargo was offloaded for transport north toward the provincial capital. Such imperial ignorance of geography (had the emperor no maps?) must have been a little unsettling. After a few more questions, the emperor fell silent and Kunhou withdrew.[7]

As was his habit, Ye Kunhou had not come to Beijing alone, but brought along his brothers and eldest son. After Kunhou's audience with the emperor, his hopes for a substantive appointment were disappointed. He was simply ordered back to Henan with his former rank as prefect, to be employed as the governor saw fit. However, this Beijing sojourn was not just for his own benefit; it was a job-seeking expedition on behalf of the entire family, designed to capitalize on Kunhou's rebel-fighting achievements and the prestigious audience with the emperor. Kunhou's eldest son, Ye Boying, had spent 1855 in Shaanxi, where he had fled with his mother. There he recovered from the ordeal of hiding from the Taiping by reading literature and books on statecraft, but he longed for the prestige of office and the chance to serve the dynasty in its hour of peril. In 1856, he preceded his father to Beijing by a few months, presumably in order to renew old acquaintances and assess employment possibilities. After his father's audience, Boying gained a position as an attaché in the Board of Revenue.[8]

His uncle, Ye Yun, had tried to reach Beijing the previous year to take the exams, but Yellow River flooding blocked the route, and he arrived too late to register. In all, he had failed the provincial-level exams six times, and his trip to Beijing was to take the exam for the seventh time, because Nanjing was occupied by the Taiping. Four times, the examiners had recommended his essays, but he never ranked high enough to pass. Now he decided that fate had not destined him to succeed by this route, and he abandoned the effort. Instead, he joined Kunhou's entourage the following year. When the latter was assigned back to Henan, Ye Yun purchased an exemption from the "law of avoidance," which prohibited anyone from holding office in the same province as a kinsman, and returned with Kunhou to Henan, working at jobs assigned by the governor. Soon the court decided that selling exceptions to antinepotism laws was a bad idea, and Ye Yun was forced to abandon his official position. He spent the next six years in militia organizing.[9] The third brother, Ye Lian, followed a more orthodox route and was reassigned as a county magistrate in Shandong, where he served until his death in 1871.[10]

These assignments added up to rather spectacular job-seeking success for the Ye men: local bureaucratic appointments (though two only as expectant officials) for all three brothers and a metropolitan appointment for Ye Boying. With Boying's brother holding a magistrate position in Shaanxi, five members of these two generations now held posts in the Qing bureaucracy. None had qualified by passing the provincial or metropolitan exams; fighting rebels had been their ticket to office. This route brought to public service men with practical experience in governance, but it also represented the breakdown of a system designed to assess and promote intellectual ability through impartial examinations. For a family whose last prominent official had served four hundred years earlier, the sudden elevation of five close relatives is unlikely to have been the consequence of each individual's objectively measured talent. Family merit provided a new route to power.

When Ye Kunhou returned to Henan, he was deputized to the Contributions Bureau (Juanshu ju), where he kept records on the sale of official titles to raise desperately needed revenue. The astonishing three million taels he helped collect in 1859 earned him promotion to the rank of circuit intendant *(daotai)*. Later he was assigned to the Logistics Bureau (Junxu zongju) and charged with controlling fraud and waste in military expenditures. The biggest challenge was disciplining clerks with long experience in the provincial treasurer's office who were particularly adept at cooking the books. Indeed, Ye claimed that with the extraordinary sources of revenue in new taxes and the sale of office and the massive antirebel military expenditures, in the ten years since the rebellions had begun, more than ten million taels had been expended without a proper accounting.

Ye Kunhou spent over a decade in Kaifeng managing fiscal and logistical affairs related to combating the Nian rebels, or working in the field with the army. The experience gave him plenty of time to think about the origins of the disastrous rebellions that were wreaking such destruction on his country. Most of his poems on this subject reflect themes that he had expressed before: long years of peace had weakened the army; the extravagant habits of the elite had alienated them from the impoverished people; the ancient virtues of humanity, humility, and sincerity had been replaced by cleverness and selfish indifference to the fate of others. But in many poems, he also points an accusing finger at officials. He wrote that people are naturally good and turn violent only when forced by circumstances; the popular distress that gave rise to rebellion was the product of official corruption and misgovernment. One poem directly addressed his official colleagues:

> Cold and hunger give rise to villains;
> People rise up and take risks when they have no recourse.
> Crime is due to circumstances and lack of alternatives;
> People seize an opportunity and rebellions erupt one after another.
> For a pure stream, cleanse the water at the spring;
> To extinguish a fire, remove the fuel under the pot.
> To recuperate, there is no need for extraordinary remedies;
> To pacify the people, we need only control official greed and corruption.[11]

In addition to the problem of official corruption, troubles arose when officials abandoned reasonable principles in settling disputes.[12] In court they should avoid harsh punishments: "If governance is fair, the people will look after themselves."[13] Above all Ye blamed oppressive clerks and officials who taxed the people mercilessly, thinking only of their own promotions. He praised one official who had been demoted for persistent arrears in his tax remissions.[14] This man was the sort of official he respected, one who would risk his career rather than press disaster-stricken peasants for more taxes.

These poems, of course, cite general principles of governance and general reflections on the causes of violent disturbances. But Kunhou and Boying, drawing on their experience in Henan, also left a number of more specific analyses of the rise of the Nian Rebellion and the fundamental dysfunction in state-society relations that provided its dynamic. Unlike the Taiping Rebellion, which was inspired by the fervent religious faith of its charismatic leader, the Nian rebels had neither a clear ideology nor a coherent leadership structure. The rebellion developed, instead, from roving bandit bands that raided the areas around their bases in northern Anhui and southern Henan. This poor area of the north China plain was frequently plagued by flood and drought, and peasants had long relied on a variety of survival strategies, from salt smuggling and itinerant begging (often in large and unruly bands) to extortion and armed robbery. It was from these bands of bandits and smugglers that the Nian rebels emerged, especially after major flooding along a wide stretch of the Yellow River began in 1851 and continued for years, completely changing the river's course to flow, as it does today, north of the Shandong peninsula. The ecological crisis that accompanied this alteration of the river's flow increased unrest, and in time, outlaw bands came together in a broad but loose alliance that became the Nian Rebellion and lasted until 1868.[15]

In 1851, while Ye Kunhou was prefect of Nanyang, the rebellion was just beginning, and his son's account gives a rather precise local perspective on how such a movement could start. In the prefectures of southern Henan, young males gathered each winter in the slack agricultural season to drink, gamble, and steal in groups that could range from a dozen or so to over a hundred. When peaceful peasants came together in temple fairs to celebrate the fall harvest with operas, outdoor markets, gambling, and other entertainment, bands of these rowdies would threaten trouble until the local gentry bought them off with food and drink. When the troublemakers needed more food or money, they robbed or extorted payoffs from merchants or wealthy folks traveling the imperial highways. Those who paid up were released; those who resisted were kidnapped for ransom. These gangs of young toughs and juvenile delinquents used their numbers and fighting prowess to operate protection rackets and buy off the local elite.

The normal official strategy for dealing with such gangs was to recruit local militia during the winter and early spring, releasing them in the second lunar month when both bandits and government troops returned to the fields to plant their crops. Summer usually brought enough agricultural work to keep most potential bandits out of trouble, and the spring harvest of winter wheat provided necessary subsistence for the robbers, who were, after all, largely driven to banditry to support their families. But by the 1850s, official neglect of militia, plus prolonged drought or persistent rains that left peasants hungry and unemployed, had led to full-time banditry in Henan. As outlaw activity spread, higher officials became alarmed and sent out urgent orders to arrest the miscreants. Ordinary peasants were caught in the middle. As Ye Kunhou learned from the local gentry, the peasants were victimized by the armed bandits, who stole their food and farm animals and abused the village women. When government forces sought help in locating and identifying the brigands, the peasants kept silent, fearing reprisals against their families if they informed on the criminal gangs. As a result, when government troops went out, nine out of ten times they came back empty-handed. When they did happen to locate the bandits, resistance was fierce, for a captured bandit faced almost certain execution. Resistance, however, especially if it involved government casualties, brought an even more determined state response as troops combed the countryside for the brigands. This crackdown in turn impelled the bandits to organize ever-larger bands to resist government suppression, eventually transforming them from occasional outlaws to outright rebels.[16]

Ye Kunhou had observed the early stages of this process while serving as prefect in Nanyang. Now, with his return to join the Qing forces in Henan, he confronted a full-scale rebellion. In between was the important time he had spent in the hills of Anhui and the sense of community he had felt with the peasants there. Somehow, he believed, the gulf that had developed between state and society had to be closed: "Officials and people must combine as one."[17] The principle of village self-defense through peasant militia was the foundation of his solution, as it was for officials everywhere confronting rebellion with little military support from the central government.[18] Gentry assistance was critical, and on one occasion, Ye appealed for the assistance of the local elites: they knew the local customs and geography, and they knew where the enemy was likely to hide.[19] Another poem addressed the common people, reminding them that government troops could not garrison every village so they would have to defend themselves. He cautioned against colluding with the rebels for temporary advantage, warning that the insurgents could turn on them in an instant. In a poem apparently for popular consumption, he urged the people to rely on their superior numbers and to surround the bandits with their farm tools. "You all know to protect rice shoots by removing harmful weeds. / Why not extend this logic and combine efforts to eliminate evil-doers, / Protecting children and grandchildren / And insuring peace for your parents? / This disaster you have brought upon yourselves. / Good fortune can also come from yourselves."[20] On another occasion, when a group of peasants appealed for help and complained that the soldiers always arrived too late to protect them, he was more supportive, promising to clear the land of bandits if the farmers would take up their tools to help him.[21]

Peasants confronted with well-armed rebel bands were unlikely to find such advice helpful. Once the Nian had organized in large armies, rakes and hoes were an inadequate defense. By the 1860s, the Nian bandits had come together in a broad alliance that occupied fortified villages across a wide swath of northern Anhui and southern Henan. Although the Taiping relied upon large standing armies based in occupied cities, the Nian soldiers rarely attacked large cities, preferring to operate in the villages and towns of the north China plain, combining in ever-larger armies to attack and loot such targets of opportunity as customs posts, river crossings, or densely populated areas. Such raids generally took place in the winter, when little agricultural work was available, or in the late summer, when sorghum stalks stood high in the fields and provided cover for highway robbery. These pillaging forays became so common in local practice that among the Nian, raiding was simply known as "going down to the countryside," and after they had loaded themselves down with the grain and loot necessary to survive, they would "return to the nest."[22] The scale of these operations was far greater by the late 1850s, but the basic Nian mode of raiding built on years of established routine.

Combating such large rebel forces required a more organized strategy and a better armed force. The coordinator of this strategy in Henan was Mao Changxi (1817–82), who in 1860 was appointed militia commissioner for the province. Just forty-three years old at the time, Mao was the son of a metropolitan official and had earned the *jinshi* degree (which his father and brother also held) before he was thirty. As a censor and prefect in the capital, he had attracted attention by his deft handling of several complex criminal and corruption cases. Having submitted thoughtful memorials on the current crisis, he was ordered back to his home province to organize militia.[23] In all likelihood, the Mao and Ye families had become acquainted when Ye Kunhou was first deputized in Henan, for Mao passed his provincial exam in Kaifeng in 1839 when Kunhou and his family were there. (Later, Mao wrote one of the prefaces to Ye Kunhou's collected poems.) While Ye Boying worked in the Board of Revenue, he met frequently with Mao, who invited him and his uncle, Ye Yun, onto his staff. Both readily accepted. For Boying, this opportunity and Mao Changxi's patronage provided a better chance to advance his career than did a menial position in the metropolitan bureaucracy.[24]

The twenty thousand imperial troops in northern Anhui and southern Henan were woefully inadequate to control the tens of thousands of rebels in hundreds of bands raiding throughout the area, all of whom could scatter and blend into the local population whenever imperial forces attacked. Mao Changxi's strategy of "strengthening the walls and clearing the fields" (jianbi qingye) built on an ancient model and had become a standard approach to combating major rebellions by the Qing period. The population was concentrated in fortified stockades where all grain, fodder, and animals were kept as soon as the harvest was in. The peasants dug deep trenches to slow the advance of the cavalry that served as the Nian's shock troops. They set up signal systems: one shot warned people of rebels nearby and meant they should stop work in the fields; two shots summoned the population back into its stockade; and three shots ordered the closing of gates and arraying of defense forces on the mud walls. Under this strategy—similar to the "strategic hamlets" advocated by counterinsurgency experts in Vietnam in the 1960s—over ten thousand stockades were built in Henan, plus hundreds of watch towers and stone-fortified outposts, all manned by hundreds of thousands of militiamen.[25]

Ye Kunhou was not altogether happy with the social effects of this strategy, and he wrote a long critical poem. He began with his usual critique of official misgovernment: "If the state's offices are full of jackals and wolfs, the fields will produce outlaws." As bandits become more powerful, the officials retreat to their walled cities. "The officials no longer care for the people; officials and people live in separate worlds." So the people look after their own defense, and several villages combine to build stockades with high walls and deep moats, which of course was precisely Mao Changxi's strategy, and not entirely a peasant initiative. These stockades were armed not just with farm tools but also with guns and cannons. What began as a defense against rebels ended up emptying the villages and leaving the roads abandoned. As a result, travelers and merchants were vulnerable to highway robbery, and officials could find no witnesses when they came to investigate. As an official, Ye Kunhou was clearly suspicious of these powerful stockade communities and their leaders: "We defend against mice and end up nourishing a tiger."[26]

The danger posed by such fortified rural communities was particularly great if leadership fell into the hands of a dissident group. As government authority deteriorated, numerous unorthodox groups emerged, including religious sectarians. Many arose from a loosely defined White Lotus tradition, which promised salvation for believers in an age of disasters and disorder. To these core beliefs were added various martial-arts traditions, chants, spells, and occasionally rituals of invulnerability. In times of trouble, martial-arts practices were essential, and their practitioners often rose to leadership roles in the sects.[27] The core members of these groups were much like the Taiping in their fanatical devotion and fearless resistance. Ye Boying helped subdue one such group, which had occupied a village that he called Golden Brazier Stockade.[28] This heavily fortified village was surrounded by moats and dikes with bamboo spikes and had withstood successive Qing cavalry assaults and artillery barrages. It was finally taken after a tight siege cut off all food supplies and prompted defections by some of the less committed. The defectors were fed and then led to the front to urge their besieged brethren to follow their example. When the fort was finally stormed after a hundred days, not a single defender survived, and the only remaining food was said to be dried human flesh.[29]

Ye Kunhou's Confucian training had taught him that people were by nature good. Only the pressures of poverty and misfortune led them into evil ways. Even the Nian rebels were still the emperor's subjects, who should return to their wives and children, resume their work in the fields and thus escape punishment.[30] He was convinced that most of the rebels had been coerced into joining the insurgency, and he fully endorsed the imperial edicts promising lenience and amnesty to reluctant rebels who surrendered peacefully. "Those who have been coerced may be pardoned; / Those who disperse shall receive amnesty. / If you can seize one of your leaders, you shall receive a rich reward."[31] At the same time, Ye's years confronting persistent rebellion convinced him that some people had become hardened in their evil ways, and for them, no lenience or mercy was possible. A pivotal moment had come early in his career, when he was prefect in Nanyang. Several hundred men from a bandit gang had been captured after a sweep of the countryside, and the leaders were subjected to the most extreme torture: their skin was peeled, bones broken, chests cut open, and bellies burned. Throughout this ordeal, they never cried out. Their obduracy convinced Kunhou that they were so evil that they merited the most extreme punishment. He would not hesitate to have them chopped into little pieces.[32] With this logic, he justified the horribly destructive "scorched earth" policy that the Qing adopted toward the rebels.[33]

When traveling with the army in battle, Ye Kunhou observed the terrible suffering and destruction of war, and the experience hardened him. He spoke of the rebellion as a cancer that was too far advanced for even harsh punishment of a few leaders to cure it.[34] After a battle, he observed a field strewn with rebel bodies and wrote reprovingly of men who neglected their families to become rebels, who now perished far from home to become nameless ghosts.[35] Following a victory over the rebels, he celebrated the fires lighting their fallen bodies and had no pity for the wounded and dying whom he heard whimpering in the distance.[36] Another victory caused the rebels to drop their weapons and flee over forty kilometers, the army in pursuit and killing anyone it could capture, leaving the road littered with corpses.[37] Later Ye looked back at the slaughter and compared the killing of rebels to cutting down hemp.[38] Kunhou's collection contains dozens of battle poems, and though he was obviously pained by the destruction of war, and on occasion allowed himself the thought "Aren't bandits also human?" in the end he was convinced that only thorough eradication of the rebels could restore peace to the land.[39]

He reserved his greatest sympathy for the common people. He wrote movingly of an old man, hunchbacked, deaf, and injured, who was cursed by soldiers when he failed to yield quickly enough as they rushed to battle. On the army's return, Kunhou saw the hunchback's stiff body dead beside the road.[40] As battles raged across the plains, the roads filled with refugees, tottering along shoeless in tattered clothes, begging for food with little success.[41] Those who remained in their villages were stripped of food and clothing by the rebels, then harassed by the government for taxes to support the army.[42] When government troops were on the move, they collected grain and fodder and conscripted peasants to help with transport. The burden on the peasants was unbearable: "The [war] preparations are exhausting Henan."[43]

Ye Kunhou recognized, of course, that the soldiers suffered as well. Most of them were simple peasants recruited into the army, and they endured terrible casualties in the bloody battles that he witnessed. On their behalf, he wrote a "soldier's lament" addressed to Heaven, the emperor, and the man's commander, asking why these superiors did not care for his suffering in the ranks, the five years enduring the hardship of war away from his family.[44] Kunhou was aware that the soldiers were often short on supplies and ill fed and that in some cases their ineffectiveness in battle was due to this lack of provisions.[45] Having shared their hardship, when they were victorious,in battle and returned singing in triumph, he joined their celebration and endorsed their looting: "Clothes stained by the blood of battle, / Gold, silver, silk, and treasure / In bags strapped around their waist, / Rewarded by beef, lamb, and pork, / And people lining the road to offer wine."[46] This was the way wars were fought in the nineteenth century, and loot (an Indian word that passed into English through the British imperial armies) was a common way to reward soldiers.

Writing in the immediate aftermath of battle, Ye Kunhou seemed to accept the soldiers' conduct. Later, in more reflective poems, he was more critical. One particularly biting pair of poems, "Fleeing soldiers" and "Fleeing braves," contrasted the troops' cowardice in the face of the rebels with their harsh treatment of the people they were supposed to be defending. The lack of discipline among locally recruited militia "braves" was scandalous.

> In victory they do not defer to each other,
> In defeat, they do not rescue each other.
> In confusion they advance, retreat, disperse.
> Like animals who call themselves braves,
> They show no courage before the public enemy,
> But only in their private battles.

In normal times, they seek merit in killing people;
When the rebels come, they recoil in fear.
Their attire is new and strange, their language deceitful and boasting.
Their food is rich and sweet, their provisions ample.
When happy there is raucous laughter; when angry, curses fly.
If they are the least bit dissatisfied, they cuss and swear.
If there are no bandits, they harass the villagers;
When there are bandits, they abandon their post.[47]

On the subject of the soldiers, Ye Kunhou was less colorful but a bit more analytical:

The rebels are like a coarse comb.
The local bandits like a fine-toothed comb.
But the government troops are like a razor.
The soldiers do not kill the rebels,
But instead profit from the rebellion
. . . . . . . . . . . . . . . . . . . . . . . . . . . . . . . .
Wherever the rebels are, the soldiers do not come;
Going instead where the rebels are not.
The soldiers seek revenge on the people not the rebels,
Stripping them of their wealth, their clothing, their bedding.
Day and night they seize people as the villagers cry out,
Women go into hiding, and the young and weak are detained.[48]

Ye Kunhou was perhaps indulging in a degree of poetic exaggeration here, but the Qing forces' routine abuse of the ordinary villagers is undeniable.

In all, Ye Kunhou spent some thirteen years dealing with rebellion in Henan, from 1853 to 1866. Sometimes he was with the army, but in most of the later years, he was in various logistical and fund-raising offices in the provincial capital. Not surprisingly, given his concern for the overburdened peasantry, he often found the revenue work distasteful, at one point resigning in frustration, saying that raising money in disaster-stricken Henan was like "seeking fish in a tree."[49] But soon he accepted another appointment.[50] When the rebellions finally came to an end, the sense of exhaustion and desolation was palpable. On one occasion, two colleagues returned from the field in Henan with tales of abandoned fields, dry wells, and deserted roads. The strong men had been taken captive and disappeared without a trace, whereas the old and the sick struggled to survive.[51] Returning to his old post in Nanyang, Kunhou found only destruction, poverty, and starvation.[52] When he traveled through an area recently visited by the rebels, the homes were all abandoned and he could find no place to stay.[53]

In his home province of Anhui, the impact of the Taiping and Nian rebellions was devastating. Official population figures show a fall in the Anhui population from more than 37.6 million in 1852 to 14.5 million in 1873. The 37.6 million figure may overstate the antebellum population, but specialists agree that the province lost 50 to 60 percent of its residents. In the Anqing area, losses probably exceeded 60 percent. (By contrast, even after the devastation of Sherman's march through Georgia in the American Civil War, the 1870 census showed a 12 percent increase over the state's 1860 population.[54]) There were reports of deserted villages and fallow fields, of wolves prowling at night in a classic sign of civilization's retreat. Homes were burned and looted; livestock was stolen, killed, and eaten; schools and temples were destroyed; bridges were burned; irrigation networks were disrupted and fields abandoned. It took decades for this area to recover from the devastation.[55]

The cost was enormous, but the Qing dynasty had survived. The Confucian elite had rallied behind the Manchu overlords when confronted by the Christian-inspired heresies of the Taiping Rebellion, the equally threatening Islamic rebellions of western China, or the ravaging peasant bands of the Nian. The banner troops that had swept the Manchus to power in the seventeenth century had decayed into utter ineffectiveness by the nineteenth, and the Han Chinese Green Standard garrisons were not much better. The dynasty was saved by a new type of military formation, the regional armies of Hunan and Anhui. These forces were regular armies of full-time soldiers, many armed with rifles and new artillery, which had been built upon the foundation of local militia and were led by locally recruited gentry who had proved themselves as commanders defending their own provinces. In the aftermath of the rebellion, these commanders were rewarded with titles, honors, and official positions, and they dominated the Qing bureaucracy for the remainder of the nineteenth century.[56]

Early in 1869, after the Nian Rebellion was finally suppressed, an imperial edict granted promotions to Ye Kunhou, his brother Ye Yun, and his son Ye Boying for their contributions to the struggle against the Nian. Kunhou had long served in Henan in a variety of posts, and now he was given the rank of lieutenant governor, though the actual posts that he held were never higher than circuit intendant. He was one of four intendants in the province, each presiding over three or four prefectures. Kunhou's connections to Mao Changxi, the Henan militia commander, had helped his brother and son gain positions on Mao's staff. Now Ye Yun was also promoted to intendant rank, and he soon received a plush post in the salt administration at a port on the Yangzi River not far from his home in Anqing. Ye Boying received the greatest promotion, to the rank of provincial judge, along with orders to serve in the metropolitan province of Zhili, where his superior and patron would be Zeng Guofan, the former commander of the Hunan Army and by then the most powerful and respected official in the country. These promotions were a family triumph, and the fact that they were granted in a single edict is telling. Ye Kunhou saw the recognition as a just reward for ancestral virtue and an example to the next generation.[57]

These men had risen to their lofty positions by a process that was typical for the mid-nineteenth century, but unusual for late imperial China. Despite repeated attempts, none of them had passed the provincial or metropolitan examinations that normally qualified a man for office. They were highly educated men, well versed in the classics and history, and Ye Kunhou was an accomplished and prolific poet. But their learning was not what had earned them promotions; they won their posts because of their service in suppressing rebels. Their long hard years with the army and in the military support staff had earned them prominent appointments, and their experience during the rebellions and the tremendous suffering they had observed would shape their approach to governance.

One lesson, repeated often in Ye Kunhou's poems, was that rebellion was caused by corrupt and oppressive government. Kunhou's months of refuge in the hills of Anhui strengthened his conviction that the government that governs least governs best. Left to their own devices, people would form a harmonious community. If disputes arose, they should be settled by reasoned mediation, not harsh sanctions. Above all, taxes must be kept low, for by pressing impoverished peasants to pay, tax collectors drove them to desperate acts and even to rebellion. Ye Kunhou's concern to keep the burden of government light reflected the fundamental Confucian obligation to serve and protect the emperor's subjects, to "nourish the people." That obligation was manifest in a range of state policies (many of which we will examine in the next chapter) to prevent floods, promote agriculture, and succor the people in times of natural disasters. The problem was that China's land taxes were already very light by international standards, amounting to only some 2.4 percent of the national product.[58] In the long run, any modernization of the Chinese state would require far more resources to build infrastructure, develop education, promote industrial development, and strengthen the military. The Confucian priorities of men like Ye Kunhou or Ye Boying made it just that much more difficult for future generations to modernize.[59]

A second important conviction that these men carried from their experience of this era was that however much the people suffered from taxes and official corruption, they suffered even more from the chaotic disruptions of domestic unrest. An official's first duty was to prevent rebellion by not oppressing the people. But if rebellion should break out, it must be mercilessly suppressed. In his reading of history, Ye Kunhou paid increasing attention to rebels, men notorious for violence, sworn partisans *(sidang)*, and troublemakers *(luanren,* literally "men of disorder"). He concluded that such people were incorrigible. They simply had to be wiped out.[60] The unprecedented toll of the nineteenth-century rebellions—perhaps as many as fifty million lives lost—left a searing imprint on future generations.[61] Disorder must be checked at all cost. It is a lesson that officials in China follow to this day. The purpose of government is to maintain a harmonious society. Ye Kunhou and Ye Boying could now serve as officials in times of peace. Let us see how they pursued this goal, and how officials lived in the final years of China's imperial age.

# 5

# Official Life in the Late Qing

The late nineteenth century was a critical era in world history. In Europe and America, technological change was transforming life at an unprecedented pace. Steam-powered factories, ships, and railways produced and moved goods at speeds unimaginable just a couple generations earlier. Telegraph cables circled the globe and carried news and information in a matter of minutes, where overland post or sailing ships just a few decades earlier had required weeks or even months. Great industrial cities produced textiles, steel, machines, chemicals, and a host of new consumer goods—from soap to sewing machines, boots to bicycles. Political reforms brought constitutional government, parliamentary elections, and political parties to western Europe and the Americas, along with a vibrant civil society of civic and professional associations and an active and widely read popular press. Brimming with confidence in the superiority of Western Christian civilization, enabled by the new weapons of war that came with the West's technological superiority, and impelled by national competition and a jingoistic press, the Western powers moved aggressively to seize colonial empires and open markets in Asia, Africa, and the Middle East.

The Western effort to "open up" China began in earnest with the Opium War of 1839–42. In the aftermath, Britain claimed Hong Kong as a colony and forced the opening of additional "treaty ports" along the Chinese coast, the most important of which was Shanghai at the mouth of the Yangzi. When these ports failed to generate a significant increase in trade—Chinese handicraft textiles proved as cheap as and more durable than the products of Lancaster's mills—the British and French launched the second Opium War in 1856, culminating in the 1860 occupation of Beijing and the destruction of the Yuanmingyuan Summer Palace (which had so impressed Ye Kunhou following his audience a few years earlier). Again China was forced to sign a humiliating treaty with the Western barbarians, opening additional ports, permitting missionaries to proselytize in the interior, and allowing Western diplomats to establish permanent legations in the Chinese capital. All these developments would radically change the context of modern Chinese history and the challenges that China faced. As we have just seen, however, it was domestic rebellion, not the foreign threat, that preoccupied the officials of the Ye family.

Ye Kunhou and Ye Boying, father and son, and Ye Kunhou's brothers and their sons began their official careers fighting rebels, then turned to the tasks of reconstruction and the restoration of order. Though they never rose to the highest levels of the bureaucracy—their names are scarcely mentioned in any general history of this era—their careers are important precisely because they were unremarkable. Their concerns and achievements were so conventional that they can be regarded as "typical" of the late Qing officials who emerged during the Tongzhi Restoration, the era in which the rebellions were finally quelled and some accommodation was reached with the Western powers following the second Opium War.[1] Ye Kunhou's large collection of intensely revealing poems and Ye Boying's autobiography afford us a more personal view of official life than the bureaucratic documents on which most histories are based. We now turn to their official careers and consider the nature of governance in late nineteenth-century China.

When the rebels were finally pacified in the mid-1860s, Ye Kunhou, his sons, and his brothers were all rewarded with substantive appointments, Kunhou remaining in Henan and Boying serving in the metropolitan province of Zhili (renamed Hebei in the republican era). Although Ye Kunhou held the relatively exalted rank of lieutenant governor, he was never promoted beyond local bureaucratic positions. As a friend later wrote, in the postbellum period, the road to power was murky: "some are recommended for merit; some advance based on monetary contributions, taking shortcuts to high position."[2] Over time, Ye lost his youthful ambition to become a famous statesman, writing that while he once aspired to be a towering cedar, now he was content to be a humble boxwood.[3] By and large, he blamed himself: "In 16,000 days I have not succeeded one time out of a hundred."[4] On occasion, however, he felt underappreciated, even discriminated against because of his humble origins. In former times, he believed, the humble scholar in a peasant's hat could enjoy true friendship with a powerful official in a cart (liche meng); and he cited the example of the Ming scholar and statesman Wang Yangming who had proved himself as a local official before his rise to prominence. Now times had changed. People like himself, without distinguished official pedigree, were tainted by their rural origins. "My generation must rid itself of the scent of the vegetable garden."[5]

Ye Kunhou served as a local official in Henan for over thirty years, and during that time he developed a fairly consistent philosophy of government. At its center was the dictum that officials should treat the people like members of their own families.[6] Disputes should be resolved by encouraging compromise; conflict could be halted by promoting humanity. To ensure that the people would not go hungry, officials should promote agriculture and sericulture but also encourage frugality, so the people would have something saved up in the event of poor harvests. The state, for its part, should restore attention to public granaries to prepare for times of scarcity.[7] To gain the people's affection and support, one must be impartial and restrained, showing no sign of either joy or anger.[8] Like every Qing official, he particularly warned against corrupt, selfish, and scheming clerks, the petty functionaries of the Chinese bureaucracy who depended for their livelihood on the fees and bribes that they extracted from the people. Kunhou had nothing good to say about these people, comparing them at various times to tigers, wolves, and mosquitoes.[9] He also realized that an official must guard against misconduct by his own servants and staff, but his solution here was notable: beware the clever servant; better that a servant be dull.[10] Cleverness was never a virtue; a quick intelligence was cause for suspicion. Loyalty, honesty, and a straightforward simplicity were the virtues one sought in oneself and one's staff.

The longer Kunhou served in office, the more cautious and conservative he became. Looking back at his career, and perhaps thinking of his zeal in pursuing bandits beyond his jurisdiction during his tenure as prefect in Nanyang, he faulted himself for excessive haste in his early days and his failure to heed warnings.[11] On another occasion, he recalled the ancient philosophers' counsel of restraint: "Pulling back is not cause for embarrassment; / Moving forward may bring much humiliation. / Advancing or retreating without good reason, / This is the source of failure."[12] His favorite analogy for judicious governance was chess. The skilled chess player pays attention to the whole board, assessing how each actor will be affected by any given move.[13] In these bits of poetic counsel, he deliberately conflated personal and political virtues, but in either case, his aversion to activist government was clear. Instead, he valued patience and persistence. On one occasion, he cited the parable of the old man who moved the mountains, who, by excavating a small piece every day, illustrated the merit of stubborn persistence in a single task.[14] (Years later, Mao Zedong would famously use the same parable for a quite different revolutionary purpose.) Though Kunhou acknowledged that times were changing, when he visited a local academy he praised its adherence to the centuries-old academic regimen devised in the Song dynasty.[15] He wrote a long poem to celebrate the final victory over the Taiping Rebellion, praising the court and the regional officials who had restored peace to the realm and welcoming the return to the old ways. Another poem from the same time declared that after all the troubles, the dynasty was now safe and "there is no need to cast a new tripod." The bronze tripod was the ultimate sacrificial vessel of the court in ancient China, and the symbol of imperial rule. Now that the rebels had been defeated, Ye Kunhou saw no reason to alter the old modes of rule.[16]

As his sons, nephews, and later grandsons and grandnephews entered official life, Kunhou readily dispensed advice to guide their official careers. His advice centered on matters of morality, reflecting his conviction that in times of peace, an official governed primarily through the force of his character. An upright character, personal probity, and dignified manners were the foundation for a successful life, and he urged future generations to "uphold the virtues and merit of our ancestors; / Do not let their contributions be offset by your failings."[17] Not surprisingly for a man who wrote so many poems, Kunhou stressed the need to uphold the family's reputation for poetry and ritual. However, family members should never presume upon or boast of their ancestors' accomplishments: "a steadfast simplicity is the basis for respect."[18] Those who began as county magistrates should not disdain their petty position but seek the people's approval as their reward.[19] A poem addressed to his grandchildren and grandnephews nicely summed up the kind of behavior that he expected of the younger generation:

> The cultivation of character has always begun with sincerity.
> You must never display cleverness before others.
> Only a properly molded heart/mind can be useful.
> If something looks suspicious it is best not to do it.
> If you are trustworthy and keep your word, you will have few worries.
> If you make agreements lightly, they will be violated.
> Favors must be fully repaid, but grudges forgotten.
> In loyalty and consideration for others, there is no harm in being emotional.[20]

This sort of moral advice, while utterly commonplace, was far more important to Ye Kunhou than specific policy proscriptions. When Boying took up an important new post in Zhili, he composed a series of poems for his edification: "Do not govern with a lot of words, but through vigorous effort. . . . Do not abuse your power and ruin your reputation . . . [An official's] first duty is clean government." Any effort to squeeze the people and fatten oneself was unconscionable. In addition to this commendable but quite conventional advice, he noted that Boying's post was an important one and near the capital. He would be closely observed and he needed a clear plan of action. Beyond that advice, however, Ye Kunhou would not go, saying explicitly, "I do not have a program to offer you."[21] Success, in his view, would not depend on clever or innovative policies but on sincere, steadfast, and economical adherence to established Confucian values and principles of government.

Such were the virtues that were supposed to guide official conduct in this era, but how did local officials actually live? We know the wide range of duties that a local official performed. Office holders were expected to be omnicompetent in their governance, combining the functions of local judge, tax collector, fiscal officer, superintendent of education, overseer of public works, sheriff, militia commander, and intercessor with the gods in monthly sacrifices and times of disaster.[22] How did one balance the multiple roles of an imperial official?

Ye Kunhou's experience gives us a sense of the tenor of official life. During his various postings as a local official, Ye Kunhou spent a remarkable amount of time on the road. This mobility was a structural feature of official life. Young men traveled to take the exams. If they received official appointment, they had to move away from their home province. One of Kunhou's favorite metaphors for a local official was a swallow, migrating from its home each year.[23] The most welcome travel was surely to the capital for an imperial audience, but the arrival at a new post, with the local gentry and notables arrayed along the road with carts and banners to greet the new prefect, was surely gratifying as well.[24] Such constant travel widened the horizons of Qing officials, both acquainting them with the diverse geography of the empire and reminding them of China's long history. Kunhou's poetry about his journeys focuses mostly on his visits to historic sites or famous temples. On occasion, as when he stopped at the Buddhist grottoes and magnificent stone sculptures at Longmen, he seemed to be just sightseeing.[25] More commonly, he was traveling back and forth to the provincial capital, patrolling his jurisdiction, or surveying the effects of or defenses against a natural disaster. As we saw during his service as Nanyang prefect, he also used these travels to settle law cases and resolve local disputes. When he stayed at temples or inns, he met people and learned about the locality or sometimes encountered other officials on the road, even former colleagues or friends, with whom he shared experiences.[26] Ye Kunhou frequently visited temples and monasteries, despite his Confucian skepticism toward religion. Occasionally he was repelled by the experience, as when he stopped at a temple complex built by eunuchs of the late Ming. These eunuchs, he was sure, only "pretended to believe in these fantasies" and exploited the sweat and toil of the common people to construct temples in transparent efforts to promote their own reputations.[27] As a local official, however, he dutifully set up an altar and prayed for rain in times of drought and offered thanks to the gods when it came.[28] Despite his personal skepticism, he recognized the social efficacy of religious practice. The people expected such rituals, and if rituals satisfied and pacified the people, they should be faithfully performed.

Much of the work of a local official was pure drudgery. In busy times, Kunhou might have to write reports late at night and have little time for his family and friends.[29] When his duties were particularly boring, he longed to retire and regretted that he had too little money to do so.[30] Especially toward the end of his career, he grew tired of the monotonous nature of his official duties, comparing his life to that of a donkey turning a millstone.[31] By this time, however, he was spending most of his time in Kaifeng, where he lived in semiretirement, still called upon for temporary local assignments but usually answering summons to duty in the provincial capital.[32]

Judging from Ye Kunhou's poetry, the life of a senior official in a provincial capital involved a good deal of networking, much of which took place at banquets, birthday celebrations, and other refined but pleasurable forms of entertainment. A gathering of elderly officials, all over seventy and including one governor-general, provided the occasion for one poem.[33] Officials traveling to distant posts would visit and share news on these occasions.[34] A tribute mission of Gurkhas from Nepal passed through Kaifeng, and he was proud to welcome this embassy from the frontiers of empire responding to the emperor's warm embrace.[35] Those who had passed the exams in the same year *(tongnian)*, "classmates" in effect, were a particularly important group of associates, and Ye Kunhou frequently met and exchanged poems with these colleagues of examination life.[36]

At times, all this entertaining became tiresome. At one point, he complained of the forced conversation and empty ritual with his many unwanted guests. His heart was not in it, and he was tired of bowing.[37] Later he adjusted to the routine and was even willing to take advantage of it: "Sometimes I use kind words to profit from fools. / A jug of white liquor and people have no complaints. / Add some green apples and there is no lack of guests."[38] With the return of some prosperity after the rebellions, these banquets became increasingly sumptuous, and Ye Kunhou was reminded of how much his diet had changed since the meager meatless fare of his home back in Anqing.

> Since I entered official life,
> I have experienced a great change.
> On one meal you spend ten thousand cash,
> But still [politely] declare that it is [so poor it is] hard to swallow.
> You gather your colleagues to drink together,
> Arraying all kinds of fancy delicacies,
> Everyone boasting and competing in extravagance.[39]

Ye Kunhou specifically associated such sumptuous banquets with official life. Networking was important to a successful bureaucratic career, for it provided critical information on the inner workings of an always secretive court and bureaucracy, and forged relationships with allies who could promote one's advancement. It also performed an important social function as a marker of elite status: "It is the custom of the times that people are only impressed by wealth and status."[40] But the extravagance also made him uncomfortable. At one New Year party, his house was full of guests, lanterns hung from the pavilions in the garden, and the halls echoed with music, and noisy celebration. But he worried, "Who would think that the expense of one evening's music and dance / Could save ten thousand poor folks from cold and hunger?"[41] He was even more uncomfortable at the lavish birthday celebration of a high official that took place while the rebellions were still in progress. Music floated from within the walls and the guests' carts lined the road outside, but beyond the city walls, the rebels ravaged the countryside, and the villages were full of suffering peasants.[42]

Music, food, and drink provided the most visible accoutrements of social networking, but the quieter pleasures of art and poetry also played a role. We know so much about Ye Kunhou's life largely because he kept the thousands of poems he wrote for pleasure or exchanged with friends. Elegant poetry full of allusions to historical figures and ancient texts was the mark of a literate man and a required part of the examination regimen. Exchanging poems on ceremonial occasions was a critical token of respect. Ye Kunhou was also an avid art collector, filling his Kaifeng home with scrolls and antique pottery. Officials purchased and exchanged such art objects as gifts and brought them to colleagues for learned inscriptions, something Ye Kunhou did frequently late in life.[43]

Ye Kunhou's semiretirement eventually passed into full retirement. In his final years in Kaifeng, he lived the life of a prominent former official, with all the attendant trappings. In about 1868, he moved to a new home in the south of the city, a property that attracted him because of its extensive garden, to which, as always, he devoted great attention.[44] He expanded the home into a large compound that stretched across an entire block of what would eventually be prime real estate in the provincial capital. Fifty servants cared for the extended family. The compound had ponds and gardens, a central hall for elaborate rituals of ancestor worship, and a two-story residence in the rear. The library held thousands of books, eight hundred scrolls of rubbings, painting, and calligraphy, and many ancient bronzes. Despite his advocacy of frugality and clean government, Kunhou's many years in local and fiscal administration had enabled him to accumulate a handsome fortune.[45]

He composed poetry, wrote essays, and edited old texts. The garden, named the "Suitable Garden" (Yiyuan) was always a source of great pleasure, offering places and vistas appropriate to each season.[46] Here he entertained guests, with whom he wrote poetry, played chess, drank tea, and examined works of art.[47] A high official who visited him in 1863 wrote, "He had the air of the ancients."[48] When Ye Boying visited his father over New Year in 1882, he strolled in the garden; relaxed with one of the classical commentaries, histories, or works of philosophy; and admired the calligraphy of famous historic or contemporary luminaries. The front courtyard was large enough to host private opera performances, which by the 1880s were largely active martial tales, for Kunhou's hearing was failing and he could no longer appreciate the arias of the more refined operas.[49] This aural impairment could sometimes be useful: when he wished to relax by himself, Kunhou locked the gate and pretended not to hear unwanted visitors.[50]

Although Ye Kunhou was joined and assisted by his brother, Ye Yun, and his son, Boying, during the military phase of his career, he was separated from the rest of his family until he settled down in Kaifeng. His wife, children, and grandchildren were in Shaanxi with his second son, whose magistrate post provided the only secure refuge and financial support for the extended family. His wife joined him briefly in Kaifeng in 1857, then went back to Shaanxi to marry her daughter to a promising young scholar. Not until 1861 did Kunhou's wife return to Kaifeng, where she lived until overcome by illness in 1865. Kunhou wrote a properly laudatory testimonial to the virtuous life of this literate daughter of a gentry family. He praised her diligence and uncomplaining sacrifice while he was young and struggling to establish himself and noted her humane counsel during the early years of his official career. She certainly did her wifely duty to advance his career, and her life recalls lines from a poem by another woman who married into the Ye family: "In my youth, I drew pleasure following his ambition to ascend the clouds; now with white hair my sadness shows in traces of parting tears."[51] Kunhou had corresponded regularly with her, and although many of his poems of spousal separation can be discounted as conventional laments, he continued to write touching poems years after her death, which testify to his real affection for her.[52] Prolonged separation and even the concubines that Ye Kunhou took in his mature years were not inconsistent with a genuine mutual respect and emotional bond between husband and wife.

Sometime during the long period of physical separation from his wife, Ye Kunhou acquired two young concubines, one of whom bore him a daughter in the year of his wife's death. At least one of these women (most likely the "singing girl" presented to him by a colleague around 1861) was probably in her teens or twenties at the time, as she lived on into the 1920s.[53] However, these details are discreetly hidden in the genealogy, which records precise birth and death dates for wives but not for concubines. Kunhou continued an active procreative life with his concubines, with sons born in 1866, 1872, and 1874, the latter two conceived when he was in his seventies. In addition to providing for these concubines and children, Ye Kunhou continued to support and enjoy the company of grandchildren and grandnephews who lived with him and whose upbringing and early education he supervised.[54] One daughter returned from her husband's home in Shaanxi to care for her mother in her last years and again to look after Kunhou for many years in his old age.[55] Another daughter ended up saddled with her husband's debts when her parents-in-law absconded, and she too returned to her father's home.[56] These daughters' extended close attachment to their natal home is notable and certainly founded on enduring bonds of affection. Clearly, the second daughter's relations with her husband's family (at least in economic terms) were less than ideal. Whether the same was true of her sister, or whether her well-off parents afforded her a more comfortable lifestyle, we do not know. There were, finally, dozens of servants to take care of the large household, including elderly family retainers who had been with the family since their days in Anqing, kept on despite the infirmities of old age. One had such bad hearing that she often misunderstood simple commands.[57]

As Ye Kunhou's official career gradually came to a close, the task of serving the Qing passed to his two elder sons, especially Ye Boying.[58] Following Ye Kunhou's crucial 1856 audiences with the emperor, Ye Boying was allowed to purchase a position in the Board of Revenue in Beijing and was appointed as an attaché. Such petty appointments provided little opportunity for either wealth or notable achievement, so for six months, he rarely went to the office, instead staying home to study for the exams. In time, his superiors convinced him that this appointment offered a chance to learn the details of administrative work, and he spent the next half year reading documents and assisting the department heads. In the spring of 1858, with the triennial metropolitan examinations scheduled for the fall, he took leave to prepare for the more prestigious degree-based path to office. A young relative joined him in Beijing, sleeping on a cot in his room, and the two studied together, talking day and night about the exams. They exchanged poems and practice essays on classical themes—a quite different and no doubt more intellectually challenging form of learning from the type he had gained at work. But Boying failed again, and soon he was back perusing tax documents at the Board of Revenue.[59]

When he was not working at the board, Boying took every opportunity to meet with high official acquaintances in Beijing. Some were of his father's generation, some of his own. His autobiography does not tell us exactly how he made these connections, but the Ye family had risen high enough in the official world to permit informal visits to the homes of important people. There Boying could discuss contemporary affairs: the state of the insurrection in the south (where the news was mostly bad), the Qing strategy to suppress it, and the techniques of statecraft and nourishing the people.[60] These conversations allowed Boying to keep up with affairs of state and provided valuable connections for his later career.

In the fall of 1859, Ye Boying was assigned to a team auditing records in an office for government money orders. There were several hundred chests filled with money orders from all over the country, in all sizes and shapes, for sums from a few taels to several thousand. These money orders provided ample opportunity for venality among the experienced clerks who handled disbursements, and the team's task was to uncover evidence of embezzlement. Two senior metropolitan officials supervised the inspectors, but they were too busy with their regular duties to devote much attention to the audit. Most of the others were young men from prominent families, who preferred entertaining and visiting acquaintances to sifting through musty receipts. Ye Boying found one capable collaborator, and soon the two devised a system to complete, with their assistants, two chests of money orders per day. Once they began to make progress, the other young gentlemen returned to join the effort, but they were rebuffed on grounds that too many inspectors would add to the confusion. In all likelihood, Boying and his coworker now saw the prospect of reward for their labor and were reluctant to share it. In any case, after nine months at a task they were ordered to finish in two, the results were sufficiently impressive to earn Boying a commendation from the president of the board and promotion to second-class secretary.[61]

Before he could take up his new position in the capital, Boying was presented with a better opportunity, an offer to serve as an aide to Mao Changxi, who had just been appointed militia commissioner for Henan. As we have seen, the Mao and Ye families were acquainted through Ye Kunhou's long service in Henan, and Mao Changxi was one of the officials with whom Boying had been discussing affairs in the capital. Mao not only took Boying as an aide, he also added Boying's uncle, Ye Yun, to his staff and thus became a significant patron for the careers of these two in Henan.[62]

In the spring of 1860, Ye Boying set out for Shaanxi to visit his mother (and his wife—though his autobiography makes no mention of this). He paid his respects, enjoyed some of the sights, including climbing the scenic and spectacular Mount Hua. By leaving the capital in the spring, Boying managed to escape its invasion and occupation by an Anglo-French army later in 1860. This expedition drove the emperor from the capital to exile in the summer retreat in Chengde, just beyond the Great Wall, where he died the following year. Meanwhile, the Europeans looted and burned the summer palace to punish the court for attacking the British fleet and seizing an envoy sent to ratify the settlement of the Second Opium War.[63] These were traumatic events in the history of modern China, but Ye Boying not only managed to escape them, he gave them no notice in his autobiography. Foreign affairs were not his concern. His focus was on defeating the Qing's domestic enemies, and he spent the next several years under Mao Changxi on this assignment.

Ye Boying's rebel fighting lasted five years, from 1860 to 1865. Along with his uncle, he served in Mao Changxi's headquarters, writing reports, handling logistics, and occasionally going out with the troops in battle. After important victories, he was recommended for promotion, but the ranks and positions that he received were either in the capital or in a distant province. The antinepotism laws prevented his holding office in the same province as his father, but since Henan was the province he knew best, the court allowed him to continue serving in Mao Changxi's command. This was a fairly typical late Qing adjustment of dysfunctional regulations, but the regulations remained on the books and the resulting compromise gave an ad hoc quality to much of the empire's governance. Extrastatutory and informal arrangements became more important than the constitutional provisions of Qing law. The empire survived, but not without jeopardizing some fundamental principles of imperial rule.

In the mid-1860s, the Qing finally gained the upper hand against the rebellions, and the empire turned to the task of reconstruction. Ye Boying had a brief hiatus in his career, for his mother died in 1865 and he entered the obligatory period of mourning. He stayed in Kaifeng for a year studying the commentaries on the *Book of Changes*. He found comfort in this ancient divination text as a guide to the auspicious and the evil, and to the inner meaning of virtue and vice, shame and greed. Then in 1867, his father got news that some neighbors had encroached on the family graveyard, and Ye Boying was ordered back to Anhui to take care of the problem. He brought his mother's beautiful and carefully sealed coffin with him. Boying was now forty-two years old, married with children, and the holder of substantial official rank. But he remained at his father's beck and call in family matters, and off he went to Anqing.[64]

The city was a depressing sight. Outside the walls, people were still living in thatch huts. Inside the town, only the gates and rooms facing the main streets had been repaired in the six years since the Qing retook the city. Beyond these thoroughfares, all was rubble. Only the commercial suburbs along the riverfront displayed signs of normal life. The old house on Close-to-the-Sages Street had been looted and vandalized, but Boying was able to repair it. Managing the graveyard problem was more difficult. The family's relatively exalted official status proved remarkably ineffective in expelling the rival claimants or acquiring alternative land. Those who had stayed in Anqing were more successful in garnering local support for their claims. Eventually a settlement was reached, and three generations of Boying's ancestors—his mother, grandparents, and great-grandparents—were all buried (or reburied) with proper rites and expensive coffins at an auspicious site with beautiful trees in a geomantically suitable setting.[65] The funeral was an expensive affair, for the poor came to beg, neighbors to borrow, and guests to eat. All were accommodated, for such were the obligations of a prominent official family.

While in Anqing, Boying was asked to edit a new edition of the Ye family genealogy. Sixty years had passed since the last edition, and many family members had died or scattered during the years of rebellion. With the help of several younger relatives to check and verify the descendants of those listed in the 1807 genealogy, Boying compiled a new edition, including extensive autobiographical sections by Ye Kunhou and his brothers, as well as obituaries for their wives and mothers. He solicited prefaces from prominent officials—including the Mongol Grand Secretary Woren, one of the leading conservative officials of the age—to whom Ye Kunhou evidently had some unspecified connection. Woren praised the genealogy project as a return to the fundamentals of the family system, whose breakdown he deemed responsible for the rebellions that had wracked China. Ironically, Woren's preface extolled the virtues of the lineage system in binding people to their homes and preventing the sort of mobility that he found conducive to rebellion, but no sooner had Boying completed the project than he left Anqing to rejoin his father and the rest of his branch of the family in Henan.[66]

The compilation of the genealogy elicited discussions of rebuilding a lineage hall, and Ye Boying promised that when he had advanced in his career (and accumu-

FIGURE 4. Ye lineage hall. Photo from Ye family genealogy, seventh edition, 2001.

lated enough funds), he would build one for the lineage. Another decade passed before the hall could be built, but in 1875, Ye Boying sent 3800 taels to buy appropriate land in the Anqing suburbs and construct the structure. More time was required to purchase land rights to the selected site from both landlord and tenant, but these tasks were accomplished before the decade was out, and a fine building was constructed with three central halls and several on the side, providing a place to worship ancestors, feast, and deliberate. An endowment of land produced rent to pay for maintenance of the hall and the annual sacrifices. Just as Ye Hua's official position had inspired the compilation of the first genealogy and construction of a lineage hall in the sixteenth century, now the second series of prominent officials, led by Ye Kunhou and Boying, produced a new and much larger hall, achieving appropriate local status and recognition for the Ye family of Anqing.[67]

At the end of 1867, Ye Boying completed his period of mourning and, upon his petition, the governor of Anhui wrote to the Board of Appointments recommending him for assignment. During Boying's service on Mao Changxi's staff in Henan, his formal appointment had always been elsewhere, first in the metropolitan bureaucracy, and later as an expectant prefect in the northwestern province of Gansu. In

1864, with the suppression of the Taiping Rebellion, the court began to exercise stricter controls over such practices. Rather than accept appointment to a frontier post in Gansu, a poor and arid province that had been devastated by the Muslim rebellions, Boying purchased the right to specify Zhili (the province around Beijing) as his choice for appointment.[68] When he returned to duty in 1868, he visited his family in Kaifeng for a few months before his father urged him on to the capital, where he met with Mao Changxi (who was now president of the Board of Works) and other capital officials he had come to know. He was appointed expectant intendant in Zhili, and in the following year, soon after his arrival in the province, his rank was elevated to provincial judge on the basis of the family's merit in quelling the Nian. Given that this merit had in fact been accumulated years earlier, in all likelihood, the final suppression of the Nian in 1868 together with Boying's appeals to his friends in the capital had generated pressure to recognize the Ye family's contributions to the defense of the Qing. At the same time, his uncle Ye Yun was promoted to intendant rank and then to positions in the salt administration and finally as Xuzhou prefect in northern Jiangsu. The latter was a troubled bandit-infested post, where he served until his death in 1880, apparently after catching cold while proctoring the prefectural examinations.[69]

Boying's superior in Zhili was the governor-general, Zeng Guofan. Zeng was without question the dominant statesman of his age, a respected scholar of impeccable rectitude who had organized militia in his native province into the Hunan Army, the new type of regional army that was instrumental in quelling the Taiping Rebellion. In his final years, Zeng was a leader of the Tongzhi Restoration, named after the reign of the young emperor who ruled (at least in name) from 1862 to 1875. Zeng charted a conservative course for the restoration of order in the provinces after the long years of civil war. Though he recognized the superiority of Western firearms and founded an arsenal in Shanghai to manufacture rifles and artillery, he was loath to adopt anything more from the West. The remainder of his program sought to revive Confucian learning (reprinting the classical texts and commentaries, rebuilding academies, resuming the examinations in the rebel-occupied regions); uphold the age-old virtues of probity, rectitude, and respect for the ancients; promote agriculture; reconstruct infrastructure; and restore the rural order.[70] These were policies to which the Ye officials also subscribed.[71]

When Zeng Guofan left his post in Zhili, he allegedly told his successor, "In two years, I have found only this one [reliable man,] Ye [Boying]. He is meticulous in his work and keeps his feet on the ground."[72] Boying was the type of methodical, down-to-earth official that Zeng preferred. In this sense, Ye Boying's career of service in Zhili—thirteen years during which he rose from temporary appointments in the provincial capital to intendant and finally to provincial judge—gives a fair indication of the Tongzhi Restoration at the local level.

As always, Boying's father was ready with career counseling. A few years earlier, in a particularly relaxed mood, Ye Kunhou had written a poem advising his sons and nephews to take it easy:

> Do not follow in the dust of conventional ways;
> A cup of wine or a poem will lighten your spirits.
> Your words (and your silence) to others can bring success or failure.
> There are reasons for one's rise or fall in the world,
> But a little drink can mend whatever troubles your mind
> Or cure what ails your body.
> Official position, wealth, and fame may not be related to each other.
> In times like these, what need is there to be so conscientious?[73]

Now that substantive appointments were at hand for his son, Ye Kunhou wrote a series of eight poems offering more characteristic and serious advice: Boying must be cautious in his first post. He would have few friends and would have to rely on himself. He should be practical: "Set your feet on level land," but also read history as a guide—the biographies of the Han dynasty of ancient China were particularly recommended. Deep learning was less important than basic moral principles. To avoid the jealousy of colleagues, Boying was advised to "restrain your cleverness and adhere to simplicity and honesty." Standing out above others was always dangerous: the tall tree would be blown down by the wind; a flower in full bloom would fade or be cut. Boying should be prepared to endure all forms of abuse: "Even if people spit in your face, you should show no alarm, for that is great virtue." Personal comfort should be no concern for a young man: a crane and a zither (simple pleasures of nature and music) were all that was necessary. In governance, Boying should seek the middle way between harsh policies and weak resolve. Finally, Ye Kunhou noted that his own career was ending with no major distinction, and the family's hopes now rested on Boying's shoulders.[74]

As Boying took up his new post in Baoding, the provincial capital, one early priority was recovery from the rebellions and management of the transition from civil war to a time of peace. Restoring the area called for controlling military expenditures, demobilizing troops, improving training of those who remained, and eliminating the corruption that had allowed many military officers to get rich while civil officials were just getting by.[75] Such important infrastructure as the post roads that fanned out from the capital and passed through Zhili had fallen into disrepair, and counties were ordered to protect them from washouts by digging ditches on the sides and using the dirt to raise the roadbed.[76] In his position, Ye Boying also had ritual obligations to honor the loyal martyrs of the rebellion, so he obtained an accounting of 39,307 martyred officials, officers, gentry, and common people in Zhili (a list that certainly undercounted the commoner casualties) and 8,384 "loyal and filial" female victims (many of whom probably committed suicide rather than sub-

像公卿冠夫大祿光

壬辰翰林世愚姪陳樹屏頓首拜撰

FIGURE 5. Ye Boying. Drawn
for the 1906 edition of the Ye
genealogy. At the top are his
title, Grand Master for Splendid
Happiness and his courtesy
name, Guanqing.

mit to the rebels) and had their names engraved in steles in separate memorial halls
in the capital. If a suitable hall existed in their home counties, these martyrs were
honored there as well. The Qing establishment thus ensured that its loyal defenders were properly remembered, and the institutional memory of their righteousness was carved in stone.[77]

Education was always a top priority, and everywhere officials established schools
and academies to train the next generation for the examinations. We have seen Ye
Kunhou's commitment to these bulwarks of Confucian values, and Ye Boying helped
raise funds and donated his own money to endow a local academy with a sum of
two thousand taels, which, when lent at interest, provided the operating expenses
for the school.[78]

Encouraging Confucian philanthropy was a long-term obligation of a Qing restoration official. Two of the most common philanthropic institutions were homes
for orphans and widows, two vulnerable groups whose numbers had been much
increased by the rebellions. Widows' homes were necessary to protect poor women
from remarrying to support themselves and their children. Such remarriage, though
quite common, violated a woman's Confucian obligation to remain chaste and loyal

to her late husband.[79] Ye Boying sponsored several orphanages and widows' homes, donating money and raising funds from other officials to build or acquire the necessary buildings, drawing up regulations, and then turning the homes over to local gentry to operate and maintain. Official initiative was necessary to start the project, but an official's tenure in a locality was brief, and only the commitment of the gentry could sustain the enterprise.[80]

Benevolent governance was a fundamental obligation of Chinese imperial officials. Ye Kunhou had expressed this obligation in numerous poems comparing an official's role to that of a parent, echoing the conventional reference to local magistrates as "parental officials" (fumu guan).

> Governing the people is like governing a family.
> Being an official is like being a mother.
> To the pitiful millions,
> We offer our tender support.
> The people are naturally good;
> Only the officials are shameless.
> If we just refrain from loving money,
> We could accomplish eight or nine tenths of the job.
> When we work just a little on the people's behalf,
> They are moved to eternal gratitude.[81]

One of the more unusual projects that Ye Boying supported was a "refuge for vagrants" with an infirmary outside the south gate of the provincial capital. Every winter, poor peasants flocked to the cities to beg or hustle to survive through the agricultural slack season. To care for these homeless poor, ten inns were opened outside the south gate of Baoding each winter; but in fact, Boying complained, these shelters became "venues for gamblers and villains to hide and evade arrest." In addition, the inns were unsanitary places, and disease spread easily among the impoverished residents. The uncaring innkeepers, fearing the expense and trouble of an investigation into a tenant's death, would not even wait for a sick vagrant to die but would cast the body into the open fields where wild dogs fed on it even before the person had expired. To remedy the grim plight of these poor vagrants, Ye Boying founded a refuge capable of housing seven hundred to eight hundred men (crowding about twenty men into each room) over the winter months. A soup kitchen provided basic sustenance, and an infirmary cared for up to one hundred patients. We have no idea how effective the medical care might have been, but the basic intent to nourish the homeless poor while they were still reasonably healthy and care for them when they fell sick was certainly an appropriate manifestation of benevolent rule.[82]

Natural disasters were unavoidable in rural China, posing a challenge to the imperial government. In 1877 and 1878, drought and famine afflicted much of north

China. Boying was charged with managing relief around Baoding, and he followed all of the established procedures. Local residents received grain, and camps were established outside each gate for famine victims seeking relief in the city. There the poor refugees were fed a thin diet of gruel each morning and evening. Males and females had separate camps, and a third camp surrounded by a mud wall protected the weak and elderly from victimization by younger competitors for food. To keep too many peasants from flooding toward the city, the local government provided four camps at the city gates and eight camps surrounding the city at a distance of about five kilometers. When drought continued for a second year, the surrounding counties established soup kitchens, and the government sent out mobile relief carts to sell gruel for a modest fee so that those with a little money could survive at home and not overburden the camps. When rains finally relieved the drought, the camps were closed, and the refugees were given a modest allowance to return to their villages. This handout reflected a guiding principle of all such relief efforts: they wanted to avoid becoming permanent institutions attracting the destitute to the cities. Every effort was made to get people back to their villages to work the land.[83]

Inevitably, disease spread in the wake of the famine, so another center dispensed medicine to the sick. Women and young children lived apart from others, and children with smallpox were strictly quarantined. Not everyone could be saved, of course, and many died by the road, to be buried in shallow graves, which were soon dug up by animals, leaving the mauled corpses exposed. Deputies were dispatched to rebury thousands of such victims. In all, Ye Boying claims that eighty thousand famine victims were cared for—certainly a small proportion of the millions affected by the drought but still a substantial effort in the area around the provincial capital.[84] He even attempted to address some of the social problems that came with natural disasters, issuing orders to prohibit the sale of wives in times of hardship and targeting unscrupulous rogues who sought to profit from the sale of women.[85]

One critical responsibility of officials in many parts of China was water control. In a predominantly agricultural economy, water could mark the difference between prosperity and poverty. Too much water meant floods and waterlogged fields; too little meant drought and dry rivers and canals. For centuries, the Chinese had developed hydrologic techniques—diking rivers, dredging canals, digging wells, irrigating fields—to meet the challenges of climate and defend against the vagaries of weather. On the north China plain, the biggest challenge was coping with the heavy runoff from the summer monsoons, which came down from the mountains and had to find a way across hundreds of kilometers of virtually flat alluvial plain. Unless the rivers were kept dredged and diked, great marshes formed, fields were waterlogged, and river transport became impossible.[86] Such water-control measures were Ye Boying's primary responsibility when he held the post of Qinghe intendant and was responsible for a circuit that stretched across forty-seven counties on the western side of Zhili where the Taihang mountains met the wide plains. In the end, this aspect of his job provided his greatest official achievement, as well as a handsome income.

Success was by no means guaranteed. Indeed, when Boying was appointed to the Qinghe circuit, his father warned of the dangers that faced him: several large rivers, hundreds of kilometers of waterways. He would require dozens of capable deputies and several hundred thousand taels in funding. The risk of failure was great, and a major disaster could ruin his career. The task also carried political dangers, as Boying would quickly learn. The Qinghe circuit was a desirable post, for it gave access to substantial state funds for waterworks. Boying had been recommended by a colleague and examination classmate of his father, who also provided key advice on how to manage the waterworks.[87] Soon after he was appointed, an imperial censor (charged with investigating corruption and malfeasance in office) impeached Boying for "conspiring to worm his way into office." The precise charges are unclear but seem to suggest that Ye Boying had gained this plush post through improper influence. Boying was quickly cleared by Zeng Guofan's successor as Zhili governor-general, Li Hongzhang, then a leading power in late Qing politics and, like Ye Boying, a native of Anhui.[88] Li Hongzhang and another senior official later proposed competing plans to solve Zhili's flooding problems, with Ye Boying caught in the middle. Only by patiently inspecting the river work with Li's haughty critic was Boying able to deflect the criticism and carry on his work. Clearly Li and Ye worked well together, as patron and client, protecting each other from criticism.[89]

The details of the various water-control projects need not concern us, but we can note that almost every year in the 1870s, Ye Boying spent months in the field overseeing the work. Rivers were dredged and straightened to ease travel by water from the capital in Baoding to the treaty port of Tianjin, the political and economic centers of the province, respectively. Elsewhere marshes were drained to reclaim farmland. In one such project, Ye Boying introduced foot-pedaled waterwheels operated by soldiers from the south, where the technology was commonly used to irrigate rice fields. Sometimes local peasants had built dams to protect their fields or provide irrigation, but the dams caused flooding elsewhere or blocked transport and had to be removed. Boying had willow trees planted to prevent erosion of the dikes and promoted well drilling in times of drought, partly because wells provided water for irrigation, but also because he had been told that connecting the water ethers of earth and heaven could help bring rain.

Year after year, during his long tenure as Qinghe intendant, Ye Boying toiled to improve water control in his jurisdiction. He certainly did not solve the problem of flood and drought, but he did stabilize the hydrology of the area. He also made money. Water-control projects were costly, and a circuit intendant could count on disbursements from the provincial government as well as taxes collected in the localities. Because an official in charge of waterworks had to hire his own staff, he had discretion in much of his budget. That Ye Boying was able to profit from this arrangement is obvious from the large personal contributions he made each year for water-control and other projects. The annual official salary of an intendant was only about two thousand taels, from which he had to support not only his family but also his personal secretaries and staff. Between 1873 and 1879, however, Ye Boying donated fifteen thousand taels (more than his total salary) for river works and additional large sums for his philanthropic projects and the lineage hall back in Anhui. If he gave such amounts to the public and to charity, one can imagine that he also kept substantial sums from the discretionary funds that he controlled.[90]

As should be evident from this discussion, the responsibilities of a local official were extremely broad. Public security, social welfare, education, tax collection, disaster relief, and water control were all the responsibility of county magistrates and the prefects, intendants, and provincial officials who supervised their work. But one of the most time-consuming duties of a Chinese official was the adjudication of civil disputes and criminal cases. In addition to all his other duties, the local magistrate was the local judge. Because many cases required review by higher officials, the system was easily overburdened. When Ye Boying served as acting provincial judge in 1878, one of his proudest achievements was setting up strict schedules for judicial review, as a result of which he managed to remove 12,300 cases from the backlog in nine months—a rate of almost 50 cases per day. He also sought to reduce the number of lawsuits by ordering the arrest of pettifoggers, the legal specialists who helped people prepare complaints. Recent scholarship has shown that these pettifoggers performed a useful service, helping vulnerable people gain access to the courts, but in the eyes of Qing officials, they were scheming profit seekers (the ambulance chasers of their day) who were responsible for the large number of lawsuits that overwhelmed the legal system.[91]

Like his campaign against pettifoggers, most of the legal reforms that Ye Boying proposed represented conventional themes in Qing statecraft. He advocated, for example, the revival of the *baojia* system of household registration. If these population registers were kept up to date, then miscreants could be easily located (for *baojia* was originally a public security system that held people responsible for the conduct of their neighbors), and officials would know immediately the number of people affected by a natural disaster. The problem, of course, was that such a census, even if carried out by local constables (or runners) from the *yamen*, as he proposed, would be extremely time-consuming and costly. Ye Boying explicitly made the registry an unfunded mandate: local officials were to count households at their own expense, to keep their clerks from using the task as an opportunity to burden the population with fees. Boying also specified that a separate register be established for certain déclassé elements: actors, musicians, opium-den operators, and convicted thieves—a grouping of people of dubious morals that made perfect sense to any Qing official.[92]

Some of the most interesting reforms that Ye Boying pressed as a provincial judge related to the prison and detention system. He first focused attention on people summoned as witnesses to cases under review in the capital. Many witnesses, though guilty of no crime, had to travel hundreds of kilometers from their home, with inadequate food, clothing, or medical attention. Some fell sick and died while waiting for their cases to be settled. Thus, Ye Boying established an Office to Await Interrogation, which would house, feed, and provide medical care for witnesses and defendants worthy of pity.[93] County-level problems came to his attention when he received a report from local magistrates that Zhili's county jails housed fourteen hundred prisoners, and in the first five months of the year, over three hundred had died from illness while in custody, a mortality rate of about 20 percent in this short time. He ordered a number of reforms to eliminate such cruel incarceration. Magistrates should keep their jails clean and warm in winter and make sure that corrupt clerks and constables did not hold people in detention to extract bribes. Prisoners were to be provided adequate food, clothing, and medical care. Innocent witnesses were to be housed separately from common criminals, in an office similar to that in the provincial capital. To avoid recidivism, petty thieves should receive work training in such skills as spinning, belt weaving, or rope making. Finally, he proposed that cruel conditions and an unusual number of deaths in jail should be grounds for a negative evaluation of county magistrates, a sanction that could end their official careers.[94]

Near the end of his tenure in Zhili, Ye Boying again turned his attention to prisoners' rights, ordering that cotton quilts be provided to those in jail. The Zhili governor-general was then Li Hongzhang, China's leading statesman of the late nineteenth century, who would soon become a major promoter of railroads, steamships, and China's first large state-supported industrial enterprises. By the usual terms of reference, Li was a relatively progressive figure in his promotion of technical modernization in China. But Ye Boying's solicitude for prisoners moved him to joke, "First you gave them food; now you give them clothes and covers. 'Ample clothes and enough to eat.' I'm afraid the prisoners in the jails will not want to leave!" Li's modernizing agenda had little place for the compassionate treatment of prisoners. However, Ye's reforms had nothing to do with modernization. Indeed, to the extent that he justified his policies with anything more than general counsels of humane governance, his appeal was to classical etymology for terms like "in bonds" or for an obscure character for "to feed a prisoner." These terms, he argued, showed the ancients' concern for treating prisoners humanely, which was sufficient justification for doing so in the present.[95]

In 1879, after six years' service as Qinghe intendant, Ye Boying was called to an audience in the capital. The eight-year-old Guangxu Emperor reigned at this time, but real power lay with his aunt and regent, the wily and powerful Empress Dowager Cixi. When officials were called to audience, it was the empress dowager who interrogated them from behind a screen, for it would have been improper for a woman to meet directly with her officials. Ye Boying's audience with the empress dowager took place before dawn on November 20, 1879. His verbatim record of the encounter (obviously written from memory, presumably just after the audience) is worth quoting:

### REVERENT RECORD OF IMPERIAL AUDIENCE

On the seventh day of the tenth month, I went to the Hall for Cultivating the Mind. I kowtowed to thank the Heavenly Grace for receiving me in an Imperial Audience. The Sovereign asked: "When did you arrive in the capital?" This minister responded: "I arrived in the capital on the twenty-first day of the ninth month [November 4]."

The Sovereign asked: "And when appointed?" This minister responded: "I was appointed to fill a vacancy as the Qinghe intendant in the 12th year of Tongzhi [1873]."

The Sovereign asked: "How many localities does the Qinghe intendant oversee?" My response: "It oversees 47 counties and departments."

The Sovereign asked: "I suppose the area is all peaceful and quiet." Answer: "Extremely peaceful and quiet."

The Sovereign asked: "The Qinghe intendant is responsible for many rivers. Report in detail so that I can hear about the condition of these river works." My answer: "The Qinghe intendant is responsible for the Daqing River, Zhulong River, North Juma River, Western Lake, and Hutuo River. Upstream there are also many smaller tributaries. When this minister was first appointed acting Qinghe intendant in 1872, the river works had long been neglected. The various rivers ran together to form a vast lake extending for hundreds of *li*. On the orders of governor-general Li Hongzhang, I traveled to inspect and begin repairs. First we devised a plan to return the rivers to their original courses. In cases where we feared the flow was too great, we opened the Luseng River and the King Zhao River to absorb the runoff. From 1872 through 1877, crops could be planted throughout the area and the harvests were good."

The Sovereign observed: "This year there are again floods." My response: "This year there was too much rain. There were some places affected by disaster."

The Sovereign asked: "I suppose there is some plan to handle this." My response: "The governor-general Li Hongzhang has for several years instructed the local officials to dredge many shallow rivers; and in normal years, they flow smoothly within their banks. But when unusual floods come down from Shanxi, Henan and beyond the pass, flowing down like water in the channels of roof tiles, some flooding is unavoidable in summer and fall. But if the winter wheat can be planted, the effects can be overcome."

The Sovereign asked: "What plans are there for construction next spring?" My response: "I have already received the instructions of the governor-general. Upstream, we will construct a low-water dam on the Daqing River in Xiong County; repair the Thousand-*li* dike; and dredge the outlet of the Zhulong River. Downstream, we will dredge seventy *li* of river near Xinnong Town and connect to the Southern Canal."

The Sovereign asked: "How did you assist and care for the areas stricken by disaster this year?" My response: "In all, 23 counties and departments were affected by floods. By the grace of The Empress Dowager and The Emperor 60,000 piculs [about

3,600 metric tons] of tribute rice were allocated. In addition governor-general Li Hongzhang added 30,000 piculs from provincial reserves. In places to which it was difficult to transport grain, it was converted to over 20,000 taels in cash. These will be distributed this winter. But I fear that next year, before the spring harvest is in, we will request Your Majesties the Empress Dowager and The Emperor for further assistance."

The Sovereign responded: "The people's lives are bitter. We should of course assist."

The Sovereign asked: "You have served as provincial judge." My response: "I twice served as acting provincial judge."

The Sovereign asked: "Was there a backlog of cases?" My response: "In Zhili, since the clearing of lawsuits, there has not been any backlog of cases. But with over a hundred counties and departments, there are still many cases. In my two terms, I concluded in all over 24,000 cases."

The Sovereign asked: "Are there any foreign affairs in the Qinghe Circuit?" My response: "There are churches in Zhengding and Ansu. Since this minister has been in office, I have instructed the magistrates to be scrupulously fair when conflicts arise between the people and the Christians. In the last years, things have been quite peaceful."

The Sovereign observed: "Li Hongzhang has had a very difficult time in Tianjin handling foreign affairs. Now he has returned to Baoding." My response: "The governor-general waited in Tianjin until the rivers were secure before returning to the provincial capital. Now I have received a letter from Tianjin that on the 3rd of this month he left for Baoding."

The Sovereign stated: "Flood and drought come repeatedly to Zhili. Conditions among the people are very bitter. After you return to your post, you should be sure to show pity on the common people. You must instruct the magistrates to devote their entire effort to the people's affairs. They must not be casual about this." My response: "This minister will reverently obey The Sagely Command."[96]

At the time of the Mid-Autumn Festival in 1881, Ye Boying read in the *Beijing Gazette* (an unofficial digest of imperial edicts) that he had been appointed provincial judge in Shaanxi. Some three weeks later, the imperial orders were forwarded to him by Li Hongzhang. (Apparently the imperial bureaucracy was a good deal slower than the privately distributed gazette.) Boying was of course ordered to Beijing for an audience before proceeding to his new post. This time he had separate audiences with the empress dowager and the young emperor. These encounters were shorter than the audience in 1879 but still notable.

His January 3, 1882, audience with the empress dowager was again in the Hall for Cultivating the Heart. After the usual questions about his past posts, his previous audience, and his work on the rivers, the empress dowager asked, "Do you use machines to dredge the rivers?" Answer: "We have only two mechanized dredging boats. For the rest, we use human labor. We hire laborers, or order the people to make repairs, or mobilize soldiers to dredge the rivers." Then after some questions on his service in the militia and as a judge, she turned to two questions related to foreign affairs: "Do you know how we can add *likin* [commercial] taxes to opium?"

to which Ye answered, "This minister has heard the governor-general [Li Hong-zhang] say there is a proposal to add 100 taels tax per chest. But this has not yet been permitted." She then asked about the whereabouts of the British minister Thomas Wade, who had been on leave, and Ye Boying reported that Wade had returned to Beijing.[97]

Ye Boying had never displayed, in any of his writings or official papers, the slightest interest in foreign affairs or technical modernization. He appears to have been a bit more enlightened than his father, who, following a major missionary incident in 1870, concluded that commercial opening to the West had only resulted in the introduction of "evil and seditious teachings" to China. (An early example of this influence was certainly the Taiping Rebellion.) The remedy, in his view, was that "Foreign trade should be prohibited."[98] His ideal model for relations with foreign lands was the tribute system of old, and one can sense the extreme measure of cognitive dissonance that the modern world presented to him when a friend brought a globe for his friends to write poems about. Ye Kunhou struggled with obscure classical allusions as he tried to fit the countries on this modern globe into his conception of how the world should be ordered.[99] Ye Boying at least understood that to avoid foreign meddling in Chinese affairs, conflicts between Christians and ordinary commoners must be prevented. Even he, however, was far behind the empress dowager. She wanted to know about mechanized dredges. She was also searching for a mechanism to overcome foreign objections to taxing the inland transport of opium. And she wanted to know where the British minister was. Boying was able to answer, but he found none of these matters worth reporting in his autobiographical account of his career. The empress dowager, by contrast, in addition to having a detailed command (and skeptical view) of the water-control issues covered in the first audience, was clearly concerned about foreign affairs and interested in questions of mechanization.

The audience with the emperor is intriguing. Though the questions were utterly conventional and perfunctory, one sees signs that the ten-year-old emperor was being trained to conduct a proper audience. Here is Ye Boying's account:

> On the 29th day of the 11th month [January 18,1882], asking for Imperial Instruction, I received an Audience with the Emperor in the Hall for Cultivating the Heart.
> The Sovereign asked: "From what office have you come?" [Boying's answer summarizes his career: Board of Revenue, militia under Mao Changxi, Henan military, intendant assigned to Zhili.]
> The Sovereign asked: "How long were you Qinghe intendant?" Answer: "This official in 1873 received The Heavenly grace of an appointment as Qinghe intendant. I served for 9 years."
> The Sovereign asked: "I suppose the work of the Qinghe intendant is very busy?" Answer: "The post supervises 47 counties and departments. In recent years I leave Baoding in the second month to supervise river work and return only in the 11th month."

The Sovereign asked: "By what road will you go to Shaanxi?" Answer: "Via Henan."
The Sovereign asked: "When will you arrive in Shaanxi?" Answer: "It is now winter; but if the snow on the roads is not too deep, I should arrive in time for the opening of the office after New Year."
The Imperial Sage's instructions: "After you arrive, you must completely reform
the situation [there], bear all responsibility and blame, and lead the subordinate officials to exert themselves to manage the people's affairs." After a while The Sovereign
ordered: "Kneel in peace!" Obeying The Edict I kneeled and kowtowed, asking peace
for The Sagely One.[100]

There was nothing very insightful in this imperial colloquy, but it shows that the
boy-emperor had mastered the basic interrogation of a high provincial official.


Though Ye Boying had promised the emperor that he would arrive at his new appointment after the lunar New Year, he did not hasten straight to Shaanxi. First he
went home to Kaifeng, stopping on the way to confer for a few days with Li Hongzhang in Baoding. Li had recommended him for promotion and given him favorable triennial reviews of service, particularly noting his careful, conscientious, and
uncorrupt administration.[101] We have also seen how Li and Ye protected each other
from criticism in factional bureaucratic struggles. Li was Boying's patron now, and
the fact that they both came from Anhui certainly helped. In Kaifeng, after three
days entertaining guests who had come to congratulate him on his new appointment, Boying feigned illness to pass the New Year with the extended family of sons,
nephews, nieces, and grandchildren who gathered at his father's home. As a provincial judge, Ye Boying now outranked his father in the official hierarchy, but he bowed
to the old man anyway: filial respect prevailing over official rank. After a pleasant
month with his family, relaxing and reading in his father's vast library, Boying headed
west for Shaanxi, arriving at the end of April after an uneventful journey that took
almost a month.[102]

Ye Boying was no stranger to Shaanxi. His younger brother had been a magistrate there twenty-five years earlier, and the family had sought refuge with this
brother in Shaanxi during the Taiping Rebellion. Boying's wife had remained in
Shaanxi, bearing a son named Qinsheng ("born in Shaanxi"), but he did not survive infancy. His sister had married a Shaanxi scholar, and Boying had visited his
mother in Shaanxi in 1860, staying long enough to take in some of the scenic sites.
Through the 1860s and 1870s, his brother had had a fairly successful career as a local official, winning merit defending against a Taiping incursion and fighting Muslim rebels. But with Ye Boying's appointment as provincial judge, the antinepotism
laws forced his younger (and lower-ranking) sibling to seek assignment elsewhere,
and he went back to Henan to finish out his career.[103]

The Shaanxi that Ye Boying was to govern in the 1880s was just beginning to recover from years of war and a devastating drought. The 1862–77 Muslim rebellion of the northwest had brought bloody ethnic cleansing to the province. A substantial Chinese-speaking Muslim population in the Wei River valley in the center of the province had been wiped out in pogroms led by Han Chinese militia; and Muslim attacks in the north had left some counties with only a fraction of their original population. After the rebellions were finally quelled, the drought of 1878–79 brought further misery and millions of casualties to the province. In some counties, half of the land lay uncultivated, and in the entire province, six hundred thousand acres of farmland had been abandoned.[104]

The officials responsible for the province's recovery were not always of the highest rectitude. When Ye Boying was appointed provincial judge, the governor was Feng Juyi of Guangdong. Less than a year later, Feng was impeached for favoritism and corruption: his son had received improper gifts; deputies were profiting from their positions; friends and family retainers had abused their connections to the governor. Feng was cashiered, and Ye Boying served his first term as acting governor until a replacement arrived.[105]

In six years of service in Shaanxi, Ye Boying held all the high provincial posts: provincial judge, lieutenant governor, and governor. Especially when he was governor, he submitted numerous memorials to the court, many of which survive in the archives and published documentary collections. From them and his autobiography, we get a clear sense of the responsibilities of a provincial official, and also of Ye Boying's concerns and priorities. As provincial judge, he pursued the same reforms of the jails, provisions for witnesses, and simplified baojia local security procedures that he had initiated in Zhili.[106] As lieutenant governor and governor, he spent much time on the provincial budget: putting the accounts in order, collecting taxes, dealing with tax remissions for areas affected by natural disasters.[107] Shaanxi was a poor province, but when floods struck the area around Beijing and his patron Li Hongzhang appealed for disaster relief, Boying was quick to send twenty thousand taels in provincial funds, and another ten thousand of his own and his colleagues' contributions.[108] Part of being a successful official involved maintaining good relations with powerful patrons.

Many of the problems that Ye Boying faced in Shaanxi related to recovery from civil war and natural disasters. In the depopulated areas of central and northern Shaanxi, he, like his predecessors, pressed local officials to follow long-established policies to attract migrants from other provinces to reclaim abandoned farmland. Such migrants were given title to the land free of taxes for several years (usually three) until it could be made profitable and once again provide needed tax revenues. Boying even proposed providing an ox for each small farm. However, reintroducing taxation on holdings that had once been tax free was difficult, especially in the hilly and sparsely populated counties of the north, where a farm's boundaries were difficult to establish, and poor but enterprising migrants were adept in the ways of evasion.[109]

Memorials on homicide cases (which were routinely reported to Beijing for approval of the sentences) reveal a remarkably violent frontier environment in these vast areas of small scattered settlements and many migrants. Shaanxi in the 1880s did not match our usual picture of Chinese rural society—it was quite different from the Ye family home in Anhui, where villages were long settled by extended families with deep roots in the land and established conventions for handling community conflicts. Granted, reports on murders are likely to emphasize violence, but the context of these murders is striking. In many cases, the murderer was the victim of an earlier misdeed who sought recourse by killing his persecutor—apparently seeing no prospect that his grievances might be redressed through community mediation or the officials' court. Two examples are representative of the problems of local justice.

In the first case, a poor migrant by the name of Liu had borrowed eleven strings of cash at an interest rate of 3 percent per month, for which a wealthy Mr. Fang had acted as middleman and guarantor. When Liu was unable to repay the loan, Fang paid in his place, but Liu died seven years later, before he was able to repay Fang. At that point, Fang pressed Liu's brother for repayment, sending his sons to demand compounded payments totaling ninety-five strings and to beat up the brother when he objected. Although the brother was also a migrant, he had apparently been more successful, and he sold some land and repaid the entire ninety-five strings. Fang, sensing that this Liu was an easy mark, then claimed that the Lius' father owed another sixty strings of cash, a sum that, through mediators, was negotiated down to thirty. By this time, Liu's brother decided that he had had enough of this overbearing loan shark. He invited Fang and his sons to come for a final formal settlement, then (with some accomplices who had also been victimized by Fang) ambushed them on the road and killed them.[110]

In this unsettled society of weak community bonds, even the conventional reliance on local militia to preserve order frequently went awry, as a second case shows. In the hills south of the Wei River valley, militia in a town on a well-traveled road had remained active after serving against the rebels and bandits of the 1860s and 1870s. Five poor migrants from Sichuan to the south were in the area seeking work. Having few resources beyond their numbers, the five had threatened several travelers on the road, extorting rice, clothes, and opium. Several of their victims happened to stop at the same inn in town, and their accounts of their troubles were overheard by the local militia head. The militia set out, arrested the five miscreants, recovered the stolen goods, took the five into custody, and apparently beat them up. As the county *yamen* was some distance away, the five thieves were held at the militia head's house overnight. Then things began to go wrong. Two of the victims of the highway robbery decided that since their stolen goods had been recovered, they would not waste time filing depositions in court and so they went on their way. Then one of the poor robbers succumbed to the beating he had received. With this development, the militia leaders realized that a court case could be very troublesome and decided to do away with the remaining captives. So they took them to an isolated spot and shot them, except one who managed to escape. The escapee found some temporary work and eventually got home to Sichuan, where he told the tale to the brother of one of the deceased, who returned to report the crime to the authorities.[111]

Ye Boying's response to such lawlessness was distinctly hard-line. He believed in swift, harsh punishment that would strike fear or induce shame in the hearts of potential wrongdoers. Spreading violence could spark a revival of the chaos and disorder of the midcentury rebellions, and such a recurrence must be prevented at all costs. In one long memorial, he bemoaned the widespread banditry, gangs, sworn brotherhoods, secret societies, feuds, and revenge killings in the southern hills, as well as the problems caused by migrants and demobilized soldiers in the sparsely populated north. He warned that such lawlessness could lead to the sort of local conflicts that gave rise to the Taiping Rebellion in the 1850s, and he complained that past Board of Punishment standards were too lenient in dealing with these criminals, releasing prisoners early and meting out light sentences. He was particularly critical of the system that exiled criminals to the care of local authorities at some specified distance from their homes, whence many soon escaped. Ye Boying wanted to show the consequence of crime at the scene of the offense, so he advocated two penalties: for the worst criminals, beheading, with their heads then hung for display; for others, instead of exile, long periods (three to five years) chained to a large rock, with the name of their gang tattooed on their face, or for lesser offenders, on their right forearm. Repeat offenders should be summarily executed. Instead of completing the time-consuming requirement of provincial and imperial review, officials would prepare only a quarterly summary of those so punished. At the heart of his policy was a belief in the deterrent value of swift, sure, severe, and very public punishment.[112]

Judging from the memorials Ye Boying submitted to the court, most of his time as a provincial official was taken up with routine administration. He submitted the required quarterly reports on rainfall and grain prices and on the state of local granaries. He reviewed and reported local tax receipts and arrears and requested remissions for areas afflicted by flood, drought, hail, or (in the north, near the desert) blowing sand. There were plenty of judicial cases to process and report: quarterly summaries of banditry and executions and records of capital cases for review. Local officials were appointed, reviewed, transferred, and occasionally disciplined in a process that left little doubt of the substantial autonomy with which provincial officials operated. Sometimes officials held up appointments made by the court in Beijing for long periods of trial service or even rejected them as unsuitable.[113] Ye Boying made at least one extended tour of the province to check on local governance and defense forces. He noted the repair of various temples and academies and requested honors for particularly filial and virtuous subjects. Finally, of course, he sent the required ritual messages: New Year and birthday greetings to the emperor and empress dowager and profuse thanks to his majesty for the gift of imperial calligraphy of a large character "*fu*"—good fortune.[114]

On only one occasion did Ye Boying present a comprehensive program for the governance of Shaanxi, and this plan is notable mostly for its cautious, conservative, and indeed conventional proposals. In December 1885, eight months after his appointment as governor, he presented an eight-point program for the recovery of Shaanxi after decades of warfare and natural disasters. The first four points related to agriculture: encouraging the reclamation of abandoned farmland, carrying out water-control projects, promoting sericulture in southern Shaanxi, and reforming granaries. None of these proposals was particularly original, and the sericulture one was manifestly impractical. Despite the ancient precedents that Ye Boying cited, Shaanxi was too isolated from easy transportation links to compete with the silk industry of the lower Yangzi and south China.[115] His call for reform of the commercial *likin* tax was also open to question, because this tax on goods in transit was most easily collected when tax stations could be placed along well-traveled waterways, which scarcely existed in Shaanxi. In the area of public security, he called for the suppression of opium and reform of the *baojia* system of population registers. But most striking was his proposal on education. After noting Shaanxi's proud tradition of scholarship as the site of China's ancient and medieval capital, he bemoaned the fact that "After the wars and drought, it has been ever more difficult to make a living. Poor landlords have turned to commerce. The respect for scholarship and esteem for the Confucian way is not what it used to be." To correct this situation, he proposed adding rooms and books to the academies and an extra monthly poetry session to the curriculum. Expectant officials with strength in the classics would be called upon to offer classes. At a time when officials and reformers in the coastal provinces were promoting industry, commerce, railways, and telegraph lines, Ye Boying was lamenting the turn to commercial pursuits and seeking to revive the literati ideals of classical scholarship and poetry.[116]

These commitments are equally evident in his autobiography. There he notes a variety of publications of which he was proud: his father's poems, which had been carefully protected through the years of flight from the rebellions; a preface to a commentary on the *Book of Changes*; another preface to a Yuan dynasty agricultural manual; a work on ancient ritual vessels; and one on music and dance performed at the Confucian Temple. He also saw to the repair of the musical instruments used in temple performances—instruments that had been neglected during the years of warfare. To preserve the architectural and cultural heritage of Shaanxi, he sponsored the repair of many temples, including one dedicated to the Tang dynasty poet Du Fu and the City God temple of Xi'an. In Ye Boying, we see an official steeped in the culture and history of his country and determined to preserve this tradition in all its splendor.[117]

Despite his active role in temple repair, Ye Boying apparently did not diverge from his father's agnostic pragmatism on the subject of religion. Kunhou was entirely skeptical about the alleged influence of the gods. To him, the secular and spiritual worlds were separate: "Men govern this world; the gods govern the other world," and the two were totally unrelated. On another occasion, he was openly disdainful of those praying at a temple: "Disaster or good fortune come from oneself. / The gods deserve no credit."[118] Despite this skepticism, however, he recognized that simple folks' fear of retribution in the afterlife could help promote good behavior in this world. For that reason, he acknowledged that the frightening temple images of torture in the eighteen layers of hell served a useful social purpose. Thus he concluded, "The ancients had a saying: the way of the gods can be used to educate the people."[119] Religion was not so much something he believed in as a useful way to lead people (primarily through fear) away from the path of evil.

It seems only fitting that Kunhou's son should spend his final days as a devoted Confucian official proctoring the provincial exams. Fortuitously, the questions for the exam and the answers selected as the best survive in a small publication. In a pattern that was common in the nineteenth century, the same candidate was judged to have the best essay for each of the first three questions. In all likelihood, only the first essay on a passage from the Four Books (by Confucius and his disciples) was carefully graded, and the others were simply awarded the same score as the first.[120] The critical first question asked the examinee to interpret and comment on a line from the Analects of Confucius: "If the calf of a plow ox be red and horned, although men may not wish to use it, would [the spirits of] the mountains and rivers put it aside?"[121] The passage is traditionally taken to mean that a fine calf (or man) of humble parents should be put to use—as an official, in the case of a man; as a sacrifice, for the calf. The favored essay expanded on this reading with a discussion of cultivating talent, which was conflated with such virtues as humanity and filial piety. To a modern reader, the critical contribution of the essay is difficult to detect. But Ye Boying was impressed: "the heart is refined and the effort effective, the language simple but the meaning exceptional. He begins by rectifying classical models and so he does not fail."[122]

The examinations were held in the fall of 1888, and the weather was cold and rainy. Ye Boying spent over two weeks at the examination hall and came down with a cold, and then a fever and respiratory problems (most likely pneumonia), which left him coughing. When the prescribed medication had no effect, he prepared a memorial asking for medical leave. Several days later, as he grew weaker, he prepared a final will that introduced his sons and grandsons to the emperor in hopes they would be honored with official appointments. Then, on October 1, 1888, Ye Boying breathed his last.

Back in Kaifeng, the family could not bear to tell the eighty-six-year-old Ye Kunhou that his eldest son had died. His own health was already frail, and he too passed away a year later. The two most famous members of the Ye family had left the scene. They had served the Qing loyally for many years, but they were truly officials of the old style. In their writings and their actions, one can hardly sense that a new world was growing up around them. The history of late nineteenth-century China is usually written in terms of self-strengthening efforts, in which the technology of the West was adopted to build shipyards, arsenals, factories, and railroads to strengthen the Qing and defend it against Western and Japanese imperialism. Most striking in the careers of Ye Kunhou and Ye Boying is the fact that self-strengthening efforts receive no mention at all. Neither the threat of Western power nor the power of Western technology seems to have impressed them. Born, raised, and serving out their careers in the interior of China, they devoted themselves to Confucian scholarship and practical statecraft: water control, land reclamation, militia and *baojia* security forces, disaster relief, and swift, sure punishment of wrongdoers. They led their branch of the family to wealth and power. But the time for such officials had come and gone. As a new century approached and a new age dawned, the old order in China was crumbling and would soon fall. To survive and continue to prosper, the family would have to change.

6

# A Time of Transitions

In 1891, a small, solemn, but no doubt well-appointed party set off from Kaifeng carrying coffins. The carefully preserved bodies of Ye Kunhou and his sons Boying and Jingchang were being returned to Anqing for proper burial. They were escorted by Ye Yuanqi, the forty-two-year-old son of Ye Boying, and his twenty-three-year-old uncle, Ye Jiquan, born to Kunhou and his young concubine late in the old official's life.[1] Kunhou and his sons had died between 1887 and 1889, in the reverse order of their ages. The three men had all been officials, and their coffins were elaborate and carefully sealed. Indeed, when their tombs were broken into seventy-five years later during the Cultural Revolution, Boying's body was found perfectly preserved, clothed in his official Qing dynasty robes, a sword at his side.

The date for the removal of the bodies to Anqing would have been carefully calculated for the most auspicious moment, and the two-year delay between Kunhou's death and this joint burial may have resulted from the difficulty in finding a date that fit the astrological requirements for each of the three deceased. A proper burial is all about choosing the right time and place. The time having been chosen, the proper place was assumed to be the lineage cemetery near the ancestral home outside of Anqing. But Ye Yuanqi and his party were in for a rude awakening.

Kunhou and Boying were the most illustrious members in the history of the lineage. Their official careers had brought fame to the Ye family, and they had contributed generously to the new genealogy and lineage hall. They were not, however, from the most senior branch of the lineage, and they had not fully conformed to the lineage's normal marks of ritual unity. Notably, males of Kunhou's generation should all have had Zhao as the first character of their given name. Aside from Kunhou and his brothers, virtually all of the 150 Ye males of this generation followed this convention, but Kunhou's original name was Fa, and his brothers, Lian and Yun, also had distinctive single-character names. Similarly, in Ye Boying's case, the generation character should have been Ji, but this was not the case for Boying, his brothers, or his first cousins. Indeed, Kunhou's father, Ye Yuting, was the last of this line whose name included the characters specified in the genealogy. All of Yuting's descendants adopted a distinctive naming system. Somehow, even before Ye Kunhou started this branch on the road to official prominence, it had separated itself in important ways from the rest of the clan.[2]

Ye Kunhou's long years in office in north China had further attenuated the bond to his ancestral home. He left an interesting poem, probably dating from the late 1840s, recording his sentiments after one visit back to Anqing:

> Although I was born in this town,
> I left my old home when young.
> Now I return in old age
> To pay respects to the ancestral tombs.
> I find the local dialect difficult to understand.
> I don't remember my way around.
> I have no property here.
> I am not used to living here.
> It is best to offer your regrets to your townsmen,
> And bid farewell to your old home.[3]

In 1891, the estrangement that had been festering between Kunhou's branch and the rest of the family burst into open conflict. When Ye Yuanqi arrived at the ancestral home, his relatives detained him in the lineage hall and refused to release him until he agreed to certain conditions. First, the lineage elders insisted that the three coffins not be buried in the family cemetery: Kunhou, Boying, and Jingchang were such eminent officials that they would completely overshadow the ordinary folks buried there and deprive the others' descendants of good fortune. Second, Yuanqi and his young uncle should share some of their immediate family's wealth with the poor relatives who were left behind in Anqing—buying land for the landless, homes for those without proper shelter. Ye Yuanqi held the rank of circuit intendant in recognition of his father's contributions, and one might wonder how these ordinary peasants dared to detain such a lofty servant of the emperor, but the explanation passed down through the generations of the Anqing branch of the family was simple: "The state has its laws, but the lineage has its rules." And among the rules of the lineage was the principle that "No matter how great an official may be, he is no greater than the lineage."[4]

Eventually, a settlement was reached (the terms were not recorded), and Ye Yuanqi spent some time searching the county for an appropriate burial site for his father and grandfather. He found an auspicious site at the base of Yellow Dragon Hill, some distance northwest of Anqing. An elaborate grave site and ritual hall were constructed and provisions made for a local family to look after the graves. The entire ordeal was both mentally and physically taxing for Yuanqi, and for the rest of his life he complained of aching legs from traipsing around the countryside looking for a proper burial site.[5] No descendants of Ye Boying ever returned to Anqing—until the research for this book brought the family together a century later.

The fallout from the break extended to other close relatives of Kunhou. In 1880, Kunhou's younger brother Yun died after years of profitable service in the salt administration and then as Xuzhou prefect in Jiangsu province. The following year, Yun's son Shuliang brought the body back for burial, but a boat accident on the way and an explosion at the Anqing arsenal near where the family was staying unnerved him and left doubts about whether the burial was truly auspicious. Through his father's connections, Shuliang managed to obtain a number of lucrative salt appointments in the 1880s, eventually settling in the key salt distribution center of Yangzhou, where he also (in his late thirties) took three teenage concubines. Then in 1893, not long after Yuanqi's troubles in Anqing, he gave up on finding a proper permanent burial place for his family in Anqing and returned to unearth the coffins of Ye Yun, his wives, his concubines, and his son (Shuliang's elder brother) and took them to Yangzhou for reburial. Such removal of the dead from their ancestral home was extraordinary. Shuliang justified it by arguing that Yangzhou was close to Anqing and the climate was similar, so the spirits in heaven should not object to the transfer of his family members' earthly remains. But the act only underscored the extent of this branch's break from its roots in Anhui.[6]

Ye Yuanqi was Boying's eldest son. Born in 1849, when Boying was just twenty-five and still subordinating his ambitions to his own father's career, Yuanqi began life in the large and comfortable prefect's mansion in Nanyang, where Kunhou was then serving, surrounded by four generations of extended family. After surviving the period of flight and concealment during the rebellions, Yuanqi stayed mostly in Kaifeng with his grandfather while his father advanced through the official ranks. Teachers hired by the family tutored him for the examinations, but in eight attempts he never obtained even the lowest *shengyuan* degree. His friends blamed this failure on "the unfairness of the new age," but another characteristic of that age was the declining importance of examination degrees as a route to official position. Indeed, Yuanqi's official career was built upon the purchase of degrees and office, and his initial appointments were only temporary: in 1877, a minor appointment in the Beijing Board of Punishments; and in 1880, an assignment as an expectant local official in Hubei province, where he never actually served and may never have even gone. These positions were undoubtedly granted in recognition of his father's and grandfather's service, and through connections the family had established in the bureaucracy.[7]

In 1871, Ye Yuanqi married Miss Zhang, the daughter of a Henan magistrate descended from the most prominent family of scholars and officials in Anhui's Tongcheng county.[8] She efficiently bore him two sons in rapid succession (1873 and 1874) and two daughters, who died in infancy. Although we know nothing of the nature of this marriage, Yuanqi was unusual in not taking a concubine, and his wife seems to have accompanied him on his later official postings. These postings did not begin until after his father's death in Shaanxi in 1888. Until that time, Yuanqi seems to have remained in Kaifeng caring for his grandfather, though he did make a number of trips to visit his father in Xi'an. The final act of Ye Boying's life was the memorial he wrote commending his sons to the emperor's attention. After the obligatory mourning period, Yuanqi volunteered for military service against a Muslim uprising in the far western province of Xinjiang. There he earned sufficient merit to have his appointment shifted to the metropolitan province of Zhili, where his father had served and Boying's patron, Li Hongzhang, was governor-general.

Under Li, Yuanqi distinguished himself mainly as a money manager. He first served in the Office of Training and Revenue, responsible for logistical support of the army in Zhili. He worked there for several years, handling millions of taels with precision. He had some success in limiting embezzlement and misappropriation of funds by subordinates before he was forced into temporary retirement by the death of his mother in 1896. Yuanqi used this mourning period to collect reports on the customs and governance of foreign lands, which he edited into a volume entitled *Collected Essentials on the Entire Globe.*[9]

This volume, which regrettably has not survived, is perhaps the clearest indication of the gap that separated Yuanqi's generation from those that came before. Neither Boying nor Kunhou displayed the slightest interest in foreign affairs, and Kunhou's poetry had a strong xenophobic strain. By the 1890s, however, the threat from abroad could no longer be ignored. In 1894–95, Japan and China fought a brief but bloody war from which the Japanese emerged fully victorious. The war broke out in a dispute over Korea, a country that had long been a tributary of China, sending regular missions to the Chinese court and acting like a loyal vassal of the emperor in Beijing. Japanese interests had been gaining influence in Korea, and eventually friction between the two East Asian powers led to war. When the better-armed and -trained Japanese navy sunk or captured the entire Chinese northern fleet and the Japanese army drove Qing forces from the Korean peninsula, China's defeat was complete and its position in Korea came to an end. Fifteen years later, Japan annexed the country as a colony. Even more threatening to the sovereign integrity of the Chinese empire was the loss of Taiwan, which for two hundred years had been an integral part of the Qing domain, had recently been elevated to the status of a province, and now was made part of the Japanese colonial empire. Finally, the Japanese extracted an enormous indemnity of 230 million taels and the right to build factories in China, a right immediately shared by all the Great Powers under the "most favored nation" clauses in their treaties.[10]

The humiliating defeat by Japan had an enormous impact on China. The Japanese seizure of Taiwan was the first major loss of territory suffered by the Qing, aside from the ceding of the small island of Hong Kong after the Opium War. Furthermore, defeat had come not at the hands of the European powers but at the hands of Japan, which had only recently emerged from seclusion and embarked on a vigorous program of economic, military, and political reform after the Meiji Restoration. For many Chinese, the Japanese example proved that the military power and technological superiority of the West could be learned and used to reform and strengthen an Asian country in a fairly short time.[11]

From this time forward, reform (and soon revolution) became the dominant theme of Chinese politics and society, and Ye Yuanqi was very much part of this new tide. His book on global politics and culture was certainly designed to introduce Chinese readers to the foreign powers threatening the empire and to improve understanding of the sources of foreign and Japanese strength so that China could emulate them. He recommended to Li Hungzhang the establishment of a Japanese-language school and the purchase of Western books to train the next generation of students. The days in which China's leaders were chosen for their mastery of the Confucian classics were coming to an end.[12]

But China's road to reform was not an easy one. The enthusiasm for change that followed the Sino-Japanese War had brought a strong reformist group to power and prominence in Beijing. The Guangxu Emperor (1871–1908, reigned 1875–1908) was just emerging from years of subservience to his aunt and regent, the Empress Dowager Cixi (1835–1908). In the summer of 1898, the reformers gained the emperor's ear, and a flood of edicts for the modernization of administration, education, industry, and the military issued from the court in the Hundred Days of Reform. The Meiji Emperor and Peter the Great of Russia were cited as precedents for thoroughgoing imperially sponsored reform based on European models. But the radical reformers moved too far too fast. Conservative gentry in the provinces and Manchu princes at court felt threatened, and they rallied behind the empress dowager to depose and confine the Guangxu Emperor and bring the reforms to a halt.[13]

As the failure of the 1898 reforms returned a conservative group of Manchu princes to power and Chinese politics lurched from reform to reaction, the threat from Western and Japanese imperialism escalated. China's defeat by Japan not only shocked the Chinese political elite, it also alarmed the European powers. Journalists, statesmen, and business elites concluded that the Qing dynasty was too weakened to survive, and the powers prepared for the division of the empire. Just as Africa was being cut up into European colonial possessions, now China was divided into "spheres of influence," a process the Chinese described as "carving up the melon." These "spheres" were not yet colonies, but they were agreements extracted from the weakened Qing state to guarantee mining, railway, and other economic rights to the foreign power claiming the territory. The fact that France demanded the territory adjacent to its new colonies in Indochina, Japan claimed Fujian across the straits from its colony in Taiwan, and Russia sought ice-free ports and railway rights in Manchuria to connect to the Siberian railway made it clear that these countries viewed the spheres as preparation for future colonial expansion.

Chinese reactions to this new level of imperialist aggression soon sparked another major crisis. On the one hand, the conservative forces at court saw all Western influence as a threat to their position and encouraged local officials to resist any foreign interference. On the other hand, the Western nations' demonstration of their willingness to use superior military power to work their will in China had important consequences. The most critical repercussion began in Shandong, a province southeast of Beijing stretching from the Yellow River plain to a long coastal peninsula. In 1897, Germany had used the murder of two German missionaries as a pretext to claim the province as its sphere of influence, seize a coastal port as a coaling station for the German navy, and force the removal of the popular but antiforeign governor. Terrified that other instances of anti-Christian violence could lead to similar threats to its sovereignty, the court issued orders that all conflicts involving Christians were to be speedily and amicably resolved. Unfortunately, the consequence of this order was an increase in such conflicts. Converts and their missionary sponsors realized that by claiming anti-Christian persecution as the cause for every insult, injury, or loss they suffered, they were likely to gain a favorable settlement in court. So Christians became more aggressive in pressing their claims in small disputes, and a Chinese reaction was soon to follow.

The reaction was a movement known in English as the Boxer Uprising. The Boxers practiced a form of Chinese martial arts, an amalgam of earlier practices that involved possession by the spirit of martial deities, which would render the adherent invulnerable to the superior weapons of the West. Soon the Boxers took up the anti-Christian cause, defending ordinary villagers in disputes with Christians. Chinese Christians were never more than a tiny minority (less than 1 percent) of the Chinese population, but they were often concentrated in certain villages, and these villages now came under attack by the Boxers. By this time, conservative Manchu princes and officials dominated the court and many north China provinces, and they were loath to suppress the Boxers' loyal opposition to foreign meddling.

The crisis came to a head in the summer of 1900. A drought plagued the entire north China plain, leaving peasants without work in the fields and a hungry populace ready to believe Boxer propaganda that the rains had been withheld by gods angered over the Christian presence in China. Under the slogan "Support the Qing, Exterminate the Foreign," Boxer bands began to stream toward Beijing and spread their message in the capital and the nearby treaty port of Tianjin. The European diplomats and Christian missionaries were alarmed and called for military protection from the powers. As foreign troops moved in, the court felt threatened and offered ever-more-overt tolerance and support for Boxers. Violence broke out, several foreigners were killed, the foreign legations were put under siege, and the crisis escalated through the summer until a massive expedition of European, American, and Japanese troops moved in to brutally suppress the uprising and drive the court from Beijing.[14]

Throughout the Boxer crisis, Ye Yuanqi was an official in Zhili, one of the provinces most affected by the movement. He was no fan of the Boxers. He saw them spreading a dangerous form of heterodox practice and urged vigorous suppression of their activities. He was not alone in this opinion, but it went unheeded by Zhili's new conservative governor-general. Having failed in his attempts to avert the crisis, Yuanqi devoted himself to damage control. As foreign troops occupied Beijing and Tianjin, then moved south toward the provincial capital in Baoding, Yuanqi acted to protect the provincial treasury. Gathering funds from all the offices in Baoding, he collected four hundred thousand taels and brought the monies under guard to a safe location deeper in the interior. Later, some of this money was used to disband poorly trained soldiers hastily recruited during the crisis. When an officer of this force threatened mutiny if officials did not allocate more money to the cause, Yuanqi faced him down and carried out the demobilization. He made sure the funds were saved to support the regular army and keep the peace until the foreign troops withdrew.

Yuanqi had certainly performed a major service to the dynasty in saving these funds from foreign confiscation or domestic predators, but he received no particular reward. Having lived in some hardship on the road for months, he was bitter and resentful when other officials returned to Baoding with carts and carriages laden with their well-dressed dependents and precious possessions. Ever critical of the corrupt excess of the day, he seems to have spent his final years as a lonely and unhappy man. Even his eulogy admits that he had no true friends.

Two years later, at the relatively young age of fifty-three, Ye Yuanqi died. The new governor-general of Zhili was Yuan Shikai (1859–1916), the military and administrative reformer who would rise to the presidency in the early years of the republic. Yuan reported unconvincingly that Yuanqi's death was the result of exhaustion from his labors in 1900. According to family lore, when Yuanqi fell sick, Yuan Shikai dispatched a Japanese doctor attached to his army to operate on him. The operation failed, and Yuanqi's wife never forgave the future president. In any case, in posthumous recognition of Yuanqi's service to the dynasty, his son, Chongzhi, was made a student of the Imperial Academy and granted the rank of magistrate. Thus would the family serve the Qing for one last generation.[15]

Ye Chongzhi was born in Ye Kunhou's home in Kaifeng in 1873. We know very little about his early life, but he presumably remained in Henan with his father and great-grandfather through his youth, receiving the usual classical training from private tutors in the elegant family compound with its large library, hundreds of antiques and scrolls, and beautiful garden. He moved to Zhili and enrolled in a Confucian academy in Baoding in the 1890s, while his father was an official in that provincial capital. There the curriculum included, in addition to the traditional subjects, an introduction to the new learning from the West.[16] Chongzhi seems not to have taken the local exams, for which he would have had to return to the ancestral home in Anqing, but instead purchased the right to take the exams in the capital. Some examiners were reportedly impressed with his essays, but he did not pass. Consequently, his official career did not begin until the early twentieth century, following his father's death.

Ye Chongzhi's patron was Yuan Shikai. According to a story passed down in the family, at the funeral of Ye Yuanqi, his widow lost her composure and blamed Yuan Shikai for her husband's death. Yuan apologized and promised that he would look after his son, Chongzhi, and in fact the latter's first employment was on Yuan's staff. Yuan then sent Chongzhi with one of Yuan's protégés to Shandong. Chongzhi impressed the populace with his filial devotion (and no doubt his wealth) by escorting his mother to their new home, riding ahead of a two hundred–person entourage and an elegant sedan chair for the matriarch, carried by eight men.[17] In Shandong, he distinguished himself by suppressing bandits while on temporary appointments. This accomplishment earned him a rank of intendant, and after a while, he was sent back to Zhili and appointed to the same Qinghe intendant post that his grandfather Boying had held decades earlier.

While Ye Chongzhi was tracing this ill-documented course up the bureaucratic ladder, China was undergoing a process of momentous change. In the aftermath of the Boxer debacle, conservative and antiforeign forces were decisively eliminated from influence at court. The occupation of the capital, the onerous indemnity demanded by the powers, and the humiliating garrisons of foreign troops (and limitation on Chinese forces) in the capital area had convinced the court, including the empress dowager, that the dynasty must undertake fundamental reforms. Many of these reforms—the modernization of the military, construction of railways, founding of steamship companies, extension of telegraph lines, opening of mines, and establishment of industrial enterprises—had begun tentatively in the late nineteenth century. But the pace picked up markedly in the first decade of the twentieth, as the Qing established ministries of commerce and communications, organized local chambers of commerce, and began revising the legal code to protect and encourage economic enterprise.

An important stimulus for this burst of economic energy was the great increase in foreign enterprises after China's defeat in the Sino-Japanese War, which brought a treaty permitting foreign investment in industry, transport, and mining. As fear spread that foreigners would control China's mineral resources, railways, and modern industrial economy, Chinese officials, gentry, and merchants rushed to form their own companies in these sectors. Before 1895, only about 100 Chinese mining and manufacturing firms were using some form of steam or electrical power, and many of these were very small-scale enterprises. The years 1895 to 1913 saw 549 new enterprises formed, primarily in silk reeling, cotton textiles, food processing, public utilities, and mining. Railway construction showed an even more striking increase: only 288 kilometers of rail were laid before 1895; 9,244 kilometers were in place by 1912. Modern industry and commerce still represented a tiny proportion of the total Chinese economy, but this era was, in important ways, the beginning of China's industrial revolution.[18]

In most areas, the government took the lead in promoting the so-called New Policy reforms. The scope of the program was sweeping, and though the effect was greatest in the cities and along the coast, few areas of China were unaffected. The New Army, as it was called, introduced modern weapons, Western uniforms and drill, and military academies to train a professional officer corps in a country that had long given little status to a career in arms. After a thousand years in which the political elite had largely been selected through examinations in the Confucian classics, the exam system was abolished altogether in 1905 and replaced with a Western-style education system in which mathematics, science, geography, and world history supplemented core courses in Chinese language, classics, and history. Because Chinese teachers for the new curriculum were scarce, many able and ambitious young men traveled to Japan for training, becoming the first generation of Chinese students to study abroad. The experience introduced them to Japan's experiment in forced modernization and the new knowledge that informed it, and it exposed them to new political ideas of nationalism and people's rights.

Within China, the most dramatic reforms were in the political arena. Once again, a critical stimulus came from Japan. In 1904–05, the Japanese scored a stunning victory over the Russian empire in the Russo-Japanese War. In Asia, the Japanese victory was greeted as exhilarating proof that an Asian nation could defeat a great European power, but more importantly, it seemed to demonstrate that Japan's parliamentary system was more effective in rallying the people to defend the nation than the autocratic rule of the Russian czars. The Qing state got the message and dispatched a mission to study constitutional models abroad. Unsurprisingly, the members of the mission were most impressed by the German and Japanese models with strong monarchial powers, but the reforms they adopted empowered gentry in local and provincial assemblies whose deliberative and oversight roles gave institutional expression to critical voices in a manner never before seen in China.[19]

Within China, the enthusiasm for reform was infectious and touched virtually every aspect of life. Cities were transformed with paved streets, gas and electric lights, rickshaws, streetcars, and police officers enforcing traffic and sanitary regulations. New schools drew the most promising students to the cities, where they participated in debates of current affairs, organized clubs, and occasionally launched strikes and demonstrations. Newspapers and journals sprung up in all the major cities, challenging centuries of censorship and permitting a much greater variety of viewpoints on public affairs than had prevailed when the *Beijing Gazette,* whose major content was edicts and memorials, was virtually the only published source of news. An air of urgency and national crisis dominated the new media, and progressive voices called for young people and women to mobilize to save the nation.[20]

The permeation of this new national spirit is evident in the 1906 edition of the Ye genealogy. The preface by the new editor, Ye Shanrong, speaks of the "tides of nationalism *(minzu chaoliu)*" of his era, an age that he identified not by the emperor's reign name but as "the twentieth century." He recounted the ten years he had spent studying in Japan and the impact the experience had on him: "I observed the beauty of its broad and elegant parks, the imposing statues along its boulevards." Mechanization inspired him: "riding on buses and street cars I felt exhilarated. There are lutes [probably player pianos] which play by themselves; plows [tractors] that till by themselves; looms that weave by themselves, and machines that make things by themselves. Things are so finely made that dust dissolves with washing and they glisten when polished." "What is the cause," he asked rhetorically, "for the majestic and radiant appearance of this new society? It all stems from a people being organized on the principle of the nation-state *(guojia zhuyi de minzu)* and not on the principle of the extended family."[21]

What a contrast to the preface to the previous edition of the genealogy! Woren had praised the family as the basis of the Chinese social order. Ye Shanrong extolled the nation and described his reluctance, on returning from Japan, to undertake the editing of a new family genealogy. He justified the project in the new language of the age: "I undertake this fifth edition just as the fatherland is establishing constitutional government, and the first light is shining on the opening of a new era of politics. It is an age in which a national empire is being created. The clamor of patriotism fills the ears. But if we probe the source of things, it is a universal principle of civilization that you cannot have a country rich in the concept of nation and weak in the sentiments of family. . . . We must join the friendship and love of kin, establish standard rules of conduct, build on the organic collectivity of family, and progress to a perfect and well-ordered nation-state." His essay thus moves from a rather disparaging view of the family as a passing stage in the evolution toward the nation-state and world unity to a popular modern notion of the family as a building block for broader national unity.[22]

This was not empty rhetoric. Citing the social Darwinian logic of "survival of the fittest" in an age of competition, Ye Shanrong proposed a new set of family regulations appropriate to the times. He envisioned a "Ye family primary school" in the lineage hall, with the aim of universal education as in Japan and the West. In their later schooling, children should specialize, moving beyond humanistic education in the classics to specialized study of law, criminology, or business. As in Japan and the West, girls should also be educated, for they were the future mothers of the nation. China could not go on in the old way, he said, "raising girls as we raise pigs" (a distinctly modernist interpretation of how young women were treated). Nor should girls be taught only home economics. With skills and training, they could become teachers, help in commerce, or work in medicine. To become full members of society, women must not have bound feet, for footbinding cripples; and mothers should not bind their daughters' feet just because their own are bound. Just as radically, sons, once educated, should choose their own wives—a proposal justified by the usual refrain that this was the custom in Japan and the West.[23]

Politically active Chinese agreed that fundamental change was both necessary and desirable, but what form should it take? Some wished to transform the Qing state into a constitutional monarchy; others wanted to overthrow the Manchu dynasty and establish a republic. Both sides in the sharp debate spoke of constitutionalism and people's rights, citing these reforms as the "modern" and "civilized" means to foster patriotism and strengthen the nation. But the advocates of constitutional monarchy argued that revolution meant civil war and carried the threat of imperialist intervention and further loss of sovereignty. Partisans of revolution argued that China was twice enslaved—by both Manchus and foreign imperialism—and unless the Manchus were removed, the Chinese nation could never grow strong and independent.[24]

Within China, the revolutionary camp was weak and poorly organized in small cells of students and intellectuals. Open advocacy of revolutionary ideas was of course prohibited, and revolutionaries were subject to police raids, arrest, and often execution. Among Overseas Chinese communities, and especially among the students in Japan, where revolutionary propaganda circulated widely, the anti-Manchu party found a much wider following. The most important figure in this group was Sun Yat-sen (1866–1925), a Cantonese doctor educated in Hong Kong and Hawaii. Sun had been advocating revolution and organizing uprisings since 1895. A man more comfortable in Western dress than Chinese gowns, who communicated in English as effectively as Chinese, Sun's early efforts depended heavily on support from English, French, and especially Japanese sympathizers, not all of whom had

China's best interest at heart. But after 1905, as the number of Chinese students in Japan increased sharply, he gained more student and intellectual allies, and they in turn carried revolutionary ideas and publications back for clandestine diffusion in China.[25]

Revolutionary ideas gained particular force in the final year of the dynasty. After the death of the Guangxu Emperor and the empress dowager in 1908, the court was dominated by a regent who proved remarkably inept at adjusting to the times. First, as the preparations for constitutional rule progressed, the court appointed China's first cabinet in the spring of 1911. This long-anticipated move was an important step on the road to constitutional rule in which national leaders would reflect the will of the people. But reformers' hopes were utterly frustrated when only four of the thirteen ministers were Chinese, and the Manchu majority was dominated by undistinguished members of the imperial clan. Second, at almost the same time, the court nationalized the country's railways and took out foreign loans to build the key trunk lines. With this act, a decade of struggles to keep China's railway infrastructure under local control and out of foreign hands came to naught. With these acts, the court seemed to flout Chinese aspirations for representative government and national independence. It turned the two most powerful political forces of the day—constitutionalism and nationalism—against the Qing dynasty itself.[26]

The conflict between Qing and revolutionary forces engulfed the Ye family in unexpected ways. Among the activists in the Ye family was a certain Chongju, greatgrandson of Kunhou's brother Ye Lian. The only son of an expectant magistrate in Jiangsu, he lived with an uncle in Nanjing while young and was exposed to Western learning and urgent discussions of current affairs. In his Nanjing school, he came in contact with some of the future leaders of the revolutionary movement and became convinced that only the expulsion of the Manchu "barbarians" would permit the revival of China. He followed a group of revolutionaries to Hunan, where a failed revolt convinced him of the need for military participation if future putsches were to be successful. So in 1906 he enrolled in the army and was sent for further study in Japan, where he met Sun Yat-sen and renewed contacts with other revolutionary leaders. He was selected to infiltrate the army in Beijing and served in the Army Ministry, sufficiently impressing his superiors to receive an honorary rank as "Master of Court Discussions." But in the spring of 1911—immediately after another failed revolutionary uprising in Canton, and just as the court was finalizing plans for the railway loans and the new cabinet—Ye Chongju was dismissed for "spreading rumors" and ordered back to Anhui. As a returned student from Japan, he had apparently been under suspicion for some time, and perhaps he had carelessly revealed his revolutionary sentiments at a time of growing political tension in the capital.[27]

In July 1911, Ye Chongzhi (Ye Boying's grandson) was appointed police *daotai* for Zhili province. This position was the equivalent of a provincial chief of police, but in fact his office was in the port city of Tianjin, and his duties were primarily confined to policing that city. Tianjin was north China's most important treaty port, handling most foreign trade for Beijing, the north China plain, and even northwest China and Inner Mongolia. Administratively, it was a confusing agglomeration of multiple sovereignties—with separate foreign concessions controlled and policed by the British, French, German, Japanese, Belgian, Russian, Italian, and Austro-Hungarian authorities in addition to the Chinese-controlled portion of the city. The treaty that had ended the Boxer incident excluded Chinese military garrisons from the city, which made the police the only armed force available to maintain public security. In addition, police officers were a critical force in the modern adminis-tration of Chinese cities, with responsibilities extending well beyond the usual traffic- and crime-control duties to include tax collection, health and sanitary reg-ulations (which covered everything from public urination to garbage disposal to prostitution), the promotion of proper civil behavior, and censorship and limita-tion of improper political activity.[28]

In October 1911, a revolutionary coup took place in the central China city of Wuchang. An accidental bomb explosion had exposed the local revolutionary or-ganization. Forced to act prematurely, the revolutionaries were nonetheless able to seize the provincial capital of Wuchang with unexpected ease and then to carry the revolution to the neighboring treaty port of Hankou, and soon to the entire prov-ince of Hubei. A popular New Army officer was made military governor of the rev-olutionary government, and the head of the provincial assembly joined the cause to head the civil administration. Soon New Army officers and prominent gentry members in the provincial assemblies, with critical support from students in the new schools and merchants in the chambers of commerce, led other provinces of southern China (plus a few in the north) to declare their support of republican rev-olution and independence of the Qing court. Within a few months, Qing author-ity evaporated throughout much of the empire, as the institutions of military, edu-cational, economic, and constitutional reform came out to support the revolution and to dominate the new revolutionary governments.[29]

For a time, north China remained solidly in Qing hands. Yuan Shikai (who had been forced into retirement by the new regent) was recalled to serve as prime min-ister. Yuan had trained most of the Beiyang (northern) Army's officers, and they remained loyal to him. But revolutionary plotting continued in the north, and with the Tianjin police a critical defense against subversion, Ye Chongzhi soon fell un-der suspicion. Although Yuan Shikai had supported his early career and remained close to the Ye family, some feared that Chongzhi had known of his cousin Chongju's revolutionary activities. Others reported that the armbands worn to identify the police uniforms in Tianjin were suspiciously similar to those used by revolutionary soldiers in the south. As a result, just a few months after he was appointed, Ye Chongzhi was dismissed as police commissioner, and the official career of this last servant of the Qing came to an end.[30]

On February 12, 1912, the last Qing emperor abdicated. Soon thereafter, Sun Yat-sen, who had been chosen as president of the revolutionary government in Nanjing, resigned the presidency of the Republic of China in favor of Yuan Shikai. China's imperial age had ended, but with the last prime minister of the Qing becoming president of the new republic, the break with the past was far from complete. The conflict between the revolutionary forces and Yuan's new Beijing government proved much sharper than the peaceful transition from Sun's to Yuan's presidency would have suggested. Yuan's commitment to democratic principles was limited, and he was immediately challenged by members of the revolutionary party, who, with their allies, dominated the parliament elected in 1913.[31] Ye Chongju was among Yuan's radical critics, and in 1912, he returned to Beijing to operate a newspaper called *China News*, which supported the parliamentary forces and was sharply critical of Yuan Shikai.

Although no copies of the *China News* seem to have survived, the intensity of public debate in the capital can be gauged in the pages of a conservative paper from the times, the *Patriotic Vernacular News*. It condemned the revolutionary forces as "lower-class hoodlums" and criticized members of parliament for collecting their salaries and then spending the day playing mahjong, watching Peking Opera, eating, drinking, and visiting brothels. One of the revolutionary leaders was quoted (indeed surely misquoted) as saying, "I would rather give China to the foreigners than follow the central government." The closing of progressive papers that published "false" news was reported with approval by this conservative mouthpiece. With little consensus on the meaning of democratic governance, the Republic of China was off to a very rocky start.[32]

In 1913, the conflict came to a head. First, Yuan had the architect of the revolutionaries' parliamentary victory assassinated as he prepared to board a train for Beijing. Then Sun Yat-sen and his allies in the south led a brief and abortive "Second Revolution" against the Beijing government. Ye Chongju left Beijing during the revolt, then returned to resume his opposition work in the press. On the evening of September 7, he was arrested. The charges were unclear and somewhat contradictory. On the one hand, he was charged with organizing a group to welcome the new parliament; on the other hand, he was said to be conspiring with die-hard members of the Qing imperial party. Despite his service in the Qing Ministry of the Army (which was noted as the basis for this latter charge), his long and increasingly public links to the revolutionaries make this charge implausible. In all likelihood, the accusation of conspiring with royalist elements was fabricated to obscure the issue. In any case, at dawn on September 24, without any public trial, Ye Chongju was taken to an execution grounds in Beijing and shot.[33]

According to family lore, when Ye Chongzhi heard of his cousin's arrest at Yuan's order, he made the short trip to Beijing, sure that his long relationship with Yuan Shikai and his father's and grandfather's relationship with Yuan's patron, Li Hongzhang, could get Chongju released. When he heard that Chongju had been executed, he realized that the politics of the new republic would be played by new and bloody rules. He was not prepared for this tough new brand of politics in which summary execution and political assassination were becoming routine. He immediately returned to Tianjin, and when Yuan Shikai invited him first to serve as police commissioner of Henan and then to be director of Civil Affairs (in effect head of the civil administration) in his native Anhui, he politely declined: he preferred to stay in Tianjin to care for his aging mother.[34]

For some seventy years, members of the Ye family had served the Qing. They had devoted their young lives to the examinations, the approved route to office. Later, when Kunhou's official and military achievements offered his brothers and descendants the opportunity to serve without passing the exams, one after the other of the Ye men eagerly pursued official careers. Office was a reliable source of both status and wealth, and the social standing and material resources of the family clearly benefited enormously from these official posts. But in the republic, politics was played by different rules that were both unsettled and unsettling. Ye Chongzhi was too cautious for such a career, so he retired to a life in business and raised the next Ye generation to pursue very different sorts of careers.

# PART II

# Republican China

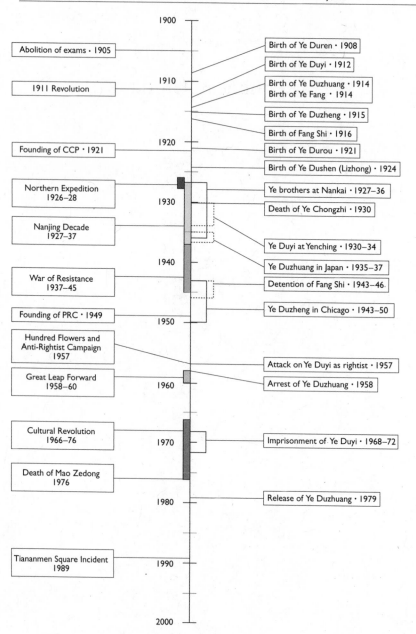

China              Ye Family

1900

Abolition of exams · 1905

Birth of Ye Duren · 1908

Birth of Ye Duyi · 1912

1910

1911 Revolution

Birth of Ye Duzhuang · 1914
Birth of Ye Fang · 1914

Birth of Ye Duzheng · 1915

Birth of Fang Shi · 1916

1920

Founding of CCP · 1921

Birth of Ye Durou · 1921

Birth of Ye Dushen (Lizhong) · 1924

Northern Expedition
1926–28

Ye brothers at Nankai · 1927–36

1930

Death of Ye Chongzhi · 1930

Nanjing Decade
1927–37

Ye Duyi at Yenching · 1930–34

1940

Ye Duzhuang in Japan · 1935–37

War of Resistance
1937–45

Detention of Fang Shi · 1943–46

Founding of PRC · 1949

Ye Duzheng in Chicago · 1943–50

1950

Hundred Flowers and
Anti-Rightist Campaign
1957

Attack on Ye Duyi as rightist · 1957

Great Leap Forward
1958–60

1960

Arrest of Ye Duzhuang · 1958

Cultural Revolution
1966–76

1970

Imprisonment of Ye Duyi · 1968–72

Death of Mao Zedong
1976

1980

Release of Ye Duzhuang · 1979

Tiananmen Square Incident
1989

1990

2000

FIGURE 6. Twentieth-century timeline.

# 7

# Doing Business in Tianjin

Like most late Qing officials, the Ye men who served China's last emperors were products of the interior. Local and provincial positions in the late nineteenth century were frequently filled by men who had risen to prominence in the Hunan and Anhui armies of Zeng Guofan and Li Hongzhang, earning merit in battles against the Taiping and Nian rebels. Born and raised in Anhui, rising through the official ranks in Henan, serving in Zhili and Shaanxi, Ye Kunhou and Ye Boying were men of this mold. They spent their entire lives in the agricultural provinces of China's interior—fighting peasant rebels, controlling floods, promoting irrigation, collecting agricultural taxes, encouraging land reclamation, and relieving famine.

The twentieth century witnessed a new breed of leader in China: men of the coastal regions who made their mark in the treaty ports, the cities opened to direct trade with the West.[1] Shanghai was the largest of these treaty ports, becoming China's most important industrial, commercial, and financial center. It came to represent a cosmopolitan modernity—trade and industry, department stores and movie theaters, newspapers and journals, dance halls and casinos—that stood in stark contrast to the life and customs of the rural interior.[2] Not far behind Shanghai, and by far the most important treaty port in north China, was Tianjin. Tianjin was home to Ye Chongzhi and his family during the last years of the Qing and through most of the republican era.

Tianjin began as a military garrison in the Ming dynasty, then rose to prominence from the seventeenth century as the "throat of the capital," a commercial entrepôt at a key junction on the Grand Canal, the strategic waterway that carried grain and products from the Yangzi valley to provision the official establishment in Beijing. It was also the salt distribution center for most of north China, and early

Western visitors marveled at the great straw-covered mounds of salt bags that lined the river connecting Tianjin to the sea. The imperial salt administration had its regional offices in Tianjin, and many of the city's most successful merchants grew wealthy off licenses from the Qing salt monopoly.[3]

In 1860, Tianjin was opened to foreign trade by the treaty that ended the second Opium War. The English and French victors in that conflict compelled the Chinese to lease in perpetuity land along the river south of the walled city to serve as their concessions. Other powers followed suit, so Tianjin ultimately had English, French, Japanese, German, Russian, Italian, Belgian, and Austro-Hungarian concessions—each administered by the foreign residents on the authority of their diplomatic consuls. Even the Americans, who had followed the British and French belligerents in the war to claim equivalent rights according to the "most favored nation" clause of their treaty, got a small concession, but they soon decided that such territorial claims were unbecoming of a young republic. Rather than return their concession to the Chinese, however, they turned it over to the British to administer.

The foreign concessions sat on swampy land, which was slowly raised several meters above the surrounding countryside by the deposit of thousands of wheelbarrow loads of mud and silt. By the 1880s, the British Concession in particular began to show the classic face of colonial modernity: macadamized roads, gas (and later electric) lights, an impressive town hall, a public park (named after Queen Victoria), a racecourse, an English-language press, a library and literary society, and telegraph connections to the world. A number of foreign banks with imposing neoclassical marble facades lined Victoria Road, which was sometimes referred to as north China's Wall Street. Foreign trade increased at an impressive rate, as the Hai River connecting Tianjin to the sea was dredged, and a fleet of icebreakers kept it open through the winter.[4]

The foreign population in the late Qing was quite small—only about fifteen hundred Westerners at the turn of the century, but this alien presence was a novel addition to the culture of the port.[5] The foreigners' unusual customs attracted attention from Tianjin's Chinese residents, and in order to educate visitors on these matters, an 1884 Chinese guidebook, observing that "in Tianjin, Chinese and Europeans live in close contact with each other," devoted a section to "The Different Customs of Chinese and Foreigners."

> Chinese braid their hair in a queue and shave their forehead to improve their appearance; Westerners regard short hair as beautiful and only shave the face.
>
> Chinese drink and rinse their mouths with warm water; Westerners all use cold water.
>
> Chinese read and write from right to left; Westerners read and write from left to right.

The Chinese compass is called a "south-pointing needle;" the Western compass points to the north.

Chinese regard long fingernails as an adornment; Westerners regard short fingernails as attractive.

In Chinese etiquette, one greets friends wearing a hat; in Western etiquette one removes one's hat before a guest.

Chinese favor the left; Westerners prefer the right.

At banquets and dinner parties, Chinese drink tea before the meal; Westerners drink tea after the meal.

Chinese shoes are high in front with low heels; Western shoes have high heels and low tips.

Chinese wear red for festive occasions and white at funerals; Westerners wear black for funerals and white for celebrations.

Chinese tea cups have a lid on top; Western cups have a saucer on the bottom.

When Chinese take a wife, they follow the mandate of their parents, and once an engagement is made, there can be no change regardless of the beauty or ugliness [of the bride]. When Westerners take a wife, it is entirely their own choice, and the affection of the couple is always harmonious.

On her wedding day, the Chinese bride is all tears; the Western bride joyfully joins the festivities.

Chinese favor males, and in child-rearing and education, boys take preference over girls. Westerners favor both boys and girls, and in child-rearing and education, boys and girls are treated equally.

When Chinese invite people for drinks, men and women are seated at separate tables and never speak to each other. When Westerners invite people for a drink, men and women sit together, laughing and talking, treating the women the same as the men.

Chinese bind girls' feet when they are young, so all their life it is difficult for them to walk. Westerners do not have this custom, and from birth girls can wander about freely. . . .

The differences in Chinese and Western customs are greater than the similarities. As we come into contact with each other, we must know these things.[6]

This catalogue of cultural differences has an amusing charm, and one can imagine its utility for Chinese coming into first contact with strange Western customs. One of the historical functions of the foreign concessions was to present China with an alternative template for human intercourse, and Tianjin's concession unquestionably played a substantial role in introducing new patterns of social, economic, and political behavior. Significantly, once this commentary on foreign customs gets beyond the superficial exoticism of hairstyle, fingernails, and teacups, it focuses mostly on gender relations. Despite an impartial tone, this Chinese commentator seems to find merit in the Western practices—a fair indication of one way in which Western influences began to change Chinese society.

Of course, the foreign concessions could also arouse resentment and opposition among the Chinese. With their own police and judicial systems, the concessions were sites of foreign power, and the Western residents' arrogant confidence in their cultural superiority could make the foreign zones a source of humiliation for many Chinese. The early twentieth-century press reflected an intense desire to achieve a modernity that would spare Chinese from insult. In a particularly mundane example, one article urged people to be careful of the new tramways but to avoid shouting out this warning, for "if the foreigners hear, they are sure to laugh at us for not keeping our eyes open and being untutored in the ways of the world. They will say that we Chinese are not as good as foreigners."[7] Increasingly, the press bitterly recorded incidents of mistreatment of Chinese. When a group of women gathered to watch a lantern show on the occasion of King George V's coronation, a "civilized Englishman" ordered a Sikh policeman to drive them off and then came to push and kick them himself. The paper urged people to avoid such festivities: "Don't you know this is an age of power and not justice?"[8]


Although the New Policy reforms following the Boxer catastrophe brought dramatic changes throughout China, the transformation of Tianjin in the first decade of the twentieth century was particularly noteworthy. After the foreign armies expelled the Boxer bands from Tianjin in the summer of 1900, they set up the Tianjin Provisional Government to administer the Chinese city and its suburbs for the next two years. This foreign-imposed administration wasted no time in transforming the Chinese city to eliminate any further threat to the concessions and to establish a regime of Western-style modernity. First, the Provisional Government tore down the high walls of the Chinese city from which Chinese forces had fired at the concessions during the Boxer disturbances. This move produced wide straight streets where the walls once stood, creating the framework for the tramways that soon ran there as part of a modern transit system. The new government also attacked sanitary conditions in the city, building public latrines, organizing a water company, collecting garbage, and paving and cleaning the streets and lining them with storm drains. It built roads and strong quays along the Grand Canal north of the city and established public buildings such as a Chinese library. To maintain order in the city, the government recruited and trained north China's first modern police force and sent the recruits forth to patrol the streets in sleek military-style uniforms.[9]

Many of Tianjin's elite residents welcomed these reforms as much as they resented the foreign occupation that brought them. When the Qing regained control of the

Chinese city in August 1902, the Zhili governor-general, Yuan Shikai, continued the reforms. He had already trained a new police force to patrol the city, and the constables from the Provisional Government were added to this force. The sanitary and urban renewal efforts were extended, and he devoted considerable energy to developing a new district north of the Grand Canal. Since 1870, when Li Hongzhang's appointment had begun, the Zhili governor-general had spent most of the year in a Tianjin office north of the canal. This office quickly became the locus of political power in Tianjin, eclipsing the walled city to the south. Under Yuan Shikai, this area became a major focus of urban renewal, "Tianjin's new world," in the words of one guidebook, with wide straight boulevards, parks, and a steel drawbridge connecting it to the old city and concessions.[10] The new railway station was built here, along with an industrial college, a college of law and administration, and an army medical school. So Tianjin came to have three distinct districts: the foreign concessions to the south, the commercial districts in and around the former walled city, and a political center in the north. This last area was where Ye Chongzhi established his home and raised his large family.

During Li Hongzhang's long tenure as governor-general of Zhili, his Anhui Army garrisoned the city, and many Anhui men filled positions in the civil bureaucracy. As was the custom when merchant and official sojourners from distant provinces came to live in a Chinese city, these Anhui men built a guildhall (huiguan) to serve their community as a meeting place, hostel, trade association, and philanthropic society providing aid for distressed fellow provincials and a temporary resting place for the coffins of the dead.[11] The Anhui Guildhall was built north of the canal, directly across the bridge from the old city, and right next to the governor-general's yamen, a small temple to Anhui Army martyrs, and the spot where a shrine and park would be constructed in memory of Li Hongzhang. As a prominent member of the Anhui elite, Ye Chongzhi served on the board of the guildhall; and on Third Street, directly behind the hall, he made his home.

The three courtyards of the Ye compound housed Ye Chongzhi, his mother, his wife and two concubines, their nine sons and five daughters, some other relatives, and about thirty servants. The compound formed an inverted L shape, with the first two courtyards arranged from south to north and the third courtyard for the two concubines and their children directly west of the inner courtyard. The large compound was surrounded by an outer wall, which was entered from an alley north of the Anhui Guildhall. At the height of the family's power, a policeman stood guard at the gate, no doubt a holdover from Chongzhi's service as police commissioner. As the family's wealth and position declined, this guard patrolled with decreasing regularity and eventually disappeared altogether.[12] On either side of the imposing front gate were four large characters in a couplet that read "With Heaven's protection, renewing the ancient." Lining the entryway were long lacquered benches where servants relaxed in the shade and hoped for some breeze in the hot summer months.

Directly inside this entrance and blocking any prying view from the outside, was a wide four-leaf screen, lacquered green and sprinkled with gold dust, on which four even larger red characters were pasted each New Year, exhorting all to be "respectful and upright."[13]

The first courtyard was filled with potted persimmons, oleander, tuberose, and lotus. The rooms on the entrance side were the servants' quarters and the kitchen; to the east were storerooms, and to the west was the family school. To the north, separating this courtyard from the inner one, was the main reception hall, flanked by two studios lined floor to ceiling with bookcases. In one studio was a fine woodblock-printed set of the twenty-four dynastic histories. The rooms were equipped with electric lights, but Chongzhi preferred to use kerosene lamps, though servants had to clean the soot from the glass every day. In the winter, heat was provided by Western-style potbellied stoves. Another concession to Western ways was two large clocks, but neither worked. A Chinese aesthetic dominated the rooms. The main hall was lined with valuable artwork and antiques, glass-framed landscape paintings by Qing masters, calligraphy presented by Zeng Guofan and Li Hongzhang, an inkstone given to Ye Boying by the emperor, and porcelain from the Kangxi and Qianlong eras of the early Qing.

Guests were received in this impressive hall. A servant would announce each guest's arrival by carrying his large red greeting card with both hands above his head and calling out his name and official title. Chongzhi would entertain with tea and conversation or, on major occasions, with banquets and mahjong parties. On one rare occasion, when the provincial governor was guest of honor, courtesans were invited to keep the men company. The family chef was among the best in the city, so Tianjin's elite of businessmen and retired officials were happy to attend. Thus were the personal relationships so essential for success in business confirmed and revitalized.

In the inner courtyard, one entered a more domestic and feminine realm. Instead of ornamental flowers, this courtyard had three utilitarian cisterns: one with drinking water bought and delivered by cart from the water company, one with river water for washing clothes, and one with waste water, which two servants emptied every day. The rear apartments included the bedrooms of Mme. Zhang (Ye Yuanqi's widow and Chongzhi's mother) and the two servants who tended her wardrobe, combed her hair, and accompanied her when she went out. Next to her was the bedroom of Chongzhi's wife (daughter of an official in Shandong) and his eldest son. All these rooms had metal beds and frames for mosquito netting in summer. A sitting room next to Mme. Zhang's bedroom was the social center of the household—the site of many happy family gatherings and of mahjong parties to which the old matriarch invited the wives of the Tianjin elite. Mahjong, which developed from earlier card games only in the late nineteenth century, became a popular form of social gambling in republican-era urban families. An important form of female socializing, the Ye women's mahjong parties provided complementary links to Chong-zhi's business and official connections.

In the third courtyard to the west, a two-story building housed Ye Chongzhi's two concubines, their children, and the children's nannies, and a single-story build-ing on the side sheltered their female servants. The first concubine had been an or-phan in Shandong who was rescued by an official family and later given to Chongzhi. Her eldest son and one daughter lived next to Chongzhi's wife, while her other four sons and two daughters occupied the first floor of the west courtyard with their mother. On the second floor was the second concubine, a former opera actress, with her four sons and two daughters.[14]

Across the alley in front of the compound was a carriage house with a sedan chair for transporting the women, a rickshaw to carry the older boys to school, a cart for provisions, a hooded carriage that Ye Chongzhi rode to work, and three horses. A man of steady and inflexible routine, Chongzhi began each day with a breakfast of two eggs, a deep-fried *youtiao* (a pastry like a straight donut), and a *shaobing* (a sesame-sprinkled wheat cake). He would leave for work promptly at nine o'clock, the main servants standing at the entrance way as he strode through in his long robe, fingers spread to keep the wide stiff sleeves up. At noon, a servant delivered lunch to his office; and Chongzhi would return at five in the evening. On his return, after a quick trip to a latrine reserved for his personal use, he would repair to his mother's sitting room to visit for a while, then to his study to smoke one Three Castle ciga-rette in a long cigarette holder and read the Tianjin and Shanghai papers. He took dinner with his mother, then read history or poetry after the meal. By the time the family had moved to Tianjin, he never slept with his wife, instead rotating between the two concubines and a room of his own on a regular ten-day schedule.[15]

What Chongzhi did at work is less clear, but he held a number of directorships and managerial positions in the industrial empire of Zhou Xuexi. Zhou Xuexi (1866–1947) was the son of Zhou Fu (1837–1921), an Anhui native and protégé of Li Hong-zhang who rose through the Anhui Army to become governor of Shandong and ultimately governor-general in Canton. Xuexi earned the *juren* degree in 1895 and soon entered the entourage of Yuan Shikai as his industrial expert. After impress-ing Yuan by quickly establishing a modern mint that helped alleviate Tianjin's post-Boxer shortage of cash, Zhou was sent to Japan in 1903 for a study trip, and he re-turned committed to the cause of industrial promotion. He organized China's most successful cement company and a coal mining enterprise, financed by a combination of public and private capital. He took the lead in promoting technical schools and industrial expositions to develop the human capital and technical expertise neces-sary for China's industrialization. In the new republic, under Yuan Shikai's presi-dency, he twice served as minister of finance (using the ministry's resources to in-vest in industry), then retired to Tianjin to direct a variety of industrial and banking enterprises.[16]

Zhou Xuexi was the classic bureaucratic capitalist, and the businesses that he organized were typical of Tianjin's modern industrial and financial establishment. In contrast to Shanghai, where most of the modern industrialists rose from merchant or local gentry families, Tianjin's industrialization was largely financed by officials and military officers. Having accumulated substantial fortunes in their official roles (much of this wealth certainly ill-gotten gains), they now invested in profitable industrial ventures. The major burst of industrialization came during and immediately after World War I, when the European powers were preoccupied with war and the diversion of shipping to wartime purposes cut deeply into exports to China. The Chinese cotton textile industry was the biggest benefactor, as the high cost of imports made Chinese factories instantly profitable. Most of Tianjin's major spinning mills were established in this period, and they were followed by flour mills, match factories, refined salt and soda enterprises, and a host of smaller factories and workshops.[17]

At the start of this industrial expansion, Ye Chongzhi made the provident decision to abandon politics for business. As a former protégé of Yuan Shikai and a fellow provincial of Zhou Xuexi, he had instant connections with two of the most important men of the era. Zhou Xuexi was notorious for keeping key managerial positions in the hands of trusted associates, and Ye Chongzhi was certainly counted in that group. In addition, as the Tianjin business community split into an Anhui faction around Zhou and a Henan faction around Yuan Shikai's family (especially after Yuan's death in 1916), Ye Chongzhi had convenient ties to each: he was a native of Anhui who was born and raised in his great-grandfather's home in Henan. Zhou Xuexi's businesses were full of such former officials, and it is said that their entryways were lined with the "tiger-head tablets" that announced the presence of an official.[18]

At one time or another, Ye Chongzhi seems to have held a position in each of Zhou Xuexi's enterprises. In the early republic, he was a manager in the Zhili Provincial Bank, where he sought to control currency issue and maintain confidence in the bank's notes. When the textile industry took off in the wartime period, he managed factories in Tangshan and in Henan, where he dealt with worker unrest at a time of growing labor activism. He served as a director in the Qixin Cement Company, one of north China's most successful enterprises, supplying cement for the expanding railway system and urban modernization. In the 1920s, he worked mostly in the banks that Zhou established to hold funds and arrange financing for his many enterprises. The most important was the National Industrial Bank of China, of which Ye Chongzhi was director.[19]

During the European war and the immediate postwar period, Ye Chongzhi prospered in business. His sons recall his going out to banquets many times each week, socializing with the elite of Tianjin. Cao Kun (1862–1938), who was briefly president of the new republic in the 1920s (chosen by the parliament in a notoriously corrupt election), and his brother, Cao Rui (1866–1924), governor of Zhili, were guests for dinner. Xu Shichang (1855–1939), another president of the republic, was also a friend, the author of Ye Chongzhi's eulogy, and an in-law: Chongzhi's eldest son married his adopted daughter (and niece). But after 1924, Zhou Xuexi's Anhui faction lost out in the clique struggles that plagued both the warlord-dominated governments in Beijing and the Tianjin business world, and Ye Chongzhi's fortunes fell.[20] Zhou made him manager of day-to-day business in his General Office for Industrial Affairs, which he had established to manage his investments, but the office proved powerless against the rival shareholders in the various companies. At the end of Ye Chongzhi's career, the National Industrial Bank provided his main income, but his earnings were sufficiently reduced that his children noticed he was going out less, spending more frugally, and on one occasion, taking out a substantial loan from Zhou Xuexi to arrange a proper celebration of the Mid-Autumn Festival.[21]

The decline of Ye Chongzhi's business ventures was not unique to the family. The wartime industrial boom continued into the early 1920s as the European economies struggled to recover from the Great War. But by 1924, foreign imports into China revived while a liquidity crisis in Europe hurt China's exports. Chinese agriculture failed to keep pace with industrial modernization. Raw-cotton prices rose as supply failed to keep pace with rising demand in the mills, cutting into profits in the textile industry and hampering its ability to compete with imports.[22] The effects of these global economic conditions were exacerbated by political instability and civil war in China. Yuan Shikai's presidency had brought a measure of order to the early years of the republic. But in 1915, Yuan sought to solidify his power by restoring the monarchy and having himself selected emperor of a new dynasty. The attempt failed disastrously when even his own generals abandoned him, and Yuan died a frustrated failure in the following year.[23]

For the next decade, China was wracked by a series of civil wars, large and small, as regional warlords formed shifting alliances in attempts to seize control of the central government. The constant conflict and disruption of trade, which were particularly pronounced in the region around the national capital—the prize that ambitious warlords all sought to occupy—only added to the difficulties of Tianjin's business community.[24] The unruly armies also threatened the lives and property of the city's elite. The Ye family endured a further threat when poor demobilized soldiers from the old Anhui Army, frustrated by the lack of response to their demands for relief, made threats against the property of the Anhui Guildhall. Ye Chongzhi resigned from the guildhall's board of directors, but his home's proximity still left him exposed.[25] As a result, whenever war threatened to engulf the city, the entire Ye family packed up its belongings and headed for the safety of the foreign concessions, leaving a few servants to look after its empty home. Eventually warfare became such a constant threat that the family rented a home in the Japanese Concession.

In peacetime, the house held one hundred empty trunks ready to speed the next evacuation.

In 1923, toward the end of the family's most prosperous years, Ye Chongzhi's mother celebrated her seventieth birthday. The old lady was the ceremonial head of the family. When the children were young, they began their day by offering her their morning greetings. On his return from work, Chongzhi always stopped first to look after her. When she went out to play mahjong at the homes of the wives of Tianjin's business and retired official elite, every departure was greeted by throngs of beggars, for whom she would prepare a handful of copper coins for a servant to distribute. Perhaps overly used to a life of plenty and insufficiently mindful of her poor skills at the mahjong table, she routinely lost money and overspent the monthly allowance that Chongzhi gave her. Then she had to borrow from her servants, pawn some jewelry, or (if she was really desperate) become ill enough to rouse her son to loosen his purse strings. But everyone from children to servants benefited from her generosity, and the afflictions of old age—which included aching legs for which a masseuse was hired—were relieved by a mild opium addiction and much love from the family.

Her seventieth birthday was an elaborate affair, an event that captured much of the flavor of this Tianjin elite family. A two-day opera was staged at the Anhui Guildhall, with top Beijing opera stars brought from the capital for the occasion. Family members, guests, various luminaries, and even family servants presented couplets of calligraphy—the servants' contributions given pride of place in a markedly democratic inversion of the status order. Cao Kun, president of the republic, sent an honorary plaque, but Ye Chongzhi was hurt that his own "sworn brother" relationship to the president was not acknowledged, and he declined to greet the president's envoys at the railway station. He did, however, respectfully bow three times when the plaque was hung in the hall. On the day of the performance, nearly a thousand guests were served food at a hundred tables, and Ye Chongzhi spent thirty thousand dollars on this display of filial devotion.

Mme. Zhang was seated in the balcony with the other women. Her arrival was greeted with great ceremony: outside ten thousand firecrackers exploded, and on the stage, the action stopped for the singing of a special aria. She was escorted by her goddaughter, the wife of one of Yuan Shikai's sons. When prominent guests arrived, they were announced and their cards carried forward held high by a servant. For particularly prominent officials—some of whom arrived in their embroidered Qing official robes—the performance stopped and a welcoming aria was sung, which the honored guest would recognize by a gift to the troupe of perhaps one hundred dollars, the generous sum publicly announced to all by a servant from the stage. Such prominent guests were seated in a special section in front of the stage, to which the family's head servant escorted them. On this occasion, the Chinese agent (comprador) of the Hong Kong & Shanghai Bank, one of the wealthiest businessmen in

Tianjin, approached the VIP section only to be asked by the servant to sit with the regular guests. Some might have regarded this slight as scandalous in the new age of business and modernization, but Ye Chongzhi later praised his majordomo for this action. This comprador, after all, had money but not status—he was neither a former official nor holder of an examination degree. In addition, he made his money working for foreigners.[26]

Such was the world of Ye Chongzhi. Much later, his sons would refer to the family in which they grew up as "feudal." Certainly, Ye Chongzhi—with his three consorts and many servants, his house full of antiques and old books, his preference for oil lamps and horse-pulled buggies over electricity and motor cars—was a man reluctant to part with the old ways. His treatment of the Hongkong & Shanghai Bank's comprador spoke clearly to his adherence to the old status system. But he was also a man of business. His income came from salary and stockholdings in the new world of banking and industry. In a sense, he had a foot in both worlds, and he raised his children for the world to come.

# 8

# Growing Up in Tianjin

Before the twentieth century, Chinese commentators paid little attention to childhood. Confucius's classic capsule autobiography does not start until fifteen, when the great philosopher "set [his] heart on learning," and then proceeds, decade by decade, from ages thirty to seventy.[1] If a traditional biography says anything about a prominent man's boyhood, it usually describes the precocious mastery of such adult skills as reading the classics. A rich tradition of pediatric medicine and scholarly writings on the early education of children evince some attention to the specific biological and intellectual conditions of childhood. An informative genre of paintings shows children at play, but literary sources provide precious little discussion of children acting and growing up *as* children.[2] In the twentieth century, intellectuals and educators began to pay attention to childhood development, and the early years came into much clearer focus as a distinct period of life.[3] For the Ye family, recollections of the men and women who grew up in the early years of the Chinese republic provide an intimate look at this critical period of change for China and the Chinese family.

When Ye Chongzhi moved to Tianjin in the last years of the Qing dynasty, he already had a wife and two concubines. His wife may have borne him one daughter (others say this daughter was the first concubine's child), who died at a very early age—perhaps from overprotective confinement to dark and stuffy rooms. At some point, apparently before the family moved to Tianjin, Chongzhi ceased to share his wife's bed, though his ten-day rotation among the three consorts contained a stay in a bed just outside her room.[4] Chongzhi's two young concubines carried the reproductive responsibilities of the family, and they acquitted themselves well. Indeed, their fecundity was so widely recognized that one of Yuan Shikai's sons, a business associate of Chongzhi, had his only son brought to the Ye family for a ritual rebirth by one of the consorts. The child was brought out from beneath the consort's auspicious red skirt and thereafter counted as Number Eleven of the Ye sons, in hopes that this association might increase the number of sons in the Yuan family. In later years, this boy made ceremonial visits on all the major holidays bearing gifts for his Ye family. The Ye boys usually made themselves scarce when the president's grandson arrived with his clean and neatly coiffed nanny, who was a cut above the rural women who took care of them.[5]

All three of Ye Chongzhi's consorts came from Shandong, where he had served as an official around the turn of the century. His wife, Mme. Cang (pronounced Tsahng), was the eldest daughter of an expectant magistrate. Born in 1873, she was the same age as Chongzhi, and was probably over thirty by the time her short-lived daughter (if the child was indeed hers) was born. Chongzhi's mother brought Miss Liu into the family as a concubine for her son, presumably to provide the heir that his wife had failed to produce. Miss Liu was an orphan, a servant in an official family, where Mme. Zhang apparently spotted her at a social occasion. Liu was quite young at the time, perhaps only fifteen (she was born in 1889), and family lore holds that she hid under the table when Ye Chongzhi (then over thirty) first came to sleep with her.[6] Mme. Cang returned for a time to the family home in Kaifeng, leaving Chongzhi and Miss Liu alone in Shandong for a period of conjugal intimacy that Liu remembered fondly.[7] The second concubine, Miss Chen, was an actress and singer, four years older than Liu. If Miss Liu had been acquired for procreative purposes, Miss Chen was a love match. Ye Chongzhi courted her himself, and her first child, a daughter, was probably born before she was brought home as a concubine.[8]

Miss Liu bore Chongzhi five sons and two daughters. The boys were the eldest, Ye Duren (1908–80); the fourth, Duxin (1912–81); the fifth, Duzhuang (1914–2000); the tenth, Duquan, who died young of scarlet fever (1919?–29?); and the twelfth, Dushen (1924–99). The daughters were the fourth, Dusong (1916?-79?); and fifth, Durou (1921–). The actress Miss Chen also had five sons and two daughters. Her first son, Duzhi (1909?-15) was Number Two. He was bright but sickly, and the family feared that he would share the fate of earlier second sons of the Ye line and die young. A fortuneteller confirmed that a son would die shortly after Duzheng, the seventh son, was born, so to protect Duzhi from his doubly endangered position, he was moved to the more auspicious Number Eight in the birth order. The ruse was ineffective, and he died as a child, though continuing to occupy both the second and eighth positions among Chongzhi's sons. Miss Chen's other sons were the third, Duyi (1912–2005); the sixth, Dulian, who would later change his name to Ye Fang (1914–2005); the seventh, Duzheng (1915–); and the ninth, Ducheng, who would later be known as Fang Shi (1916–). Her daughters were Dushi, the second, whom she brought with her into the family (1907?–29?), and the third, Duya (1910?–79?). (See table 2).

TABLE 2  Children of Ye Chongzhi

| Name | Birth Order | Dates | Mother | Career/Marriage |
|---|---|---|---|---|
| (unknown) | First sister | 1906?–9? | Cang | Died in childhood |
| Dushi | Second sister | 1907?–29? | Chen | Married landlord |
| Duren | One | 1908–80 | Liu | Banker |
| Duzhi | Two/Eight | 1909?–15 | Chen | Died in childhood |
| Duya | Third sister | 1910?–79? | Chen | Married an official's son and heroin addict |
| Duyi | Three | 1912–2005 | Chen | Leader in the Democratic League |
| Duxin | Four | 1912–81 | Liu | Businessman |
| Duzhuang | Five | 1914–2000 | Liu | Agronomist/translator |
| Dulian (Ye Fang) | Six | 1914–2005 | Chen | CCP cadre |
| Duzheng | Seven | 1915– | Chen | Scientist |
| Dusong | Fourth sister | 1916?–79? | Liu | Married a Cornell graduate/businessman |
| Ducheng (Fang Shi) | Nine | 1916– | Chen | CCP journalist |
| Duquan | Ten | 1919?–29? | Liu | Died in childhood |
| Durou | Fifth sister | 1921– | Liu | Teacher, married a translator |
| Dushen (Lizhong) | Twelve | 1924–99 | Liu | Entertainer |

SOURCE: *Ye-shi zupu* [Ye family genealogy] (n.p.: 1944), 7:17, 42–44; Ye Duzhang, 1991 mss, 84–114; interviews with Ye Duzheng, Durou, and Chen Cheng.

The names that Chongzhi chose for his sons represent a veritable catalogue of Confucian virtues. Following the generation character "Du" (earnest) came "-ren" (humane), "-zhi" (wise), "-yi" (righteous), "-xin" (trustworthy), "-zhuang" (respectful), "lian" (honest), "-zheng" (upright), "-cheng" (accomplished), "-quan" (complete), and "-shen" (discreet). The girls' names, of course, were chosen from a different feminine register: "-ya" (refined), "-song" (singing praise), and "-rou" (gentle). These names could hardly have been more conventional coming from an orthodox scholar-official schooled in the classical texts, but in the rapidly changing world of twentieth-century China, they had a somewhat anachronistic flavor. It is thus unsurprising that the two sons whose student radicalism led them into the Communist Party would change their names: the "earnestly honest" Dulian becoming Ye Fang, and the "earnest and accomplished" Ducheng even changing his surname to become Fang Shi. (To avoid too many similar and confusing names, I consistently call these two boys by their adult names.) Mme. Cang jealously (but properly) guarded her status as Chongzhi's official wife—perhaps more so after she ceased to enjoy his sexual attention. She controlled the domestic purse strings: regulating expenses; helping out her own family, which had fallen on hard times; and deciding what gifts the family would give at weddings and festive occasions, yet keeping the two concubines on a tight allowance. In the Tianjin high-society world of women's mahjong parties, only Mme. Cang and Chongzhi's mother went out; the two younger women stayed at home. When the games took place in the Ye home, Miss Liu and Chen shared a place and played for lower stakes, while Mme. Cang played with the big spenders, and usually won. At home, she dined at a separate table with her husband, first son, and mother-in-law, while the concubines ate with their children. Her birthday was celebrated but never those of the concubines. All of these distinctions between wife and concubine were entirely proper in the Confucian order, but especially after the boys started going to school, the discrimination grated on their modern sensibilities.[9] Most galling, from the perspective of the children, they were to address only Mme. Cang as "mother." They called their birth mothers "Second Aunt" and "Third Aunt"—using the term *yi*, which in the precisely distinguished Chinese kinship terminology was normally applied to one's mother's sisters. Thus, the children's own mothers were technically treated as sisters of their father's wife.

Despite her favored status, Mme. Cang was not a happy woman. She had a drink every afternoon, and as time went on, she became something of an alcoholic. She often smoked a water pipe with her liquor. Without children of her own, she took Duren, the eldest son, as her favorite, serving him a special diet at her own table—unequal treatment that earned the resentment of the younger boys. Toward them, she was often surly, and they learned to stay clear of her, especially after she had had a few drinks.

Miss Liu, the senior concubine, was a favorite of Mme. Zhang, Chongzhi's mother and the matriarch of the family. The old lady practiced a Buddhist vegetarianism, and Miss Liu was in charge of the family menu, giving the orders for the day's dishes to the cooks and sometimes overseeing their preparation. She knew well enough, when the old lady seemed tired or weak, to sneak some meat or chicken into the dishes and take responsibility for the transgression. Having grown up as a family servant, she was more adept in the kitchen than the other two consorts, and she got along well with the staff, also insisting that her children treat the servants with respect. With no formal education (she later learned enough characters to write a simple letter), she was more relaxed toward her children's education and probably spoiled them. Miss Chen was stricter. A former actress, she was literate and enjoyed reading romantic novels. While a servant combed her hair in the morning, she instructed her children on the importance of school, and her boys proved disciplined students. Somewhat weak and sickly (probably from tuberculosis), she had a sad elegance that made her Chongzhi's favorite.

As a prosperous family with a large residence, Ye Chongzhi's Tianjin household took in relatives from other branches of the Ye clan. The least attractive of these was Ye Chongshi, another grandson of Ye Boying. Born in 1903, the year his father died, Chongshi was orphaned when his mother passed away three years later, leaving him to Mme. Zhang to raise. The old matriarch spoiled him rotten. Never a good student, he attended a vocational school but seems to have had no real job, living off his inheritance and spending freely on fancy clothes, a diamond ring, a Swiss watch, and the family's first radio. Married at about twenty, he had two sons, who were counted as numbers Thirteen and Fourteen in the family. He abused his wife terribly, beating and cursing her to the distress of the whole compound, and had an affair with one of the wet-nurses—leading to her dismissal and that of the maid who stood watch during the trysts of the miscreant pair. In 1930, Chongshi died an appropriately miserable death, driven crazy in his last years by venereal disease he had contracted in the brothels of Tianjin. During his time with the family, he provided a vivid negative example for the young boys contemplating their own futures.[10]

Another relative was Yao Niu, whose mother (a cousin of Ye Chongzhi) had grown up in the same household with grandmother Zhang. When her father died, Yao Niu was brought into the family and slept in the room next to Mme. Zhang. Her brother, Yao Zengyi, was a frequent guest at the Ye household and became the best friend of the third son, Duyi, and later the husband of Durou.

By the 1920s, the Ye home on Third Street was full of children—sixteen in all at its peak. Their births were so closely concentrated that when the last of Chongzhi's children was born in 1924, his eldest brother was only sixteen. The children were addressed by their birth order within each gender, the adults calling the girls "Second Miss" (Er xiaojie), "Third Miss" (San xiaojie), and so on and their siblings calling them "Second Sister" or "Third Sister." The boys had similar forms of address. For example, Ye Duyi (Number Three) was called "Third Master" (Sanye) by the servants, "Third Brother" (Sange) by his siblings, and "Third Pup" (Sangou) by his elders in the family.

The most important person in the children's early lives was their wet-nurse. Neither mother nursed her own children, which is one reason the two concubines were so frequently pregnant. Breastfeeding tends to delay the resumption of ovulation, so women who nurse their own children usually have births that are spaced at least two or three years apart. The Chinese elite commonly employed wet-nurses for their newborns, and this practice, together with the polygamy that came with concubines and the ability of wealthy families to support more children, tended to make elite families unusually large.[11] In Tianjin, the hiring of wet-nurses was institutionalized, and the Ye engaged theirs through an agency. The women were usually from the surrounding countryside and were ready to nurse, which meant that they had just borne children of their own who had died, been weaned early, or been given to someone else to nurse. Such employment offered a secure livelihood to poor peasant women, but at considerable cost to their own families. One wet-nurse "signed" a contract for three years' employment with her thumbprint, only to have her husband appear the next day to beg for her return. She was not released (whether she wished to leave is unknown) until her husband reappeared three years later to take her back.[12]

These wet-nurses were the newborns' closest companions. They were mother figures, and the young ones often called them "mother." In addition to nursing the children, they bathed them (infrequently), fed them rice or wheat gruel as they grew older, toilet trained them, and took them to the nearby Li Hongzhang shrine to play. At night, the nannies slept with the children. One of the boys recalls that his wet-nurse always slept naked, following a rural habit in which nightgowns were unknown. Naturally he followed her practice, and grew accustomed to sleeping comfortably naked next to her large, warm, dark-skinned body. After he was weaned, he continued to resist pajamas, and when his mother insisted that he wear them, he would put them on for bed but secretly remove them once he was under the covers. When his mother discovered this deception, he endured many spankings before he finally changed his childhood habits.[13]

The children might not be fully weaned until they were five years old and ready to start school. The process could be quite sudden and formal. One boy remembers being called into his grandmother's room just before his fifth birthday. There was his wet-nurse, her large dark nipples exposed, together with his grandmother and mother. His mother told him, "Your 'mother's' nipples have gone bad. You can't nurse any more." He was encouraged to try them and got only the acrid taste of ink mixed with a bitter herbal medicine with which they had been smeared. That was the last time he nursed.[14]

After the children were weaned, either their wet-nurse would be replaced by another maid, or she would stay on as a nanny to look after her young ward's needs. These servants would wash clothes and also help make them. Even the youngsters' cloth shoes were made at home. Only their silk caps with a red button on top were bought at a haberdashery.

The children's principal contact with their own mothers was at dinnertime. As babies, they were fed on their beds by the wet-nurse, but after they were old enough to sit at a table, they ate with their mothers and siblings. The eldest son (later joined by the third and fourth) was always special: he ate with Chongzhi's wife and mother at their small table and received a special diet, supposedly because he was sickly. He ate delicacies denied the others: eggs, chicken broth, and such special Western imports as Carnation milk, American sugar, and cod-liver oil from Norway. His favored treatment was much resented (and well remembered) by the younger boys.

The children and their mothers ate at a separate large table (or when the family reached its maximum size, at several tables) in the eastern rooms near the kitchen, or outside in the courtyard in summer. The fare was simple, mostly rice, vegetables, and half a preserved egg for each child. Except for banquets or special celebrations, meals were not an occasion for extravagance. Although the family had lived in north China for several generations, it continued the southern China diet of rice, no doubt following the custom of Chongzhi's mother, who came from Tongcheng County in

Anhui. Only Chongzhi's wife ate the steamed wheat buns favored by northerners. Even the concubines, despite their northern origins, adopted the southern preference for rice.[15]

Ye Chongzhi was a typically distant patriarch. During the most prosperous period of his business career, he often ate out, and later, when he commonly dined at home, his mother and wife, not the children (except his eldest son), shared his table. After dinner, he would inquire about the boys' lessons, and sometimes ask one to massage his back as he sat reading classical essays from his library. On rare occasions, he would take some of the boys to see a movie, a novel form of urban entertainment (almost always a Hollywood film) that he came to enjoy.[16]

Some of the clearest memories of childhood surround special annual rituals. The New Year was the most important holiday. To begin the preparations, the family dined on a special stew, prepared from an old Anhui recipe. Then everyone gathered to hang large portraits of illustrious ancestors in the front hall. These portraits featured officials in formal robes, with emblems and buttons on their hats indicating their rank in the imperial hierarchy. As the children grew older, they learned to recognize the distinctions and pay special attention to the most important, especially Ye Boying. After making offerings to the spirits of each ancestor, first the men and boys, in order of age, and then the women bowed three times to each picture. This ritual was repeated by all the family on New Year's day and again when the portrait scrolls were stored away in the middle of the first month. In between, one son was sent each day to represent the family in performing this ritual. This ceremonial acknowledgment of the family's august ancestry was the serious part of the New Year celebrations. The rest of the time was given over to family feasts and visits to friends and relatives. On New Year's eve fireworks and firecrackers were set off at the main gate; then the boys joined their father for a card game, one of the rare occasions on which he would play with them. He served as banker for modest stakes and always managed to lose everything, then left the boys to play on their own.[17] At the end of the evening, a servant went around to each room to collect a small sum of "selling sickness money" from each person and then threw these coins out the front gate, which was then locked until the dawn of the new year. Whoever picked up the scattered money would get the illness destined for the family.[18]

Other happy family occasions were associated with special seasonal foods. In the summer, when walnuts were harvested, the family would gather in grandmother Zhang's room to shell and eat walnuts. In the fall, everyone would congregate in the same place for a few special meals of fresh crab, prepared by Miss Liu. But the watermelons of summer provided the happiest treat. Every evening from mid-July to mid-August, during the thirty hottest days of summer in the Chinese calendar, Miss Liu would cut up three or four watermelons for the children to eat their fill. The crowd of boys grabbed the slices so eagerly that she had to warn them to watch their fingers around the knife, while the girls ate more sedately in a separate room.[19]

When the children were very young, before they started in the family school, they began each day with a visit to their grandmother Zhang, then to Chongzhi's wife, and then to their biological mothers to bid them good morning. Escorted by their nannies, the boys would bow politely and accept a few coins from the matriarch (and a few more from their mother), with which they could buy snacks during the day. After this morning ritual, they had plenty of time to play. They had precious few toys: only wooden swords and masks at New Year, for as long as they lasted. Perhaps appropriately for an era of unbroken civil war, the most common game for the boys (and some of the girls) was playing soldier. They would march about in military drills or hide in ambush behind the furniture of the living room or in the courtyards and play there during the day.[20] In the summer, the children kept crickets in small wicker cages, considering them treasured pets. When the boys were teenagers, the family obtained a Ping-Pong table, which was set up in a front room, near the servants' quarters.

The servants' quarters were an area where the children often gathered to listen to stories, which might be heroic tales of storytellers or even bits of Ye family history from the older servants. The younger staff might throw in bawdy tales and sexual jokes. As the boys grew older, these interactions with the male servants complemented their earlier close relations with wet-nurses and nannies. When they went to bathe in the public bathhouse, it was the male servants who took them. Living in a large household full of servants brought the children in close personal contact with members of the lower classes—something that would not occur in a middle-class nuclear family. The influence of these servants was not necessarily progressive. Indeed, the greatest wish of the senior servants was to have the boys' father return to official life. They remained attached to the old status system in which serving a businessman was less prestigious than working in an official household. But in their interactions with these servants, the children acquired a sense of the poorer classes' very different lives. From their stories, they learned that people of little formal education could be wise in the ways of the world. And on the rare occasions when they went out with these servants—as when the fifth son, Duzhuang, visited the home of his wet-nurse in a rural migrants' shantytown on the edge of Tianjin—they experienced the poverty-stricken world from which their closest adult companions came.[21]


As each boy reached the age of five, his daily routine changed abruptly. Escorted by his father, the young lad began his first day at the family school. There the new student bowed three times to the tablet of Confucius and then to the teacher, the holder of the *gongsheng* degree in the imperial examination system who had once taught at the Lotus Pond Academy in Baoding, which Ye Chongzhi had attended years earlier. Once the boys were thus formally "enrolled," they began each day at school, reciting their lessons from shortly after dawn until they broke for breakfast. Breakfast was purchased for them (with their spending money) by a servant boy attached to the school, who went out to the neighborhood food stalls. After breakfast, lessons resumed until a longer lunch break and then continued in the afternoon until about four o'clock—though the school had no clock, and the schedule was entirely regulated by rough reckoning from the sun.

The students started out by tracing characters with a brush and then progressed to memorizing simple sentences and spending long hours of calligraphy practice. They began with simple textbooks published in Shanghai in the early 1910s (already dated by the time most of these Ye boys used them), then moved on to the Four Books and other classical texts. Because the boys were of different ages and learned at different rates, instruction was individualized, but their education basically consisted of rote memorization. Those who failed to recite a text correctly could expect to have their hands slapped, though the brothers would help each other by leaving their books open to the proper page so that the reciting student could peek if necessary, a simple ruse that the nearsighted teacher rarely detected. Proper handling of a brush was important, and the boys grew to recognize the fine quality of the old teacher's calligraphy. Their father praised it and asked the old man to write the calligraphy that graced the entrance to the compound and the couplets that hung around the courtyard each New Year. When the fifth son, Duzhuang, was ten years old, his calligraphy was good enough that he was asked to write these characters— an honor of which the young boy was justly proud.

The teacher's classical learning was sound, and in time Chongzhi's sons came to appreciate his knowledge of China's ancient texts and the virtues of the Confucian learning they contained. Late in his life, Duzhuang hung a pair of scrolls in his living room with a couplet written by his teacher: "Only when you come to apply your knowledge do you regret learning so little. Only when you have experienced things can you recognize their difficulty." As the boys' Chinese improved, they were given essay topics from the classics. Although sometimes these assignments included passages or allusions that utterly baffled them, in the end, the old teacher imparted to the young men a deep commitment to Confucian values of righteousness, humanity, scholarship, and sacrifice. He also lectured on the great statesmen of the late Qing, reminding the boys of their distinguished ancestry and the high expectations the family had for them. Duzhuang kept a simple couplet on his desk as a daily reminder: "Unless you endure the greatest of hardships, you cannot become a man above others."[22]

By the mid-1920s, the old teacher was afflicted by a worsening opium addiction. His young charges noticed him coughing, his nose running, and his body starting to shake as he waited in the morning for their father to leave. Then he would rush to the servants' room in the front, where a boy would prepare his opium. This hit would keep him until the afternoon, when he needed another one just before their father returned. Chongzhi was not fooled by this effort: he knew of the old man's addiction. But by confining his smoking to the hours when the master of the house was away, the teacher made it easier for his employer to look the other way. The old man was assisted by his son, whose learning was sufficient only to help the younger boys with character recognition. But the son came to resent the large portion of their rather generous forty dollar per month salary that went to serve his father's addiction and often took out his anger in harsh physical punishment of the boys, once sitting on the rebellious ninth son's back and forcing his face to the ground when he resisted bowing to Confucius's tablet in punishment for failing a recitation exercise.

In addition to his opium addiction, the old teacher had distinctly unmodern personal habits. He was extremely nearsighted but refused to wear glasses, holding a book right up to his nose to read. He never bathed, merely wiping summer sweat and dirt from his body with a towel, and smelled terrible. He constantly spit on the ground—or against the bedroom wall when lying in bed. As he entered his final illness, the family's Japanese doctor came to treat him and left his room holding his nose and saying, "This man is not fit to be a teacher, not fit to be a teacher!" Despite his classical learning, the old man certainly did not meet modern Japanese hygienic standards for a proper schoolteacher.[23]

In the late 1920s, the teacher died, having been moved to the carriage house for his final days so that the main house would not be contaminated by an inauspicious death. His son was let go at the same time. By then, most of the boys had already started middle school outside, but the younger ones were still taught at home by a new teacher, whom they called Bad-Breath Yuan. Yuan had been a petty official in Beijing, but after the capital was moved to Nanjing in 1927—and Beijing ("Northern Capital") became Beiping ("Northern Peace")—he was left without a job. With a large family to support in Beiping, he readily accepted employment in the Ye household.

Under Bad-Breath Yuan, one of the girls attended the family school for the first time. The older daughters had learned only a few basic characters, sewing, and embroidery from Mrs. Jin, the widow of a petty official. Although many voices had been advocating women's education since late Qing times, and a small suffragette movement was active in the early republic, Ye Chongzhi did not believe in educating his daughters. His conservatism in this matter was pronounced and stood in marked contrast to the calls for women's education seen earlier in the Ye family genealogy. Only in the mid-1920s, as appeals for women's rights became more insistent, did he allow his youngest daughter to attend school—first at a neighborhood primary school and later, when the winter chill in the unheated classrooms left her feet so cold she could barely walk, at the family school with her brothers.[24]

Bad-Breath Yuan represented a fresh change from the old scholar who had preceded him. Unlike the old teacher, he read newspapers and showed an interest in current affairs. His classical learning could not match that of his predecessor, but he was able to write and assign essays on such current topics as Sun Yat-sen's Three Principles of the People (nationalism, people's rights, and people's livelihood), which formed the governing ideology of the Nationalist Party and the new national government. In this respect, he represented a curricular adjustment, even in this Ye family school, to the national agenda of the day. But Ye Chongzhi's most important concession to the educational requirements of the modern era had begun well before the hiring of Bad-Breath Yuan. Every day, after the old teacher finished drilling the boys on their classical texts, they moved to another classroom on the east side of the courtyard and turned their attention away from the old exam curriculum to study English and mathematics in preparation for careers in business or one of the modern professions. When one boy confessed his love of Chinese and his hope to become the secretary of a prominent official, or perhaps to enter a military academy (he admired the fancy dress uniforms favored by republican-era warlords), his father was not pleased. An official or military career was too dangerous. He saw his sons' future in science and engineering. When Duyi, the talented third son, graduated from high school with honors in science, Chongzhi boasted that his son would become a scientist working in a laboratory, like those featured in popular Hollywood films.

To prepare the boys for the high school and college education necessary to undertake such a career, a special teacher was hired from the outside, arriving each afternoon at four. For the last few hours of the school day, the lessons were in arithmetic, algebra, geometry, and English. The teacher was recruited from a local primary school and was a graduate of Nankai Middle School, the most prestigious middle school in north China. Later Chongzhi also paid for special tutoring by a moonlighting Nankai teacher who came for a half day on Saturday and Sunday, a step that helped most of the boys pass the Nankai entrance exams.

These teachers were clearly a new breed. The Nankai graduate came every afternoon by trolley. He wore thick glasses, smoked cigarettes, and dressed in the long gray gowns and short jacket favored by students of that era. He was a great soccer fan and had been a defensive back on Nankai's soccer team. Physical education was an important part of the Nankai educational experience, reflecting the twentieth-century nationalist dedication to strengthening the body in addition to cultivating the mind. Under this teacher's influence, the Ping-Pong table was added to the room off the servants' quarters. Sports, English, and mathematics made a natural combination in republican education, the practical ingredients in the training of modern citizens.[25]


Perhaps the most important contribution of the teachers from Nankai and even Bad-Breath Yuan was the tenuous link they established with the outside world. Most of the family lived in remarkable isolation from the world beyond the compound's front gate. Ye Chongzhi (and, to a lesser extent, his wife and mother) were notable exceptions. Chongzhi circulated among the business and banking elite of Tianjin, which included many former officials, warlords, and members of their families. His wife and mother played mahjong with the women of these families, which strengthened ties and created another channel of communication to this group.

Social ties to the Tianjin elite were further cemented by marriages arranged for the older boys. The eldest son was engaged to the adopted daughter (a niece) of former president Xu Shichang. The third son was engaged to the daughter of a Bank of China manager (and niece of a finance minister). The marriage of the fourth was arranged with the daughter of an official family (her grandfather had been a governor) that also had marriage ties to the family of Yuan Shikai, the first president of the republic. Ye Duzhuang, the fifth son, was the last to have a marriage arranged by his father, which was to a granddaughter of Zhang Xiluan (1843–1922), a former governor-general of Northeast China (Manchuria) then living in luxurious retirement in the Tianjin concessions. In the late 1920s, Chongzhi considered a match for his sixth son, but this time, instead of seeking an alliance with official families in Tianjin, he contemplated a union with the daughter of the Shanghai capitalist Liu Hongsheng (1888–1956). But Chongzhi was not quite ready for the new ways of Shanghai. The Liu family sent a studio photograph of the daughter leaning casually against the back of a chair with one foot on the seat. That pose was too modern for Ye Chongzhi, and he canceled the arrangements forthwith. The three eldest surviving sisters were also betrothed to descendants of official families, though each of these families was clearly on the decline. In arranging his daughters' marriages, Ye Chongzhi paid more attention to his in-laws' pedigrees than to the character and accomplishments of his future sons-in-law, and none of these marriages was particularly happy.

Such marriage arrangements created important social connections for the older generation but few new contacts for the children. On one occasion, when warlord fighting forced the family to flee to the safety of the foreign concessions, the former governor-general Zhang Xiluan offered his mansion as a refuge. But the fifth son was not allowed to go: it would create too much talk were he (though only a boy of twelve) to stay even a few days with his fiancée's relatives. Marital matters were so exclusively a concern of adults that these relationships limited, rather than enhanced, the social world of the children.

The youngsters had remarkably few occasions to escape the confines of the family compound. Though two other families lived on their lane, the children hardly ever played together. When very young, the boys were sometimes taken to the Li Hongzhang shrine to play, and the male servants took them to a neighborhood bathhouse for infrequent baths—rare enough in winter that the boys remember black feet that stuck to their socks. On the afternoon break from their lessons, they went down the lane to a small shop to buy snacks, but rarely did they go any far-ther. The boys enjoyed occasional trips to the movies with their father, and once or twice a year, Ye Chongzhi took the entire family to a Shandong restaurant for a big meal out. With two buggies and several hired rickshaws, the group made quite a procession. But even here, the family went by itself and as a unit, and even this cus-tom was abandoned when the household finances became more straitened in the late 1920s.

The confinement of the girls was especially strict. They were even barred from the servants' quarters and the kitchen.[26] Dusong, the fourth sister, was the favorite of Chongzhi's wife, and Mme. Cang once took her out shopping. Somewhere on this expedition, a young man took an interest in the young lady, found out who she was, and wrote to request an introduction. Chongzhi was outraged! This sort of spontaneous romantic attraction between young people—such insulting interest in his daughter from a complete stranger—was highly improper. He forbade his wife to take the girls shopping again or to allow them to be seen in public.[27]

Ye Chongzhi lived in a world that in many respects was passing him by. By re-stricting his children to the family compound, he was protecting them from that new world; but total insulation from the tides of change was impossible, nor did he reject all innovation. He sought to update his children's education, and he al-lowed the introduction of some modern medical practices. Although the boys' old teacher prescribed Chinese herbal remedies for minor complications (and the old lady and Miss Liu smoked opium when they were uncomfortable), the sickly eld-est son was given Carnation milk and cod-liver oil. For more serious illnesses, the best Western-trained doctors, often Japanese (like the one who treated the teacher), were called. A Chinese graduate of Edinburgh University treated the eldest son's tuberculosis.

New material things inevitably found their way into the home. The toilette of the ladies combined Chinese face powder and rouge with French sandalwood soap and Ponds Face Cream. Miss Liu did her hair in a modern figure-eight bun instead of the traditional tight coil. Several technologies reflected the transitional charac-ter of this age, but also the fact that Ye Chongzhi was a little behind the times. The house was lit with kerosene lamps (an innovation much promoted by Standard Oil); the electric lights installed in the compound and increasingly common in homes of the wealthy were rarely used. Chongzhi traveled by horse-drawn buggy while many of his peers had cars, and the rickshaw that carried the boys to school was a classic new-yet-old technology of the day—an innovation made possible by paved streets and pneumatic tires but relying on plentiful cheap human labor power. The house had no telephone, but one servant's duties included going out to use a pub-lic phone.[28] Chongzhi did spend eight hundred dollars to buy a large RCA radio, which picked up music and popular entertainment from Tianjin's several new radio stations, though only through heavy static. The radio sat in grandmother Zhang's room until she had it removed as an annoyance.[29]

Slowest to penetrate this world were the new cultural influences of the age. The 1910s and 1920s were one of the liveliest eras in the history of Chinese culture, though this vitality was born of intense disillusionment with China's predicament. The high hopes for China's revival that had greeted the new Republic of China quickly dissipated in the ensuing years. Yuan Shikai, an effective reformer under the Qing, became an autocratic dictator as president of the republic. When his supporters lost the election for China's first parliament, he arranged the assassination of the opposition leader, banned the opposition party, then disbanded parliament altogether. Finally he decided to make himself emperor, but even his own army turned against him. Following Yuan's death in 1916, the disarray in China's central government intensified with a brief attempted restoration of the Qing emperor and then a succession of warlord governments that made national politics look like a game of musical chairs with guns.

The weak and ineffective governments that followed the 1911 Revolution proved even less capable than the Qing in defending China's national sovereignty. First the former Qing empire began to crumble along its frontiers as Tibet and Mongolia declared independence, with the encouragement and support of Britain and Russia, respectively. When World War I preoccupied the European powers, Japan moved aggressively to claim a role as East Asia's preeminent imperial power. It seized the German position in Shandong, then forced Yuan Shikai to accept the humiliating Twenty-One Demands giving Japan special economic rights in Shandong, Manchuria, and on the southeast coast opposite its colony in Taiwan, along with partial control of a major coal and iron complex in the Yangzi valley. Both domestically and internationally, China seemed on an inexorable trajectory of decline.

Chinese intellectuals responded to this crisis with increasingly trenchant critiques of China's cultural heritage. The social Darwinist logic of the day taught that only the fittest nations would survive, and China was looking markedly unfit. The political institutions of the new republic had proved utterly ineffective in reviving China's fortunes. The time had come to search deeper for the roots of failure. If changing China's political institutions from monarchial rule to republican governance was inadequate, then perhaps the hierarchical principles of Confucian culture and society had to be replaced as well. The advocates of republican revolution had argued that giving political rights to the people would mobilize their energies to improve governance and strengthen the nation. Now that argument was extended to promote a New Culture movement to rouse and empower youth, women, and common people to transform the very fabric of Chinese culture and society.

The flashpoint that energized and lent its name to this movement was the May Fourth incident of 1919. On that day, three thousand students assembled in Beijing's Tiananmen Square to protest the provision of the Versailles Peace Treaty that awarded Germany's colonial possessions in Shandong province to Japan, rather than returning them to China. Two years earlier, China had joined the Allied cause with the explicit purpose of gaining a seat at this peace conference and recovering its sovereign rights in Shandong. Tens of thousands of Chinese laborers were sent to Europe to serve the Allied cause in factories and on docks, replacing the young Europeans sent to the front in the Great War. But Britain, France, and Italy secretly agreed to support Japan's position in Shandong. Even more galling to the students, their own warlord government, in return for Japanese loans to fund their armies, acquiesced to the Japanese claim. China's hopes for the recovery of lost territory—encouraged by Woodrow Wilson's lofty ideals of national self-determination—were dashed by the realities of warlord self-interest and Great Power politics. The student demonstrations and strikes drew support from merchant, worker, and professional organizations across the country. In China's first truly national movement of mass urban protest, the government was forced to back down. It refused to sign the Versailles Treaty and dismissed the ministers responsible for signing away China's rights to Shandong.[30]

The May Fourth incident had repercussions well beyond the issue of Shandong and the Versailles Treaty. The students and their intellectual supporters recognized that if China was to avoid future victimization by the Great Powers, it would have to arouse its population for thoroughgoing and even revolutionary change. The hundreds of journals and magazines spawned by the movement offered myriad proposals for reform. Language reform was one of the most popular causes, and perhaps the most successful. Out of the May Fourth era came a new vernacular language, a written language much closer to spoken Chinese than the obscure and difficult classical Chinese. By 1922, the vernacular was mandated for school textbooks, making the written word far more accessible to ordinary Chinese and encouraging mass education of the citizens of the republic. The new journals were filled with translations of Western works, and articles contrasted the Western ideals of individualism, democracy, and the emancipation of women to the Confucian "three bonds" that subordinated subject to ruler, son to father, and wife to husband. "Mr. Science" and "Mr. Democracy" were the heroes of one famous article, and Western notions of scientific progress were contrasted to China's idealization of its ancient classical verities.

One of the most enduring cultural images of the day was Nora of Ibsen's play *A Doll's House*. An entire issue of *New Youth*, the most influential journal of the day, was devoted to Ibsen; and Nora's dramatic walking out on an unfulfilling marriage became a powerful symbol for young women seeking more control over their destinies. China's practice of arranged marriage was a particularly common target for attack, for it seemed to violate all notions of young people taking responsibility for their lives, controlling their fates, and acting as mature individuals in a modern society. Love marriages—and even some radical experimentation in "free love"— became popular, and a few daring radicals wrote openly about sexual matters in books and articles whose scientific parlance masked their erotic appeal.[31]

The iconoclasm of the age was largely confined to college campuses, high schools, and a cosmopolitan sector of the urban classes. But the newspapers and journals of the day were broadly affected by a new spirit of criticism directed at Chinese customs and culture, which were increasingly seen as products of the "old society" or even "feudalism." How was this new critical spirit to be translated into political action? One force that reemerged on the political scene was Sun Yat-sen's reorganized Nationalist Party, or Guomindang (Kuomintang in an older spelling, or KMT). Sun Yat-sen had been advocating and organizing national revolution since the late nineteenth century, and if nothing else, his persistence and dedication were beyond question. Out of power since he had ceded the presidency to Yuan Shikai in 1912, he had been driven into exile a year later and been seeking allies for a political comeback ever since. Sun greeted the May Fourth demonstrations with enthusiasm, and by the early 1920s, he was back at his Canton base, maneuvering for political advantage among local warlords and seeking to capitalize on the new nationalist sentiments of China's youth.

In 1922–23, Sun was presented with a fresh opportunity when representatives of the newly established Soviet Union came to visit. The Russian Revolution of 1917 had aroused considerable interest among some Chinese intellectuals, to whom it seemed a dramatic throwing off of imperial rule and resistance to foreign intervention. When the Soviet Union renounced czarist Russia's claims on China under the unequal treaties, Chinese nationalists were impressed. Here was a revolutionary model of anti-imperialist foreign policy that stood in dramatic contrast to the sordid deals of the Great Powers at Versailles. The Soviet emissaries assured Sun Yat-sen that they were not interested in promoting communist revolution (which Sun opposed as encouraging class warfare instead of national unity). Instead they wanted to support his national revolutionary movement in order to weaken the imperialist powers then encircling the Soviet Union and to secure a friendly ally on their southern border.[32]

While the Soviets were negotiating with Sun, they were also seeking to establish a Communist Party in China. In the summer of 1921, the small groups of intellectuals inspired by the Russian Revolution to study Marxism came together and, with careful Soviet prodding and advice, formed the Chinese Communist Party (CCP). Marxism-Leninism combined "scientific socialism" with a systematic critique of imperialism as the "highest stage of capitalism." The failures of the Chinese republic could be explained from the weakness of "bourgeois democracy" and the residual influence of China's "feudal" past. A Communist Party could organize young activists into a revolutionary vanguard, leading workers and peasants in a broad revolutionary movement to throw off the yoke of foreign imperialism and feudal warlordism.[33]

When the Russians and Sun Yat-sen sealed their agreement to cooperate two years later, members of the CCP were instructed to join Sun Yat-sen's Nationalist Party. The United Front coalition of the two parties proved beneficial to both. The Communists gained experience in practical politics in Sun's Canton base, and the Nationalists gained dedicated revolutionaries committed to organizing workers and peasants for national revolution against imperialists and warlords. More importantly, the Nationalists received critical support from the Soviet Union to fund, arm, and train their own party army in Canton.[34]

While Sun Yat-sen was alive, the United Front worked reasonably well. But after Sun died suddenly of liver cancer in March 1925, the strains in the alliance began to show. A series of dramatic strikes and demonstrations in the summer of 1925 revealed the considerable influence of the CCP among workers and students in many Chinese cities. Conservatives in the Nationalist Party were alarmed. At the same time, the commander of the Nationalist military forces, Chiang Kai-shek (Jiang Jieshi in the new spelling), grew increasingly resentful of the Soviet advisors to the revolutionary alliance. In 1926, Chiang Kai-shek launched the Northern Expedition in which the revolutionary forces moved on three broad fronts from its southern base toward the Yangzi valley. By early 1927, the central China city of Wuhan was already in revolutionary hands, and Chiang's army was sweeping toward Shanghai.

Then the alliance fell apart. Chiang's forces and his allies in the Shanghai "Green Gang" underworld fell on the Communist-organized workers who had seized control of Shanghai and slaughtered them. In a broad movement to "cleanse" the Nationalist Party, Communists and their leftist sympathizers were arrested, executed, or driven into hiding in city after city across China. By the end of the year, the Chinese Communist Party had lost 90 percent of its members to death, arrest, defection, or withdrawal. Most of those who survived headed for the safety of the hills and the hinterland, where Mao Zedong and other survivors of the purge began the long process of reviving the party as a rural, peasant-based revolutionary and military force. Chiang Kai-shek, meanwhile, consolidated his control of the Nationalist Party and established a new national government in Nanjing. In 1928, he continued the Northern Expedition through a series of strategic alliances with friendly warlords until the warlord government in Beijing fell and the entire country was, at least nominally, unified under the Nationalist banner.[35]

All of this drama barely touched the Ye family. In 1919, when Tianjin students demonstrated in sympathy with their May Fourth comrades in Beijing, they marched on the governor's office, which was right next to the family compound.

The young boys went outside to look and could hear the shouted slogans, but they soon returned to their lessons in classical Chinese.[36] Nine years later, the Northern Expedition caused a somewhat greater stir. As the Nationalist armies approached, Chongzhi alarmed his consorts with rumors that the revolutionary forces were threatening to carry out a radical program of "common property and common wives." This classic anti-Communist propaganda led the family to take refuge once again in the foreign concessions. The older boys, however, were already enrolled at Nankai Middle School, and the Nankai Boy Scouts (which all male students had to join) marched in uniform to a mass meeting to welcome the Northern Expedition. The event was the first mass meeting they ever attended, and as they marched, they shouted the popular slogans of the day: "Down with the Great Powers! Eliminate the warlords!" The meeting stage was filled with men in uniform, one of whom (wearing fashionable dark glasses) gave a long but unamplified speech, which was inaudible to most of the crowd.

At Nankai Middle School, the boys began to experience the social and political currents that were sweeping through China at this time, but only in small doses. They were only day students, who missed the after-school sports and drama that were important parts of the Nankai experience. Though their history and science classes introduced new ideas, the impact on their lives was still small.

The girls were even more isolated. Until the youngest sister, Durou, was allowed to attend primary school in the late 1920s, they were offered no formal education and scarcely allowed out of the house. The two eldest daughters even had their feet bound for a time, though not so tightly as to hamper mobility. This practice had been under attack by progressive Chinese since the late nineteenth century and had stopped in most cities by the early republic. The girls wore their hair in an old-fashioned braid until the fourth daughter, in a dramatic act of independence, took a pair of scissors and cut her hair in the short bob then popular among school-girls. And, of course, Chongzhi insisted on arranging marriages for his daughters to "proper" official families. One of the most important themes of May Fourth era writings was the liberation of women from the bonds of patriarchy, and Ye Chongzhi was clearly out of step with progressive thinking in his treatment of his daughters.

The family's comfortable isolation from the outside world soon changed. A series of cruel shocks struck the Ye household and transformed the young folks' world. First came the death of Uncle Chongshi, the syphilitic playboy whose passing was little mourned. Then came the death of two children. Dushi, the eldest surviving sister, was struck with a sudden paralyzing illness while visiting Tianjin. Despite receiving the best medical attention, she died in her natal home—no doubt a happier place than the home she had shared with her abusive husband, but an inauspicious omen according to Chinese customary beliefs. Next the bright and promising tenth son died of scarlet fever, which brought a Japanese disinfecting team to spray his room. The loss of two children so suddenly, the first to die since the second son had passed away years earlier, was a blow to the family, but far less than what was to follow. One morning in the summer of 1930, Ye Chongzhi left for work as usual promptly at nine. But he felt poorly and stopped at the family doctor on the way. The doctor prescribed some medicine and sent him home. As a banker, he was likely working under some stress because the value of China's silver-based dollar was falling rapidly in 1930 as the depression brought a collapse of the world silver market.[37] On the way home, the horse bolted in a narrow alley, and the elderly driver, himself recovering from a stroke, was unable to control the animal before the buggy struck and injured a rickshaw coolie. A policeman brought the horse and buggy under control and, recognizing Chongzhi, sent the shaken banker home in a rickshaw. He slumped in a chair in the family room as his mother asked what brought him home so early. He said he was feeling ill, mumbled something about the old driver being a worthless fellow, and died—apparently of a heart attack.

His mother was beside herself. The doctor was called immediately, but it was too late. She summoned a medium to bring her son back from the dead but without effect. Finally she broke down and berated him for dying and leaving her alone. She refused to leave the room, right next to her own, in which he had died, and barely a month later, she followed him to the grave, her will to live exhausted by his passing.

Ye Chongzhi's funeral was suitably elaborate, and the coffin was so well made that his body in its Qing robes was still intact fifty years later when the grave site outside Beijing was disturbed by new construction. The coffin lay in the front courtyard for three weeks as guests came to offer their respects with funerary couplets of calligraphy and floral wreaths. A band of Chinese musicians welcomed guests at the gate, and Buddhist monks and Daoist priests performed their rituals in the courtyard. The funeral procession was more modern than Chongzhi's life had been—with a Western band and two white horses pulling the hearse with the coffin, the boys following in hemp robes. After a banquet for guests at the large Guangdong Guildhall, the coffin was taken to Beiping for burial.[38]

Just a year and a half after Chongzhi's death, his most beloved concubine, Miss Chen, died. The mother of five fine students destined for distinguished careers, she had just one request in her final days. She asked Chongzhi's widow to bury her in the red headdress and gown of a properly married bride. She wished in death to enjoy the status of wife and mother that had been denied her throughout her life. This once, her wish was granted. After a simple funeral, she was buried next to Chongzhi.[39]

In a few short years, the family lost the key people and the vital force that had held it together. Duren, the eldest son at age twenty-two, inherited his father's position and soon followed his career in banking and business. As the most conservative of the sons, he was best suited to head the family, but his privileged childhood as the favorite of Chongzhi's wife made him unpopular with his younger brothers. He never commanded the unquestioned authority that his father had enjoyed.

The death of the family matriarch, Mme. Zhang, left another void. If Chongzhi was the authority figure to whom all were subordinated, she was the emotional heart of the family. Her room was the site of family gatherings. She was the senior figure to whom all paid their respects and the one who dispensed love and favors to all. Her passing left Chongzhi's wife as the senior female in the home. As alcoholism made her temper ever more volatile, she enjoyed little affection or esteem from the younger generation. The center of gravity of the family was gone. Soon the centrifugal forces of the larger society would pull the younger generation in a variety of new directions.

# 9

# Student Life in the 1930s

When Ye Chongzhi planned the schooling of his sons, there was one obvious choice for their secondary education: Nankai Middle School. As we have seen, he paid scant attention to the education of his daughters. Once they acquired basic literacy and learned to sew and embroider, they were married off to old scholar-official families, where they were expected to devote themselves to domestic duties. (Only his youngest daughter, who grew up after his death, managed to escape this fate.) The boys were another matter. For them, he envisioned jobs in science, engineering, or business—practical careers for which a modern education was necessary. To prepare for these occupations, there was no better school in all of north China than Tianjin's Nankai Middle School. The boys' special tutoring in English and mathematics was specifically directed at passing Nankai's highly competitive entrance examinations.

Nankai was the creation of Zhang Boling (1876–1951), one of modern China's most progressive and innovative educators. Trained at Beiyang Naval Academy, Zhang abandoned his naval career after witnessing China's humiliating defeat in the Sino-Japanese War. Thereafter, he devoted himself to the long-term goal of educating the next generation of China's youth for the task of national self-strengthening. Working with prominent members of the Tianjin gentry elite, and traveling to Japan and the West to study foreign educational models, he established Nankai in the years before the 1911 Revolution. A large man with unbounded energy and a flair for dramatic rhetoric, he gave weekly lectures at school assemblies to imbue his students with a distinctive "Nankai spirit." Zhang's aim was to nurture a modern Chinese elite that was both cosmopolitan and patriotic, a generation of leaders endowed with scientific training, physical strength, and public spirit. To this end,

Nankai provided a rigorous education in mathematics and natural sciences, which were taught with English-language college textbooks. Solid preparation in English was essential for admission, and a second foreign language was required for graduation. The regimen was sufficiently demanding that in many years, only one-fourth of those who started the lower middle grades would graduate from the high school.

Sports and physical education were a hallmark of the Nankai experience, and Zhang Boling maintained close relations with the YMCA, which was one of the important conduits through which Western team sports were introduced to China. The members of Nankai's basketball team from the 1920s, the "five tigers," became national heroes when they won the all-China championship and then defeated a touring Filipino team that was the reigning power in Asian basketball. Nankai's "five tigers" were a symbol of China's new commitment to training strong bodies as well as keen minds, and to sports as a vehicle to instill discipline and teamwork in China's youth.[1]

An active campus life of drama and music clubs, speech contests, student unions, and a school paper helped foster civic concern. As a private school with rigorous entrance requirements (the English exam being the greatest hurdle), most of the students came from elite families with access to special preparation either at home or at private (usually missionary-run) schools. To raise the social consciousness of these elite youths, Nankai in the 1920s required two courses of social investigation in which students visited local factories, prisons, government offices, and civic institutions and wrote research reports on their findings.[2]

Nankai offered an educational experience entirely different from that which the Ye boys had received in the confines of their home, and worlds apart from the classical training given to generations of Ye scholars before them. The six grades of middle and high school included about one thousand students in a modern campus of Western-style classrooms and dormitories south of the old walled city and west of the Japanese Concession. Though most of the students came from the Tianjin area, the school's reputation attracted boarders from across the country, and even Overseas Chinese from Southeast Asia and the United States. Many of the teachers were foreign trained (especially in the United States) and later went on to distinguished scholarly careers. The school's graduates were even more impressive, from the Communist leader Zhou Enlai (1898–1976), whose urbane manners and steely resolve charmed Chinese and foreigners alike, to Cao Yu (1910–96), modern China's most famous playwright, and Wu Dayou (1907–2000), the physicist who later headed Taiwan's Academia Sinica. Hundreds of the Ye boys' schoolmates became prominent scientists and scholars or embarked on political careers with either the Nationalist government or its Communist rivals.[3]

The Nankai experience was different for the older Ye boys than for the younger ones. The eldest three, Duren, Duyi, and Duxin, all commuted to Nankai as day students during their father's lifetime, whereas after Chongzhi's death, the younger brothers boarded on campus and enjoyed the full range of Nankai student life. Among the older boys, only Duyi graduated from Nankai, passing his college entrance exams in the year his father died and going on to the elite, American-affiliated Yenching University in Beijing. The eldest son, Duren, tested into Nankai but was diagnosed with tuberculosis. Despite Chongzhi's attempt to bribe the school's medical examiner, Duren was refused admission. For several years, he was treated at home by Tianjin's premier Edinburgh-trained doctor and ate the preferential diet that his brothers so resented. After this, he went by a special horse-drawn carriage to the preparatory school for Nankai University, Zhang Boling's new venture in higher education, established in 1919. Just as he was about to enter the university, his father died. He quit school to assume a position in the Industrial Bank of China, basically inheriting his father's career in banking and business.

Duxin, the fourth son, was never a particularly diligent student. Though he tested into Nankai, he mostly indulged his love of sports and soon flunked out. After a few years at the Tianjin School of Industry and Commerce, he took a job as an accountant at the Kailan Mining Company, the large Anglo-Chinese coal company north of Tianjin. He too was afflicted with tuberculosis and was soon forced to quit. Always good at games of chance—when the boys played cards, he always won—Duxin turned to China's volatile stock market, making and losing large sums and establishing a reputation as an able speculator with a taste for fancy Western suits. Thus, Duren and Duxin followed their father into the world of business. In their brief time at Nankai, they absorbed far less of the school's independent spirit than their younger brothers did.

The middle sons—Duzhuang (Number 5), Ye Fang (6), Duzheng (7), and Fang Shi (9)—all boarded at Nankai, and this experience led to widely divergent lives after graduation. The four were only two years apart in age, all born between 1914 and 1916, and for them student life meant a major step toward independence. They were not particularly eager to accept their elder brother as family head, and boarding at Nankai provided the perfect way to escape his supervision. All participated in sports, though the only evident talent was for Ping-Pong, at which Duzheng and Fang Shi excelled. Years later, the Tsinghua University student newspaper recorded a memorable tournament between Tsinghua and several Tianjin teams. Duzheng led the Tsinghua team to several close victories; but in the final pairing, he faced off against his younger brother Fang Shi (who was still at Nankai) in a fraternal rivalry to decide the bragging rights of China's premier athletic powers, and Fang Shi led Nankai to victory.[4] All these boys joined the Boy Scouts and went on camping trips. They sampled their first Western food and watched movies. They participated in speech contests and student government and contributed to the school paper. When educating modern women became part of Zhang Boling's progressive vision and he established a girls' school next door, they also experienced coeducational classes at Nankai. With teenaged boys and girls mixed together, the natural action of youthful hormones and the New Culture movement's stress on releasing the individual from "feudal" constraints combined to make affairs of the heart an important part of student life. Love poetry graced the pages of the student paper, and the exchange of love letters and closely chaperoned visits to the girls' dorms initiated new rituals of courtship into adolescent life.

For this middle group of Ye brothers, the Nankai experience came at an important juncture in their family and national history. Their father and grandmother had died in the summer of 1930. Soon, with Miss Chen's death, Duyi, Ye Fang, Duzheng, and Fang Shi lost their mother. The family lost its key breadwinner and its emotional center. It was forced to economize by selling off the horse carriages and canceling the leases on the rickshaws that had carried the boys to and from school. A number of servants were let go, as the smaller family had less need for their services. The family, now headed by a member of their own generation, had much less influence on the boys' development than their new life at school.

Just as student life became more important, it was dramatically transformed by the national crisis created by renewed Japanese aggression. Japan's 1895 seizure of Taiwan, its 1910 colonization of Korea, the occupation of the German possessions in Shandong, and the Twenty-One Demands of 1914–15 were proof enough of the island nation's imperial ambitions in Asia, but these events did not yet threaten critical parts of China proper. Then came the Mukden Incident of September 18, 1931: the Japanese army in Manchuria (Northeast China) blew up a portion of the railway, then blamed the incident on Chinese saboteurs and used it as a pretext to occupy the region. Chiang Kai-shek believed that China was still too weak to resist Japan, and he ordered Zhang Xueliang (1901–2001), the Chinese commander in the Northeast and the son and successor of a warlord assassinated by the Japanese in 1928, to avoid confrontation and withdraw his forces. The abandonment of the Northeast, a center of heavy industry and plentiful natural resources for China's modernization, outraged patriots across China and aroused a series of student demonstrations, boycotts of Japanese goods, and petitions to the national government to mobilize against Japanese aggression. When Chiang Kai-shek failed to respond adequately, nationalist sentiment became relentlessly critical of his Nanjing regime's "appeasement" policy.[5]

The effect on Nankai's students was direct and immediate. As the Japanese advanced across Manchuria, refugees fled down the railway to Tianjin, where their tales of woe further inflamed anti-Japanese sentiment. Then in early November, the Japanese Special Services recruited some two thousand plain-clothed Chinese agents from Tianjin's gangs to attack Chinese police outposts and government offices in the city. This so-called plain-clothed corps launched its assault from the Japanese garrison, which was just a few hundred meters from Nankai Middle School. The operation was a diversion to allow the Japanese to spirit the last Manchu emperor out of Tianjin and install him as nominal head of the Manchukuo puppet

FIGURE 7. Japanese artillery closes Nankai. Cartoon drawn by Sun Song, from *Beiyang huabao* [North China pictorial], 25 February 1933.

regime that Japan was setting up in the Northeast. While the Chinese police exchanged fire with Japanese troops and their Chinese agents, Nankai was forced to close for a week and send its students to safety.[6] In later years, as Japanese agents caused repeated disturbances, the school enforced frequent blackouts in the dorms at night or cut off electricity at the first sound of gunfire.[7]

With Japanese aggression literally at their front gate, Nankai faculty and students eagerly participated in the national tide of patriotic anti-Japanese activity. The first efforts were in support of General Ma Zhanshan, the Northeast army commander who led a brief but heroic resistance to Japanese aggression in the far north of Manchuria. The Tianjin press led a campaign to raise donations in support of Ma's forces, and the Ye boys contributed—Duzhuang offering the money he had been given for a winter coat and also buying a photo of Ma on horseback to hang in his dorm room.[8]

Zhang Boling and the school authorities enthusiastically supported such patriotic activities, and Zhang was selected chair of Tianjin's Anti-Japanese National Salvation Alliance. He was an appropriate choice, for he had a long interest in the Northeast, frequently traveling there to consult on educational reform. At Nankai, he had organized a Northeast Research Committee to help plan economic development in the resource-rich region. After the Mukden Incident, this committee

FIGURE 8. League of Nations
debates as Northeast China
suffers. Cartoon drawn by Sun
Song, from *Beiyang huabao*
[North China pictorial], 28
February 1933.

edited a text on the geography of the Northeast, which became a required part of
the Nankai curriculum. Raising national consciousness had always been central to
Nankai's educational mission, and the school made sure its students understood
that Manchuria was an integral part of China. Through the social investigations
course and other pragmatic parts of the Nankai curriculum, Zhang Boling also
sought to integrate the classroom experience with China's pressing social problems.
As a result, in the classroom and out, the Manchurian crisis had an enormous influence on the lives and thinking of Nankai's young students.[9]

In 1932, the conflict spread to Shanghai, where anger at Japan's aggression set
off a series of attacks on Japanese civilians. Japan responded with a marine landing
and aerial bombardment that caused great destruction. Unexpectedly stiff resistance by the Chinese troops in the city raised national morale, and after several weeks
of fierce fighting and heavy casualties on both sides, a truce was arranged and the
Japanese withdrew. In Tianjin, Nankai responded to the national crisis by adding
an afternoon of military drill each week. An officer from the Chinese navy led the
drill and combined marching and basic military skills with a strong dose of patriotism. The nearby Japanese garrison—which was there because of a provision imposed on China after the Boxer Uprising giving foreign powers the right to station
forces near the capital—was a considerable source of aggravation, with the sound
of Japanese marching and target practice audible from the Nankai classrooms. Japa-

FIGURE 9. Nankai military drill. From the 1933 Nankai Middle School yearbook.

nese troops openly drilling on Chinese soil were a constant reminder of the structures of imperialist privilege built on past Chinese weakness and defeat, evidence of a national humiliation that this generation of young patriots was determined to erase. As one article in the student paper asked plaintively, "Is China an independent country?"[10] The young naval officer fueled the patriotic zeal of his student charges by facing his drill classes directly at the Japanese soldiers whenever they marched nearby.[11]

In the immediate aftermath of the Mukden Incident, the students' anger focused on the Northeast commander Zhang Xueliang, whose opium addiction and playboy lifestyle were well-known and much despised.[12] His retreat before the advancing Japanese army was viewed as a sacrifice of national territory by the degenerate son of a Chinese warlord. When the Ye boys and their Nankai classmates marched in their trademark blue gowns, their banners and slogans called on Chiang Kaishek to punish Zhang and mobilize the country for national resistance, and students organized delegations to Nanjing to stiffen the resolve of the national government. The government's response was at first encouraging: Chiang Kai-shek and his ministers met with the students, ordered military training in the schools, and issued resolute statements of determination to recover China's lost territory. But as time passed and no action followed this rhetoric, Chiang Kai-shek appeared more committed to eliminating the Communist insurgency in the mountains of central China than to resisting Japan. Doubts about the Nanjing government's patriotic commitment spread. As the Communists trumpeted their own commitment to fighting the Japanese (an empty boast as they were far from the front), they gained sympathy for their cause and attracted even broader support for an end to civil war and a united front against Japan.[13]

As the student movement turned to the left and toward opposition to the Nationalist regime, Zhang Boling and the Nankai authorities became more hostile toward it. They opposed the students' off-campus political activities and sought to disband the increasingly leftist student union. In 1932, the school paper was closed for a time, and some twenty student activists were expelled for suspected (and in some cases, actual) Communist activities.[14] Among the Ye brothers, the politically inclined and volatile Duzhuang was the first to evince the shift to the left. In addition to hanging a photo of Ma Zhanshan in his dorm room, he became active in the student union and was elected its secretary. Because of his activities, Duzhuang was called in by the principal and given a warning: "Don't follow those Red fellows." But his good grades saved him from punishment, and he did not heed the warning. When he graduated from high school several years later, his photo showed the shaven head that was his statement of rebellion and ascetic resolve. Duzhuang and the two brothers who later joined the Chinese Communist Party, Ye Fang and Fang Shi, all sampled communist writings passed to them by schoolmates, although they scarcely understood some of the recondite tracts on dialectics or other philosophical issues. For them, as for most students, the attraction of Marxism-Leninism was its theory of imperialism; the appeal of the Communist Party was its advocacy of resistance to Japan. This strain of nationalism is what radicalized them.

Ye Duzhuang revealed the thinking behind his radicalism in "Imperialism and the Chinese Capitalist Class," a short article published in two of the Nankai student journals. Written during the summer of 1932, when Duzhuang was just eighteen and ready to begin his senior year, the piece was full of statistics on the slow development of Chinese industry and foreign capital's domination of railways, banks, and telecommunications. He attributed this situation to the "mortal wound" inflicted on Chinese industrialization by low tariffs set by the "unequal treaties." Imperialism prevented China from erecting tariff barriers to protect its young industries. As a result, Chinese capitalism was very weak, "requiring it to compromise with imperialism and feudalism." Attacking "comprador capital and its government," the article concluded with a ringing cry to "defeat imperialism and eliminate the feudal forces; . . . struggle on . . . to destroy imperialism and its running dogs."[15]

Such Marxist analysis was extremely common in the 1930s in mainstream journals as well as student publications.[16] Duzhuang's essay reflects a familiarity with Marxist class analysis and Leninist theories of imperialism. It also reveals the impact of the social investigations course, which included visits to cotton mills where he was shaken by the unhygienic dust-filled conditions in which the workers toiled for paltry wages. His friends included several future Communists who encouraged

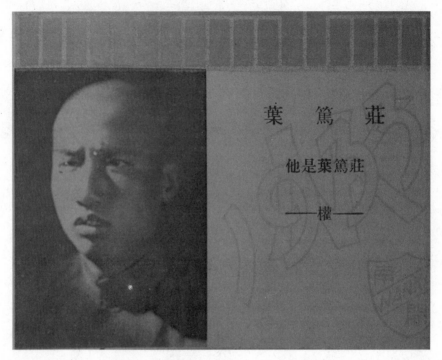

FIGURE 10. Ye Duzhuang's school photo. From the 1933 Nankai Middle School yearbook.

these radical ideas and gave him left-wing pamphlets to read, but he never participated in leftist student groups. His younger brother Fang Shi, however, was a few
years behind him in school and in the mid-1930s, had much closer contacts with
left-wing students and joined the Communist front organization, the National Liberation Vanguards, in 1936. Even before that time, his sampling of left-wing literature brought him into fateful contact with the law.

The encounter occurred on a Sunday afternoon in the fall of 1935, when Fang
Shi was returning to school on a streetcar (which had by then replaced the rickshaw
as the boys' mode of transportation) after a weekend at home. Fang Shi began to
read the *History of the Great Revolution,* a left-wing tract that described Chiang Kai-
shek as a butcher for his bloody suppression of the CCP in April 1927. The book had
a false cover, but Fang Shi failed to heed the military policeman who sat next to him
on the tram and noted what he was reading. When he got off the tram at Nankai,
the M.P. followed and stopped him, saying "Student, come with me." Fang Shi's protest
that he had to get back to school was to no avail, and he was taken to the Tianjin
garrison command. After a phone call verified his student status, he was asked about
left-wing contacts. He denied even knowing what "CP" or "CY" (Communist Youth)

meant. Asked where he got the book, he concealed the fact that his sixth brother, Ye Fang (the other future Communist), had passed it to him, and named a student who he knew lived safely in the Japanese Concession. Soon the questioning turned to his family, and when he identified his late father, the interrogating detective said, "Well! Then you're no stranger to me. Your father was my 'teacher' at the police academy."

Ye Chongzhi's career as police commissioner had been a short one, and suspicions about his contacts with an earlier generation of revolutionaries had cut it short in 1911. But in 1935, that service was sufficient to save his son from immediate danger. Fang Shi was told that if he could find a suitable guarantor, he would be released. He called home to his elder brother Duyi, who had graduated from college by this time and was working with the Tianjin Sanitation Bureau. Duyi went with a servant to Tianjin's most famous old-style piece-goods store, Ruifuxiang, where the family had long bought material for clothing. But Ruifuxiang—presumably realizing that many scions of elite Tianjin families were involved with left-wing organizations—was unwilling to guarantee a young man about whom it knew nothing. So Duyi went back to a neighborhood shop from which the Ye family bought its oil, soy sauce, and other staples, and the owner readily offered his guarantee. Fang Shi was released and returned to school, where his friends told him to dispose immediately of all left-wing literature in his dorm. He did, and sure enough, a plainclothed officer came to search his room the next day.

Fang Shi graduated from Nankai the following spring, the last of the Ye boys to attend that remarkable institution. His father's connections had saved him from any immediate consequences of his careless reading habits. But years later, the fact that he had been released from custody so quickly would cause suspicion among the Communists (a story we will leave for later).

In the years after they left Nankai, the differences between the younger and older Ye boys' adolescent experiences became even more pronounced. Though each child's situation was naturally distinctive as he or she forged a path in the world, certain patterns did distinguish the experiences of three groups: the three older brothers, the three surviving daughters, and the younger boys.

Studies of birth order and its influence on the personalities of children suggest that firstborn sons tend to be socially conservative and defensive of their status, whereas younger sons are more often "born to rebel." Age gives older children a natural advantage in family dynamics and sibling rivalry, and they tend to develop the social skills and behavior patterns to protect that advantage—learning to display their relative maturity in ways that will curry favor with parents and other authority figures. Younger children, by contrast, often strike out in new and different directions in their effort to establish their niche in the family. They are more likely to innovate and even to rebel as adults.[17] Although such general rules can never explain particular cases, the Ye boys conformed to this pattern to a remarkable extent. Ye Duren, the eldest son, was the conservative, responsible elder brother, who moved easily into his father's place in the Tianjin business world and took his duties as family head seriously. Although he was once engaged to the daughter of an official family, the girl's family called off the match when his tuberculosis delayed the marriage. The Ye family retained a lawyer to handle this embarrassing break and handsomely rewarded his discreet settlement with a valuable scroll from Chongzhi's collection. This event occurred in the year before Chongzhi died, so a director of the Industrial Bank was the one to arrange Duren's marriage to the niece (and adopted daughter) of the former president Xu Shichang. This was a favorable match, and the bride's dowry included a home in the British Concession, a foreign-style house with a piano that she rarely played. Duren's sole condition for the marriage was that his wife speak proper Beijing Mandarin, so he was quite disappointed when, after the wedding, he heard her thick Henan accent.

In the mid-1930s, Duren left the old home behind the Anhui Guildhall and moved to the safety of his wife's house in the British Concession. He continued to take care of his mother and Chongzhi's wife, but relations with his younger brothers were strained. His siblings had resented his favored treatment as a child and now chafed under his role as family head, questioning the equity of the privileged position he inherited in the Tianjin business world, especially after their own academic qualifications far surpassed his meager credentials. He seems to have had the accounting mentality of a banker, which engendered behavior that his brothers regarded as excessively stingy. Their leftist views predisposed them to look skeptically at his bourgeois lifestyle; and his personal life, which apparently included a certain amount of extramarital dalliance, offended their progressive morality.[18]

The fourth brother, Duxin, also went into business, but maintained much better relations with his brothers. His relative poverty earned their sympathy, and he was more generous when he was successful in his stock speculations. His marriage had been arranged to the daughter of an official family, but the wedding in 1934 was something of a hybrid affair, and the combination of Chinese and Western customs did not go smoothly. First came a small dispute about the couple's prenuptial meeting. Such meetings of the two families—often with the couple sitting silently on separate seats—were becoming conventional with arranged marriages. Because the new republican marriage law required the consent of both bride and groom, these encounters became the occasion for the young people to register any objection to the match.[19] But to Duxin's fiancée, the new practice seemed demeaning: "It's like shopping," she said. "Take it if it's good, turn it back if it is not." But her relatives talked her into two encounters with her husband (though the two hardly talked), and the process went forward.

The selection of a wedding gown created another problem. By the 1930s, elite urban families had abandoned the traditional belief that white was the color of mourning, as young women showed a clear preference for elaborate Western-style wedding gowns with lots of lace. Still, the groom's family was expected to provide the dress, and the Ye family sent over the wedding gowns of Duren's and Duyi's wives and asked the bride to choose one. The bride's aunt, wife of Yuan Shikai's grandson, was with her niece when the Ye servants delivered the gowns, and she threw them back, hectoring the poor fellows fiercely: "This is not a second wedding for our young lady. Damned if she's going to wear an old gown." So they went to the most expensive Western store in Tianjin, ordered a gown, and sent the bill to the Ye family.

Once these difficulties were overcome, Duxin's wife proved exceptionally kind and supportive. After leaving school and then losing his job at the Kailan Mining Company, Duxin retired to Beiping (as the former capital was known after 1928) for treatment of his tuberculosis. There his wife's relatives supported him until his health and business fortunes recovered and he was able to buy a house in Tianjin. Stock trading was for him an extension of his youthful talent for gambling. When he made money, he indulged his taste for fancy Western suits and visits to the racetrack but was also generous to friends and relatives. The marriage was childless, but he remained close to his younger brothers and looked after their inheritance while they were in school or in the interior during the war.[20]

Ye Duyi, the third brother, was the last of the older group that finished Nankai before his father's death, but he was a far more gifted student than Duren or Duxin. He studied at Nankai from 1925 to 1930, which were relatively peaceful years on the political front, and graduated from high school near the top in the natural sciences track. He was the first to graduate from high school, and his father was delighted, viewing the achievement as the equivalent of passing the provincial examinations in the old system. Chongzhi was particularly pleased that his son had selected the science track and envisioned him as a white-coated researcher in a test-tube–filled laboratory. Duyi traveled to Beiping for the entrance examinations to Tsinghua University, a school with a reputation as China's MIT. Then, while he was home waiting for the results, his father suffered his fatal heart attack.

The day after his father died, Duyi received his letter of admission to Tsinghua, but he turned it down in a fateful decision that he came to regret but could never explain. He decided to attend Yenching University, located next to Tsinghua in the Western suburbs of Beiping. Yenching was a private university supported by American missionary and philanthropic institutions, and Nankai's top students automatically qualified for admission. Duyi's best friend from childhood (who spent his vacations with his sister in the Ye household), Yao Zengyi, was also a classmate at Nankai, and he was going to Yenching. Perhaps the sense of loss and loneliness occasioned by his father's death made Duyi more anxious to stay with his friend. In any case, his decision meant forgoing the scientific career for which he had shown such talent. Yenching's strengths were in the social sciences and humanities, and those were the subjects Duyi would study.

There were fewer than fifty thousand college students in all of China in the 1930s, roughly 0.01 percent of the population. In entering Yenching, Duyi was joining a particularly privileged group within this tiny elite. The parklike Yenching campus was the former estate of a Manchu nobleman. Classrooms and dormitories had been designed by an American architect in "Chinese Renaissance" style, which combined modern materials and interiors with Chinese-style tile roofs and décor. The buildings were gracefully sited around a small lake and several ponds, and a famous water tower beside the lake was cleverly disguised as a five-story pagoda. The dorms had all the modern comforts: baths and showers with hot and cold running water, kitchen and laundry facilities, and servants to clean and care for the students' needs. The president of the university was the American missionary and later diplomat Leighton Stuart, and most of the faculty were either Westerners or graduates of American universities. Along with St. John's University in Shanghai, Yenching was the most Westernized campus in China, with a reputation as the "academic playground for the hedonistic, English-speaking scions of South China's treaty-port bourgeoisie and wealthy émigré businessmen."[21]

Duyi fit in quite comfortably. Even at Nankai, while his brothers wore the blue gowns and cloth shoes favored by most students, Duyi sometimes went out in Western suits and leather shoes, even having his hair cut by an expensive barber in a downtown department store. At Yenching, he majored in political science but displayed little interest in the political movements of the day. Although Yenching students would play a crucial role in the student demonstrations of 1935–36, while Duyi was there in the early 1930s, the campus was relatively quiet—isolated by its suburban setting and comfortable in its cosmopolitan culture. Duyi devoted himself to his studies, adding French to his already solid command of English.

The best indication of his thinking is the B.A. thesis he wrote in 1934, "The Development of International Organizations." The 150-page manuscript is written in flawless English and is based entirely on Western-language sources. It is a remarkable document for a time when continuous Japanese aggression was fueling a fierce spirit of patriotic resistance across the country. Duyi's thesis portrayed nationalism in an entirely negative light. Linking national consciousness to notions of racial superiority, he declared, "Nations are most likely tempted to impose their racial superiority upon other nations. . . . The idea of nationalism is merely endeavoring for one's own benefit at the sacrifice of others." Expressing the naïve conviction that "nationalism is past and cosmopolitanism is still in the invisible future," he placed his hopes on a "transitional stage" of internationalism: "Opposed to the idea of nationalism is the idea of internationalism. . . . International affairs are conducted by the principle of justice, not of force, by mutual help and by conciliation. Each nation or state preserves its own rights and at the same time does not injure others. All principles of self-sufficiency, protectionism, militarism, and imperialism should be done away with."

Particularly striking in this internationalist vision is the hope that Duyi placed in a strengthened version of the League of Nations. When Japan invaded Manchuria in 1931, China immediately appealed to the League of Nations. Although the League issued a report condemning the Japanese aggression, Japan simply withdrew its membership and suffered no sanctions for its actions. Duyi's hopes still lay with some form of international organization: "The present League is inadequate to the needs of the case and a closer form of international government is necessary. The conclusion is simply obvious. Such is the argument for an international federation. And such is our future prospect."[22]

In the long term, one cannot help but be impressed by Duyi's idealistic hopes for peace through a new global order—reminiscent of the goals of progressive American advocates of world federalism in the postwar era. But in an era when the world's attention was consumed by the calamity of the Great Depression, an aroused Chinese nationalism was far more likely to provide effective resistance to Japan's aggression than any international organization. In the cosmopolitan precincts of Yenching's parklike campus, that conclusion was not obvious to Ye Duyi. The fact that his cosmopolitan stance was at such odds with the patriotic passions of the day says something about the education he received from his Yenching mentors.

These political views were not the only contradiction in Ye Duyi's life. He also displayed a curious combination of modern education and old-fashioned superstition. One of the hallmarks of Zhang Boling's promotion of scientific training was his conviction that superstitious beliefs in ghosts and spirits were a barrier to China's modernization. Indeed the attack on "superstition" was a common feature of Nationalist policy at the time.[23] But such modern ideas did not deter Duyi. With his mother terminally ill midway through his college career, he returned to Tianjin to see her. Thinking her well enough to hold on for a while, he returned to Beiping only to learn a few days later that she had passed away. He missed her dearly and felt terrible that he had not been at her side when she died. He went to a spirit medium in the effort to contact her spirit, and in his Yenching dormitory he tried to put himself into a trance to speak with her. One can only imagine what his American missionary professors would have thought of these "superstitious" practices by their talented and idealistic student of world peace through international federation.

Even more remarkably, when Duyi graduated from Yenching University at age twenty-two, he accepted the marriage his father had long since arranged with the niece of a former minister of finance. In the Westernized atmosphere of Yenching, where young couples strolled along the shaded paths by No-Name Lake, such arranged marriages were commonly regarded as a relic of a dying culture. The most popular novel among college students of this generation was Ba Jin's *Family*, which was a wholesale attack on the patriarchal family's denial of true love and individual freedom.[24] Not surprisingly in this environment, Duyi thought seriously of renouncing this arranged marriage. However, the young lady acted to save the engagement, traveling to Yenching to confront Duyi, an encounter that left him rather discomfited. In the end, his elder brother talked him out of any change of heart. Duren argued that his own first engagement had been broken by the bride's family, and their fourth sister had also been turned down. For Duyi to reject this marriage would bring irreparable harm to the family's reputation. Always eager to please, never inclined to risk conflict, Duyi accepted his brother's advice. He met the young lady a couple of times in awkward tête-à-têtes at her spacious Western-style home in the Tianjin concessions. She was the proper daughter of a very wealthy Tianjin family who had received a good classical education at home—especially in poetry, the favored literary form for women—but she made a poor match for this distinguished graduate of one of China's most Westernized colleges. Their marriage was a loveless union that he would regret all of his life. But he never renounced it, and they lived together for some sixty years, until her death in old age.

After his graduation and marriage, Duyi worked for a short time with the Sanitation Bureau of the Tianjin municipal government, then moved to nearby Tangshan to take a job with the large Sino-British Kailan Mining Company. There he stayed, living off a comfortable salary until midway through the war years. Thus, despite the college education that set him apart from Duren and Duxin, he fell into the pattern of the older boys in sticking with his arranged marriage, entering the world of business, and staying in the Tianjin area even during the period of Japanese occupation.[25]

Ye Chongzhi's conservative ways were most evident in the raising of his daughters, who had bound feet (though only loosely), received no schooling beyond instruction at home in basic literacy and embroidery, and entered into arranged marriages to old official families. The first daughter having died as a child, the second daughter was the first to be wed. Married in the early 1920s when the family was most prosperous, Dushi was sent with eight trunks of clothes and jewelry as a dowry. At her fiancé's wish, the wedding was held in Shanghai, at an expensive hotel. The bride begged her father's wife to accompany her, hoping her presence would enhance her status, but the wife refused, and in the end Dushi left with her own mother, a cousin, and two servants, one male and one female. After the wedding, her husband forced her to walk with him along the streets of Shanghai's International Concession. She found such public intimacy embarrassing, and the high-heeled shoes she wore to compensate for her short stature were extremely uncomfortable. The marriage improved little from this inauspicious start. Her husband was an opium addict who treated her badly, and, as we have seen, Dushi passed away in her natal home just before her father's demise.[26]

The husband of Duya, the third daughter, was no better. Also the scion of an old official family, he had never been a diligent student, and as the date for this long-

arranged marriage approached, various Ye family members heard disturbing rumors of opium use, whoring, and even venereal disease. A servant was sent to make
discreet inquiries and devised the stratagem of inviting the young man to join him
in a public bathhouse. The prospective groom easily guessed his companion's intent and offered a handsome bribe to cover up his misdeeds. This ruse worked:
the servant attested to the prospective groom's good behavior and even bragged
to the Ye boys about his clever bathhouse investigation. This report was a great relief to Ye Chongzhi, his wife, and his mother, who were much opposed to breaking
the engagement.

The wedding was held in Beiping, and this time the bride was accompanied by
both her father and mother. It was another hybrid affair: the bride wore a white
bridal dress and veil, but she arrived in a red sedan chair. She too received a substantial dowry worth several thousand silver dollars. This money became the key
source of support for the family, for her husband was indeed an opium (and later
heroin) addict and had no regular job until after the war. But he had the cultivated
air of someone from an elite family and was polite, so Duya put on a brave face and
endured the disappointment and poverty that the match had brought. The couple
lived simply at his home in Hebei before moving to Beiping, and Duya's economical ways, plus some help from her brothers, allowed the pair to get by.[27]

Dusong, the fourth sister, had her arranged marriage renounced after the
prospective groom entered Tsinghua University and was infected with new ideas
about love marriages. Following her father's death, family friends arranged a marriage to a Nankai graduate from a wealthy Tianjin family, who later studied engineering at Cornell. During the marriage negotiations, the boy's family provided a
photo of him, which Dusong was allowed to peek at over her mother's shoulder.
Then the couple was escorted to a Chinese opera performance, where the two sat
in the same box but not in the same row. The groom-to-be sat in the back, where
he had a better view of his prospective bride, and his elevated seat concealed his
short stature. Before the wedding, the yellow press in Tianjin carried a story about
him visiting brothels, which Dusong's brothers showed to her. She was devastated,
crying for several days, but went ahead with the marriage, which involved a Western feast (a first for the family) in a fancy Tianjin hotel. Her radical brother Duzhuang startled the guests by shouting out anti-Japanese slogans at the end of the
ceremony. Dusong also received a substantial dowry, but this time it was not chests
full of clothes and silk but the passbook of a savings account. She lived with her
husband in a large house in the Japanese Concession, and he took a job at Beiyang
College, then transferred to the engineering section of the Beiping-Fengtian Railroad until the Japanese occupation. His weakness for prostitutes never ceased, and
he later took one as a mistress, who bore him several children.[28]

The break from this pattern of arranged and generally unhappy marriages did
not come until the fifth daughter, Durou, who was much younger than the others,

born in 1921. By the time she was six, her father's opposition to educating girls had weakened, and she attended the family school and a nearby primary school. After her father's death, she passed the examinations for Nankai Girls' Middle School, which she attended until the Japanese bombed the school after the outbreak of the war in 1937. She did not board, however; she lived with her eldest brother and his wife in the British Concession and went back and forth in a leased rickshaw. Though she did not participate fully in the Nankai experience—regularly shirking the physical education requirement, for example—she did go to movies and read foreign (especially Russian) novels in translation. She had little interest in politics and did not become involved in the political movements of the day. Still, this youngest daughter broke the mold by which her sisters had been raised and exemplified the new life patterns arising in the family (and in China) at the onset of the 1930s.

The new pattern among the younger children was even more pronounced in the sons. Duzhuang, the fifth son, was recognized by all his brothers as the rebel of the family. His political activism (and article on imperialism) was only one side of that radical streak. Even more dramatic in the family dynamics was his decision to renounce his arranged marriage. Duzhuang had been engaged as a boy to the granddaughter of Zhang Xiluan, a former governor-general of Northeast China who was then living in luxurious retirement in Tianjin, where he was famous for a stable of horses that he raced along suburban roads. With a Manchu-style queue and embroidered Qing robes that he wore on ceremonial occasions, he remained an imperial official of the old style. His only son had no job but lived off his father's great wealth and gained a reputation as a collector of antiques. The Zhang family and their wives were close friends of Chongzhi's family, and the women often played mahjong together.

The young lady to whom Duzhuang was engaged had a good deal more formal education than his own sisters did. She had attended a Catholic middle school, which represented a very respectable level of education for a girl at this time. But Duzhuang had been affected by all sorts of new ideas at Nankai, and a bright and perky young co-ed had attracted his attention. His father had already died, so the family lacked a clear authority figure to enforce the prior engagement. Duzhuang's political leanings were also relevant. His critical attitude toward the "capitalist class" was evident in his essay for the school paper, and he was influenced by left-wing literature that painted the blackest picture of the corrupt and parasitic nature of the old elite. It was common knowledge that his prospective father-in-law was an opium addict, and this fact raised doubts about the upbringing of his fiancée. So he wrote a letter asking to meet her.

His fiancée, being a proper young lady, brought the letter to her parents, who were furious. They took their private auto to the Ye compound to meet with Duzhuang's mother and brother. Deeming a private meeting of the young couple abhorrent, the young lady's father made a counterproposal with two stipulations: the couple should meet only in the company of the elder generation, and no rejection of the engagement was to be entertained after the meeting. To these hard conditions, the father offered a substantial incentive to preserve the match: if the couple married on Duzhuang's graduation from Nankai, the Zhang family would finance his college education in the United States.

Now it was Duzhuang's turn to be outraged. If the condition for a meeting was agreement that the wedding must go forward, then the whole point of first getting to know the young woman was lost. Even more offensive to Duzhuang's youthful sense of amour propre was the bribe of an American education. The Zhang family was using its great wealth to gain his consent, but he was not to be bought. He resolved to call off the match. The arrangements were made in a lawyer's office, the two families signing papers in separate rooms, but Duzhuang's request that the annulment be announced in the newspaper was rejected. The decision was a dramatic break for the Ye family, a move reluctantly accepted by the eldest brother and family head. When the meeting was over, Duzhuang returned to the family home and danced around the courtyard shouting (in English) "I'm free! I'm free!" From then on, all the Ye matches were "love marriages" arranged by the couples themselves.

Duzhuang was responsible for another major family transition when he proposed, in 1936, that the brothers formally divide their patrimony. The longtime Chinese custom was that after daughters received their dowries and provision was made for the support of any surviving parents, the family property would be equally divided among the surviving sons (or the heirs of those sons). Sometimes this family division came only after the death of the father, but often it occurred after one or more of the brothers married and began to establish families of their own.[29] In this case, the eldest brother was already married, his wife had just borne his first child (a daughter), and tensions were growing about the payments he was making to support his brothers' education. On one occasion, after an argument about how much money was left from their father's inheritance, Duren slammed the account books on the table and told his brothers to check them themselves. His wife, from the wealthy family of a former president, had brought to their marriage an extensive dowry that included the large house they lived in along with a wealth of jewelry and other household items. She was concerned that supporting her brothers-in-law would soon start eating into her own dowry, and her grumbling added to the pressure that her normally mild-mannered husband was feeling. She enthusiastically supported the idea of a family division.[30]

The Ye family division was unusual in that no effort was made to ensure an equal division of Chongzhi's accumulated wealth. Instead, each of the younger sons received a lump sum of ten thousand silver dollars in stocks and government bonds.

The family home, over one hundred acres of farmland in Jiangsu, and all of their father's extensive collection of antiques, books, and artwork were left in the hands of the eldest brother. He was clearly the big winner in this deal, but his brothers were the ones pushing for the division so that they would not have to keep begging him for tuition money. To the younger boys, ten thousand dollars was an enormous amount of money. Even at the elite Yenching or Tsinghua universities, annual expenses came to only three to four hundred dollars.[31] Most of the brothers left their funds in the care of either Duyi or Duxin to manage and dole out as needed (none, significantly, left their money with Duren). Their needs were not great, and only much later, when Duren sold all the family's books and artwork and kept the proceeds, did they resent the financial killing he made off the division.[32]

The financial independence of the younger sons and their liberation from arranged marriages gave rise to a new life pattern as they entered adulthood. Not only did they marry women of their own choosing, but the weddings did not take place until during or after the war when most of them were already well into their twenties. If we compare the experience of Ye Boying, still living under his father's wing long after he was married, the novelty of this generation's rather prolonged period of bachelorhood is particularly striking. Most likely, the independent spirit of this group—an independence encouraged since their schooling at Nankai—was further strengthened by these years in which they made their own way after finishing high school.

After graduating from Nankai in 1933, both Ye Duzhuang and Ye Fang took and passed the exams for Nanjing University. They were drawn to Nanjing because it had China's premier school of agriculture. The school was an unusual choice, and Duzhuang's mother certainly did not understand: "You are going to college to learn how to farm?" But the two were convinced that China was weak because it was poor, and poor because of the backwardness of its peasant economy; so transforming rural China was essential to the progress of the nation. In the 1930s, the Chinese public was paying increasing attention to rural China with all sorts of schemes— rural education, land reform, credit cooperatives, or agricultural extension for new strains of cotton or silkworms—to rescue the Chinese peasantry from persistent poverty.[33] The two boys' interest in rural China reflected this general public concern. At this time, the Chinese Communists were leading a peasant-based revolutionary movement in the Chinese hinterland, so the boys' interest in the rural economy had a political dimension. If their leftist political commitments were leading them toward revolution, they would have to learn more about peasant agriculture.

Nanjing University, however, proved a great disappointment. Known as Jinling in Chinese, it was a missionary college with a conservative orientation. Its location in the nation's capital allowed the Nationalist government to keep a tight rein on students' political activities. Both boys found student life stultifying after their experience at Nankai, offering little more than boring book learning. The academic curriculum ill suited their radical political agenda, for the faculty members in the College of Agriculture and Forestry were virulent anti-Communists who were convinced that the reform of Chinese agriculture would come not from land reform but from technical improvements, mechanization, and larger, more "efficient" farms.[34] After one semester, both boys decided that Nanjing was not for them, and they packed up and headed home.[35]

The boys headed for Beiping, but their objectives were quite different. Duzhuang went in pursuit of Sun Song, the co-ed he had fallen for at Nankai and could not stop thinking about. She had entered Yenching, where she made quite a splash as one of an inseparable trio known as the "Three Modern Girls" (the title of a popular 1933 movie) from Nankai. The other two were Liang Siyi, daughter of the eminent turn-of-the-century reformist intellectual Liang Qichao, and Wang Ruolan, who later joined the Communist Party and achieved fame as Zhou Enlai's English secretary. In his junior year in high school, Duzhuang had a class in classical Chinese philosophy with Sun Song, where his seat was next to hers. When she came in just before the bell, she asked his name with a characteristic directness, and he responded with such a blush that his classmates immediately teased him: "The Sage [his nickname] is cooking!" Duzhuang succumbed to love at first sight, and after a time, he wrote asking to be her "friend." Following a proper delay, he received a positive reply, with the modest warning, "My talent is slight and learning shallow; I hope I do not disappoint you." Years later, he discovered that Wang Ruolan had written this reply on Sun Song's behalf without her friend's knowledge.

Sun Song's family was from Wuxi, in the lower Yangzi valley, and her father was an English-trained railway engineer. The family was far more Westernized than the Ye family, and Sun Song, in addition to being a young woman of striking beauty, carried the confident superiority of the new elite. Her sharp tongue earned her the nickname "Pepper," and she had quite a reputation as a cartoonist, seeing several of her patriotic and progressive drawings published in the Tianjin illustrated magazines (see figures 7 and 8). Every time Duzhuang was in her presence, he felt embarrassed and tongue-tied, but he pursued her with dogged persistence, competing for her attention with several handsome and stylish classmates and visiting her dormitory for closely chaperoned and highly awkward chats in the sitting room.

In Nanjing, his friends sent news of "Pepper" at Yenching, and once back in the north, he went to visit her. The Three Modern Girls met him together, Sun Song dressed in a fashionable short silk dress and straw hat, while Duzhuang made a point of going in a simple cotton gown and cloth shoes. With his shaven head, he looked particularly out of place among the Westernized students of Yenching, but his attire was a deliberate attempt to appeal to Sun Song's unconventional and progressive taste. Duzhuang studied that spring in the Beiping Public Library, going every day on a new Japanese bicycle, and supplemented his income by tutoring a high school student in mathematics, the first money he had earned on his own. He aimed to take the exams for Tsinghua University, next door to Sun Song at Yenching, but he proved overconfident, spending more time reading progressive books and magazines than reviewing for the exams. He did not pass. Having been a top student at Nankai, he was disappointed and ashamed. Then he heard that Sun Song was going to Tokyo to study art, and he decided to follow her.

That these two patriotic youths should continue their studies in the capital of the national enemy seems, on its face, difficult to explain. Both had been active in the anti-Japanese student movement, yet here they were choosing to study in Japan. They were not alone, however: 1934–35 witnessed a wave a Chinese students headed for Japan—the largest number since 1905–06 in the wake of Japan's victory in the Russo-Japanese War, and 1913–14 in the first years of the republic. In the fall of 1935, some 6,000 to 6,500 Chinese students were studying in Japan, a number that surprised Chinese and Japanese commentators alike. The Japanese government did everything possible to encourage this trend, hoping to win the friendship of China's future leaders. It required no passports or visas, only a high school diploma and four hundred yen to support a year of study. Many Chinese students went to learn Japanese, a language that was certain to be important in the new Asian order. Some were looking for careers working with Japanese businesses or in Japan's puppet state in Manchuria, but even more came with the intent of "knowing thy enemy." The main reason for this flood of students, however, was that study in Japan was incredibly cheap. After 1931, China's silver-based currency more than tripled in value over Japan's gold-backed yen, propelled in large part by the U.S. Silver Purchase Act, which drove up the price of the metal. As a result, a university education in Japan could be even cheaper than one in China.[36] Because both Sun Song (who had hoped to go to a celebrated art academy in Hangzhou) and Duzhuang had been unable to pursue their chosen academic paths in China, Japan provided an ideal alternative. Both, in the end, got their wish: "Pepper" studied art at a prestigious women's art college, and Duzhuang (or "Sage") soon tested into the Agricultural College of Tokyo Imperial University.

In Tokyo, Duzhuang continued his courtship of Sun Song, inviting her to lunch at the YMCA but (in characteristically unconventional manner) suggesting that they go Dutch. He took her to a left-wing discussion group, but she confessed that her interests were in art, not politics. Duzhuang joined a progressive drama group and was surprised to see Sun Song in the audience as he read one play, and then was moved by her kind words after the performance. They exchanged letters in which he confessed his love with increasing openness, and she responded sometimes with encouragement and sometimes with cryptic parables that seemed to highlight the difference in their priorities: "A dog likes bones, a horse likes grass. If a dog told a horse that bones taste good, the horse would not understand. If a horse told a dog that grass tastes good, the dog would not understand." In the end, she made clear that she intended to finish her studies, and though his love for her never slackened, he devoted more attention to his academic concerns.

In Tokyo, Duzhuang first lived in a dormitory for Chinese students, taking his meals at a nearby Chinese restaurant. Every day he went by trolley to an intensive Japanese course at the East Asian Japanese Language Preparatory School, an institution designed to teach Japanese to foreign students from Asia. After a few months, he rented a room in the home of a greengrocer who sold vegetables from a cart. Here he was able to escape the Chinese-speaking environment of the dorm and practice his Japanese. His relations with the family were cordial and correct, but when the letter announcing Duzhuang's admission to Tokyo Imperial University arrived, he was instantly transformed from a simple Chinese lodger into an elite student of Japan's premier institution, and the family greeted its young Chinese boarder with deep bows and unprecedented respect.

In 1935, when Duzhuang entered the school of agriculture, it had just been separated from the rest of Tokyo University to become the Tokyo College of Agriculture and Forestry. He managed to pass the entrance exams after only a half year studying Japanese by memorizing the essay his Japanese teacher helped him write (the subject, "my home town," had not changed for years) and carefully practicing some standard answers for the oral exam. Like the other Chinese students, he was listed only as an auditor—though the school later recognized him as a distinguished Chinese alumnus.[37] His Nankai training had fully prepared him for the English, math, and biology sections. The education at the college was rigorous and thorough, with notable professors in botany, entomology, cropping, and soil sciences. A geology field trip took him into the Japanese countryside, where he saw the poverty of the mountain villages but also observed Japan's advances in the use of chemical fertilizers, pesticides, and improved hybrid crops. Though he attended the school for only two years before the war interrupted his study, Duzhuang's agronomy training in Tokyo provided the foundation for a significant monograph on north China cotton cultivation that he wrote in the postwar years.

This education in Japan gave Duzhuang a basic command of Japanese and firsthand familiarity with Asia's rising power, but it did nothing to reduce his Chinese nationalism. As a Chinese college student in Japan, he was eligible for scholarship support from a fund established with monies from the Boxer Indemnity. The indemnity, imposed on China as reparations for the destruction of foreign property during the Boxer Uprising, was a much-resented example of the Great Powers' extraction of scarce funds from impoverished China. After a few years, Japan, following the lead of the United States, began using this money to support Chinese students studying in the country, part of a broader project to promote goodwill among an elite group of students who were expected to become opinion leaders on their return to China. In this case, however, the Japanese intentions were a little too transparent for Duzhuang. The scholarship exam required an essay on "East Asian coexistence and coprosperity," Japanese euphemisms to cover their imperialist project in Asia. Duzhuang was not about to write a fawning essay on this theme, and he simply walked out.

While Duzhuang was studying in Japan, Ye Fang and Duzheng, the next two younger brothers and his close contemporaries, were at Tsinghua. After leaving the School of Agriculture in Nanjing, Ye Fang passed the exams to enter Tsinghua; he was joined in 1935 by Duzheng, who tested in straight from Nankai. Located right next to Yenching University, Tsinghua shared much of that missionary college's reputation for an academic life of privileged isolation in the idyllic surroundings of a former Manchu villa. But Yenching was a missionary college; many of its students came from treaty-port Christian families and missionary-run high schools. They were known for their attention to stylish Western fashions and for a certain delicate sensitivity. A visiting American scholar was struck by their pale complexions and physical frailty, which they sought to remedy with cod-liver oil, countless bottles of which cluttered the dining-hall tables.[38] Tsinghua had been founded to train students for study in the United States on Boxer Indemnity funds. Even after becoming a national university, it still received generous support from a Boxer Indemnity endowment. As China's answer to MIT, Tsinghua offered a strong science curriculum, and its laboratories were the best equipped in the nation. Its stone, brick, and concrete buildings looked like an American midwestern university, in sharp contrast to the Chinese Renaissance style of Yenching next door. Student life was active, with a large variety of clubs. Moreover, a daily requirement of an hour of physical education (during which time dorms, libraries, and laboratories were locked up) and rigorous graduation requirements in running, jumping, and swimming made Tsinghua men renowned for their physical fitness (in striking contrast to their Yenching colleagues next door). Not surprisingly, the college's sports teams (including Duzheng's Ping-Pong team) consistently excelled.[39]

Designed as a preparatory school for study in the United States, Tsinghua oriented campus life toward the American academic model. Among the customs that it picked up from American campuses was the practice of freshman hazing. At Tsinghua, the ritual was known by an English name: "freshman-toss." A 1930 article in the student paper described it as the "greatest event and most important fun" for non-freshman. The school's physical education department conspired in supporting the practice, which immediately followed the physical exam for entering students. As the freshmen exited the gymnasium, they were greeted by upper classmen who pushed and swung them about, forced them to crawl under various obstacles, and finally picked them up by their four limbs and tossed them onto a mat. The terms used for the participants in this hazing ritual acquired a certain Chinese flavor: the sophomores were known as *shafumo* (father-killing devils) and the freshman as *fulanshimen* (rotten corpses). The entering class of 1934 knew of the ritual and did not consider it Tsinghua's "greatest event." Many of these freshmen had experience in the anti-Japanese student movement of the early 1930s and knew something of the power of organization. So a core group, including Ye Fang, mobilized to resist the hazing and successfully stopped it. At the time, this success seemed a petty campus victory, but many "Anti-Toss" activists later became prominent in the anti-Japanese student movement. They had learned that organization and unity could turn students into effective agents of change. This event was a small example of the ways in which campus controversies could spill over into the realm of national politics.[40]

The freshman Anti-Toss movement brought Ye Fang together with a number of left-wing students who joined the Socialist Alliance, a secret organization that ran study groups on Marxist writings and current affairs. But coursework in chemistry consumed most of Ye Fang's time. Tsinghua was one of China's most competitive colleges, with only one-tenth of the applicants passing its rigorous entrance examinations, and Ye Fang was one of the top chemistry students.[41] As he took his required science courses, the 1934–35 academic year passed relatively quietly on college campuses. The Nationalist Party had effectively clamped down on dissent, prohibiting anti-Japanese demonstrations and expelling and arresting known leftists. Many students simply withdrew from politics, and those who maintained their political concerns did so quietly. But 1935 would prove to be another matter, and Ye Fang was soon drawn decisively into the political maelstrom.

Japanese aggression in the 1930s did not stop with the occupation of Manchuria. The Mukden Incident of 1931 and the Shanghai incursion the next year were followed by an endless string of petty incidents and a relentless Japanese advance in north China. The Japanese imperial army in Manchuria provoked much of the conflict, and civilian and moderate authorities in Japan proved both unwilling and unable to check the military's expansive agenda. Again and again, Japanese agents created incidents as pretexts for further military action. Typically, the trouble would begin near one of the twelve Japanese garrisons maintained in north China as a result of the Boxer Protocol. In early 1933, Japanese forces turned a blind eye to (and probably encouraged) their countrymen's smuggling and drug trafficking along the Great Wall that separated China and Manchuria. When Chinese authorities attempted to check this illegal trade, the Japanese garrison at Shanhaiguan attacked, and a major battle broke out at this historic gate where the wall meets the sea. Soon the entire province of Rehe was in Japanese hands, thus completing the conquest of the Northeast. By May, the Japanese had pressed well south of the wall, occupying a large chunk of eastern Hebei province and coming within twenty kilometers of Beiping. With Japanese planes regularly buzzing both Beiping and Tianjin, Chiang Kai-shek was forced to negotiate a truce that demilitarized the area north of the two cities.[42]

The press and many political leaders throughout China responded bitterly to the so-called Tanggu Truce, but Chiang responded forcefully against his domestic opponents, putting down several challenges from patriotic rivals in the south and vigorously suppressing all opposition. Several activists were assassinated, apparently by Chiang's agents, and soon a degree of normalcy returned to relations with Japan. Rail and postal services were resumed with the Japanese puppet regime in Manchuria, and Chinese and Japanese diplomats met in Nanjing to negotiate a new relationship. The Nationalist government prohibited boycotts of Japanese goods and even banned the publication of anti-Japanese articles in the press, though such censorship proved difficult to enforce.

By 1935, the brief relaxation of tensions came to an end. The Japanese stirred up dissident Mongol princes to declare autonomy from China under Japanese protection. In June 1935, they forced the Chinese minister of war, He Yingqin, to agree to withdraw Nanjing's troops and prohibit all anti-Japanese activities in the Beiping-Tianjin area. Still Japanese provocations continued: their military police arrested Chinese officials, their troops carried out threatening maneuvers, and their bombers overflew Beiping. By November, they had engineered the establishment of the East Hebei Anti-Communist Autonomous Council through which pro-Japanese politicians claimed control of the area northeast of Beiping. There was a fatal consistency to Japanese policy each step of the way. In Manchuria, Inner Mongolia, and now north China, the Japanese enticed or coerced collaborators to declare autonomy from the national government in Nanjing and to enter into close economic, political, and military cooperation with Japan's ever-expanding web of imperial operatives. Step by step, the northern regions of China were being drawn under the umbrella of Japanese dominion.[43]

The Chinese student response to this relentless process was far from uniform. Many despaired of finding a solution to China's predicament and fell prey to "pessimism, passivity, and a sense of helplessness and meaninglessness."[44] This passivity of the student majority was much decried by leftists, who attacked their classmates' "nihilism, hedonism, fatalism, and pessimism."[45] The student publications at Tsinghua, which were dominated by left-wing students, were full of such talk, criticizing those who were more concerned about conditions in the dormitories or romantic liaisons than about the national crisis.[46] The left was certainly frustrated by the relative quietude of the student movement after the activism of 1931–32, but we should not assume that the silent majority was completely inured to China's sad fate. The revival of campus activism in 1935 suggests that many students had been heeding their professors' appeals for a long-term program of "saving the nation through study" and were simply waiting for the right opportunity to display their patriotic commitment.[47]

This was certainly the case with Duzheng, who entered Tsinghua in 1935. Duzheng was the scholar of the family, later earning a Ph.D. in atmospheric physics from the University of Chicago. At Tsinghua, he devoted himself to his books and lab work, with Ping-Pong his only notable recreation. Ye Fang and Duzheng roomed together and took many of the same courses. But by the fall of 1935, Ye Fang's political activities were consuming more and more of his time. Several of his friends from the 1934 anti-hazing movement were active leftists and members of the Socialist Alliance. As these political groups became more active in 1935, Ye Fang had difficulty completing the steady stream of homework assignments and lab reports required in his science courses and resorted to copying his younger brother's work to keep up. This strategy worked for a while, but eventually he could not even get to afternoon lab sessions on a regular basis. So Ye Fang abandoned the scientific career for which he had shown such aptitude and switched to history.

Tsinghua had a distinguished history department, whose eminent faculty included the medieval historian Chen Yinque and the modern Chinese historian who chaired the department, Jiang Tingfu; but its curriculum included a heavy dose of European and ancient Chinese history, both of which were quite distant from Ye Fang's contemporary political concerns. Indeed, the modern Chinese history course was not even offered that year, and the Russian history course (which might have attracted a left-wing student) stopped with the Revolution of 1917.[48] In any case, Ye Fang was attracted less to the history curriculum than to the lack of regular homework or lab reports, which gave him more time for political meetings. In fact, he was part of a general pattern: few activists came from the science departments; most majored in the humanities, which allowed more time for the political activities that governed their lives.[49]

The revived student movement in the fall of 1935 was centered in Beiping. Whereas the 1931–32 movement began and found its strongest base in Shanghai, Beiping students took the lead in 1935. Within Beiping, the most important sites of activism were the suburban campuses of Tsinghua and Yenching. At Peking University, the historic breeding ground of student movements since the May Fourth era, a hostile administration and stronger police presence within Beiping's walls made organizing much more difficult. But the suburban isolation of Tsinghua and Yenching, the protective presence of missionary-educators at Yenching, and the counsel and support that the students received from such left-leaning foreign faculty as Edgar Snow and his wife, Helen (Nym Wales), gave some political space for students to organize quietly. In addition, the June 1935 agreements with Japan that He Yingqin had entered into on behalf of the Nanjing government called for the withdrawal of the military police and the anti-Japanese "Blue Shirts," the protofascist Guomindang organization that was the main rival to the student leftists. With the suppression of the Blue Shirts, the government lost its best source of intelligence on leftist students to target for arrest.[50]

Though many of the early leaders of the student movement later became prominent members of the Chinese Communist Party, few were Communists at the time. Place of origin more than party affiliation seemed to motivate the early activists. Students from Manchuria and Hebei province were prominent, driven by a desire to recover their homeland from Japanese domination or protect it from imminent threat. They were incensed by harsh government suppression of patriotic protest, which seemed to them both treasonous appeasement of the aggressor and a fascist denial of civil liberties. Radical student rhetoric caused the government to regard the movement as a Communist plot, but in fact many of the activists—though aware of the similarity between their patriotic ideals and the Communist Party's recent call for a united front against Japan—had yet to make contact with the underground party organization. Still, the more the authorities accused the students of being Communist agents, the more the students became convinced that the party was the only group that truly shared their commitments.

Government surveillance and suppression of student activism accounted for much of the movement's loose organization. If a student were arrested, he or she needed to be able to say that the group had no leader, that it was only a like-minded group of students concerned about the fate of the nation. So the students organized in secret, without open meetings or elected leaders. They first appeared on the scene in November 1935 when they issued a dramatic and inflammatory manifesto decrying the Nanjing government's denial of civil liberties to patriotic students and intellectuals, a manifesto that reached the censored Chinese press first through foreign reports from the United Press, and then from newspapers in the treaty ports that picked up the story. Soon the protesters formed a federation of student groups from colleges and middle schools in Beiping, but the organization was still a self-selected core, with no claim to represent the formally constituted student unions at the various schools.

In December 1935, the minister of war, He Yingqin, returned to Beiping to manage the crisis with Japan, and the students used his visit as the occasion to act. At dawn on December 9, an overcast Monday morning, bugle calls roused the Tsinghua and Yenching students from their sleep. The previous night, activists in each dorm had advised the students of a planned demonstration. As a result, some one thousand students from Yenching and Tsinghua, fully half the enrollment of the two schools, assembled on their respective campuses and then set out across the barren fields to walk the six miles to Beiping. Ye Fang was one of the organizers, but his studious younger brother, Duzheng, recognized that this demonstration was important enough to abandon his courses for a day, and he too joined the march. Bundled up in cotton-padded coats against the winter cold (or even fur coats for some Yenching co-eds), the group belied the axiom that youth only demonstrate in the warm weather of spring. Avoiding the main roads where the police might block their progress, they reached the walls of Beiping around noon but found all of the gates securely locked. Inside the walls, students from colleges and middle schools in the city had also been roused to take to the streets, but the two groups were never able to link up. Eventually, the Tsinghua-Yenching contingent headed back to the two campuses, while those inside the walls attempted to deliver a petition to He

Yingqin. They were met by police and soldiers who beat them with rifle butts and the flat side of large broadswords and then dispersed them with fire hoses, a chillingly effective technique in the subfreezing temperatures of winter.

This was the march that gave its name to the December 9th Movement, but it was only the beginning. On returning to their campuses, the demonstrators declared a student strike and demanded that study of China's national crisis replace the regular curriculum. With campus activities now essentially under the control of the students, they planned an even larger demonstration for a week later. On December 16, the two Ye brothers and hundreds of other students set out again. With a bicycle brigade preceding them as scouts, they repeated their march across the fields to Beiping, but this time they managed to force open a smaller gate across a railway opening and headed for a planned rendezvous in the lower-class entertainment district of Tianqiao. The students had printed handbills to explain their patriotic purpose, which they pressed into the hands of any who came out to watch; but onlookers were distressingly few, most hiding in their houses in fear of the authorities. Subsequent student attempts to organize a boycott of Japanese goods were similarly unsuccessful. Merchants were unwilling to forgo their profits to support the patriots' cause. At this point, the students were clearly several steps ahead of the general population in their national consciousness. Perhaps sensing the students' isolation, the police again fell on the demonstrators, arresting several, beating many, and turning the dreaded fire hoses on the group, though this time the students were prepared and promptly cut the hoses.

The students sent manifestos and news of their protests to the Chinese and foreign press and to schools across the country. As word spread, students by the thousands demonstrated in all of China's major cities and called for boycotts of classes at their schools. In Tianjin, the students marched forth on December 18, two columns snaking out from the schools north and south of the Hai River. At Nankai Middle School, young Fang Shi (who had been arrested earlier that summer for carrying leftist literature) helped organize some eight hundred Nankai students for the demonstration, roughly 80 percent of the student body. Shouting the popular slogans of the day—"Down with Japanese imperialism!" "Oppose north China autonomy!" "Oppose the traitorous capitulationist policy of the Guomindang!" "Chinese should not fight with Chinese!"—they overpowered the police trying to keep the two groups apart and marched on to Nankai for a mass meeting and speeches. As usual, left-wing students were prominent in the leadership, but at the mass meeting, pro-Guomindang students carried the day with a proposal to send a delegation to Nanjing to urge Chiang Kai-shek to stiffen his opposition to the autonomy moves in north China. Once the December 1935 protests moved from the realm of secret plotting to open marches, the ability of the leftists to manipulate the agenda was limited, and the student movement took on a life and direction of its own.[51]

Late in December, Ye Fang joined several hundred students from Tsinghua and

FIGURE 11. Ye Fang with female students, 1935. Family photo.

other Beiping and Tianjin campuses who marched into the countryside to spread their anti-Japanese message to the peasant masses. Each school formed its own company of agitators, which, led by scouts on bicycles (and tailed by plain-clothed police cyclists), traveled from village to village to give speeches, sing songs, perform simple patriotic dramas, and distribute handbills. Usually the local school teacher was receptive, and his young pupils provided an attentive audience, but the peasants listened impassively, and the local authorities were uniformly hostile, often locking the students out of walled towns. The students slept on straw scattered across the floors of schools or temples—men and women in separate rooms—with their bedding carried on ox-carts that followed the dedicated band. When they reached Gu'an county about fifty kilometers south of Beiping, they were joined by the students from Tianjin. There some five hundred students engaged in an animated debate on tactics. They recognized that Manchuria was an unknown land and that "China" was a vague abstraction to most peasants. Burdensome taxes and high interest rates were the peasants' real concerns, and when the students added economic appeals to their message—"Refuse to pay unnecessary taxes!" "Organize to resist the invasion of Japan *and* the encroachment of your landlord!"—they found a much more enthusiastic audience. Some peasants even asked the students to stay and help them organize—which many would return to do after the war with Japan broke out.[52]

The students hoped that their trek would eventually bring them to Nanjing, but in mid-January they were rounded up by police and agents from the provincial government and sent back to their schools. Their propaganda crusade had been too brief to have a lasting effect on the villages through which they passed, but for most of the students, it was a novel experience in the countryside and a lesson that rousing the nation and its rural masses to national resistance was not going to be easy.

Back in Beiping and Tianjin, the students found their schools closed early for vacation—the authorities' response to their class boycott. The administration's hard line continued with a declaration from 164 university and middle-school chancellors calling for "the suppression of such student activities as will tend to upset school order and discipline."[53] In mid-February, the Nanjing government followed with the harsh Emergency Law to Maintain Public Order, which banned all marches and protests and threatened any participants with arrest. At Tsinghua, now a hotbed of political activity and sharp conflict between left- and right-wing students, the situation was complicated by a conflict with the faculty over semester examinations. As Ye Fang's example shows, many student activists were having difficulty keeping up with their studies, so the leftists' call to cancel exams in favor of patriotic "emergency education" was undoubtedly motivated by a degree of self-interest. But here the left clearly overplayed its hand. The faculty insisted on holding the exams, and most students were like Duzheng: they joined the demonstrations and fervently opposed Japanese aggression, but they also wanted to earn their degrees. In the end, the radicals relented, and the examinations were scheduled for February 29.

Now the government overplayed its hand. Before dawn on the twenty-ninth, busloads of police arrived to surround the campus and search the dormitories for radical activists. The day was apparently chosen because all students would be present for the exams, but similar raids had occurred at other Beiping campuses in the preceding days. Forewarned of the danger, the students had posted sentries at the Tsinghua gates, and these lookouts roused their sleeping classmates at the first sign of the police. A throng of students rushed forth to overpower the lawmen, destroying their buses and pelting them with the steamed bread (mantou) they had brought along for lunch.

The students' victory was brief. That evening, a larger force returned to search for forty-seven students on a Public Security list of dangerous activists. All students were herded into the gymnasium, where they were confined until each could be identified and released. Like most leaders of the student movement, Ye Fang had already gone into hiding, but Duzheng was in the gym with the others. A politically savvy classmate (an underground party member, he later learned) approached him with a warning: the two brothers were roommates, and Ye Duzheng's name was very close to Ye Fang's (then still called Ye Dulian). Ye Dulian was likely to be on the list, and Duzheng would be arrested and forced to reveal his brother's activities. So his friend supplied Duzheng with the name and student number of a classmate known to be off-campus. When his turn came, Duzheng used this alias and got through—but not before glancing down and seeing several red circles beside "Ye Dulian" on the policeman's list.[54] The police were not misinformed. On this very day, while hiding with the other leftist leaders, Ye Fang filled in the forms to enroll in the Chinese Communist Party.[55] Thus did the Ye family gain its first official recruit to China's new revolutionary elite.

Through the spring of 1936, a "reign of terror" gripped the Beiping campuses. Arrests and expulsions decimated the ranks of the activists, but the students still managed to mount periodic demonstrations. On March 31, Ye Fang, Duzheng, and their brother Duzhuang (back on spring break from Japan) joined a march in memory of a middle school student who had died in prison, quite possibly as a result of police abuse. Ye Fang also traveled to Shanghai as part of a group seeking to establish a national student union. He met with students from other cities for several days to plan for such a union, but the group never got as far as agreeing on a charter. In Tianjin, their younger brother Fang Shi participated in a march of several thousand students on May 28—a commemoration of the May 30th Incident of 1925, held two days before the anniversary to avoid police interference. As he was distributing leaflets and yelling slogans, a plain-clothed agent approached to ask him about the march's purpose, but the same man had questioned him after the December demonstrations and he knew well enough to ignore his inquiries.

As the 1935–36 school year drew to a close, the student movement was badly fragmented. Most faculty and pro-government students accepted the Nanjing government's argument that although China could never accept Japanese occupation of the Northeast or any long-term "autonomy" of north China, the time had not come for all-out war. The government was urgently building up its military forces and developing a military-industrial complex to support a conflict that it too saw as inevitable, but it needed more time. To the impatient radicals of north China, "This so-called long-term resistance, so-called mature strategies for the country are just the stinking dog-fart theories of a bunch of vulgar dog-shit-eating traitors and VIP scoundrels."[56] Such scatological rhetoric from the Tsinghua student paper (while rare in printed sources) reflected the angry passions of many activist students. But it did not endear them to their elders, and as time passed, more and more voices spoke up for moderation, especially from the Communist Party itself, which sent its top organizer of underground work and later number two man in the party, Liu Shaoqi (1898–1969), to direct party work in the region.

Progressive student writings argued that the time had come to move from symbolic demonstrations to practical action. An editorial in the Tsinghua student paper, "Carrying on the Student Movement," put it this way:

> Now north China is no longer the front line of national defense. It has become the rear area of the enemy. All illusions of peace and tranquility have been smashed to

smithereens. The present stage of the student movement is no longer about 'display-ing' some 'point of view' or 'protesting' some 'policy.' Every student in north China and in all of China should cast off the habit of dreading difficulty and living in a fool's paradise, should enter the ranks of the masses and join the practical efforts of the war for national salvation.[57]

For left-wing students, their practical efforts focused on organizing the Chinese National Liberation Vanguards. The Vanguards grew out of the rural propaganda brigades of January, and during the most intense periods of suppression, their unity was strengthened by rising early each morning for calisthenics, and dining and study-ing together. Both Ye Fang and Fang Shi (the two future Communists) joined the Vanguards, and the organization became the focus of their political activity.

When Ye Duzhuang returned from Japan for summer vacation in 1936, he led the brothers in another practical venture: the Knowledge Bookstore in Tianjin. Duzhuang proposed that the brothers pool funds from their inheritance to open a progressive bookstore in a busy part of Tianjin's French Concession. Though Du-zhuang was officially the manager, the actual operation of the bookstore was in the hands of two underground Communists, one of whom was a former editor at Tian-jin's leading newspaper, the *Dagongbao*. In addition to selling stationery, the book-store sold Communist and progressive literature, acted as north China agent for progressive publishers in Shanghai, and put out its own journal, *International Knowl-edge*. With elegant furnishings and comfortable sofas on which customers could sit and read, the bookstore was quite popular until forced to close by the war, just a year after it had opened. One of the Ye boys' Communist partners, however, may not have been an entirely scrupulous businessman. Later investigations of the vice-manager's activities revealed that he had embezzled funds from his partners to buy jewelry for his wife.[58]


With the students moderating their rhetoric and behavior, and with leftists adher-ing ever more faithfully to the new Chinese Communist Party call for the broadest possible united front, the young radicals slowly began to overcome their isolation. On campus, the Tsinghua leftists easily dominated the 1936 elections for the stu-dent council.[59] When the students in Beiping began shouting slogans to resist the Japanese *and* support the Twenty-ninth Army (the force garrisoning Beiping, which was stiffening its resistance to Japan), the support they received from onlookers (and from soldiers) was in sharp contrast to the passivity that had greeted them in De-cember 1935. During the March 31 demonstrations in Beiping, after the police dis-persed the marching students, Duzhuang and his friend ducked into the nearest courtyard, and the mistress of the household readily concealed them when the gen-darmes came to search.[60]

The change in the popular mood was partly due to the students' more moderate line, but far more important were incessant Japanese provocations. As one observer wrote, "The most effective anti-Japanese propaganda was furnished by the Japanese themselves." Throughout 1936, the Japanese strengthened their garrisons in north China to levels several times those allowed by the Boxer Protocol. At the Fengtai garrison outside Beiping, they added an airfield. In June, they staged a military parade through Beiping, and in November, they practiced an occupation of the old capital, with Japanese army tanks lumbering through the streets. The Japanese military seemed to be doing everything possible to antagonize the population, and sympathy for the Nanjing government's appeasement policy simply evaporated.[61]

The dramatic breakthrough came with the Xi'an Incident of December 1936. Xi'an was the capital of Shaanxi province, in the northern portion of which Mao Zedong and the Red Army had established their base at the end of the Long March. Confronting the Communist armies was the Northeast army of Zhang Xueliang, which Chiang Kai-shek had ordered to the area after its retreat from Manchuria. To these soldiers, Chiang's slogan "to repel the invaders we must first have internal pacification" rang hollow. Their homeland had been lost. They wished to fight the Japanese, not other Chinese. As the Chinese Communists moderated their own policies, downplaying class struggle in favor of a united front against Japan, the Northeast army's will to attack them crumbled. The two armies began fraternizing across the battle lines, and Zhang Xueliang began secret talks with Communist emissaries. At the same time, Zhang Xueliang, as titular head of Northeast University, moved the school from Beiping to Xi'an. Soon these Northeastern students, who had eagerly participated in the December 9th Movement, were demonstrating in Xi'an for a united front of all Chinese against Japan.

Chiang Kai-shek, meanwhile, was secretly pursuing a complex mix of conflicting strategies to confront the national crisis. On the one hand, his agents were meeting with Communist emissaries representing both Mao Zedong and Stalin (the USSR being the most likely source of aid in the event of a Japanese attack) in hopes of reaching some settlement of the civil war; on the other hand, he ordered maximum pressure on the Communists in Shaanxi to strengthen his hand in the negotiations or (he hoped) wipe out Mao's forces if the talks failed. All this plotting failed disastrously when Chiang Kai-shek flew to Xi'an to order the Northeast army to press the attack on the Communists. As students protesting Chiang's policies filled the streets, Zhang Xueliang, on December 12, placed the Generalissimo under arrest. The "kidnapping" of Chiang caused a brief but intense national crisis, which ended with Chiang's oral agreement to Zhang's demands to terminate the civil war and unite all forces to resist Japan. Zhang Xueliang spent the next sixty years in confinement for his insubordination, but the campaign against the Communists ended, and China moved irreversibly toward a united front against Japan. The era of appeasement was over.[62]

War with Japan was now just a matter of time, and the younger Ye boys began to make appropriate preparations. Ye Fang was now a member of the Communist Party, and the party decided his course. Early in 1937, he left school and traveled west to the neighboring province of Shanxi, where Yan Xishan (1883–1960), the local warlord, was making peace with patriotic leftist forces in order to confront the approaching Japanese. Yan sponsored the formation of the Sacrifice League, whose leaders included the Communist activist Bo Yibo (1908–2007), released from prison to aid the national struggle. Ye Fang was among the young patriots who joined the Sacrifice League, adding youthful energy to Yan Xishan's regime.[63]

In the summer of 1937, Ye Duzhuang packed up his books in Tokyo and headed home. In Tianjin, he devoted his energies to the Knowledge Bookstore, and then he too headed to Shanxi to establish a link with progressive book dealers there. He met with Bo Yibo and other Communists, including, of course, his brother, and was there when war broke out in July.

Fang Shi graduated from Nankai in 1936 and went on to National Beiping University's College of Law and Commerce, where he devoted much of his energy to political activities. He had already joined the Communist front organization, the Chinese National Liberation Vanguards and was responsible for organizing middle school students in the vicinity of the college. His recruits included several young girls from a nearby middle school, including one who became his wife a few years later. In 1937 their relationship was strictly political, but the fact that politics had brought them together was a sign of change in youthful gender relations.

One writer has observed that among Chinese youths in the 1930s, "the outcry for individual development" that characterized the May Fourth Movement had "changed to one of collective struggle."[64] This statement certainly applies to the younger Ye brothers. On the eve of the war with Japan, Ye Duzhuang, Ye Fang, and Fang Shi had all either joined the Communist Party or were working closely with its front organizations. Even the studious science major, Ye Duzheng, though he stuck to his academic career, was active in the student demonstrations and always on the edge of more intense political involvement. However, these tendencies affected only those who were in school as the national crisis intensified. The three older brothers, Duren, Duyi, and Duxin, were already out of school by this time, married and working in Tianjin. The intense politicization of college life had little effect on them. As for the older sisters, all trapped in unhappy arranged marriages, there was little question of either individual development or collective struggle. Denied the opportunity even to attend school by their conservative father, they were part of a generation of women that enjoyed none of the liberating effects of student life. Thus did the effects of age and gender intersect with the broad currents of social change as China sat poised for war with Japan.

# 10

## War

In the hot sticky summer of 1937, the students of Tsinghua University were undergoing military training on the outskirts of Beiping. It was not Ye Duzheng's first experience with the army. During the winter vacation of 1936–37, he had traveled to Shanxi with a couple hundred Beiping students for training in a "student army." His involvement was as much personal as political: he was following a girlfriend, a Tsinghua classmate who was deeply embroiled in left-wing politics. In Shanxi, the students received political education and basic military training, including their first live-ammunition firing of real weapons. The growing threat of Japanese aggression had made military drill a regular feature of student life. Back in Beiping in July, Duzheng was again drilling under the direction of a patriotic officer of the Twenty-ninth Army garrisoned in the old capital when their commander came with news of serious fighting with the Japanese south of Beiping. With the sound of artillery booming in the distance, the students headed back to Tsinghua to collect their belongings, then scattered before the advancing Japanese troops.

July 7, 1937, was a watershed in modern Chinese history. On that date, the Japanese army was engaged in night maneuvers near the Marco Polo Bridge, a crucial rail junction controlling Beiping's communications with the south. Someone fired on the Japanese soldiers, and a fierce firefight erupted with Chinese forces in a nearby walled town. A local solution to the incident was soon negotiated, and for a time, the encounter seemed no different from scores of minor skirmishes provoked by the Japanese army's aggressive maneuvers in north China. This time, however, both the Japanese government in Tokyo and Chiang Kai-shek's Nanjing regime were unwilling to make concessions to preserve a fragile peace. Even before the local settlement was reached, Tokyo mobilized five divisions for dispatch to China. Chiang, meanwhile, began moving his own forces north along the railway. Soon China and Japan were engaged in a full-scale war that would last for eight long bloody years.[1]

The consequences of the war were enormous. For all its failings, Chiang Kai-shek's Nationalist regime had made remarkable progress in the prewar decade. It had united the country, unified the Nationalist Party around an authoritarian version of Sun Yat-sen's legacy, strengthened the military, reformed the legal system, established municipal governments, extended the railway network, built roads, reformed the currency system, promoted industry, extended education, and promulgated health and labor regulations. Though many rural areas in the interior were scarcely touched by these reforms, efforts to modernize the economic, political, military, financial, and legal system were moderately effective in the coastal cities and the lower Yangzi valley, where the Nationalists' power was greatest.[2] The outbreak of war wiped away all of these gains, as Japan occupied the coastal cities and main railway lines, driving the Nationalists into the less-developed interior. Eventually Chiang Kai-shek would establish his wartime capital in Chongqing, on the banks of the Yangzi River in Sichuan province.

In the early years of the war, the United Front between the Nationalists and Communists worked reasonably well. The national government recognized and gave financial assistance to the Communist government in northern Shaanxi and to its Eighth Route and New Fourth armies. The Communists established an office and newspaper in Chongqing, and an office in Xi'an served as an assembly point for students headed for the Communists' schools in Yan'an or armies in north China. For a brief time, political differences were put aside as patriotic students and intellectuals of all stripes worked together in propaganda teams to rally the nation to resist the Japanese invaders.[3] But even the national crisis could not erase the memory of a decade of civil war. Mutual suspicion ran deep, and in the rural areas behind Japanese lines, each party sought to establish its own regime with its own army and exclusive control. By January 1941, a major clash erupted between Communist and Nationalist forces in the New Fourth Army Incident, bringing an effective end to the United Front.[4]

By the time the United States entered the war following Japan's attack on Pearl Harbor on December 7, 1941, China was effectively divided into three zones: the Japanese-occupied areas in the east, where a puppet government was installed under the former Nationalist Party leader Wang Jingwei; the Nationalist areas in the west and much of south-central China; and the Communist region in the north, including rural areas behind Japanese lines. Chiang Kai-shek's forces were always much larger and better armed than the Communists, having received extensive aid from the Soviet Union in the early war years and from the United States after 1941. But the Nationalists suffered the most from frontal assaults by the Japanese, and became increasingly passive and riddled with corruption as the war dragged on. The Communists, by contrast, launched small-scale guerrilla attacks on Japanese

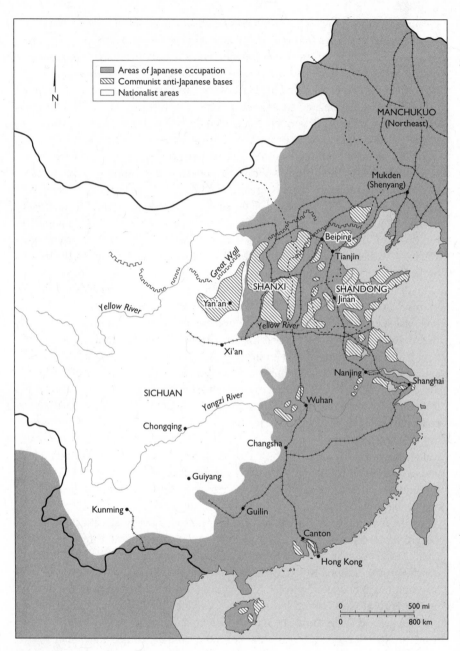

MAP 2. China at war, c. 1944.

outposts and puppet forces as they expanded their rural bases behind Japanese lines. In the opening months of the war, the Nationalist government simply collapsed in much of north China, and the Communists became the main force waging anti-Japanese resistance. As they carried out popular economic policies to reduce tax, rent, and debt burdens on the poor, they earned widespread popular support and greatly expanded the rural areas under their control. By the end of the war, the Communists commanded armies with over a million men (having begun the war with fewer than forty thousand poorly armed soldiers) and controlled roughly ninety million people. Momentum in the long political competition between Nationalists and Communists had shifted irreversibly in the Communists' favor.[5]

In retrospect, these consequences of the war are clear. At the time, nothing was clear. Even as fighting spread after 1937, the Nanjing and Tokyo governments continued negotiations to resolve the conflict. In Chinese domestic politics, the United Front against Japan blurred internal conflicts and led to a vast array of local configurations of political competition and cooperation. The confusion within north China was mirrored in the movements of the Ye brothers, whose paths crisscrossed much of the country as they sought an appropriate outlet for their patriotic passions.

In time, out of all this confusion, each of the brothers found the personal commitment and institutional home that would govern the rest of his life. In this sense, the war years were decisive on a personal level. In part, this was simply a product of age: most of the brothers were in their twenties and at a point in life when critical life decisions are made. But the progressive hardening of political divisions during the war years meant that a path once chosen—to join the Chinese Communist Party or the Nationalists, to follow an academic career or work with liberal intellectuals in the Democratic League—would have a decisive impact on one's prospects for the future.

All of the Ye brothers passed through Tianjin in the first weeks of the war. They stayed at their eldest brother's house in the safety of the foreign concessions; but for the younger ones, it was less a home than a convenient place to hold political meetings with activist classmates before heading off to join the resistance against Japan. Duzhuang, home on vacation from Japan, was in Shanxi on July 7, then passed through Beiping and Tianjin on his way to Shanghai. Returning to Tokyo to finish his degree in agriculture was never an option. His Knowledge Bookstore was closed down, a farewell notice on the door attracting a small crowd. Ye Fang had returned from his party assignment to Shanxi, where he had contracted pneumonia. He, like Duzheng and Fang Shi, stayed quietly in Beiping for a few weeks in July before taking the train to Tianjin. Significantly, after gathering in Tianjin, each of the boys left with his own group of friends and classmates—the bonds of school and political struggle now stronger than those of family. The contrast to the 1850s, when Ye Kunhou and his family fled the Taiping together, was unmistakable. None of the brothers had a clear sense of where he was going, just somewhere to join the resistance. None had any idea how long the war would last. Each took some money and a change of clothes, but Duzheng ignored his leftist girlfriend's savvy advice to bring along winter clothing.

The oldest three brothers stayed in Tianjin. They were all married and had jobs, and two were starting to raise families. The eldest brother's first son had just been born, and he lived comfortably through the war in his wife's house in the British Concession, supported by his job at the bank. The fourth brother, Duxin, never had children but worked first as an accountant at the Kailan coal mines, and then when tuberculosis forced him to quit, spent the rest of the wartime and postwar years as a stock speculator in Beiping, sometimes nearly penniless, eventually borrowing from his wife's relatives and making enough money to live in some comfort.[6] Duyi, the only college graduate among them, briefly joined Fang Shi and his friends in Shandong, but they urged him to return to his family, his first child (a daughter) having just been born.[7] He went back to his secure and gainful job with the British Kailan mines, and two more daughters were born in quick succession. With the outbreak of the Pacific War in 1941, the Japanese took over the mines, and Duyi quit and moved to Beiping, where he shared a courtyard with his third sister. He eked out a living teaching English, but his income was not enough to support his family, which by the end of the war included four children, a son having been added in 1944. This son marked the end of Duyi's procreative life, and in the ensuing years, each parent shared a single bed with one of the children. Cramped into a single room, the family survived on a diet that included meat perhaps once a week, with cornmeal substituting for wheat flour. This way of life was particularly difficult for Duyi's wife, given her wealthy and privileged upbringing. In the end, she had to sell stocks and jewelry from her dowry to support the family, and in later years, she often reminded her husband of this sacrifice on their behalf. The issue became a constant source of friction in their always troubled marriage.[8]

The older sisters stayed with their husbands in Tianjin and Beiping. The youngest sister, Durou, was at Nankai Girls School when the war broke out, but in the early days of the conflict, the Japanese bombed Nankai—a provocative act of revenge against this hotbed of patriotic activity—and the school was forced to close and relocate to the interior. Durou continued her studies in the Tianjin concessions for a time, then went on to the Catholic Furen girls' school in Beiping. Having commuted to Nankai, she had difficulty adjusting to dormitory life and resented the compulsory classes in Japanese. More importantly, she had fallen in love with Yao Zengyi, Duyi's best friend from Yenching, whose sister had grown up in the Ye household and who often stayed there in the summers. In his usual old-fashioned way, her big brother tried to arrange an alternative match with a local banker, but Durou resisted and halfway through the war, she married Yao in a large formal ceremony in Beiping. She was the only Ye sister to receive formal schooling and the only one to marry for love.

Also staying in occupied China was the youngest brother, Dushen, the black sheep of the family. Born in 1924, he was seven years junior to Duzheng and Fang Shi (his closest male siblings) and only six years old when his father died. As the fatherless youngest child, he was spoiled by his mother, Miss Liu (always the more indulgent of the two consorts), and incurably naughty. He abused the young servants, shot rubber bands at Bad-Breath Yuan in the home school, and ran from the room when disciplined. As a teenager, he chafed under his eldest brother's attempts to control him and openly challenged the privileged status of his father's wife, not hesitating to point out that the two concubines had borne all the children. After his father's death, he attended a local primary school for several years, once enlisting a servant in a crude attempt to alter the poor marks on his report card. By the age of twelve, he became fascinated by the demimonde of popular entertainment. An opera staged for the sixtieth birthday of his father's widow had enthralled him, and after dinner he would listen to the storytellers and popular ballads on the radio that his eldest brother's wife had brought with her dowry. Soon he was cutting school to hang out at the teahouses where these entertainers performed, currying favor with the waitresses and actors by sending gifts in the manner of a wealthy young gentleman, borrowing and memorizing their scripts instead of completing his classical lessons, and occasionally performing for fun.

Proper Chinese have long regarded actors and entertainers as the dregs of society, banning them (with their descendants) from the examination system for much of the imperial period. Though many members of the elite enjoyed the more refined forms of what would later be called Peking Opera, the acting profession was associated with vulgar (and popular) performances and questionable moral standards.[9] The Ye family tried everything it could to save Dushen from his fascination. During the war years, he was sent to high school in Beiping. There too, he slipped away to the popular entertainment quarter, and he dropped out in his junior year. Up to this time, the family had supported him, but now Dushen demanded independence and his share of the family inheritance. In general, he had as little contact with his elder brother as possible. On this occasion, Duren presented him with a bundle of stock certificates and cash wrapped in a newspaper. Without even counting the money, the young rebel said "Fine! Goodbye!" and turned on his heel and left.

Then just eighteen, Dushen left home for good. He moved to the fancy International Hotel in the concession area, went nightly to consort with his actor friends, and within a year, spent his entire ten thousand dollars. During this time, he was formally accepted as a pupil of a leading comic, given a stage name (Ye Lizhong), and taught his trade: storytelling, comic dialogues, and popular opera. He was very good, showing a natural talent for memorizing lengthy monologues and impressing the local professionals. His eldest brother, however, could not accept Dushen's choice, and he posted a notice in the local newspaper renouncing all responsibility for his younger brother's activities. By this time, the sixth and ninth brothers were already Communists, but that fact had not kept Duren from sheltering them in Tianjin as they fled the Japanese invasion. Dushen (or Ye Lizhong, as he now was called) was a different kind of rebel. His lifestyle and chosen vocation set him apart, and they ultimately got him expelled from the family.

While Ye Lizhong, his sisters, and the three eldest brothers stayed in occupied China, the four middle brothers all headed for the interior. Each went his own way, and the choices they made in the next few years would affect them for the rest of their lives. Duzheng, the science major from Tsinghua, took the train south to Jinan in Shandong, then on to Nanjing. When the national capital was threatened by the Japanese advance that would culminate in the infamous Rape of Nanjing, he went back to Shandong to rejoin his girlfriend. From there, the two headed south again, to Changsha, the capital of Hunan province in the central Yangzi region, where Tsinghua was establishing a temporary wartime campus. But Duzheng decided not to stay in school, and soon the pair was off again, joining a group of students in Xi'an. In nearby Lintong, site of Zhang Xueliang's kidnapping of Chiang Kai-shek just a year earlier, these students organized a patriotic youth propaganda corps. Their little troupe traveled through both Nationalist and Communist areas of Shaanxi province, giving speeches in towns, performing patriotic skits, urging the population to support the war effort. This life was hard on these urban students, who walked most of the way and lived on millet gruel and pickled vegetables.

By early 1938, the group had joined the National Liberation Vanguard, and it was sent to do propaganda work with the Nationalist army in southern Shanxi province. The Japanese had occupied much of the north China plain, and the mountains of Shanxi were a crucial front line of the national resistance. The National Liberation Vanguard was a Communist front organization, but in the chaotic early years of the war, cooperation between Communist and Nationalist organizations was fairly common, and the imperiled Shanxi governor was happy to accept eager young volunteers for the war effort. The students were issued two army uniforms and a mathematics and another general textbook, with the expectation that they would continue their studies while working to raise the national consciousness and morale of the troops.

Duzheng's involvement in the Vanguards always had two sides. On the one hand, he was motivated by the same patriotism that had moved him to march in the December 9th demonstrations. On the other hand, he was drawn by his romantic attraction to an activist coed in the group. The two had known each other since their Tsinghua days, and he was first smitten by her when she unexpectedly offered him a fresh tomato on a hot day. By the outbreak of the war, their relationship was serious enough for her to suggest marriage, but Duzheng demurred, feeling they were still too young. He first wanted to finish his studies. With the Vanguards in Shanxi, the males and females were in separate camps, and she had wept when they parted. One night, word came that the women's camp was threatened by a Japanese advance, and Duzheng was sent out in the dead of night to walk fifty kilometers to warn them. Through the night and the next day he hiked past successive defensive lines being set up by the army. When he reached the last Chinese position, still far from his destination, he proceeded from village to village, picking up local guides to lead him each step of the way. Fortunately, the Vanguards' propaganda work had been fairly successful, and the peasants willingly led him along. Eventually he reached the women's camp, only to find that the Japanese were still some twenty-five kilometers away and not moving any closer.

Duzheng's relief that his girlfriend was safe was quickly shattered by an unexpected blow. She had another boyfriend and told Duzheng their relationship was over: "You want to be a scientist. I want to make revolution." Later he learned that she was already an underground party member, and because he had indicated that he did not wish to join the CCP, her superiors had suggested that their relationship was inappropriate. Her new friend was apparently another Communist and a more suitable match. This rejection was a harbinger of the new age that was dawning. Political lines were being drawn ever more sharply and starting to affect the most personal decisions. Duzheng was devastated. Exhausted and distraught, he wept and slept for much of the next day, then headed back to his own group.

Once back with the Vanguards, Duzheng realized that his life had reached a turning point. With the end of his college romance, his appetite for revolution was sapped. He left the young activist group and made his way back to Xi'an, where he ran into his agronomist brother, Duzhuang, at the railroad station. In their brief and unexpected encounter, Duzhuang urged his younger brother to go back to school. A good student at China's best technical university, he had a promising academic career ahead of him. So he boarded a train to Wuhan, then a boat up the Yangzi to the wartime capital in Chongqing. Each step of the way, Duzheng managed to link up with friends or acquaintances from whom he borrowed money and gained companionship. Eventually he made his way to Kunming, where Southwest United University had been formed from the fleeing faculty and students of Tsinghua, Nankai, and Peking universities.[10] There he resumed his studies in the fall of 1938. The break with his girlfriend left him depressed by politics, and this time he devoted himself completely to his studies and stayed clear of political activists. He would maintain this attitude for the rest of his career.

When Ye Duzhuang met his brother in the Xi'an train station, he too had just returned from the front lines in Shanxi. Duzhuang's journey to Shanxi has been typically circuitous. He left Tianjin in a great hurry, having been warned that Japanese agents were looking to arrest him as the registered manager of a left-wing bookstore.

He asked his eldest brother to liquidate all his stocks and send the money to Shanghai. Carrying only a small suitcase, he took the train to Shanghai, where he retrieved the remaining two thousand dollars of his inheritance and immediately donated five hundred dollars to a patriotic newspaper. In Shanghai, he witnessed the horrific battle for control of that city, including a furious and destructive bombing campaign. Against China's largest city and key commercial and industrial center, Japan initiated a tactic that would become a staple of modern warfare, launching devastating air raids against the civilian population and economic infrastructure.[11] One day when Duzhuang joined a crowd watching the air battle over the Japanese portion of the concessions, an errant bomb fell on a spot he had just vacated, killing hundreds of innocent civilians and leaving blood and body parts spread over the street. War was no longer an abstract ideal of repelling aggression; death and destruction were now close at hand.

In Shanghai, Duzhuang joined some student acquaintances who had just returned from Japan. Through their connections, the young men got a pass to take a small boat out of the Shanghai war area—though their decision to take a group photo on leaving the city led to a brief detention for suspicious photography in a military zone. They gladly surrendered the film and were impressed by the professionalism of the Nationalist army in Shanghai, feelings that grew stronger when a troop train of well-armed and disciplined reinforcements arrived at the station and responded enthusiastically to patriotic speeches by the young students. For years, Duzhuang had vigorously criticized Chiang Kai-shek's Nationalist regime for its failure to combat imperialism, but in these first days of the war, a sense of unified resistance to Japanese aggression overwhelmed all previous differences.[12]

From Suzhou, Duzhuang and his friends took a train north to Kaifeng in Henan, where he obtained an introduction to the office of the Communists' Eighth Route Army in Xi'an. With the outbreak of war, the Red Army had been renamed and recognized as part of China's national army, and it was allowed to open offices in several Chinese cities for recruitment and logistical support. The office in Xi'an was the most important, for it served as the gateway through which thousands of young Chinese traveled to the Communist headquarters in Yan'an and other areas controlled by the Eighth Route Army. In Xi'an, Duzhuang learned that the front lines desperately needed men with Japanese-language ability. His two years studying in Tokyo provided ideal qualifications, so he immediately went with a small group to Shanxi.[13]

After crossing the rushing torrents of the Yellow River in a small boat that creaked and groaned with every wave, he boarded a freight car on the narrow-gauge rail line to the provincial capital. The journey was slow, with frequent long stops. At one station, the group met a train filled with wounded soldiers from the local warlord's army. The soldiers' train had taken six days to travel 250 kilometers, and the dressings on their wounds had not been changed for days. When Duzhuang overheard one soldier ask plaintively, "Do you want us to recover or not?" he was distressed by the indifferent care given those who had fought for their country. Later, traveling by truck, he passed a demoralized band of retreating soldiers, and the contrast between Shanxi's Nationalist armies and the well-trained and disciplined troops on the Shanghai front was stark indeed.

The Shanxi headquarters of the Eighth Route Army assigned Duzhuang to the 129th Division, which was then fighting in the southeastern corner of the province. The journey to join his unit took many days, on foot, usually leaving before dawn and often traveling forty or fifty kilometers a day over mountain paths. The route passed through the Taihang mountain range, which runs along the western edge of the north China plain. The peasants were extremely poor, many supplementing their meager diet with husks from the harvested grain. From their bases in the mountains, the Communists waged guerrilla warfare against the enemy on the plains below and along the major communications routes. For such warfare, the support of the local population was essential, to provide intelligence on enemy movements and conceal guerrilla activities. In Shanxi, the Communists were operating far from their old bases, and relations with the local peasantry were mixed. In some villages, Duzhuang found morale high and the peasants ready to offer assistance. In others, especially where the Japanese had recently destroyed nearby villages, peasants were reluctant to help the guerrillas, refusing to provide local guides and even sending them up the wrong path. In general, they assisted the Eighth Route Army far more than they did the Nationalists. One Guomindang unit was so resented for its mistreatment of the local population that the locals led them straight into a Japanese ambush.[14]

Duzhuang joined his unit in early November and was immediately engaged in battle with the Japanese enemy. A fragment of his diary survives from this time and is extremely revealing. The core of the 129th Division was veteran Red Army soldiers, and many of the officers had endured the perilous Long March from central China. They made clear that they regarded the new student recruits from the "White" (Guomindang) areas to be soft and unable to bear up under the hardship of army life. For his part, Duzhuang was annoyed when a sudden movement of the camp in the middle of the night had them crossing a stream where he and others fell in frigid water up to their waists. He thought that building a simple bridge would have been easy. His fall in the stream and the rigors of constant marching left his knee painfully swollen so that he had to bind it to a stick for support when marching. He also suffered from an inflamed ulcer, a severe toothache, and occasional insomnia. Much as he tried to bear the rigors of army life, his periodic complaints did not escape his superiors, who soon concluded that he was not tough enough to endure the adversity of frontline combat.

Duzhuang had been sent to the front because, after two years of study in Japan, he had a rare and valuable command of the Japanese language. His job was to translate captured documents, interrogate prisoners, and teach the troops to yell in Japanese: "Give up your weapons and you won't be killed! Prisoners will be treated well." But Duzhuang was frustrated by this purely "technical" work and bored by long periods of inactivity between battles when there were no new documents or prisoners. Within a month, he had written his superior asking to resign or be reassigned. His request was forwarded to the division political section, where a cadre met him to convey its negative reaction. Duzhuang wrote in his diary that the officer "used threatening language, laid out a lot of bullshit, just like a bully. He hasn't the manner of a political officer. Why does the Red Army have this sort of useless fellow? I'm so angry I don't know how to write. If the revolution continues like this, we'll be just like ignorant warlords!"[15]

The one person who seemed to understand how to handle this discontented young intellectual was Chen Geng, the commander of the brigade in which Duzhuang was serving. Chen was a veteran Communist from Hunan, having joined the party in 1922 (the year after it was formed), trained at the Guomindang's Whampoa Military Academy during the first United Front, traveled to the Soviet Union, fought in the Chinese soviet bases in the early 1930s, and survived the Long March. He had been wounded several times and sent to Shanghai to recover, so he understood both fierce revolutionary struggle and the treaty-port life from which intellectuals like Duzhuang had emerged.[16] Chen took Duzhuang under his wing, chatting and eating roast chestnuts with him in the evening, telling stories of the Long March, enjoying relatively luxurious meals with occasional pork and chicken, and gradually revealing more of his own life story, even the romances of his youth. He also arranged for Duzhuang to have a young aide prepare his meals and a donkey to carry his belongings. Duzhuang was clearly impressed by the veteran revolutionary and for a time abandoned his intent to resign. However, he once caught Chen Geng flipping through his diary and was hurt and angry at this violation of his privacy and the lack of trust it suggested.

He found more work writing articles for the party newspaper. One notable contribution was "The Glorious War Record of the 129th Division," a fairly long report that was serialized in three successive issues of the paper. Chen Geng had reviewed a draft and asked him to tone down some critical comments about the Guomindang armies, in the interest of protecting the United Front. Even in its published form, the article reflected many of the impressions noted in his diary. It recounted an attack on a Japanese airfield, declaring enthusiastically, "The hope of six years will be realized tonight: let's see if the Japanese devils' skulls are really made of steel!" In Shanxi, of course, the Japanese invasion was only a few months old, but for students like Duzhuang, the aggression had begun in 1931 in Manchuria. Since that time, the Japanese had appeared invincible, and the task of the Eighth Route Army was to convince people that this was not the case. The article described the battle as a great victory, with many Japanese planes destroyed in a sneak night attack, though it acknowledged the "glorious death" of over one hundred men and one company commander. The disparity in the weaponry of the two armies was obvious: Japanese airplanes were destroyed by simple hand grenades, whose explosions ignited their fuel tanks. In the hand-to-hand fighting that followed, the Communists lacked even bayonets on their rifles, and Duzhuang's article included the appeal: "masses in the rear areas: quickly donate thousands of swords."

Duzhuang concluded by commenting on the poor discipline of Guomindang troops from Sichuan, who retreated from a bloody battle that left corpses from both armies covering the mountain each had fought to control (no doubt the section Chen Geng had suggested rephrasing). He included a roseate report of Japanese prisoners, realizing that they had been sent to war in the interests of Japanese monopoly capital. Duzhuang also reported his regret that many peasants failed to support the guerrilla war, saying, "In war, it is always the common people who lose." He correctly perceived an important challenge of the Communists' anti-Japanese struggle: the peasants would not automatically support the national resistance. Indeed, bloody Japanese reprisals might discourage them from aiding the guerrillas. It would take time for the Communists to build support for their movement, to convince the peasants that the party could protect them from Japanese attack (usually by temporary evacuation to secure mountain areas) and improve their livelihood with reforms of the tax and rent systems. Duzhuang's report reminds us of the challenges the Eighth Route Army faced in the opening months of the war, but by the end of the conflict, this area would be securely under Communist control.[17]

Before long, Duzhuang again decided that he had had enough of life at the front and offered his resignation. He appended a draft of the letter to his 1937 diary, and it is a poignant *cri de coeur*. He began by saying that despite the education and training he had received in his months with the Eighth Route Army, his gains were "far from the plans and desires I came with." He wrote as one seeking personal growth through revolutionary struggle, one whose background in China and Japan's elite urban schools "makes it difficult for me to accept this sort of ad hoc education." He confessed to some perplexity: why do we camp here? why do we attack there? why do we retreat now? He was particularly embarrassed when, in the heat of one battle, others felt they needed to take care of him. "All of this experience with the army leaves me feeling like a person without sight or hearing. On the battlefield I feel like a mule—a mule carrying no burden, being led about by someone running from place to place. This is what hurts me the most." With his lack of experience in guerrilla struggle, he felt like a "superfluous soldier with an empty title" who should be sent to receive proper training in the rear areas.

"Comrades, please believe me!" the letter continues. "Although I am not a Communist Party member, I am a communist, loyal to communism to the end. I fear no difficulty. Although I did not pass over the Snowy Mountains or the Grasslands [on the Long March], with my firm political beliefs and goals, I can endure all the physical suffering that other comrades can. All I ask is to be able to achieve those things that give meaning to my life. If I lose those ideals, it will hurt more than death itself." Then, in an abrupt shift, he admits that after one battle, an old ulcer had acted up again: there was blood in his feces, and he had vomited blood. Now he suffered from insomnia and he asked a chance to rest. So he requested an introduction to study at Resistance University, the Communists' cadre training school in Yan'an, or directions to get back to Xi'an. Though embarrassed to do so, he made this sincere request "for the sake of the revolution."[18]

Here was a young man who wanted so much to serve the revolution, to serve the communist cause in which he had come to believe. But after years of relatively privileged existence as a student in China's elite schools and in Japan, life at the front with a guerrilla army was more than his body could endure. Chen Geng realized that students like Duzhuang with Japanese-language ability and higher education were an invaluable resource for the Eighth Route Army, but other veteran Communists obviously found them a burden to look after and unsuited to revolutionary struggle. So Duzhuang left the front. His request to study in Yan'an was not approved. He went first to Xi'an, to recover from his ulcer and knee injury, and then to a series of jobs in the rear areas. Although each step of his journey was governed less by design than by chance and his prickly personality, his wartime activities moved steadily westward and away from the front, and ever closer to the Nationalist government and its American allies.

Duzhuang first served at a cadre training school in southwestern Shanxi, where he taught Japanese and classes on politics and "enemy work": how to handle prisoners and how to demoralize the enemy through propaganda. A prime example of the usefulness of this work was his fellow language teacher, Yoshida, a captured soldier who had been treated well and persuaded to aid the Chinese resistance. Yoshida had been an ordinary worker in Osaka, and Duzhuang's task was to teach him Japanese history from a Marxist perspective, helping him to understand the roots of Japanese imperialism. The school mostly trained former students as political officers for the New Army that Yan Xishan had formed from activists in the left-wing Sacrifice League. Many of the teachers were Communists, and Duzhuang included some of Mao Zedong's recent essays in his courses.

In the fall of 1939, the United Front in Shanxi broke down. Governor Yan Xishan and his conservative officers felt threatened by the growing strength and popularity of the Communists and ordered the cadre school closed. Duzhuang went back to Shaanxi, where he crossed paths with his brother Fang Shi (by then, secretly, a CCP member) before they went their separate ways. For the next few years, he bounced from place to place and job to job, never able to find a stable affiliation in the shifting alliances of the early war years. He taught at several schools in Shaanxi and soon fell in with a contingent of foreign leftists who had fled to the interior. One of these activists was working for the Communist International and recruited

Duzhuang to go to Harbin, a city in northern Manchuria with a substantial Russian population, to spy on the Japanese. But the foreign recruiter proved a clumsy agent: his letters were intercepted, he was arrested, and the plan never came to anything. By the winter of 1940, Duzhuang had moved to Chongqing, the seat of Chiang Kai-shek's national government. Chongqing was the target of repeated Japanese bombing raids in the early war years, and from his room on the south bank, Duzhuang would look across the Yangzi River at people fleeing to underground shelters as the planes approached, and witness the fires and destruction that followed each raid.[19]

In Chongqing, Duzhuang first worked in a left-wing press agency as a writer. He stayed there for a few months, receiving room and board but no salary, then shifted to the Chinese Industrial Cooperatives (Indusco), an effort to organize craftsmen into cooperatives to support the war effort. Indusco received substantial publicity and support from Chinese and foreign liberals and leftists and was much favored by those seeking a middle road between the conservative authoritarianism of the Nationalists and the Marxist socialism of the CCP.[20] Duzhuang edited the organization's newsletter for a time but found the work boring. One day the printers used a wrong character in his boss's name, and Duzhuang simply corrected the printed copies in red pencil. The head reprimanded him for not catching the typo earlier, and Duzhuang quit on the spot. He was not very good at accepting criticism.

From Indusco, Duzhuang went to an intelligence office jointly operated by the Nationalist Army and the Soviet Union. In the early years of the war, China's best ally was the USSR. Japanese imperial ideology treated Communism and the Soviet Union as the greatest threat to Japan's domination of East Asia, and Russia responded by offering military support (especially air cover) to the Chinese resistance. To assist their operations, the Russians established a special intelligence unit on Japan's activities in China. It kept track of casualties in the Japanese officer corps and translated right-wing publications from Japan. Duzhuang was given officer rank in the Nationalist army, but he also smuggled out useful intelligence to pass to the Communists, thanks to the lax security in the unit. By 1941, however, as the USSR felt increasingly threatened by Germany, it signed a nonaggression pact with Japan and withdrew its units from China. With the Soviet withdrawal, Duzhuang was unwilling to work with a purely Chinese Nationalist agency, and he left this job as well.

Duzhuang's next step was to start a business—an improbable move for this longtime critic of capitalism—but his company, Taiping Enterprises, Ltd., was formed at the suggestion of an underground Communist acquaintance, with the idea that it might prove a useful front for left-wing activities. Much of the capital came from Duzhuang's remaining inheritance and that of the other three middle brothers, Ye Fang, Duzheng, and Fang Shi, which was wired by their brother in Tianjin, presumably through Hong Kong. Taiping Enterprises was basically a trading company, with plans to hoard oil and other commodities in anticipation of price increases.

But none of the participants had any business experience, and the company barely made enough money to support Duzhuang and his colleagues. On one occasion, traveling to Guilin to make a deal, Duzhuang failed to make contact with the local agent and ended up selling his clothes to feed himself. In the end, he was reduced to the status of a petty trader, selling rubber shoes in one town, Hunan embroidery in another.

In the final year of the war, Duzhuang made two contacts that would have a fateful impact on his later life. In October 1944, he joined the Democratic League. A newly formed alliance of liberal intellectuals and politicians, the Democratic League was highly critical of the growing corruption and dictatorial tendencies of Chiang Kai-shek's Nationalist government. In the late 1940s, it would become increasingly supportive of the Chinese Communists, and indeed a number of its members were secret Communists. It was a natural political home for a progressive individualist like Ye Duzhuang, and he remained active in the League for most of his public life. In 1944–45, he edited a League publication, the *People's Weekly*.

He also met the American journalist Graham Peck, who in turn introduced him to other Americans in China. Peck was a liberal journalist who served in the U.S. Office of War Information during the war. He and Duzhuang would live together in Beiping after the war, while Peck was writing *Two Kinds of Time*, a highly critical account of wartime China under Nationalist rule. Peck introduced Duzhuang to liberal friends in the U.S. Army, which was then under the command of General Joseph Stilwell. When America entered World War II in December 1941 following Japan's attack on Pearl Harbor, Stilwell was sent to manage U.S. assistance to China's war against the common enemy. This involved supplying arms and equipment flown over "the Hump" from India and later carried by truck over the Burma Road; in addition, American military advisors were to retrain Nationalist Government troops. Stilwell was a salty field commander who was accustomed to speaking bluntly. As the war drew on, he became convinced that Chiang Kai-shek's army was riddled with corruption and that Chiang was withholding his best troops from the battle with Japan in order to prepare for a postwar showdown with the Chinese Communists. Allied war plans before the testing of the atom bomb involved driving Japan's armies from the Asian mainland and then attacking the Japanese home islands. Eager for dedicated forces to carry out this strategy, Stilwell became increasingly interested in working with the Chinese Communists to defeat the Japanese in north China. As politically sensitive Chinese became aware of the tensions between Chiang and Stilwell, they began to look on the U.S. Army with unusual favor. Even Mao Zedong, speaking to Stilwell's representatives in Yan'an, described American soldiers in China as an "advertisement for democracy," adding, "We welcome them in China for this reason."[21]

In March 1945, far to the south, Japanese occupation forces in Vietnam, then a part of French Indochina, cracked down on French expatriates cooperating with the resistance. The ripple effects of this distant operation had fateful consequences for Duzhuang. Caught up in the crackdown was an Allied intelligence unit known as GBT, which operated with the support of British intelligence and the U.S. Office of Strategic Services (OSS), the wartime predecessor of the CIA. Having lost most of its French agents, GBT turned to Asians to fill its ranks. The Office of War Information seems to have suggested many of the new recruits, who were often people of the left. In Vietnam, the most famous of these was Ho Chi Minh. In China, a far less prominent member of the team was Ye Duzhuang.[22] He cleared his decision to join the OSS team with a CCP agent in the Democratic League, but this wartime service with U.S. intelligence would later come back to haunt him. After training in telegraphy and code, he worked in the southwest reporting on the disposition of Japanese and Nationalist Chinese forces. GBT also worked with the U.S. Army's Air Ground Aid Service (AGAS), a division of military intelligence (G-2) devoted to rescuing U.S. airmen downed after bombing runs over Japan.[23] In the final months of the war, Duzhuang flew with AGAS to Inner Mongolia as an interpreter for a team seeking to rescue downed U.S. airmen in north China. When the war ended in August 1945, the team was ordered to the Beiping area, to release American prisoners of war. By this time, American relations with the Chinese Communists had cooled substantially. At Chiang Kai-shek's insistence, Stilwell had been recalled, and American policy tilted back toward exclusive support of the Nationalists. With the end of the war in Europe, the Cold War was on the horizon, and cooperation with Communists was becoming politically unacceptable in the United States. With little hope of American aid, CCP policy shifted as well. As a result, when Duzhuang and the AGAS team attempted to cross Communist-held territory to reach Beiping, they were turned back. On one occasion, when the Americans were otherwise engaged, an Eighth Route Army officer demanded that Duzhuang turn over the group's radio and rifles. This he gladly did, much to the Americans' annoyance, but he insisted that he was a Chinese citizen obeying orders from a Chinese officer. Needless to say, in the postwar environment, Duzhuang had no wish to remain with the U.S. Army, and when his unit returned from Inner Mongolia, he resigned. Soon thereafter, he was on a boat for Shanghai, where his first interest was looking up his long lost love, Sun Song.[24]

After his brief stint with the Eighth Route Army, Duzhuang had spent most of the war years in Chongqing and the Nationalist-controlled areas of West China. The only other brother with a similar experience was the black sheep of the family, the entertainer Ye Lizhong. Though his background, interests, and talents were quite different from those of his studious and politically engaged brother, he resembled Duzhuang in one respect: he was a free spirit who did not easily subordinate himself to organizational discipline. As we have seen, Lizhong had been publicly disowned by his eldest brother and used up all his inheritance in Tianjin in the early war years. His actor friends appreciated his talent as no one in the family ever had, but he was never able to make a decent living. His mother, who had received a letter from Duzhuang, suggested that Lizhong join him in Chongqing.

In 1943, Ye Lizhong bid good-bye to his mother and set off for the interior. His brother Duyi gave him two pieces of parting advice: don't smoke opium, and don't get V.D. Surprisingly, Lizhong (who had already had a brief teenage affair with a Beiping actress) took these words to heart. With some money from his mother sewed into the rim of his straw hat, he traveled to a known quiet place on the front and walked across the no-man's-land. A brother-in-law had bought him a fake high school transcript, which got him a pass once he reached the Nationalist lines. The journey was a tough trek through the hills of central China, but he received a lot of help from strangers along the way. A traveling merchant put him up when his feet were too blistered for him to walk. Once while fording a river, he slipped and was swept downstream until rescued by a passerby. For part of the journey, he fell in with a group of soldiers taking a prisoner to headquarters, and their small wooden boat carried him down to the Yangzi. From there, he stowed away on a troop ship to Chongqing, helped by an officer who took him for a patriotic youth coming to join the resistance.

In Chongqing, Lizhong looked up Duzhuang at the address his mother had given him, but by this time Duzhuang was off traveling in his failing business. From Duzhuang's Taiping Company, he learned that his sister Durou and her husband had also reached Chongqing, and he went to find them. Their journey had been somewhat easier: by train and boat to Wuhan in central China, then in a small junk across the front lines—where they told the Japanese sentries at the checkpoint that they were taking a bride to be married. With their money hidden inside a bamboo oar sweep, and later sewed into their clothes, they managed both to pass the Japanese searches and to avoid bandits in the no-man's-land between the Chinese and Japanese lines and arrived safely in Chongqing. When Lizhong located his sister and brother-in-law, he desperately needed a job. His brother-in-law suggested signing up for a Chinese army corps being trained by the Americans in India to open a land route to China through Burma. So Lizhong became a soldier.

No Chinese unit in the war suffered higher casualties than those that fought through Burma, but this time Lizhong's comic and acting talents saved him. An officer kept him in the rear to entertain at headquarters and teach in a small performing arts group. At last his talents were appreciated, and life was never better: smart khaki uniforms, plenty of food and drink, and enough salary to buy a watch and several gold rings. After a year in India, he returned safely to China and then simply walked away from the army (an interesting comment on discipline even in the best-trained Nationalist units). In 1946, he started working in the teahouses in the southwestern city of Guiyang. He achieved a local reputation for comic dialogues, and his pay for one performance almost equaled a month's salary in the army. Then he fell in love with a popular Peking opera actress. The two would meet after shows and neck in the park, but when the newspaper gossip columns spread the news, his career plummeted. Chinese audiences could not accept their favorite actress taking up with a lowly comic actor. (It was quite acceptable, and expected, for her to have wealthy officials or businessmen as patrons and lovers.) So whenever Lizhong performed, he was howled off the stage and pelted with bottles and orange peels. For months he could not work and lived off his girlfriend's income and the sale of his jewelry. She vowed to stick by him, and they planned an engagement party after Chinese New Year in 1947. Then on the eve of the engagement, she left town in the middle of the night with a young army officer.

Ye Lizhong was crushed. After all the disdain directed at him by his elders in Tianjin, he had found in the army and the teahouses of Guiyang people who finally appreciated his talents. No sooner had his career begun to take off than it was destroyed by his first true love. Then once he decided to marry, he was abandoned by his sweetheart. With his career and his personal life in shambles, and nothing more than the clothes on his back, he took a truck back to Chongqing. There, with his passage eased by letters of introduction from friends among the mafia elements who controlled entertainment venues in west China cities, he slowly made his way as a teahouse storyteller, catering mostly to northerners left behind in the wartime capital. He stayed there for the rest of his life and did not make contact with his brothers for many years. But at last the black sheep of the family had found his calling.

Two brothers, Ye Fang and Fang Shi, were already involved in the Communist movement before 1937. Ye Fang, the older of the two, had been a party member since 1936, while still a student at Tsinghua University. His activities during the war, so far as they are known, were fairly mundane, mostly involving work in education and propaganda. Like the others, he had gathered with friends in Tianjin after the war broke out, then made his way to Nanjing, where he joined the Tianjin Students National Salvation Propaganda Corps. The group spread anti-Japanese propaganda in the Yangzi valley, retreating to Wuhan as the enemy advanced. He was in Wuhan in 1938 while the national government was located there, a period of unusual political openness in the early United Front.[25] Then the party sent him to Guilin, capital of Guangxi province in the southwest, where he taught for three years at a local cadre school. Though the school was under the province's Nationalist government, its head was an underground Communist, and Ye Fang's job was to promote leftist thinking among the primary school teachers and local functionaries who studied there.[26] He mentored a small group of young cadres, following a consistent party educational line that encouraged the students to link their lessons in history or socialist ideology to their own lives. In effect, this line encouraged the students—

FIGURE 12. National Salvation Propaganda Corps, 1937. Ye Fang is at the top center, with glasses. Family photo.

who usually came from merchant, landlord, or wealthy peasant families—to believe that any doubts they had about communism or party policy were the product of their class background and should be acknowledged and overcome in criticism and self-criticism sessions.

By 1942, the United Front was breaking down all over China. Communist and Nationalist forces had faced off in a number of major battles, with accusations and recriminations on both sides. Realizing that the Communists had been unusually successful in using the United Front to build an organization and spread their message in the early years of the war, the Nationalists began to crack down on suspected leftists in their territory.[27] The Communist cell in Guilin was uncovered, and as arrests spread, Ye Fang fled to Hong Kong, took a boat to Shanghai, and then proceeded to the area between the Yangzi and Yellow rivers controlled by the Communists' New Fourth Army.

With the New Fourth Army, Ye Fang did rural work for the party: mobilizing peasants to support the war effort, carrying out rent and interest reduction, and identifying and eliminating enemy agents and traitors. By this time, the area was under fairly secure Communist control, so the party effectively ran local government in the rural areas, keeping the Japanese confined to their urban garrisons and the main railway lines.[28] Late in 1943, the party Rectification Campaign, which had started much earlier in Yan'an, came to this region. For several months, Ye Fang and other cadres met at a regional party school to investigate the background of each party member. As a college student from an elite Tianjin family, Ye Fang was unusual. Many rural cadres could not understand how someone from a family with such close relations to people like President Yuan Shikai could end up joining the Communist Party. But he frankly explained his political development from nationalism to socialism and passed muster with little difficulty. He was also able to say, in all honesty, that he had had no contact with other members of his family since joining the New Fourth Army, nor would he have any contact until after the Communists came to power. The party was now his home.

While at the party school, Ye Fang got to know a lively young woman from Jiangsu, Lin Ying, who did drama and propaganda work for the party as well as secretarial duties in the county government. The daughter of a small shopkeeper, she began the war acting and singing in propaganda performances for the Nationalist army, but she became involved with left-wing groups and had been imprisoned for over a year in Jiangxi. After her release, she fled to join the New Fourth Army. She had just had a baby, a daughter of unknown paternity, whom she had left in her mother's care. Ye Fang and Lin Ying were in the same study group and learned everything about each other's past, so the fact that she already had a child apparently did not bother him.[29] Party regulations prevented any courtship ("talking love") while they were at the party school, but after they graduated, their relationship became more serious. In the fall of 1945, the party asked for volunteers to go to Manchuria, to establish a new party base in a region that the Soviet Red Army had occupied in August 1945, just after the atomic bombs were dropped on Hiroshima and Nagasaki. Ye Fang and his girlfriend both joined up (perhaps wishing to get away to an area where no one knew of her earlier relationship), and soon they set off on a month-long trek, walking over fifty kilometers a day through villages in east China. On the way, with no real ceremony, Ye Fang and his friend married—a devoted Communist couple on their way to recover the territory where the Japanese invasion of China had begun.

The final leg of the journey was by boat from Shandong, a short trip that left the entire group seasick and miserable, but they were warmly greeted by Russian Red Army troops on their arrival. Soon, however, the Nationalists moved troops to take over the main cities from the Soviets, while the Communist Eighth Route Army streaming in from north China occupied the smaller cities and rural areas. Ye Fang was posted to the far north, where the main threat was bandits allied with Nationalist forces: Ye Fang termed them "political bandits." On several occasions, daring bandit attacks on Communist units inflicted heavy casualties on Ye Fang's comrades, but he managed to emerge unscathed. For the next two years, his task was to combine the anti-bandit struggle with land reform, to build up a rural base for the party. Ye Fang rose to the position of county magistrate and vice-secretary of the local party before he was transferred back to education work. Having been a promising student at both Nankai and Tsinghua, this bright but soft-spoken young Communist was an obvious choice for educational roles. As his political career advanced, his family also grew, with his wife bearing two sons in these cold northern lands. From late 1946, he was an administrator at party schools at the county, provincial, and regional levels, ending up as head of the education section of the party school for the entire Northeast, after the Communist forces seized this strategic region in some of the decisive battles of the Civil War.[30]

The ninth brother, who took the name Fang Shi in the party, did not rise as smoothly in the organization as his elder brother did, but he came closer to the top leadership. Like the others, Fang Shi gathered with friends in Tianjin when the war broke out in 1937, though his group included a number of middle school girls from Beiping, comrades from the student movement including one who would later become his wife. The two had become friends when they hid together from the Japanese in a house on a small Beiping alley, waiting for a chance to flee to Tianjin. From Tianjin, the group took a British ship to Yantai on the Shandong peninsula and then traveled overland and by train back to Jinan. His group called itself the Tianjin National Salvation Student Corps. This organizational identity allowed the young activists to approach the local authorities for food and lodging, and they stayed in the classrooms of a Jinan normal school. They were issued uniforms and asked to do patriotic propaganda work in the local warlord's army. After about a month, they were sent to Liaocheng, about forty kilometers north of the Yellow River in western Shandong. Here they got a taste of the chaotic military situation in the early months of the war.

The army commander in Liaocheng was progressive and welcomed the students, but soon he was ordered to withdraw south of the Yellow River by the provincial commander—a notorious figure later executed for ineffective resistance that resulted in the loss of Shandong to the advancing Japanese. About half of the students decided to stay to mobilize guerrilla forces in the countryside, and they were given twenty rifles by the departing troops. Three days later, they heard troops advancing and when they discovered they were Chinese soldiers, they threw open the town gates. Unfortunately, the soldiers proved to be an undisciplined rabble of retreating warlord troops, who put the students under house arrest and took their uniforms, guns, and ammunition. They wanted Fang Shi's leather shoes as well, but he insisted they were too small, offering one to try on. Fortunately, they accepted his argument because the other shoe had all his hidden cash. After looting the town, the warlord soldiers left. The now-unarmed students headed south to link up with the commander who had withdrawn. They found the local population suspicious and hostile, the result of years of mistreatment by government agents and unruly soldiers. At most villages, the local militia would not even allow them to enter. Organizing the peasantry for national resistance, they learned, was going to prove a challenging task.

With the situation looking hopeless in Shandong, Fang Shi and his friends took the train west to Xi'an, heading straight for the Eighth Route Army office. They wanted to go to Yan'an, but the needs at the front were greater. Like Duzhuang and Duzheng before them, they were sent to Shanxi. Most in this group were leftist members of the National Liberation Vanguards. They were assigned to the political section of Yan Xishan's army, teaching politics, doing propaganda, and organizing patriotic performances. Many of the political officers came from Shanxi's Sacrifice League and were part of Yan Xishan's attempt to use students and intellectuals to raise the political consciousness (and thus the commitment and discipline) of his troops. Through most of 1938 and 1939, these leftists in the political section engaged in an escalating struggle with conservative unit commanders for predominant influence in the army. On several occasions, Fang Shi's group was surrounded, disarmed, beaten, or expelled by hostile commanders. He often had to withdraw to the relative safety of Communist-controlled Shaanxi, but he always found a way to continue his political education work.

In 1939, while Fang Shi was teaching at a training school for young army officers, a colleague approached him about joining the Communist Party. As a former student activist from Tianjin and Beiping, he was a natural target for recruitment. He was delighted to be asked: to him the party was an elite unit of selfless activists, dedicated to resisting Japan and overthrowing the corrupt old order and committed to building a strong nation and a just society. He hesitated only because the party in Shanxi was still underground and the man who approached him was new to the unit. Perhaps this invitation was a trap by a Nationalist agent to discover his political leanings. So he went to Bai Tian, the former middle school student from Beiping who was by now his girlfriend, to ask what she thought. He knew she was a committed leftist but did not realize that she was already a party member. She vouched for the bona fides of the man who had recruited him, and two days later he filled out a form and slipped off to a nearby cave dwelling* to be sworn in as a member of the Communist Party. He was told the identity of only one member above him and one below him—in keeping with the so-called single-line command structure that prevailed where the party was still a secret organization.

As he moved from place to place in Shanxi and Shaanxi, Fang Shi had repeatedly crossed paths with Bai Tian. She was an active, healthy girl, known for her ability to ride a horse. Indeed, Fang Shi had once picked her up when she fell from her mount, a gesture they both took as a sign of serious affection. By 1939, they were

---

*Caves are the standard dwellings in this part of China. The loess soil of the hillsides is easily cut into stable arched caves, which are cool in summer and warmed by simple stoves in the winter.

already in love, but they kept their relationship discreet, informing only her political superiors. Late in 1939, with both now members of the party, they were married in a simple ceremony presided over by the local head of the Sacrifice League. They spent twenty dollars on a banquet of mutton stew and steamed bread. Then Bai Tian's roommates moved out of her cave so the couple could have some time together. This union was a disciplined, serious (and politically correct) marriage, and after a week, the two returned to their respective units. Soon they were traveling in different directions, following the orders of the party. They were together in Yan'an in early 1940, he for some quick theoretical training at the Marxist-Leninist Academy and she at another school. They managed to rent a room at an inn for one night before Fang Shi again headed for northwestern Shanxi. There he taught in a school for rural cadres, and in the spring, his wife arrived as a teacher. For the first time, they were able to live together.

By the winter of 1940–41, Bai Tian was pregnant, but just at this time the Japanese launched a major offensive which forced her withdrawal across the Yellow River to Shaanxi. Fang Shi stayed behind to mobilize support for the guerrillas fighting the Japanese, but once the offensive was over, he took leave to visit his wife. When he found her, she was living in a cold cave, wracked by fever and with one leg so stiff and swollen from the cold that she could hardly move. The area to which she had been evacuated was poor to begin with, and drought the previous year had made things worse. The local Communist Party organization was not particularly strong, so the peasants did not go out of their way to assist the pregnant stranger left in their village. No one provided fuel to heat her cave, and when Fang Shi arrived, he found the chimney blocked with ice. When the baby was born, there were no sterile instruments to cut the umbilical cord, which accounted for the mother's infection. As for the child, she was given to a peasant family to care for, but they could provide only a thin millet gruel. By the time Fang Shi arrived, the baby was pitifully emaciated and soon died. Her parents called their lost child "Black Bean" after the food (usually fed to horses) her mother had eaten during her pregnancy.

Fang Shi was able to stay with his wife for about a month. After he gathered some fuel to warm the cave and bought some noodles and chicken for food, she slowly recovered. She was covered with lice from the borrowed bedding in the cave, and he had to shave her head to get the bugs out of her hair. Her leg was the biggest problem. With no doctor in the village, the poorly trained nurse had simply bound it up like a war wound; and when Fang Shi unbound it, the flesh was rotting and the leg atrophied. In removing the decaying flesh, one of her tendons was cut. Finally, Fang Shi had her evacuated to the Communist wartime headquarters in Yan'an, where she could get better medical treatment, but she never regained full use of the leg.

In the meantime, Fang Shi headed back toward the front. It was already March 1941, and he had to help organize the spring planting to ensure that production would be sufficient to support the guerrillas. As sick and weak as his wife was after the birth and loss of her baby, his first duty was to serve the war against Japan. With the enemy so close, he could not ignore his responsibility to rejoin his unit, nor would his wife have expected or requested that he do so. They were both Communist Party members and dedicated revolutionaries. The revolution and the war must come first.[31]

By 1942, Fang Shi was back in Yan'an with his wife. A fair number of visitors were now coming to the Communist capital: Chinese and foreign journalists, sympathetic intellectuals, and also Nationalist officers and agents on official business for the United Front. A Reception Office had been established to manage their visits, and Fang Shi headed one team in the office. For a while, he led a fairly normal life and helped care for his wife, who still could not walk after the injury to her leg. He had written to his brothers, and Duzheng had replied to say he had a friend in the Eighth Route Army Office in Xi'an who might be able to help her get better treatment there, but that option was rejected.

Late in 1942, the Rectification Campaign began in Fang Shi's unit. Rectification had been raging in the schools and academic institutions of Yan'an for several months, leading to sharp attacks on some more liberal-minded intellectuals who dared to criticize the shortcomings of Yan'an's new socialist society and the privileges of the party elite. Mao Zedong and his allies used the movement to strengthen their control of the party at the highest levels, attacking the "dogmatism" and "book worship" of those who had learned their Marxism from the Soviet Union rather than through bitter experience in China's hinterland. At the same time, Mao firmly reminded the urban intellectuals who had joined the party during the war that they must subordinate their outlook to the interests of the broad masses of workers and peasants—as those interests were interpreted by the Communist Party.[32] Former students like Fang Shi were a natural target of the Rectification Campaign, but the movement in his unit began quite mildly. Party members spent most of their time reading essays by Stalin and Mao Zedong, learning more about the principles of Marxism-Leninism and the history of the Chinese Communist Party, and writing down their own personal background and political history. In recounting his story, Fang Shi mentioned his brief arrest in Tianjin in 1935. It had not seemed so important at the time—only an afternoon in detention—but now it was almost a badge of honor, evidence of his left-wing involvement even before the December 9th student movement.

In early April 1943, his boss came to tell him that the party's Organization Department had ordered him to Shanxi. "When?" he asked. "This afternoon," came the response. This order seemed strangely sudden, especially given the snowstorm outside, but he was told that another comrade was leaving that day and it would be best if they went together. So he quickly went home to pack and say good-bye to his wife. She was barely able to walk with crutches, but a small boy (a "little devil," in the terminology of the day) was there to help her. Back at the Reception Office, a guard was waiting with a horse to carry Fang Shi's roll of luggage. As they passed the Public Security Office, the guard said he had to go in to feed the horse, so Fang Shi sat down to wait in the office. Soon an officer came in and said sternly, "You have a serious political problem. You must confess fully." Fang Shi was shocked: "Comrade, you've made a mistake! The Organization Department is sending me to the front." But there was no mistake. He was under arrest.

He was taken to the detention center, which consisted of line after line of caves holding four to five hundred prisoners. The guards led him to a dark cave containing an old, bearded, white-haired man, his clothes patched so often that the original material was barely visible. Fang Shi thought he had wandered into a Daoist temple! He soon learned that the man was from the Third International, brought to Yan'an from the Northeast and presumably unwilling to accept Mao's version of Communism. He had been there for six years, he said, and had never seen anyone leave. "Once imprisoned, you can forget about going home." This chilling message was not true, but one can imagine the impact it had. The cave had no bed, only a floor of straw to sleep on, and a pot to piss in. Meals were passed through a small sliding door, and twice a day the prisoners were let out for quick trips to the bathroom. This turn of events seemed a dismal end to a brief revolutionary career.

Some time passed before Fang Shi was even interrogated, and he wracked his brain to figure out what might have landed him in prison. In his mind, the party only arrested traitors, Guomindang agents, and Trotskyites, and he could not imagine how he could be suspected of such crimes. The only reasons he could think of were his arrest in 1935 (for others had been accused of betraying the party to secure their release from prison) and the letter from Duzheng suggesting medical treatment for his wife in Xi'an. He now remembered that the letter had taken more than a month to reach him, and it arrived all crumpled up, the party's skill at opening mail being poorly developed at this time. Perhaps he was suspected of plotting to send his wife to Xi'an and then to defect himself.

In the summer of 1943, he was twice interrogated but admitted nothing. Then he joined a small group organized to "help" cadres confess their errors. Those who had already confessed came to persuade those who had yet to see the light, assuring them that they would receive lenient treatment if they came clean. At first, Fang Shi could not figure out what he was supposed to confess, but eventually he understood that his 1935 arrest was indeed the source of his problems. (Forty years later, his superior at the Reception Center, then dying in a Beijing hospital, telephoned to say he was sorry about the events of 1943. Fang Shi realized that this man had probably turned him in, under pressure from security people eager to uncover "secret agents" in the Reception Office, a sensitive unit that regularly dealt with Guomindang visitors. His superior would have known of the 1935 arrest from the autobiographical account Fang Shi had prepared during the Rectification Campaign.) Fang Shi also understood that only an appropriately embellished false confession would get him out of jail. So he said that he had indeed defected and betrayed the party to gain his release in 1935 (though in fact he was not even a party member at the time) and that Duzheng was a Guomindang agent who had sent him to Yan'an as a spy. When this story was deemed adequate, he was instructed to write it down in a formal confession. Thus did this loyal party member become the first of the Ye brothers to experience the CCP's reliance on coerced and false confessions to assert its power. He would not be the last.

With this contrived confession, Fang Shi was allowed to resume work, though he had to return to the detention center every evening. He was also permitted weekly visits to his disabled wife, who had been assigned work in a school, then sent to a sanitarium outside Yan'an for treatment of her leg. He had to walk several kilometers to see her, and he was not allowed to spend the night, but at least he could assure her that he was all right. In early 1944, he was assigned to the Security Bureau to do research on Guomindang organizations. A year later, Fang Shi was assigned to "work on" (the standard term for persistent persuasion) some captured officers from Yan Xishan's army being held in the Reception Center, first to persuade them to help his research group and then to join the CCP. As implausible as it may seem for a prisoner of the party to act as a recruiting agent, he was apparently successful, for after a time the officers were allowed to return to Shanxi in the hope that they would operate as CCP agents. Though Fang Shi was permitted to resume work (the party needed his intellectual skills), he was not fully cleared and released from detention until February 1946, nearly three years after his arrest. By that time, the party realized that its campaign to uncover "secret agents" had gotten utterly out of hand and produced mostly false confessions. In addition, the war was now over, and the party desperately needed its better-educated cadres to staff the local governments it was establishing in areas recovered from Japanese occupation. So the charges against Fang Shi and his coerced confession were found to be false, his original account was accepted, and he was reinstated as a Communist Party member in good standing. He was offered his choice of two good jobs: a teaching position at Yan'an University or an editorial job with the New China News Agency, the Communist press service.

Fang Shi chose the New China News Agency, and would remain with the organization for the rest of his career. His wife was also given a job, so at last they were able to live and work together. In the spring of 1947, a brief postwar cease-fire between the Nationalists and Communists broke down, and Chiang Kai-shek's troops launched an all-out offensive against the Communist headquarters in Yan'an. The Communist leadership split up and took cover in the hills of northern Shaanxi while the entire party apparatus packed up and left. Fang Shi and his wife bundled up their clothes, bedding, and a few books (the baggage limit was fifteen kilograms per person) and left with the others. A horse-drawn cart carried Bai Tian, who was still unable to walk, and later she rode a horse or camel when narrow trails proved impassable by cart. All this time on the road, the New China News Agency kept broadcasting, its radio transmissions becoming all the more important as the party could no longer print a regular newspaper.

By 1948, the party leaders had a relatively secure base in the village of Xibaipo in Pingshan county in the foothills of the Taihang Mountains. The news agency was headquartered nearby, and a small group including Fang Shi was selected to work in the same village with the party leadership, to undergo training in the practice of party journalism under the direction of one of Mao's secretaries. This arrangement made the agency an unusually direct mouthpiece for Mao and the party leadership, which reviewed every dispatch that the agency staff wrote. Fang Shi was responsible for military reports on the Civil War, and Zhou Enlai, as army chief of staff, reviewed most of these pieces. The news agency dispatches were the primary means of notifying China and the world of the CCP's version of the war's progress, and whenever Fang Shi entered Zhou's office with a new report, Zhou put other business aside to inspect it right away. On one occasion in 1948, Fang Shi was waiting for Zhou to approve a draft when a phone call came from the front. He soon realized that the call involved preparations for the Huai-Hai campaign, a massive operation involving millions of men that would become one of the decisive battles of the Civil War. Uncomfortable about overhearing such a sensitive call, he considered withdrawing, but when Zhou made no sign that he should leave, he stayed in the room for almost half an hour until the call was over. Zhou proceeded to approve his dispatch without mentioning the interruption. For a young man who just a few years earlier had been imprisoned on suspicion of being a Guomindang agent, this episode was an unforgettable sign of the party's (or at least Zhou's) trust, and Fang Shi was deeply moved.

Relations with the top party leadership were unusually close and casual at this time, and Fang Shi often saw Mao and the others strolling around the village with a single bodyguard, Mao invariably with a cigarette in his hand. Though his direct contact with the Chairman was minimal, Fang Shi much admired Mao's ability to dash off a penetrating article while overseeing his forces in the heat of battle and found his conversation humorous and broadly knowledgeable. This impression was first formed in Yan'an in the summer of 1942, where he had met Mao while escorting a group of "enlightened gentry" that the party was cultivating with an invitation to its headquarters. Mao had carefully asked the basic details of Fang Shi's background (work, age, hometown, education) and noted them in a small book—shades of the memos the emperors consulted for their audiences with Fang Shi's great grandfather. Then in five hours of conversation and dinner with his gentry guests, Mao held forth easily and confidently on current politics and international affairs, on China's future, and on the lessons to be learned from Chinese history and the classics, from which he freely quoted, much to the delight of his classically educated guests.

In Xibaipo, Mao often wrote articles for the New China News Agency. Early one morning he dropped off an article he had just completed. Mao habitually worked late at night and slept through the morning, so his early visit caught the staff off guard, but Mao explained that he had been working on the piece all night and still had not gone to bed. Such dedication greatly impressed the young journalists. Fang Shi had a couple more substantive encounters with the Chairman. He remembers delivering an article on an important conference for Mao's approval as the Chairman walked by the river. After glancing through the article, Mao suggested a few changes. Much to his chagrin, Fang Shi could not understand Mao's thick Hunan accent and had to ask the Chairman to repeat himself.

Life at Xibaipo was incredibly busy, with Fang Shi's normal work day running from 8:00 A.M. to midnight, seven days a week, with neither vacations nor holidays. Only on Saturday night might there be an evening off for a movie or dance. Life was simple. Housing and clothes were provided, and there was little to spend money on, especially for someone like Fang Shi who did not smoke. Food was now much better than it had been during the war, with noodles and steamed buns made of wheat and meat dishes several times a week. It was a time of great optimism, as a string of Communist victories in the Civil War heralded the final collapse of the Nationalists. Fang Shi's job was to write the battle reports, of which there were several every day, and have them checked by the party leaders. As he later recalled, "While working at Xibaipo, the clearest impression I received was that when the top leaders review a draft, they first consider the problem from a political perspective." Such was the intensive training in party journalism that Fang Shi received at the hands of the Communist Party leadership, lessons that he would follow through the rest of his career. Almost all of his career was in the headquarters of the New China News Agency in Beijing, the city that he had fled twelve years earlier with the outbreak of the war and to which he returned early in 1949.[33]

For Communist Party members like Ye Fang and Fang Shi, there was a seamless transition between the war with Japan and the Civil War with the Nationalist Party. Their revolutionary struggle to create a New China continued from the party's rural bases. For the other Ye brothers, victory in the war against Japan provided at least a temporary respite and an opportunity to pursue other interests.

When the Anti-Japanese War ended, Ye Duzhuang's first thought was to locate his high school sweetheart, Sun Song. While in Chongqing, he had learned through mutual friends that she had returned to China in 1938, after finishing art school in Japan. Her sister in Beiping had arranged a job teaching Japanese in a girls' high school, but she could not bear the thought of teaching young people the language of the occupying army and turned down the job at the last minute. She was lonely and unhappy in Beiping and discouraged by the lack of discipline and patriotic spirit in occupied China. In her diary, she wrote, "Compared to the Japanese, we are way behind. Right now, we should recognize our failings."[34] She longed for male companionship ("What I urgently need now is someone to hold me "), but soon found a purpose in patriotism: "My fatherland, my heart is yours forever."[35] With a letter of introduction from a former teacher at Yenching University, she headed south to Shanghai, then boarded a boat up the Yangzi to seek a job as an art teacher. Her plans changed quickly when she met two young textile workers who had been recruited to join the Communist resistance. These two young women and the handsome officer who was leading them persuaded her to join them. The urbane commander of the New Fourth Army was eager to recruit young artists and intellectuals like her. Still, when she arrived wearing white high-heeled shoes and carrying a wooden case holding her oil paints, she must have seemed an unlikely recruit to a guerrilla army. When winter came, her brother, the manager of the International Hotel in Shanghai, sent her an embroidered silk comforter. She spent about three years with the guerrillas doing woodblock prints—a popular form of propaganda art during the war—and patriotic wall paintings, but regrettably no fragments of her diary survive from this period.[36] Then late in 1941, suffering from a painful toothache and with the New Fourth Army under attack from both the Japanese and the Nationalists and eager to shed some of its less hardy female cadres, she was sent back to Shanghai dressed as a peasant carrying a basket of eggs to market.[37]

She spent the rest of the war in Japanese-occupied Shanghai, living with her brother in the International Hotel and feeling miserable most of the time. "Shanghai is a frightful selfish place, where no one thinks of anyone else."[38] After three years with the Communist guerrillas, "bravely and with high spirits on the battle lines," she was now living in the lap of luxury, with fine food, cars, coffee shops and movies, but she felt trapped and empty.[39] Only her love of art and painting gave meaning to her life, which was otherwise preoccupied with a frustrating search for a suitable mate. At one point, she contrasted her daily focus on her love life with the ethic that prevailed while she was with the Communist guerrillas. She reflected on the New Fourth Army commander's practical guideline that one hour per day was adequate to take care of male-female relations, and the remaining twenty-three hours could be allocated appropriately.[40] In Shanghai, Sun Song had several boyfriends, but all were involved in business. She often poured out her love for them in her diary, recording a firm embrace or first kiss, but then quickly found fault with their vulgar concern with money or inattention to her feelings.[41] Suddenly, in the spring of 1943, she received a letter from Duzhuang, who had met her cousin in Chongqing and learned her address. Her diary immediately filled with excitement and hope: "His letter is like a powerful shot that has blasted a hole in my jail." Though she admitted that her memory of him from Nankai and Japan was hazy, she was overjoyed that he had kept thinking of her through years of separation. In the past, she had never shown much interest in his attentions, but now she wrote in a free-verse poem:

He is so brave, forthright and passionate.
I am amazed that he could be so resolute,
That he should still think of me for these ten years.

She was certain that "when he embraces me, he will give me a new life." As the days passed, she became ever more impatient for his arrival: "Zhuang! Come quickly! I need you—a crazy guy who has loved me for ten years!"[42]

It never seemed to occur to her that she was living in Japanese-occupied Shanghai and Duzhuang was not likely to join her there. In any case, whatever letter she sent in return seems not to have made it across the lines to "Free China." Not until the end of the war did the two get together. By this time, Sun Song had fallen in love with a fellow painter who worked in his father's oil-pressing business. He was about to leave for the United States and wished to take her with him. They had been dating for over a year, but she was not convinced that he really understood her. Duzhuang arrived just in time, having secured passage on a U.S. chartered vessel through his American friends. When he arrived in Shanghai, he was determined to win her back. The pair spent two weeks together, meeting almost every day. She took him to Western restaurants and bought Danish pastries. They walked arm in arm along the Bund. They had not seen each other for eight years, and he broke into tears one evening telling her how much he had missed her. She was much more of a tease, saying that she had forgotten what he looked like. He bought her a new bicycle but then had to leave for Beiping, where the Democratic League wanted him to set up a new office. He was apparently uncertain whether he had won her over, for one of his foreign friends reported in a letter that Duzhuang had gone "to present Miss Sun with a bicycle and withdraw from her life."[43] He was certainly fighting against substantial odds to win Sun Song's heart. Her friends and family advised that she was foolhardy to "fall in love with a guy you have not seen for ten years and whom you do not understand," but their politics were certainly compatible as her patriotic and progressive cartoons from the 1930s and this period show. (See figures 13 and 14.) Her diary has four drafts for the beginning of a letter she had promised to write right away, but eventually she did write, and the two corresponded regularly over the next year.[44] Then, in the summer of 1946, Duzhuang was sent south on League business. He stopped in Shanghai, proposed, and brought her back to Beiping to get married. Her American-educated elder sister strenuously opposed the union, saying that Duzhuang had neither property nor a real career, but the headstrong Sun Song ignored her. The ceremony was just a simple dinner with his two elder brothers in Beiping (Duyi and Duxin); then the newlyweds went to the beach for a honeymoon.

When he first returned to Beiping, Duzhuang had shared a house with Graham Peck, thus extending the relationship with the American journalist that would get him into such trouble later. Through Peck, he met several other Americans and Europeans, who formed something of a progressive, cosmopolitan community in post-

結婚八年　　　　　左 拉作

第一碗調養的粥湯

左 拉作

FIGURE 13 (*above*). "Eight Years of Marriage." Cartoon drawn by Sun Song, from *Zhoubao* [Weekly news] of Shanghai. Undated clipping from fall of 1945. In the cartoon, the father is labeled "feudal forces"; the mother (in a Japanese kimono), "imperialism"; the son, "new aristocracy"; and the daughter, "culture."

FIGURE 14 (*right*). "First Nourishing Bowl of Porridge." Cartoon drawn by Sun Song, from *Zhoubao* [Weekly news] of Shanghai. Undated clipping from fall of 1945.

FIGURE 15. Sun Song (c. 1943).
Family photo.

war Beiping. John Hersey, who had been born in Tianjin of missionary parents and then worked for *Time* magazine during the war, stayed with Duzhuang and Peck before traveling to Japan to write his award-winning book *Hiroshima*.[45] At one point, another journalist, Barbara Stephens, joined the group. Peck was a notorious heavy drinker, and the trio of Duzhuang, Peck, and the free-spirited Stephens was particularly rowdy, often causing substantial damage to paper walls and crockery in drunken evenings that left the neighbors talking about this wild and unusual group.[46] James Burke, a photojournalist for *Life* magazine, was also in Beiping at the time, and Duzhuang helped both Peck and Burke travel about north China to get stories. It was a mutually beneficial arrangement (and always cleared with Duzhuang's Democratic League colleagues), with Duzhuang providing contacts and translation help, while the foreign journalists provided cover to move through Guomindang lines when Duzhuang was on League business.

The house in Beiping was fairly luxurious, with a bath, tile floor, and telephone for Duzhuang's Democratic League activities. After Duzhuang and Sun Song were married, Peck moved out, and the young couple had the place to themselves and one cook. In addition to his Democratic League work, Duzhuang got a job with the National Resources Commission, for which he wrote a book on cotton cultivation,

making ample use of Japanese surveys of north China agriculture that he had discovered in Beiping and saved from mindless destruction.[47] With his reputation as
an agronomist thus established, he was hired to head the agricultural economics
section of the Beiping station of the national agricultural extension service. This
station (first established by the Japanese) later became the Chinese Academy of Agricultural Sciences, where Ye Duzhuang would spend the rest of his career.

Duzhuang's academic training had been in agronomy, and he seemed finally to
have settled into a stable professional career. But the late 1940s were hardly a stable time, especially for someone as politically engaged as he was. Although he did
some of his best research in this period, his heart was really in politics and family
life. His eldest daughter was born in 1947, and during his wife's pregnancy, he
busied himself painting the crib. Sun Song's sister, the American-educated nurse
who had so opposed their marriage, supervised the infant's care. Everything was
done according to the child-care text she had brought back from America: boiled
diapers, nursing from carefully cleaned nipples, American-made powdered milk
and orange juice as soon as Sun Song stopped breastfeeding, and feeding according to a fixed schedule no matter how much the child might cry. Duzhuang was not
thrilled by these foreign methods, and his next daughter was cared for "Chinese
style"—fed when hungry and held when she cried. But for the first daughter, he knew
well enough not to question his sister-in-law.

Other than his family, Duzhuang's life was filled with political activities. The
Democratic League had long seen its role as peaceful opposition to Nationalist Party
dictatorship, a liberal democratic force in a nation where liberals were an endangered species. In the late 1940s, as the Civil War between Nationalists and Communists escalated, the League was increasingly sympathetic to the Communist
position—blaming the Nationalists for the conflict and appealing for an end to the
war and formation of a coalition government. By the end of 1947, the Nationalists
regarded the League as a hostile force and banned its activities. This move only drove
people like Duzhuang into even closer relations with the Communists.

Duzhuang, of course, had long considered himself a socialist, even a communist. He had served briefly in the Eighth Route Army and knew many of the key
underground Communists in Beiping, serving as a liaison when visitors came to
find them. These associations several times brought him close to arrest, as Nationalist agents interrogated him about his leftist contacts. When his former roommate
Peck left Beiping, he believed that Duzhuang was "beginning to make plans to go
over to the communists."[48] In the end, he changed his mind when his first child was
born, and he stayed with his family in Beiping. He continued his Democratic League
activities even after the Nationalists ordered the organization disbanded. His political sympathies were clear, and he awaited the Communist victory with anticipation, working to persuade researchers at the agriculture institute not to withdraw
as the Nationalist regime collapsed and its leaders headed for Taiwan.

His elder (third) brother, Duyi, was even more active in the Democratic League. When the war broke out in 1937, he had stayed behind in Tianjin under Japanese occupation, taking a job at the British-owned Kailan Mining Company in Tangshan. This foreign company afforded a certain amount of political protection, and through his professors at Yenching University, he was in contact with the liberal intellectuals who would later form the Democratic League, and through them, with the Communist underground. He began sending reports to CCP agents on coal production at the mines and Japanese fortifications around Tangshan. The Communists were sufficiently impressed to invite him to join the party, but he demurred, saying he did not wish to give up his personal freedom. After the outbreak of war in the Pacific, the Japanese took over the Kailan company and Duyi quit and moved to the relative safety of Beiping. He continued to serve as a liaison between the liberal intellectuals of occupied China and the CCP, traveling in 1943 to the Eighth Route Army headquarters in southeastern Shanxi. He was impressed by the confident informality of the Communist base, where the commander Peng Dehuai mixed easily with the people. On July 7, 1943 (the sixth anniversary of the outbreak of the war), he signed an agreement with Peng that the two groups would work together to defeat the Japanese and, after the war, to form a peaceful democratic government. The document was rolled up and hidden in a toothpaste tube for Duyi to bring back to Beiping.

In the spring of 1944, Duyi made his way across Japanese lines to Chongqing, where he joined the meetings that led to the founding of the Democratic League. As a key delegate from occupied China, he was elected to the Central Committee. Then he made his way back to Beiping, where a secret branch of the League was founded shortly before the end of the war. After the Japanese surrender, in 1946, he left again to work in the central secretariat of the League, first in Chongqing, then in Nanjing, where the national government returned in the fall. At this time, the main thrust of Democratic League activities was opposition to resumption of the civil war and pressure to form a coalition government of all parties. In June 1946, students and progressive intellectuals organized a massive peace demonstration in Shanghai and dispatched a delegation to petition the government in Nanjing. When the delegates' train arrived in the evening, Duyi was in the greeting party at the train station. Suddenly, a large crowd of Nationalist thugs surrounded the group, first cursing and then beating the delegates, even turning on several journalists who had come to report on the group's arrival. The delegation was trapped in the station for several hours, while the police watched passively. During the melee, Duyi was knocked unconscious and robbed, as were several others. Only after several senior generals and representatives of the Democratic League intervened were military police sent to disperse the crowd and get the injured to a hospital for treatment. While Duyi was recovering, the Communist representatives in Nanjing, led by Zhou Enlai, visited the hospital to wish him well. With several journalists among the victims, the press made much of this attack and other instances of government-orchestrated violence against liberal dissent. In the typically dramatic rhetoric of one Shanghai paper, "Their blood has not been shed in vain, but will reap its reward in the peaceful democratic movement to come. This is not only an attack on and insult to the delegates, it is also an attack on and insult to the people of Shanghai and all the sons and daughters of China."[49] Needless to say, such violent attacks (and the well-orchestrated Communist solicitude toward the victims) drove Duyi and other liberal dissidents even further to the left.

Despite his growing disillusionment with the Nationalist Party, Duyi joined an ongoing effort to mediate between the Communists and Nationalists, advocating a democratic socialist course that would combine the political democracy of the United States with the economic democracy he perceived in the Soviet Union. Many of the negotiators' efforts were coordinated with the United States, which also hoped to avoid civil war and continuing chaos in China. In 1946, when Duyi was beaten in Nanjing, General George Marshall was in China trying to head off civil war between the opposing Communist and Nationalist armies. But Marshall would withdraw in frustration in 1947, and the job would fall to the American ambassador, Leighton Stuart, who had long been the president of Yenching University. There were Yenching students on all sides of the conflict, and Stuart was constantly trying to bring them together. Not only did he wish to support the democratic intellectuals as a Third Force in Chinese politics, he also used them as an important link to the Chinese Communists. When Democratic League leaders met with Stuart, Duyi often served as translator.[50]

All these efforts came to naught. China's fate would be decided on the battlefield, and the Democratic League had no army.[51] As the Civil War between Communists and Nationalists intensified, the Democratic League joined progressive students and intellectuals in criticizing the Nationalists' effort to solve political differences by force. Convinced that the League was leaning too close to the Communist position, the Nationalists banned the organization in November 1947, surrounding the headquarters with police and ordering everyone out of the building. Duyi and the others were powerless to resist. He continued working for his democratic socialist ideals in Shanghai and Hong Kong; then when Communist victory was assured, he made his way back to Beiping.[52]

After Ye Duzheng graduated from Southwest United University, he taught briefly in a middle school, then went on to graduate study in meteorology at Zhejiang University, which had relocated to Guizhou in the southwest during the war. There he met and fell in love with a smart young co-ed, and soon they were married and had a son. Duzheng had always been the scholar of the family, sticking to his books and proving to be an outstanding student. In 1943, he took the exams for further study

FIGURE 16. Ye Duzheng. School photographs from 1935 at Nankai and 1948 at the University of Chicago. Family photos.

in the United States. He was one of three hundred students who qualified for "self-supported" study, which permitted him to change his Chinese money at the rate of twenty to the dollar, when the black market rate was six hundred to one. He easily bought enough dollars to cover his travel and living expenses. He sold his Chinese clothes to leave his wife enough money to support herself and their son, then flew over the Hump to Calcutta, took a boat to Bombay, boarded a U.S. military transport to Australia, and sailed across the Pacific to Los Angeles. A friend at the California Institute of Technology suggested the University of Chicago as the place to study meteorology. He applied and was immediately accepted.

At Chicago, he worked with a Swedish scholar, Carl G. Rossy. This was an exciting time in the field of meteorology. Longer-range weather forecasting and climate research were important to the war effort, and computer modeling was being developed for the first time. Duzheng's strong English skills from Nankai and Tsinghua (where the science textbooks were all American), his solid technical training at China's best universities, and his keen scientific mind made him a top graduate student. He received his Ph.D. in 1946 and was kept on to work as a researcher at Chicago's Institute of Meteorology. In 1947, his wife came to the United States for a chemistry M.A. at Wyoming, later joining him in Chicago. Their son stayed behind with her brother in China.

The Chinese students studying in Chicago had a student association and an Association of Chinese Scientists, which met to exchange news and talk about events in China. During the republican era, most Chinese students at American universities returned to their homeland after completing their studies, so they naturally followed the situation in China closely. Their discussions avoided sensitive political questions, focusing more on the progress of the Civil War than the relative merits of the Communists and Nationalists. Though he was always circumspect around his Chinese friends, Duzheng was also invited to speak to Americans about the situation in China, and on one such occasion he made his anti-Communist views clear, stating that he saw no difference between Stalin and Hitler.

Despite these sentiments, when the Communists emerged victorious in the Civil War and set about the task of reconstructing China, Duzheng resolved to return. He had just been offered a post at the U.S. Meteorology Bureau at a handsome annual salary of over five thousand dollars, more than many full professors were making at the time. But he was drawn back to China by a combination of nationalism—the desire to do something for his country, which was just emerging from a century of disorder—and professional ambition. He saw an opportunity to make a real contribution in China, where scientific meteorology was, in his words, "a blank sheet of paper." However he did not make this decision until 1950, and the Korean War had just broken out. The U.S. government was not enthusiastic about Chinese scientists returning to "Red China." So when he applied for a visa to pass through Hong Kong, he was turned down at the British consulate. When he asked for an explanation, he was told, "Go talk to the State Department." "Isn't Britain an independent country?" he asked. Eventually the British relented, and he returned by boat with several hundred other students, disembarking in Hong Kong, taking the train to the border, and walking across the bridge to China.[53]

By the early 1950s, four brothers—Duyi (Number 3), Duzhuang (5), Duzheng (7) and Fang Shi (9)—were all working in Beijing, as the city was again called as the capital of the People's Republic of China. The eldest and fourth brothers, Duren and Duxin, were nearby in Tianjin; Ye Fang was at the party school in the Northeast; and Ye Lizhong was working as a comic in Chongqing. Before long, they were all in contact with one another—with the exception of Lizhong, who was still smarting from his rejection as a youth and a bit ashamed of his work as an entertainer. The war years had been eventful; most of the brothers had spent a great deal of time wandering about the country finding their way politically and professionally. Their experiences carried them far from their sheltered lives in a wealthy Tianjin family. They witnessed the diversity of their country, from the peasants of mountain villages to the peddlers, traders, soldiers, workers, businessmen, and officials whom they met in the towns and cities. They saw the devastation of war, and all but the eldest came to know the meaning of hunger and poverty.

In many ways, the wartime devastation recalled the destructive rebellions of the previous century. In both eras, members of the Ye family fled their homes to escape occupation by hostile forces. But Ye Kunhou's extended family largely stayed together, the younger generations still following in the footsteps of their elders. The war with Japan had a very different effect. Each young man followed his own set of friends, classmates, and associates; each traveled a different route to a different destination; and each found his own wife to start a new type of family. Surprisingly, none of the scions of this elite Tianjin family even considered joining the Nationalists in their retreat to Taiwan. Indeed, many of them had worked actively in the revolution that created the New China. Optimistically, they welcomed the red dawn of a new era. But the war had also been a time in which each of the Ye brothers charted his distinct professional and political course. The choices that they made in this period—for an academic or a political career, for the Democratic League or the Communist Party—would decisively shape their lives in the People's Republic. In that sense, the war was a watershed for the Ye family just as it was for China.

# PART III

# The People's Republic

# 11

# Family Life in New China

Ye Duzheng was no leftist, but he returned to China within a year of the Communist takeover. If the Communists had not emerged victorious in the Civil War, he might never have returned: China under the Nationalists was too corrupt and chaotic. The founding of the People's Republic of China (PRC) in 1949 inspired new hope for the country. As Chiang Kai-shek's Nationalist armies collapsed in the final year of the Civil War, first Beijing and Tianjin were "liberated," then the Communist forces swept southward to occupy Shanghai and the Yangzi valley, and finally Canton and the far south. Duzheng followed the Communist victories in the Chicago newspapers and discussed the course of the Civil War with his Chinese classmates. In most cases, the change of power in China's major cities was accomplished with minimal violence and destruction: the local Nationalist commanders surrendered or withdrew a day or two before the Communists' People's Liberation Army (PLA) marched in to assume control. Although mop-up operations continued after 1949 against remnant Nationalist forces in the hills of the southwest, by and large the country returned to peace. It was the first real peace that China had seen since the Republic of China descended into warlordism not long after the fall of the empire, and it followed the horrible destruction of the Japanese invasion and the turmoil of Civil War. Those years had left millions dead, the nation's infrastructure in shambles, and the economy crippled by runaway inflation and critical shortages of raw materials. Now the new Communist regime promised peace and order and hope for the future. It was time for Duzheng to go home.

For the Chinese Communist Party, 1949 marked a major turning point. The party's strength was rooted in the villages of north China. From bases in the mountains, the Communists had waged guerrilla warfare against the Japanese aggressors, winning support as defenders of the homes and families of China's peasant farmers. In areas where they established stable control, they instituted highly progressive tax systems that shifted the fiscal burden onto the wealthiest households and reduced the rent and interest payments of the poor. By the end of the war, the CCP controlled much of the countryside of north China. Here, in the postwar era, the party carried out thoroughgoing land reform, confiscating the land of the rich to redistribute to the poor. The process was at times extremely violent, but it helped solidify support among those who gained from the revolution, and the party was able to conscript millions of peasants as soldiers and transport coolies for the climactic battles of the Civil War. As victory approached, the requirements for the task ahead changed. A peasant-based revolutionary army would have to transform itself into a political regime capable of building socialism in the world's most populous country.

Above all, the party needed to establish a political base in the cities. As Mao said early in 1949, the revolution was entering a stage of "the city leading the village," and the "center of gravity" of party work would now shift to the cities.[1] In the cities, the party would not rule as a "dictatorship of the proletariat," as Stalin did in the Soviet Union, but as a "people's democratic dictatorship" representing four progressive classes: workers, peasants, the urban petty bourgeoisie (meaning especially intellectuals and professionals), and the "national bourgeoisie." In this coalition, the working class (represented, of course, by the Communist Party) would take the leading role, and the reactionary classes ("feudal" landlords, for example) would be denied political rights and subject to the dictatorship of the progressives. The inclusion of the "national bourgeoisie" in this coalition was an important gesture, but the category was essentially a political one. It stood in contrast to "bureaucratic capitalists" with ties to the Nationalist regime and "comprador capitalists" linked to foreign interests. These latter two groups were both labeled reactionary elements and subject to expropriation or even arrest and execution.[2] In order to revive the urban economy, the Communists sought the cooperation of this "national bourgeoisie" in the cities; many businessmen, both to test the bona fides of the new regime and to earn the coveted "national bourgeois" label, were prepared to cooperate with their new Communist overlords.

In the spring of 1949, Ye Duren, the eldest Ye brother and a banker in Tianjin, was called to a meeting with the new Communist rulers. Liu Shaoqi, the second-ranking CCP leader, had come to north China's most important port and industrial city to meet with representatives of the business community. His main purpose was to persuade business leaders to stay and keep their money in China and to cooperate with the new regime in reviving the urban economy. The businessmen complained that although they had opted to stay and had kept their capital in the city, thus giving employment to thousands of workers, they were still being treated as "exploiters." Liu replied that he could not deny the Marxist truth that capitalist profits were derived from exploiting the labor of others, but he admitted that their efforts had "merit" (a line for which he was much reviled during the Cultural Revolution) and promised to allow private enterprises to keep and reinvest their profits.[3] Duren was sufficiently impressed by the message that when his wife's wealthy friends spoke of fleeing to Hong Kong, he urged them to stay and try to do business under the Communists.[4] Many Chinese businessmen made the same choice, and the Chinese economy in the early years of the PRC combined private and state-owned enterprises along with a large rural sector of private peasant farming.

Although the party was willing to make concessions to private businesses in the initial period of its rule, it left no doubt that its long-term goal was to build socialism. In this regard, it was not out of step with the majority view of educated Chinese. As a well-informed American observer wrote at the time, "The prevailing opinion among almost all politically conscious people in China has favored some sort of socialism adapted to Chinese needs."[5] This was, after all, an era in which the Labor Party, committed to the nationalization of industry, had just come to power in Great Britain, and democratic forms of socialism commanded a wide following in many parts of the world. Under the Nationalist government during and after the war, many of China's mining companies, railways, and leading heavy industrial enterprises were state owned, and in cities like Tianjin, the postwar confiscation of Japanese factories further expanded the state-owned sector of the economy. The Communist victory only changed the nature of the state that would dominate the urban economy.[6] If China was destined to be socialist, though, just how democratic would Chinese socialism be? For many, the answer was tied to the question of how closely the Chinese Communists would link themselves to the Soviet Union.

The CCP had been founded in 1921 under the tutelage of Soviet emissaries of the Communist International, and throughout the 1920s, the party leadership maintained close relations with the Soviet Union. That era ended in the bloody suppression of the CCP by Chiang Kai-shek after 1927, and Mao Zedong's rise to primacy in the party during the 1930s and 1940s had been quite independent of Soviet interference. Mao's strategy of rural-based guerrilla struggle owed little to traditional Marxist-Leninist doctrine, and the party's spectacular growth during the Anti-Japanese War was substantially due to its appeals to patriotism. There was, accordingly, considerable debate in the 1940s about how closely Mao's party would hew to the Soviet line. Sufficient documentation has now emerged to demonstrate that Mao's intention to follow the Stalinist model of socialism was never in doubt, but at the time, both Chinese liberals and foreign observers held out hope that Mao's nationalism would prevail over his commitment to Stalinism. Tito in Yugoslavia was another Communist who had risen to power independent of the Soviet Union, and when he broke with Stalin in 1948, Yugoslavia became a model for an independent socialist path that many hoped China would follow.[7]

The United States, fearful that Asia's largest country would fall firmly in the Soviet camp in the Cold War, did everything it could to encourage China along a Titoist path. In May 1949, as Ye Duyi was preparing to flee Shanghai for Hong Kong, he met with an American consular official who gave him a State Department–printed copy of correspondence between Stalin and Tito from the period leading up to the break. Duyi was struck by Stalin's imperious tone and overbearing attitude. He knew that China's new rulers would not welcome such an overlord, and he was apparently prepared to deliver the volume to Zhou Enlai as the American consul requested, though he fully recognized the transparent U.S. effort to sow discord between China and the Soviet Union. But when Mao's speech on July 1 spoke of "leaning to one side" in the Cold War, Duyi saw that Mao was committed to a pro-Soviet course. He would only invite trouble by delivering the Stalin-Tito correspondence, so he left the booklet in Hong Kong.[8]

Among the Ye brothers, Duzheng's return from the United States was the most dramatic evidence of the CCP's success in attracting the support of "petty bourgeois" professionals, and it signified the hope that patriotic Chinese intellectuals had for the new order. With a University of Chicago Ph.D. and training under the world's leading scholar in his field, Ye Duzheng forsook a well-paid job and a promising career in the United States to return to an uncertain future in China. By the time he left Chicago, the Cold War had turned hot in Korea. The United States sought to isolate "Red China" by refusing recognition, keeping the new government out of the United Nations, and barring trade. But the boat on which Duzheng and his wife returned was filled with young Chinese who, like him, were drawn back to their homeland not by Communism but by patriotism, and who longed for an opportunity to serve their country and make it great again. When they crossed the bridge from Hong Kong, they were greeted on the Chinese side like returning heroes. Touched by the officially organized welcome, Duzheng felt his eyes fill with tears.

Soon he was on a train to Nanjing, where he joined the Institute of Geophysics of the Chinese Academy of Sciences. The job had been arranged by correspondence before his return, and he took up his new duties eagerly. Once facilities were arranged in Beijing, the Academy of Sciences moved to the new capital. Duzheng helped to organize the Meteorology Bureau, which would coordinate weather forecasting for the nation, a critical enterprise in a largely agricultural country plagued by persistent floods and drought. He rose to the rank of research scientist (*yanjiuyuan*) and was a leading member of the Institute of Atmospheric Physics when it was established within the academy.[9]

Like all the Ye brothers, Duzheng was in the prime of life in the early years of the Communist regime. The eldest brother, still living in Tianjin, had just turned forty when the PRC was founded; the youngest, staying in Sichuan to pursue his career as an entertainer, was only twenty-five. The others were all in their thirties and eager to get to work. The third brother, Ye Duyi, was the only one besides Duzheng who had finished his college education. As a young intellectual and a leading member of the Democratic League, he had long been critical of the Nationalist dic-

FIGURE 17. Ye Duyi with Democratic League members, 1949. Ye Duyi is on the left
in the top row. The anthropologist Fei Xiaotong (Duyi's Tsinghua classmate) is second
from the left in the front row. Zhang Bojun, with whom Duyi was linked in 1957, is
third from the left in the second row, with a dark jacket and horn-rimmed glasses.

tatorship, and had extensive contacts with Communist united front operatives.
Indeed, the Communist representative in Hong Kong (where he had fled in the
spring of 1949 to escape arrest by the Guomindang) had helped arrange his return
to China. In September, he was named a Democratic League alternate member of
the Chinese People's Political Consultative Conference, the Communist-dominated
united front organization that proclaimed the founding of the People's Republic of
China on October 1, 1949, passed the Organic Law that served as a constitution for
the first years of the PRC, and gave the regime something more than revolutionary
legitimacy. In a sense, Ye Duyi was present at the creation of the new government,
but he was dissatisfied with his "alternate" status. He brought up the issue with Li
Weihan, who headed the CCP's United Front Department and was responsible
for relations with the democratic parties. Li explained that the "alternate" label was
unimportant: it meant only that Ye could not vote. As Li candidly explained, the
lack of voting rights was inconsequential, because the Communist Party would decide all important issues before the meeting anyway. Duyi, trained in politics from

American textbooks at Yenching University, had received his first lesson in the "people's democratic dictatorship" of the new regime.[10]

With his degree in political science, Ye Duyi was recruited to serve on the Politics and Law Commission (Zhengzhi falü weiyuanhui). This commission, headed by party elder and Politburo member Dong Biwu, was charged with overseeing all the ministries concerned with domestic, legal, and internal security affairs and was clearly an organ of considerable importance.[11] Duyi was a diligent official, the only full-time member of the commission, and he was soon promoted to executive secretary. Later his duties came under the jurisdiction of the Ministry of Justice, and he was provided an old-style courtyard house in a neighborhood where many officials lived, a regular salary, and quite comfortable working conditions. He was also one of the leaders of the Democratic League, which was permitted to continue its activities in the PRC as long as it accepted the leading role of the Communist Party. He was becoming one of the not inconsiderable group of Western-educated liberal intellectuals co-opted into an uneasy working relation with the new Communist state.[12] Non-party intellectuals and professionals played a significant role in the early PRC government. Eleven of the twenty-four ministers of the new government were members of the Democratic League or other minor parties, or independent "democratic personages."[13]

The agronomist Ye Duzhuang had also been active in the Democratic League, though not at the national level like his elder brother Duyi. When the Communist forces surrounded Beiping early in 1949, he had no intention of leaving and worked to persuade others to remain at the agriculture institute in the city's suburbs. With his agronomy education in Japan and his progressive politics, he too had hopes for an official position, perhaps in the administration of the institute. But he was probably too independent minded for the new Communist leadership. He was also put off by the superior attitude and hard official line of the Communist cadre appointed to head the institute. In the new leader's first meeting with the staff, he strode across the stage in a grey PLA uniform, avoided all eye contact with the assembled agronomists, and delivered a simple and not very welcoming message: "stay if you wish, go if you want." But Duzhuang's public stance in the Beijing Democratic League was consistently supportive of the new regime. In the spring of 1951, the *People's Daily* approvingly printed a statement he drafted praising the "awesome power" of recently issued laws for dealing with counter-revolutionaries.[14]

Ye Duzhuang's position (and publications) in the pre-1949 institute had been in agricultural economics, but that discipline, whose principles assumed a market economy, was deemed irrelevant in a regime devoted to building socialism. With his old department abolished, Duzhuang was appointed head of his institute's editorial committee. He felt underused, but he put out a newsletter and a journal whose main theme was the need to learn from Soviet science, especially the theories of the peasant-agronomist Ivan Michurin. Michurin's ideas had been championed by

Trofim Lysenko, a favorite of Stalin, as a theory (now discredited) showing that acquired characteristics could be inherited independently of any genetic mechanism. The embrace of these "advanced discoveries" of Soviet science certainly did nothing to improve biological science or agricultural practice in China, but Duzhuang dutifully joined a team that translated an English edition of Michurin's works and, for a while at least, found them fresh and exciting. The People's Daily hailed his translation for transmitting Michurin's important message that one should not simply accept natural phenomena as given, but "struggle with nature . . . transforming nature."[15] This optimistic transformative message of Michurin and Lysenkoism was the basis for its appeal. The People's Daily published a rather fastidious review that Duzhuang wrote of a rival Chinese translation of Michurin's most important study, closing with the admonition, "The translation of such an important work should not be undertaken so recklessly." But he must have been disappointed when a careless copy editor changed one character of his name, attributing the review to his more famous brother, Ye Duyi.[16]

When Ye Duyi had returned to Tianjin after the war, he stayed with his eldest brother and urged him to join the Democratic League. In many ways, this eldest brother should have been the most vulnerable of the Ye brothers facing a Communist revolution. A banker living in his wife's mansion in the former concession area—a house left her by her uncle, Xu Shichang, the one-time president of the republic during the warlord era—Ye Duren was far and away the richest Ye sibling. In addition, having lived and worked in Tianjin during the Japanese occupation, he was open to the charge of collaboration with the enemy. But Duren was nothing if not cautious, exceptionally effective at avoiding attention, and just as successful at collaborating with the Communists as with every other regime that Tianjin had seen. He seems to have liquidated most of his property during the 1940s. He quit his job at the bank, took a salaried position with the Democratic League, cooperated with every CCP campaign that came along, and taught his children to live simply and without display, once insisting that his daughter, who wanted a foreign watch like her friends, content herself with a cheap domestic brand. His approach worked perfectly: he and his family led an uneventful life, accomplishing little but suffering less.[17]

The other Tianjin businessman of the family, fourth brother Duxin, had been living off stock dividends for some time. After 1949, he taught for a while at a night school, but he had tuberculosis and was unable to continue. His cheerful and outgoing wife was active in the local neighborhood committee, looking after public hygiene and social order, doing propaganda work for the government, reading the newspaper aloud to illiterate women (she was good at transforming the dull official accounts into lively stories that kept her audience entertained), and serving as one of the commoner-judges on the local court. She was effective and popular at her job, even daring to complain against petty officials who abused their privileges, and was probably less the intrusive busybody than many other women in that role. The couple had no children, and after private enterprises were socialized, Duxin received fixed monthly interest payments for the stocks he had held, which provided enough for their simple needs.[18]

The youngest brother and black sheep of the family, the entertainer Ye Lizhong, stayed in western China after the war. The People's Liberation Army did not reach his new home in Chongqing until the end of 1949. One day, the Nationalist police simply lined up and marched out of town, and the PLA entered behind them. The new China brought an end to much of the discrimination against actors that Lizhong had felt in the old society, and within a year, he had a regular salaried job with the Great Masses Performing Arts Troupe. He learned the new revolutionary songs and stories and performed with his usual gusto. He did not marry until 1957, but in all, his transition to the new China was smooth. Nonetheless, still smarting from his earlier expulsion from the family, he dared not contact his brothers in Beijing and Tianjin.[19]

Of course, the two brothers for whom 1949 brought the least change were the sixth (Ye Fang) and ninth (Fang Shi), the two members of the Communist Party. They had been working for the revolution for some years, and now they simply moved on to a new stage of that project. After his bandit-fighting years as a magistrate in the Northeast, Ye Fang was appointed vice-president of the party school in one of the new provinces of the region. This post began a long period of service in such institutions, which instructed local party cadres in basic Marxist doctrine, the history of the Chinese revolution, and key CCP policies. Ye Fang's years at Nankai Middle School and Tsinghua University made him unusually well educated for a CCP member. (The party included only about 40,000 college graduates in 1949, less than 1 percent of its 4.4 million members.)[20] He had, in addition, a calm intellectual demeanor and capacity for guarded circumspection on sensitive political matters, which suited him for an administrative role in party education. In 1948, when Shenyang (the former Mukden) was taken, Ye Fang was sent to organize the party school for the entire Northeast region and headed its education department until 1955.[21]

The ninth brother, Fang Shi, stayed with the New China News Agency, following the party center to Beijing in 1949. The agency was unable to arrange housing in the city until August, at which point it located its headquarters at the same Beijing College of Law and Commerce that he had attended as a student in the 1930s. His responsibility was now political reporting, including coverage of the activities of the Communist leadership. In this role, he interviewed Zhu De, the commander of the PLA, on Army Day and covered the first meeting of the Political Consultative Conference that led to the founding of the PRC. At that meeting, he got a taste of the changes taking place among the revolutionary leadership. He ran into an old friend from his days in the student movement, who was now a governor in the Northeast. The men greeted each other in the warmest manner and quickly sought to catch up on their respective revolutionary careers. But when his friend discovered that Fang Shi was not a fellow high official or even a delegate to the conference, but only a lowly reporter, his manner turned abruptly formal and cold, and he moved off to seek a more important partner for conversation. The casual relations that Fang Shi had enjoyed with China's highest leaders at Xibaipo were a thing of the past. Hierarchy and rank and official airs would find a place in New China too.

Of the three sisters who survived to 1949, only the third, Duya, lived in Beijing and interacted much with the rest of the family. Her husband had worked in a tax bureau under the Nationalists and accumulated enough money to buy a house for the family. To protect his job, he had had to entertain his superiors, which he often did at brothels or with drugs. Duya suffered greatly from his whoring and once attempted suicide. After 1949, he managed to escape punishment for his work for the Nationalists and took a job at a local handicraft workshop. But eventually his unsavory past and penchant for speaking too freely got him arrested, and he died in prison in 1960. Duya, meanwhile, became an activist in her neighborhood committee, seeing to the peace, order, cleanliness, and political correctness of her neighbors. She raised three sons, all of whom went to college and became her primary consolation in an otherwise bitter life.

The fourth sister, Dusong, had a similarly grievous life in the southwest, where she had fled with her husband during the war. He was a Cornell-trained engineer with no sense of marital fidelity. In Yunnan, he brought his mistress into the household, where they lived in bigamous disharmony until the woman left him. Dusong had three children, two distinguishing themselves in technical careers, one becoming a successful official. Meanwhile, the fifth sister, Durou, ended up in Shanghai. Her husband, Yao Zengyi, whom she had married for love during the war, had become a prominent official in the Nationalist government and fled to Hong Kong in 1949. He was promised a high position if he followed the Nationalists to Taiwan, but his wife refused to leave China while her mother was still in Tianjin. So he returned, and they stayed on in Shanghai. She (the only sister with any formal education) became a biology teacher, while her husband, fearful that his past would be held against him, worked at home as a private translator. Living away from the new family center in Beijing, these two sisters rarely interacted with the rest of the family, and at this point, we allow them to drop from our story.[22]

With the exception of the childless and mostly unemployed Duxin, all of the Ye brothers found a role contributing to the work of the new China, whether in science (Duzheng) or entertainment (Lizhong), in government (Duyi) or party activities (Ye Fang) or with the Democratic League (Duren), or as an editor of a technical journal (Duzhuang) or journalist in the official news agency (Fang Shi). They were also all raising families of a different stripe from the one in which they had grown up in Tianjin. The large "feudal" family—with husband, wife, mother, concubines, and dozens of servants living under one roof, children confined to the household compound, and boys attending school at home under a private tutor—was a thing of the past. The nuclear family, perhaps with the addition of a surviving grandparent, had long been the norm in ordinary peasant or small merchant families; it had been embraced by the middle class in the republican era, and now even elite families conformed to this pattern.

Among the Ye brothers, as we see from table 3, the same divide that had separated older and younger siblings in the republican era was evident in the demography of their families under the PRC. The three oldest brothers, all of whom had arranged marriages, were wed before the war at the age of twenty-two or twenty-three, ages very close to the established norms for Chinese males. Beginning with the fifth brother, Duzhuang, all the others married during or after the war, usually when they were near or past the age of thirty. (The exception is Fang Shi, who married a party comrade at age twenty-three, though his first surviving child came only in 1950.) All but one of the three elder brothers' seven children were born before or during the war, whereas all but two of the younger brothers' eighteen children were born after the war. Indeed, when we consider that Ye Fang was living in "liberated" Communist-controlled areas of the Northeast from 1946 on, fifteen of these children were born under the new regime. As such, they were part of the Chinese population boom that came with the peace and order of New China.

The families of these younger brothers most interest us, for they brought a new type of child rearing, characteristic of the early years of the PRC. Not all of these families were alike, of course. The most distinctive new type was Ye Fang's large family in Shenyang, for his was a privileged provincial-level cadre family. It was distinctive in part by being very large. In the early years of the PRC, the party's policy was clearly natalist, following the anti-Malthusian theories of the Soviet Union, which held that class oppression and imperialist aggression, not overpopulation, were responsible for poverty in countries like China. One of the duties of a residence committee activist like Duxin's wife or Third Sister Duya was to encourage young couples to have more children.[23] Ye Fang and his wife certainly heeded this injunction, which may have had particular force in the Northeast, where the population was relatively sparse and Soviet influence was particularly strong following the Russian occupation in the waning days of World War II. The couple had eight children (six in their first ten years in the Northeast), and the party did everything necessary to accommodate this large family, providing a large Japanese-built house with a separate bedroom for each child and a nanny until the child was two years old and ready to begin boarding at nursery school.

The family lived in a compound reserved for leading cadres of the provincial party apparatus. Such compounds are found in every provincial capital, surrounded by high walls that were usually topped with barbed wire or broken glass and guarded

TABLE 3  Ye Families of the PRC Period

| Ye Brother[1] | Date of Marriage | Age at Marriage | Children | Child's Date of Birth | Child's Gender |
|---|---|---|---|---|---|
| #1: Ye Duren b. 1908 | 1931 | 23 | Weiqi | 1935 | F |
| | | | Weihu | 1937 | M |
| | | | Yun | 1949 | F |
| #3: Ye Duyi b. 1912 | 1934 | 22 | Weiti | 1937 | F |
| | | | Weizhen | 1939 | F |
| | | | Weiyou | 1941 | F |
| | | | Weizuo | 1944 | M |
| #4: Ye Duxin b. 1912 | 1935 | 23 | | | |
| #5: Ye Duzhuang b. 1914 | 1946 | 32 | Liang | 1947 | F |
| | | | Wa | 1949 | F |
| | | | Xiao | 1952 | F |
| #6: Ye Fang b. 1914 | 1945 | 31 | Lin | 1943 | F |
| | | | Jiamu | 1946 | M |
| | | | Boli | 1947 | M |
| | | | Binbin | 1951 | F |
| | | | Yangyang | 1952 | M |
| | | | Xinxin | 1954 | M |
| | | | Bao | 1956 | M |
| | | | Hongbao | 1960 | M |
| #7: Ye Duzheng b. 1915 | 1942 | 28 | Weijiang | 1943 | M |
| | | | Weiming | 1951 | F |
| | | | Weijian | 1953 | M |
| #9: Fang Shi b. 1916 | 1939 | 23 | Weili | 1950 | F |
| | | | Weijia | 1951 | M |
| | | | Weiqiang | 1959 | F |
| #12: Ye Lizhong b. 1924 | 1957 | 33 | Weizhou | 1958 | M |

NOTE:

[1]Ye Chongzhi's second and tenth sons died in childhood. The second son was relabeled and also occupied the eighth position. The eleventh "son" was the adopted son from Yuan Shikai's family. (See chapter 8 and table 2.)

by a PLA sentry at the gate.[24] Inside, the grounds were spacious, with plenty of trees and open space and room for children to play. The nursery school that the children attended was within the walls. There they boarded from Monday through Saturday, in dormitories with about ten beds to a room, returning home only on Sundays for a noisy meal with the family. The children spent so little time together at home that family ties were not that important when they were young. Their personalities were quite different, and during vacations or time away from school, they were more likely to play with classmates from school than with siblings. These games clearly showed the elite status of the peer group: the boys' make-believe world was filled with generals and ministers and party secretaries, reflecting the posts held by their fathers and the ones to which this new generation naturally aspired.

At nursery school, they learned revolutionary songs and dances—resisting American imperialism and aiding North Korea being particularly popular themes during the Korean War in the early 1950s. At home, their father reinforced this message, urging the children to develop their revolutionary spirit and devote their lives to China and the Communist Party. When they were ready for school, they attended the Cultivating Talent Primary School, headed for a time by the wife of Gao Gang, the powerful party boss of the Northeast region. The talent to be cultivated at such schools belonged to the children of the regional party and army leaders, and the best teachers and facilities were provided for this next generation of the revolutionary vanguard. Even during the worst years of shortages, the food at their schools was always adequate, with steamed wheat buns and noodles instead of the cornmeal that many ate, vegetables for most meals, and meat several times a week. In general, the food at school was better than what they got at home. On weekends, a great line of black sedans lined up outside the school gate, sent by the students' fathers' unit to take the kids home for a brief visit with their families. The Ye children, however, lived only a few blocks from school and walked home.

In the early years of the PRC, party and government cadres' compensation remained on the supply system inherited from the revolutionary era. In lieu of a salary, each family was provided housing, food, clothing, and other essentials sufficient to meet their needs. At New Year, two new suits of clothing were provided, the younger children receiving theirs through the nursery school. The clothes were just the colorless basics: tee shirts and pants for summer, cotton-padded jackets and pants for winter. Invariably, the younger children's simple wardrobe was supplemented by hand-me-downs from their older siblings. Until the 1960s, when rubber-soled canvas shoes became available, the Ye children wore cotton shoes made at home by their mother and maid.

The biggest annual holiday was Chinese New Year. Everybody got at least a week off from school and work, and the party supplied food for a major feast. Invariably the meal included fish (required for any New Year celebration), and Ye Fang's large family usually got half a pig as well. With no refrigeration (except the cold temperatures of the northern winter), the family quickly consumed these unprecedented provisions. Free tickets were distributed for New Year entertainment, usually a dubbed Soviet-bloc movie or revolutionary Chinese film. In the summer, Ye Fang was given a vacation at a party retreat on the beach at Dalian. The accommodations were not adequate for the whole family, so he took one or two children, usually the younger ones, leaving his wife to care for the rest. One of his youngest sons fondly remembered these vacations, including the fancy white bread he was allowed to eat.

By the time they reached middle school, the children went on school-organized holidays, with special buses and food and lodging provided. Such comprehensive care could breed a psychology of dependence in the children, hampering their ability to fend for themselves later on. One remembers that as teenagers, when they went to take a public bus, they did not know how to buy tickets.

A curious and contradictory spirit prevailed in this privileged party family. On the one hand, with spacious housing, maids and nannies, special schools, and ample supplies from the party, Ye Fang's children led a pampered, privileged life. A certain sense of entitlement took hold in this fledgling party aristocracy. Their friends all came from similar circumstances, and they were expected to pursue the same party, government, or military careers as their fathers. On the other hand, their father (and their teachers) lectured them on the hard times the party had gone through to reach this point and drilled into them the need to emulate that spirit of hard work and simple living. When one daughter brought her dirty clothes home from school for the maid to wash, she was sharply rebuked and told that henceforth she must see to her own laundry. Ye Fang was perhaps stricter with his family than many of his colleagues, rarely using an official car to take the children to a movie, sometimes allowing his complimentary movie or theater tickets to expire unused (one boy recalls his dismay at discovering a pair of tickets in a wastebasket), and prohibiting the children from reading his copies of sensitive internal party publications like *Reference News*, whose excerpted reports from foreign publications were often available to older children of other high cadres.[25]

The family of the fifth brother, Ye Duzhuang, provides a contrast to this provincial cadre lifestyle and was similar to most of the others in the Beijing area. For Duzhuang and his wife, Sun Song, children and family life were much more important, and sending their daughters to be raised by the state was unthinkable. While courting, the couple had talked of owning a farm in the Western Hills outside of Beijing, where Duzhuang would carry out agronomy experiments and his wife would raise the children, paint, and (in her romantic imaginings) raise horses. The revolution put an end to Sun Song's dreams of horseback riding on the family farm, but she eagerly welcomed her husband's assignment to the agricultural institute in the suburbs. Though the Chinese Academy of Agricultural Sciences, the successor to the institute Duzhuang joined in 1948, is now well within the urban boundaries of Beijing, at the time it was surrounded by open fields, and Sun Song loved the fresh air and closeness of nature. The area offered the healthy environment in which she wished to raise her children, and they would picnic in the orchards, or she would take her girls into the cornfields and strip them to their undergarments to romp about exposed to the sun, breathing in all the clean air that their little lungs could absorb.

They lived in a simple apartment in a square two-story compound of about

FIGURE 18. Ye Duzhuang with his wife, Sun Song, and daughters, Ye Liang (left) and Ye Wa (front) in 1951. Family photo.

twenty units, built by the Japanese during the war. Their ground-floor unit had a kitchen, bathroom, bedroom for the children, living room in which the parents had their bed, and a room with a tatami floor (made, at some expense, to suit Sun Song's Japan-derived taste) where the nanny slept and the children played. Through the early 1950s, the girls all lived at home, as neither father nor mother was willing to trust their care to the sorts of boarding nurseries that Ye Fang's children attended. At first, Sun Song stayed at home with the children, even turning down an offer to work in the film business from associates who had known her in Shanghai. Soon, however, her professional ambitions returned, though the only convenient job she could find was as an underpaid illustrator for the journals that her husband edited at the agriculture institute. He wanted another child, hoping for a son, but she was reluctant, almost terminating one pregnancy, though in this natalist period of the early PRC, an abortion required ministerial approval. By the time Duzhuang contacted an acquaintance in the relevant ministry, it was too late for the operation and the third daughter soon arrived.

By the mid-1950s, Sun Song got a job with the Beijing Film Studio as a costume designer, a position she would hold for the rest of her life. She went to work by bus and was sometimes away for weeks at a time when the studio filmed on location outside Beijing. By this time, the children were at nursery and then primary school. The older two attended as day students, coming home at noon for lunch. The youngest, who was too small for such independence, went to a boarding nursery during the week. After the eldest started primary school, Sun Song had her take the entrance exam for a selective elite boarding school. She wanted the best possible education for her daughters, and her own energies were increasingly devoted to her career. Her nine-year-old daughter passed the exam, but Duzhuang was unwilling to part with the girl. When the announcement of her acceptance came, he hid the letter until the enrollment deadline passed. Only then did he inform his wife of the exam results, so his daughter stayed at home to attend day school.

The family lived comfortably in this period on Duzhuang's and Sun Song's two salaries plus royalties from his publications. Rent was essentially free, deducted from his pay. Accounts in his wife's diary from 1955 show a monthly income of 144 yuan plus 108 yuan in royalties. From this, 20 yuan went for the nanny, 15 yuan to support Duzhuang's mother, and 12 yuan to repay some loan. In a typical month, he spent 16.40 *yuan* on books and 28 yuan for transport into the city; these business and educational expenses came to 18 percent of the total. Food was clearly the biggest expense, 81.13 yuan, or 32 percent of the total, with the remainder spent on clothes, heating, toys, and 3.80 for the one clear luxury: cigarettes.[26] This income bought a very comfortable standard of living, with meat, fish, and even shrimp frequently on the table. Sun Song insisted on a healthy diet that included an unvarying daily breakfast of warm milk, an egg, and toasted *mantou* (steamed bread) with butter and jam. The girls grew so tired of this regimen that one once sneaked off to school without eating her portion, only to have it served to her for lunch. The children went to a special new pediatric dentist, and the middle daughter even had orthodontics, a very new practice at the time. They wore colorful clothes, often created by their costume-designing mother and specially made. Books were a big part of family life, and Duzhuang bought so many children's books for his daughters that the house became a lending library for the neighborhood.

At school, the girls were model students. With intellectual parents and plenty of books at home, they excelled at their studies. Their father was also a strong supporter of the primary school at the agriculture academy, his editorial office generating income from which he could contribute to the school. This generosity helped to make his daughters favorites of the teachers. Indeed, when his second daughter began primary school, she was selected as a representative of the new students to give a short speech at the beginning of the school year, for which her mother made a special pleated white silk dress.

Family memories from this period are uniformly happy. Duzhuang frequently took his daughters to parks, the zoo, or the popular Soviet industrial exhibition hall.

They would take the bus into the city to listen to storytellers with their father, or watch movies with their mother, once a memorable special showing of the 1924 Douglas Fairbanks silent classic, *The Thief of Baghdad*, which Sun Song had seen years before in Shanghai. She knew that with its flying carpet and magic rope, it would be a rare treat for the kids, compared to the usual fare of Russian spy movies. On special occasions, such as birthdays, they ate at the Moscow Restaurant, a cavernous facility near the exhibition hall that served Russian food, a rare if not always tasty treat. Duzhuang had enough money to buy toys—blocks and puzzles and a red fire engine—and he started the girls stamp collecting with an album that they eagerly went about filling. As the girls grew older, they spent summer days swimming in the muddy pool in the academy yard. The second daughter became quite a good swimmer, whereas the eldest had a clear voice that earned her a place in a neighborhood choir group.[27]

The other Ye brothers in Beijing—Duyi at the Justice Ministry, Duzheng at the Academy of Sciences, and Fang Shi at the New China News Agency—enjoyed a family life not so different from this, though they all lived in the city, and their wives did not share Sun Song's romantic notions of pastoral life. Duzheng and Fang Shi each had three children of similar ages to Duzhuang's, and they occasionally visited each other and let the cousins play together. As a party member, Fang Shi shared many of Ye Fang's ideas about child rearing, and when both he and his wife were working and had frequent evening meetings, they found it convenient to place their children in boarding schools. They also wanted their offspring to experience collective living and to develop good socialist values of cooperating and getting along with their peers. As the children grew older, their parents encouraged lively dinner-table discussions of daily affairs and even more sensitive topics of culture and society—a practice that some of their neighbors regarded as "too democratic."[28]

The children of Duyi, Duzhuang, and Duzheng were exposed to a great deal of Western culture. Duyi loved to tell stories to his children, and the favorite authors of this graduate of the Western-influenced Yenching University were Dickens and Victor Hugo, so for days and weeks on end, with great energy and emotion, he would recount serialized versions of *Les Misérables*, *The Hunchback of Notre Dâme*, or *The Tale of Two Cities*. For Duzhuang's children, the art books that his wife had brought back from Japan introduced them to the masters of the Renaissance, the Impressionists, and modernist painters. The atmospheric physicist Ye Duzheng's home featured a scientific culture, with a blackboard on which was written the bewildering truth, "The universe has no end." The culture and values of these families differed in important ways, but all of them lived comfortably, put great stress on education, and raised their children to contribute to the progress of New China.[29]

Relations among the Ye siblings were handled with some care under the new regime. They had grown up together in Tianjin; most had studied at Nankai; the younger brothers had participated in progressive politics as students; and they had corresponded and occasionally seen each other during the long years of the war. But the Communist Party was wary of any excessive concern for family among its cadres, and the Ye party members were careful about reestablishing connections with their siblings. Fang Shi at the New China News Agency, for example, had left his inheritance with his third sister when he went off to join the revolution in 1937. In the years since, the two had corresponded occasionally, and she had sent him such scarce necessities as toothpaste when communication with Yan'an became easier in the immediate postwar period. But after arriving back in Beijing, he waited several months before going to see his sister. Even then, he made the mistake of taking a rickshaw to save time and was criticized for this forbidden bourgeois luxury. When his first child was born in 1950, he was still being compensated on the supply system and so received no salary to cover extra expenses. His sister sent him three hundred yuan from his own money. This was still a significant sum, and when it became known, a colleague accused him of using capitalist profits and thus allowing bourgeois consciousness to creep into the party. This was a serious accusation and posed a threat to his budding career, a predicament only resolved by extensive and sincere self-criticism of his bourgeois failings and donating the money to the party.[30]

As time went on and families grew, the brothers visited each other more frequently, often with their wives and children. When no political campaigns were going on, ordinary communication about family matters was easy enough, but since Fang Shi was a party member and Duyi held an important post in the Justice Ministry, they could not discuss many sensitive matters. So family gatherings involved a delicate avoidance of certain (especially political) topics, though these matters might actually be the areas of greatest common concern.


If sibling interactions were sometimes complicated, gender relations and their impact on conjugal life in the new China were even more complex. The position of women in Chinese society underwent tremendous changes in the twentieth century, and the redefinition of women's roles created new tensions in the family. For a late imperial Chinese woman from an elite family in Ye Boying's time, women's roles were clearly and strictly defined. She would marry into an appropriate family of similar status to her own, bear children, teach her daughters needlework and proper decorum and encourage her sons' classical studies, oversee the domestic economy, and eventually retire into a respected matriarchal role surrounded by grandchildren, deriving solace from family rituals and Buddhist piety. In the twentieth century, all of this was challenged and changed. Arranged marriages were condemned, women's education was promoted, and increasingly women were expected to play productive roles in society and assume full citizenship in the nation. Naturally these changes were uneven, and came more quickly in urban areas, but the

Communist Party's rhetoric supported liberating women from the shackles of patriarchy and promoted the notion (in Mao's slogan from the Cultural Revolution) that women "held up half the sky." The party itself, however, was a completely male-dominated institution, with most of its members recruited from the socially conservative countryside. Any feminist agenda of gender equality was inevitably subordinated to the cause of building socialism.[31]

· Thus, gender relations in the early PRC were a contested terrain in which no one was quite sure of the rules, and the potential for conflict and domestic discord was substantial. In the Ye family, most of the women had some education, many had served in the revolution, and they hoped for and expected to play a role in the new China. Male domination of the institutions of power and employment often frustrated them, and when their husbands (fearful of criticism for nepotism and corruption) were unwilling or unable to assist their search for a suitable job, some marital tension was inevitable. In most cases, these difficulties were overcome with time. Fang Shi's wife, for example, had joined the party even before he did and served in the guerrilla bases. Then her first pregnancy and childbirth, alone in that cold cave in the winter of 1940–41, left her crippled for life. By 1949, she had recovered enough to walk with a limp, but she was given no job and felt held back by her husband's position. So she left Beijing for Shenyang, where a friend got her a job in a rubber factory. This move toward independence forced a resolution of her problem: several months later Fang Shi went to Shenyang and brought her back to an editorial job at the New China News Agency. Domestic harmony was restored and lasted for the rest of her life.[32]

When Ye Duzhuang's first child was born, his wife wanted to stay home with the baby for a time. But she soon grew restless, especially when Duzhuang was away in the evenings for political meetings. The problem intensified when a young lady started pursuing him, writing love letters that Sun Song found in his desk. He professed his innocence of any dalliance with the woman and vowed to have nothing more to do with her, but things only settled down when he found work for his wife illustrating the journals he edited. She was grossly underpaid, and when in the criticism of Duzhuang for alleged corruption, she was targeted as the "boss's wife," she was furious. Fortunately, the job at the film studio soon came available, and she was able to achieve some professional recognition consistent with her extensive art training in Japan.[33] Ye Duzheng's wife, with her graduate training in the United States, quickly found work in the Academy of Science's Biology Institute, and their happy marriage was never affected by problems over jobs.

The wives of these three brothers all made the transition to a new order in which women of professional families had jobs, though none as prominent as their husbands'. While the women were also responsible for most domestic duties, they were helped by nannies who did much of the child care, cooking, and cleaning. All-day schools for the children also helped, and with the schools and small shops usually within the compounds where they lived, the mothers could rest assured of the children's safety while they were at work. In addition, their husbands were certainly more involved in the child rearing than had been the case in the previous generation.

In the early years of the PRC, Duyi at the Justice Ministry and Ye Fang at the Northeast Party School were the most successful of the Ye brothers in the political realm, and in part for that reason, their marriages were the most troubled. Ye Fang's wife was a pretty, young, outgoing actress when he met her with the New Fourth Army. The couple had been married on the road to the Northeast, and she immediately started having children at a remarkable rate. Though she longed to resume a performing career, her children were her first priority. In the fall of 1950, soon after the Korean War broke out, she fled to Harbin to give birth to her fourth child, Binbin—who, like most of her brothers, took her name from her birthplace. Ye Fang's wife always insisted that the move to Harbin had been authorized by the party, but the Organization Department denied any such approval and accused her of harming morale by fleeing to the north when Shenyang was threatened by the American advance in Korea. In 1951, she was expelled from the CCP. She bore the scars of this perceived injustice for the rest of her life, complaining to anyone who would listen (and many who would not) that she was a loyal and dedicated communist hounded out of the party for no good reason.

Eventually she accepted any work she could get, at a nursery school or later as a file clerk at the newspaper. But she repeatedly appealed her verdict, seemed incapable of accepting any form of party discipline, and blamed her husband for failing to clear her record. As a result, her obvious gifts as a social person with a talent for performing never found an outlet. Frustrated outside the home, she asserted her authority as boss of the domestic sphere. Her husband responded with silence to her endless complaints and bossy manner. At home, he simply kept his mouth shut. Despite the tensions between them, the two managed to keep having children, and their large family was the favorite of the kids' grandmother, who often visited from Tianjin to enjoy the noise and activity of a large family. The domestic quarrels of husband and wife did not bother her, and the old lady shared the party's idea that big families were a good thing.[34]

Ye Duyi's marriage was perhaps the unhappiest of all, though the dynamic was quite different from Ye Fang's. His wife came from a very wealthy family, and during the war, she had supported her husband and children by spending her dowry. Duyi was in Shanghai on Democratic League business when the oldest children were ready to start school. His wife wrote to ask if they should begin their studies, and without any money of his own, he wrote back, "This is like asking a beggar if he wants to eat. . . . If you can help them go to school, I will be forever grateful." She put them in the local primary school and kept the letter to remind him of this debt to her. After 1949, Duyi thought that his wife, like other women in her position, should get a job. Despite the lack of any formal education, her classical Chinese was excellent, and he thought she would make a fine teacher. She adamantly refused. She had supported him during the war; now it was his turn to support her.

As a result, she stayed home in a housewife role. But Ye Duyi's job required frequent evenings out, and in the early 1950s, for people in his position these occasions often included dances. Duyi felt he had to go, but his wife had grown up in a conservative official family, had no formal schooling, and felt quite unprepared for such modern customs as ballroom dancing. She refused to accompany him. However, afraid that he would be dancing with other women, she sent her eldest daughter in her place, to report back on her father's behavior. If she heard anything the least bit suspicious, she would hound him all night so that he could not sleep. Always troubled by insomnia, he found her harangues unbearable, and eventually Duyi moved out to live in the Democratic League compound, eating in the cafeteria. His wife became increasingly despondent, three times downing pills in attempts to take her own life. Much later, she was committed to a mental institution, where she was so heavily medicated that on her release, she seemed a completely different person: quiet and often depressed though she had been active and sociable before, extremely frugal with money though she was once an avid shopper. At that heavy price, a measure of domestic peace was achieved.

Compared to what was to come, the early years of the PRC were relatively calm on the political front. Still, a number of political movements had a substantial impact. Duyi, as a key member of the Democratic League, witnessed much of this activity, and the experiences became part of his political education. In early 1950, he led a team to inspect natural disaster conditions in northern Jiangsu, and he apparently acquitted himself well enough to be sent later in the year to spend eight months in the southern province of Guangdong observing land reform.[35] He went with a large delegation from the Democratic League, and the villages chosen were near the home of the famous turn-of-the-century reformer Liang Qichao (1873–1929). Obviously, the point was to show that even progressive intellectuals like Liang had reached their positions as scions of landlord families that exploited the poor. The trip was Duyi's first experience in the countryside, and in this area of extensive landlordism, he saw for the first time the poverty and suffering of the peasantry. He was stunned by the violence and cruelty with which the peasants responded to their oppression. Landlords were driven to suicide, and on one occasion that he found particularly painful, he watched a young activist viciously beat his own landlord father. Duyi knew that such violence was a violation of party policy and that his team was expected to report its views of the land reform experience. Nonetheless, he also understood that any objection to this violence would invite accusations that he was seeking to protect the exploiting landlord class, so he said nothing. He learned to accept such violence as a necessary excess in any class struggle. Above all, as he watched the party orchestrate the land reform process, he realized how tough and brutal the Communists could be.[36]

Back in Beijing, he experienced another side of the CCP: its skill at manipulating the democratic party leaders to gain their cooperation. Late in 1949, just after the founding of the PRC, a Democratic League congress devoted much of its energy to criticizing the "pro-American" views of some of its leaders. Duyi felt targeted in the attacks and withdrew. Several days later, as Zhou Enlai was about to leave for a critical trip to the Soviet Union to negotiate a Treaty of Friendship and Mutual Assistance, Duyi and other Democratic League leaders were summoned to meet with him. These leaders came from a generation of Western-educated intellectuals heavily influenced by American values, and the party was fearful that they might become a force opposing the alliance with the Soviet Union. Zhou met with them through the night and told them that he would not feel at ease abroad if he could not close ranks with the League at home. This sort of personal appeal by the revered Zhou Enlai was extremely effective. Duyi made his first public self-criticism, for having walked out of the congress, and when Zhou complimented him for his words, he was much encouraged.[37]

For Western-educated intellectuals, one critical task was to demonstrate that their sympathies were on the right side in the Cold War. Duyi watched as, one after the other, Democratic League leaders failed this test. One of them criticized the behavior of Russian troops in the Northeast after the war. The criticism was accurate: instances of indiscipline had occurred, especially involving the rape of Chinese women, but such "anti-Soviet" criticism was unacceptable. Another colleague thought of urging Mao to abandon his policy of "lean to one side" (i.e., the Soviet side), but the outbreak of the Korean War made this notion unthinkable. Duyi watched as those who held such views fell from grace in the party's eyes, and he was careful to hew closely to the party line. When the Democratic League issued a declaration supporting China's entry into the Korean War, condemning "ninety years of American imperialist ambition to invade China" and comparing the U.S. advance in Korea to the Japanese aggression that led to the invasion of China and World War II, Duyi's name was prominently listed in the People's Daily announcement.[38]

Journalist Fang Shi's job at the New China News Agency was to articulate this party line and produce the reports to support it. An interesting episode came in 1952, when he was called upon to travel to Korea to document charges that the United States was carrying out bacterial warfare against China by dropping rats carrying fleas infected with bubonic plague. The current scholarly consensus is that these charges were false, but their origins are interesting. A Japanese group, Unit 731, had carried out bacterial-warfare experiments on Chinese prisoners during World War II. After the war, most of this group escaped back to Japan, where the U.S. military protected the scientists from war crimes prosecution because it coveted their expertise for America's own bacterial-warfare programs. However, some members of the unit fell into Soviet hands when the Red Army overran Manchuria in 1945. Thus, the Russians learned of Unit 731 and its commander's return to Japan, and the incident became part of Cold War charges of U.S. protection of Japanese war criminals.[39] After the Korean War broke out and Chinese "volunteers" entered the conflict, many soldiers contracted a variety of unexplained diseases, and suspicion grew that they were victims of bacterial warfare, spread by the U.S. Air Force, which commanded the skies over North Korea. Mao and the Chinese leadership decided to make a propaganda campaign out of the reports before the allegations could be fully checked out, and once they started the campaign, they were forced to fabricate evidence to support it. In the spring of 1952, a wave of propaganda accused the American imperialists of violating international law and humanitarian principles. Though the Russians were certainly involved in the plot, after Stalin's death, the new Soviet leadership turned against the effort, and in May 1953, the Soviet Presidium formally complained to Mao: "The Soviet Government and the Central Committee of the CPSU were misled. The spread in the press of information about the use by the Americans of bacteriological weapons in Korea was based on false information."[40] Soon afterward, the campaign abruptly ended.

In the spring of 1952, however, at the height of anti-American sentiment accompanying the bloody conflict threatening China's borders, most Chinese were willing to believe the charges against the United States. The New China News Agency was a major source of reports on this alleged American perfidy, publishing articles on strange insects discovered by peasants and scientists' testimony on bacterial agents identified in their labs. In 1952, Fang Shi was the Chinese head of a joint Chinese-Korean delegation sent to interview two captured American airmen who had confessed to dropping germ-warfare bombs. He led a group of experts and journalists to the Northeast by train and then by truck across the Korean border at night until they reached the prisoner-of-war camp. In six days of interviews, they found the airmen friendly and cooperative. Although Fang Shi recalls no clear confession from the two, the published account has them admitting that they dropped special bombs at low altitude that were allegedly bacterial weapons and were officially reported as "duds." But the airmen may have been aware of an inherent weakness of their testimony: Chinese accusations of germ-warfare attacks date them from January 28, 1952, but the two airmen were shot down on January 13, two weeks before the attacks began. Despite such problems, Fang Shi's team was able to produce a long article and newsreel footage on the interviews. The journalists never went to the crash site or examined the physical evidence (though other Chinese scientists had), but the will to believe was strong enough that their reports were added to the evidence of U.S. crimes in Korea.[41]

The New China News Agency was China's official news agency and the mouthpiece of the party. Its daily dispatches from reporters all over the country and the world provided the main source of news for China's media, and the agency was also the official voice of China for the world. But in addition to being the mouthpiece of the party, the agency was its "eyes and ears." In this role, it produced "internal

FIGURE 19. Fang Shi, facing camera, interviewing American POW in Korea, 1952.
Family photo.

reports" *(neican)* to the party center. These secret reports were edited for distribution to the top party leaders, and they formed an important link in the party's in-
telligence-gathering apparatus. Much of the bad news in these reports (on natural
disasters, industrial accidents, or problems in the bureaucracy) never found its way
into the newspapers. But even these "internal reports" were subject to a high degree of self-censorship, a problem that grew worse over time.

From the fall of 1952 to 1955, Fang Shi was deputy head of the agency bureau
in the Northeast. By regulation, an agency representative attended all meetings of
the local party committee. As a result, Fang Shi was quite familiar with the activities of Gao Gang (1905–54), the former party boss of the Northeast who was purged
by Mao in 1953 in the most significant breach in the top party leadership at the
time. A former guerrilla leader from the party's northwestern base, Gao had an arbitrary and authoritarian style, and he was a notorious womanizer—though such
indiscretions could cost a lesser official his career. Indeed, Gao's wife was rumored
to collude in his misbehavior, procuring young girls to serve him and covering up
the liaisons. These kinds of reports were widely known in the Northeast, but muck-
raking was not in the New China News Agency's brief, and before Gao's fall, even
"internal reports" contained no such malicious gossip.

By 1955, Fang Shi had acquitted himself well enough to earn a promotion. To prepare him for his new job, the agency sent him for a year of study at the Central Party School. There he received systematic training in Marxist philosophy, political economy, social development (i.e., the inescapable historical transition from feudalism to capitalism to socialism), and contemporary domestic and international affairs. When his training was over, he returned to the news agency headquarters in Beijing as deputy head of the domestic bureau. At this time, the supply system was replaced by salary grades in the bureaucracy, and he was assigned to grade 11 out of 24. The top grades were reserved for the highest party leaders, and even a minister was only grade 8, so this rank was very high and earned him the generous monthly salary of 195 yuan.[42]

The Ye brother who had the greatest difficulty conforming to the political demands of New China was the agronomist Ye Duzhuang. His experience is a telling case study in how the Communists' successive political campaigns could finally trap a person in their fearsome logic. The process of political transformation began innocently enough (or so it seemed at the time) with a "loyal and sincere study movement" in 1950. Small groups of colleagues gathered to review each person's background and help each other overcome his prior class status and prepare to contribute to the new society. Duzhuang told his entire life history, starting with his life at the family compound in Tianjin and moving on to his early schooling at home and then Nankai, his study in Japan, his service with the Eighth Route Army during the war, his work with the Nationalists and Americans, and his relationships with American friends in Beijing after the war. He was proud of his progressive history and told his complicated story in ways that showed him in the best possible light. His wealthy class background was clearly a problem, but he emphasized that his mother was a concubine and said that he resented the unequal treatment she and her offspring received, leading him to oppose the class of his birth. He noted the leftist literature he read, his left-wing friends, and his role in the patriotic student movement. He said as little as possible about working with the American OSS.

The process was long and protracted, stretching on for over a year. Every connection with a foreigner had to be explained, and naturally there were lots of questions about his American connections in particular. By this time, the Korean War had broken out, and China and the United States were engaged in a bloody conflict on the Korean peninsula. China and the United States had been allies during World War II, when Duzhuang worked with the Americans, and his American friends were all liberals and leftists who were generally sympathetic to the revolution. There was no doubt in his mind that everything he did in the 1940s was on behalf of the struggle to defeat Japan and then the Nationalists and to build a strong, progressive, and democratic China. But a review of his dossier reveals intense questioning of his

American contacts and a verdict that he was not sufficiently humble, demonstrating a superior attitude and thinking he was above politics (*qinggao sixiang*). He even confessed to the sins of "individualism and liberalism."[43]

The first major political campaign of the early years of the PRC was the patriotic "Resist America, Aid Korea" campaign to support China's entry into the Korean War. Duzhuang had no hesitation in signing the Democratic League declaration condemning American imperialism in Korea and its threat to China.[44] Whatever friendships he had with progressive American journalists did not weaken his instinct to defend China against anything that looked like an aggressive threat. Not until the Three-Anti Movement of 1952—with its attack on corruption, waste, and bureaucratism—did a major campaign really affect work at the agriculture academy. The Ministry of Agriculture sent a representative to oversee the movement at the institute, and he encouraged people to criticize the director. When he got little response, he called on Duzhuang, who was known to be forthright in his views, and Duzhuang noted problems with the director's temper and authoritarian style but praised him as uncorrupt and knowledgeable about agriculture. The ministry representative was unhappy with this mild criticism (Duzhuang thinks because he coveted the director's job), so he turned to other targets and induced one of the agronomist's subordinates in the editorial department to criticize Duzhuang for bureaucratism. Duzhuang's initial reaction was that this was "like blaming the urinal because you can't piss." Later, in a fit of pique, he challenged, "You can find all the little bureaucratic flaws in me that you want, but you won't find any hint of corruption!" To this challenge, the ministry representative replied, "Fine! Then we'll check your corruption problems." The investigation first found problems with the financial manager of Duzhuang's editorial office, and then, starting with a gift of the selected works of Michurin to a colleague, it uncovered a series of minor transgressions, including one questionable business dinner and a long-distance phone call to Shanghai in which, after discussing an editorial matter, Duzhuang asked his colleague to send milk powder for the children. This request made the phone call a private matter, and together with the dinner, the total sum in cases judged "close to corruption" was deemed to be 45.65 yuan. The fact that Duzhuang had never pocketed any public funds proved an inadequate defense. He had not clearly separated public and private affairs, a sure sign of bourgeois thinking. He made matters worse when, under criticism, he withdrew from the study sessions and sought solace reading the eighteenth-century novel of scholar-official hypocrisy and misgovernment, *Rulin waishi* (The Scholars). In the end he was forced to make two self-criticisms at meetings of the institute's employees, swallowing his "stinky pride" and coming to "recognize more concretely the great power of the party and the masses."[45]

After the campaign, Duzhuang returned to work in the editorial department, but his pride was hurt by this attack on his probity, and his enthusiasm for editorial work was never the same. Instead, he put his energy into a personal project:

translating the works of Charles Darwin. He worked late into the night on his translation, which left him too tired to devote as much energy to his regular job. He knew that he was not putting his best effort into editing the journals, but his translations earned him several thousand yuan in royalties, which was important insurance in case things should get even worse at work.

In 1955, the government launched the Campaign to Suppress Counter-Revolutionaries, usually known as the Sufan campaign, and things did indeed get worse. In the agricultural academy and other educational and cultural institutions, the campaign developed out of an attack on the Marxist literary critic Hu Feng who had made an appeal for greater intellectual autonomy. Hu's appeal was treated as a counter-revolutionary challenge to party authority, and soon a witch hunt spread through the ranks of intellectuals, looking for hidden counter-revolutionaries.[46] Duzhuang and his colleagues were again gathered in small groups to study prepared materials on the "Hu Feng counter-revolutionary elements" and then to review their own political histories and respond to questions. At first, Duzhuang was not threatened: his name was listed in a *People's Daily* article about Democratic League members gathering to attack Hu Feng.[47] But Duzhuang's relations with the U.S. Army and OSS during the war, and with American journalists in the postwar era, were known to the party from the account he had written in 1950, and these relationships immediately became the focus of intense questioning: Hadn't Graham Peck worked for the U.S. Office of War Information (OWI)? Wasn't OWI an American intelligence agency? Hadn't Duzhuang provided information to Peck? Hadn't he taken the journalist James Burke to gather information in the guerrilla areas? Didn't such activities help the Americans spy on the Communist Party?

The questioning went on for an entire month. Nothing that Duzhuang could say would erase the suspicion that he had somehow been working for the Americans, even after the war, that there was more to the story than he was admitting, and that he was hiding something and dissimulating. Finally, in exasperation, he burst out, "There is nothing more to say!" and stood up to leave. "This is resisting!" charged his interlocutors, and that was a serious accusation. All of the party campaigns promised "lenience for those who confess fully, unmerciful treatment for those who resist." This mantra was repeated in every political movement in China, and it induced millions of people to confess fully—often to crimes they had never committed—in hopes (usually vain) of gaining a lenient sentence.

Duzhuang, however, would not confess. Finally, the party committee handling his "historical problem" proposed a verdict of "no punishment." Duzhuang would not accept this verdict. To him, it meant that he had committed a punishable offense, and he demanded that his interrogators specify what it was. When they could not, the verdict was changed to "an ordinary historical problem," referring to his service in the American OSS and AGAS. Again, he refused to accept the verdict: he had contacted his friends in the CCP before agreeing to work with the Americans, and they had approved. The United States was an ally in the war against Japan at the time. He suggested that they agree on the verdict "an ordinary *revolutionary* history problem." If Ye Duzhuang had realized that the OSS agent who had recruited him had also enlisted Ho Chi Minh, the leader of the Vietnamese communist party, it might have helped his case.[48] But he was unaware of this fact, and it may not have helped anyway.

In the end, the party reached no clear decision. Duzhuang's "historical problem" remained unresolved. He felt that at least his honor was intact. He had not agreed to any "counter-revolutionary" crime. But his wife was not pleased. She found his behavior stubborn and unreasonable and feared that in the end, the children would suffer from his recalcitrance: "Why do you insist on wearing a red dress [of a new bride, i.e., a pure one]? In the end, you're the one to lose. The kids are still small. Just sign it! End the matter and satisfy them!" But he would not, and in the end the consequence of this obduracy was as others had warned: he was left with a "pigtail" that the party could grab the next time a political campaign came along. His family life had been unusually happy in the first years of the PRC, but now politics would intervene to change everything.[49]

# 12

# Hundred Flowers
# and Poisonous Weeds

Late in the spring of 1957, Ye Duyi was summoned from his small apartment at the Democratic League headquarters to a meeting at Tsinghua University. He did not have a car at his disposal, and he had never learned to ride a bicycle, so he took a city bus to the campus in Beijing's western suburbs. Only about twenty people attended the meeting, mostly party officials and faculty at the prestigious university. They sat in overstuffed chairs and sipped tea in the heat of the afternoon. It was the sort of semiformal get-together to exchange views that the Chinese call a "sit-talk gathering" *(zuotan hui)*. It was not, however, an occasion for idle chit-chat. Indeed, it was presided over by Li Weihan (1896–1984), a senior party leader, veteran of the Long March, head of the CCP's United Front Department, and the man responsible for relations with intellectuals and the democratic parties.

When Ye Dui's turn came to speak, he suggested that relations between the Communist Party and intellectuals in the universities would improve if the party were to abandon its organizational role in the schools. The special and privileged position of party members gave rise to unnecessary conflicts. As he phrased his argument in later meetings, he did not question the leading role of the Communist Party. The party was the helmsman. But once the helmsman set the course, "it doesn't matter if the party or the democratic parties carry it out." His intent was to reduce conflict in the universities, and if there were "no party relationships in the universities, but only relations among faculty members, those relations would be much simpler, and conflicts much fewer."[1]

This was a very radical suggestion, for it would eliminate the system of party committees that had the final word on all curricular and personnel decisions in Chinese higher education. If the Communist Party organization were eliminated from elite colleges like Tsinghua, where 42 percent of the faculty members belonged to the democratic parties,[2] the influence of Ye Duyi's Democratic League colleagues would expand immeasurably. The move might help non-Communist intellectuals feel less like second-class faculty in their schools, but it would seriously weaken party control of higher education. Ye Duyi certainly did not make this suggestion lightly. He was allowed to inspect, approve, and sign the reports of his comments that would appear in the *People's Daily* and *Guangming Daily,* the national paper that in the 1950s catered a bit more to intellectuals.[3] Significantly, however, when the first article appeared on May 8, the headline read "Ye Duyi *approves of* the reorganization of the system of party responsibility in higher education."[4]

Two days before his comments at Tsinghua, Ye Duyi had heard a report on an April 30 talk by Mao Zedong. On the eve of the annual May Day celebrations, Chairman Mao and other Politburo members had met with leaders of the democratic parties in a reception room on the palace gate overlooking Tiananmen Square. In that talk, as it was reported to Ye Duyi and other cadres of the Democratic League, Mao had said, "I suggest that we first abolish the system of party committees in the schools. Let's not have everything managed by the party." He urged Deng Xiaoping (1904–97), the powerful general secretary of the Communist Party, to meet with the democratic parties to consider alternatives.[5] So when Li Weihan asked Ye Duyi for his views at Tsinghua, the latter felt quite safe in endorsing this proposal—though the confidential nature of Mao's conversation would have prevented Duyi from explicitly citing Mao's authority.

Chairman Mao's proposal to abolish party committees in the schools was not a casual or isolated suggestion. For over a year, the CCP had been debating policies toward non-party intellectuals. The process of "thought reform," the 1955 campaign against Hu Feng and "counter-revolutionaries," and the heavy weight of Communist bureaucracy had sapped the initial enthusiasm with which most progressive intellectuals had greeted the new China. Yet the party understood that building the education system and training the personnel needed to run a modern socialist economy would require the expertise of non-party intellectuals. The party itself was overwhelmingly composed of peasants with minimal education, and even the middle and upper levels of party leadership had few people with technical training in economics, finance, science, or engineering. Now, with the economy recovering rapidly and beginning a period of impressive growth under Soviet-style five-year plans, the party desperately needed to train and recruit a new generation of technicians and managers to run the socialist economy. To do so, it needed the cooperation of progressive but non-Communist intellectuals who had stayed in China to work with the CCP to build a new China.

In January 1956, Premier Zhou Enlai addressed this issue in a speech to over a thousand party cadres. "The Question of the Intellectuals" offered encouraging words, which were followed by concrete measures to increase professionals' salaries and improve working conditions. In April, Chairman Mao proposed the slogan "long-term coexistence and mutual supervision" to govern relations between the CCP and the democratic parties, and in the following month, he announced the slogan by which this entire period would be known: "Let a hundred flowers bloom, let a hundred schools of thought contend." In the succeeding months of 1956 and early 1957, Mao held meetings across the country in which he reiterated that non-party intellectuals and the democratic parties must be encouraged to speak up and criticize, to help the party rectify the errors of bureaucratism, dogmatism, and sectarianism. The successful socialist transformation of industry and agriculture had left him confident that party rule was secure and would not be subject to significant challenge. His key themes were laid out in a long, rambling speech in February 1957, "The Correct Handling of Contradictions among the People."[6]

In addition to the process of building socialism in China, the international situation was very much on Mao's mind. Two shocking events of 1956 were of paramount concern. The first was Nikita Khrushchev's secret speech in February acknowledging Stalin's dictatorial excesses and criticizing the "cult of personality." The Chinese leaders had been much shaken by this speech, in part because they were given no advance warning; and if the "cult of personality" was an error, then China's glorification of Mao's wise leadership and the guiding role of Mao Zedong Thought might be called into question. Mao himself found fault with Khrushchev's more tolerant policies—"The sword of Stalin has now been abandoned by the Russians"—and he feared that the "sword of Lenin" might also be forgotten. He saw the consequences of this weakening of proletarian dictatorship in the second shock of 1956, the Hungarian Uprising in October.[7]

The implications for China of the Hungarian Uprising against Soviet occupation (plus the somewhat less dramatic disturbances in Poland) and the de-Stalinization in Russia formed a recurring theme in Mao's February 1957 speech. He linked them explicitly, saying that Khrushchev's exposing of Stalin "provoked the Hungarian and Polish incidents."[8] At the outset of his speech, Mao admitted that in China, "some people have been delighted by the occurrence of the Hungarian and Polish incidents." They call for "big democracy" in the form of street demonstrations, and "a few naive people . . . imagine that European democratic freedoms are wonderful and we haven't enough of them."[9] "Since the Hungarian incident, has China had any disturbances?" he asked rhetorically, and then he admitted "a few small disturbances."[10] He downplayed the significance of these incidents, attributing the lack of serious challenge to Communist rule in China to the elimination of counter-revolutionaries, especially during the campaigns of 1950–52, which killed seven hundred thousand people (a figure later deleted from the published version of his speech).[11] Mao also noted that the party had stopped killing its enemies in 1956, and he pointed out that because the threat to Communist rule had been eliminated, it was now possible to permit and even encourage critical voices. Mao again harked back to Stalin's role, offering his criticism of the Soviet dictator's errors. Most serious, in Mao's mind, was that "Stalin did not admit that socialist society had contradictions."[12] Mao condemned Stalin's suppression of all criticism, which he directly contrasted to his own advocacy of a hundred flowers blooming and different schools of thought contending.

The central message of Mao's "Correct Handling" speech and other talks in this period was that conflicts and contradictions would inevitably persist under socialism, but the best way to handle them was to let people speak out and have a vigorous debate. At one point, he argued that China's "petty bourgeoisie" (a category in which he obviously included peasants) numbered over five hundred million. Did the party, he asked, want "to have them completely gagged, only letting [the gag] off a little when they eat, and as soon as they've eaten gag them again. How can that work? . . . [They] must express themselves, using various methods, staunchly—in a thousand and one ways [they must] express themselves. We cannot use coercive methods to stop them from expressing [themselves]; [we] can only debate them at the time of their expression." In endorsing debate with the party's critics, he warned against "dogmatic criticism" by party conservatives; and later in the speech, Mao warmed to his theme, proclaiming that even worker strikes and student disturbances were permissible: "I say it is better to permit disturbances." "I say let them agitate to their hearts' content."[13]

Party leaders and intellectuals held meetings across the country to hear recordings of Mao's speech, and many were charmed by his frank talk and earthy manner and stunned by his radical proposals.[14] As news of the speech spread among the politically engaged, an exciting sense of change was in the wind. However, previous campaigns made people wary of speaking out without a clear guarantee that their words would not later be used against them. Some called for the public circulation of Mao's speech, to provide definitive guidelines on the limits of dissent.[15]

Intellectuals and members of the democratic parties had been measuring the winds of change for some time. They were aware of Khrushchev's speech criticizing Stalin's errors. Coming in the midst of the Cold War, when China and Russia were firmly allied in the socialist bloc and the Soviet Union was routinely praised in the Chinese press as a socialist model and "elder brother," Khrushchev's speech had enormous impact. Foreign reports of the text were translated in *Reference News* and available to most intellectuals and party cadres. The text was read at party meetings in which members were sternly instructed to take no notes and discuss it with nobody outside the room, though there was clearly much talk about what it might mean for China.[16]

The Hundred Flowers slogan calling for a "hundred schools of thought" received great attention after Khrushchev's speech. Some read it as evidence of a post-Stalinist thaw in China, but intellectuals were still cautious. Previous campaigns against variously defined enemies of the party had made them wary of speaking out. As one democratic party leader said, "Since 1952, campaign has succeeded campaign each one leaving a great wall in its wake, a wall that estranges one man from another. In such circumstances, no one dares to let off steam even privately in the company of intimate friends, let alone speak his mind in public. Everyone has now learnt the technique of double-talk; what one says is one thing, what one thinks is another."[17] In the much-repeated metaphor of a prominent Beijing intellectual, people in early 1957 feared they were witnessing "early spring weather," which could easily be followed by a damaging "frost" that would kill any flowers that bloomed prematurely.[18]

The intellectuals' caution was justified. Many Communists were resisting Mao's calls to open the party to criticism from those outside its ranks. By the end of April, however, Mao had overcome this opposition, and he held lively meetings with intellectuals in Beijing, Shanghai, and other cities, encouraging them to speak up and help correct the ills of bureaucratism and dogmatism in the Communist Party. During May and early June, the democratic parties were invited to take the lead in offering suggestions and criticisms. Mao had long been advocating this role for the minor parties, under his slogan of "long-term coexistence and mutual supervision," and his April 30 meeting with the democratic party leaders repeated this message in unambiguous terms. In the days that followed, the democratic parties met to carry out Mao's instructions, and Li Weihan's United Front Department organized a series of public forums to solicit their leaders' suggestions and criticisms to rectify errors in Communist Party work.

As we have seen, Ye Duyi was one of the early Democratic League leaders to speak up, at the forum at Tsinghua University, where he called for the abolition of party committees in high education. Duyi had always been politically cautious, so it is not surprising that he began with a suggestion that Chairman Mao himself had already made. His comments were duly reported in *Guangming Daily* on May 8, though of course the article made no mention of Mao's views. As suggestions from the democratic parties were not only encouraged but also publicized in the CCP-controlled media, the Democratic League leadership met again on May 13 to organize its response to the Hundred Flowers Movement.[19] Three days later, the seventh of these forums with leaders of the democratic parties took place, and news of it dominated the papers on May 17. Ye Duyi was one of thirty-six people who spoke at the meeting.[20]

His comments, which were reported piecemeal in separate articles, touched on several issues. He repeated the suggestion made at Tsinghua that party organizations be abolished in the schools. He also noted that not all intellectuals were interested in politics. When forced to attend political meetings, some of the older ones simply turned off their hearing aids, so they could think about their research. He saw no reason to force political engagement on such people. For those intellectuals who wished to participate in the political process, he suggested that the proliferation of minor democratic parties be abolished and that a single intellectuals' party be formed to represent the interests of this group. This suggestion revealed the extent to which the so-called democratic parties were in fact so completely dominated by intellectuals that it would make sense to replace them with an "intellectuals' party," and it bespoke the special role that intellectuals were accustomed to playing in Chinese politics. (By way of contrast, one cannot easily imagine an intellectuals' party with any influence in American politics.)

In the headlines that followed Duyi's talk, the press reported his criticism of an "irrational state system." Articles noted that he particularly criticized the assignment of privileges according to political position and rank, so that members of the Standing Committee of the People's Congress were automatically given the very high rank of grade 5 cadres, which allowed them to ride in their own imported car. He also noted the unease of Democratic League members like himself, who had important positions in the state bureaucracy but had no role in setting policy, which remained a monopoly of the CCP.[21]

In his comments at Tsinghua, Ye Duyi was eager to eliminate the distinction between CCP and non-Communist faculty in the universities, and he continued this theme of "breaking down walls" in a forum on May 22, with an interesting suggestion for reform of the political language of the day. He noted that whenever a prominent CCP leader addressed an audience of party and non-party people, the address would begin "Comrades! Friends." The idea, of course, was that party members were comrades, while the others were only friends. Noting that the democratic parties all accepted the leadership of the CCP, to the degree that the Western press routinely characterized them as "fellow travelers," he wondered why everyone could not be considered a comrade.[22] In this plaintive plea for a change in the terms of political discourse, one hears the dominant theme in suggestions by Ye Duyi and many others in the spring of 1957. His aim was not to oppose the Communist Party; he wished only to be taken seriously and to be included as a full participant in the political process of the new People's Republic.

Because of his position in the national leadership of the Democratic League, Ye Duyi was the most prominent Ye family participant in the Hundred Flowers Movement, but his voice was only one of many. Across the country, forums were organized for intellectuals and democratic party leaders to propose ideas for the reform of politics, culture, and education. These forums were widely reported in the press, which was filled with an unprecedented range of criticism of Communist rule. Many of the critics were Western-trained intellectuals, and they expressed distress at the Chinese leaders' uncritical following of Soviet precedents. Complaints against party domination of all important decision making and criticisms of arrogant party cadres, arbitrary judgments, and dictatorial behavior were commonplace. Many objected to party leaders who were ill-educated apparatchiks heading technical ministries, schools, and research institutes, who were unwilling to heed the advice of experts.

The privileges and favoritism enjoyed by party members were another target of criticism, and many objected to the excesses of past political campaigns, which had subjected colleagues to severe and often unjust public struggle sessions.[23]

The publication of these criticisms in the party-controlled press inspired ever-wider debate on China's campuses. Peking University had always been a center of student activism, and beginning on May 19 (two days after the prominent press coverage of comments by Ye Duyi and other Democratic League leaders), the brick walls of the central meeting places were plastered with posters by faculty and students in a massive outbreak of participatory democracy. The students, demonstrating the impetuosity of youth and their lack of experience with previous campaigns, were a good deal less cautious than their elders. They began to launch direct attacks on the Communist Party and on Marxism-Leninism, posing an unprecedented challenge to proletarian dictatorship. At the end of May, the People's Daily reported a speech by one particularly outspoken young lecturer at People's University in Beijing. China, he argued, belongs to the Chinese people, not to the Communist Party. "If you carry on satisfactorily, well and good. If not, the masses may knock you down, kill the Communists, overthrow you. This cannot be described as unpatriotic, for the Communists no longer serve the people. The downfall of the Communist Party does not mean the downfall of China."[24]

With colleges in turmoil across the country, Ye Duyi and other Democratic League leaders met on June 6 to consider their options. They were deeply concerned that the student movement would spin out of control and move off the campuses into street demonstrations. They were already hearing reports of strikes and disturbances among workers, and if these two volatile groups should link up, the consequences could be serious.[25] Recognizing that the Communist Party, with its tight control of the security apparatus, had the power to crush any challenge to its authority, the Democratic League leaders were intent on restraining the students' excesses. They also saw an opportunity to speak as representatives of the campuses in the League's ongoing dialogue with the party, so they contacted Zhou Enlai for advice on how to proceed, but Zhou gave no reply.[26]

Zhou Enlai did not respond because he and the other party leaders were busy planning the party's counterattack. By mid-May, Mao realized that his plan to use non-party critics to help rectify problems in the party's work had spun dangerously out of control, and he saw the emboldened democratic party leaders now threatening the Communist Party's monopoly of power. On May 15, he angrily signaled that he had heard enough, drafting a secret circular to the party leadership: "The Situation is Changing." He allowed the criticisms to continue, but now with the purpose, as he would later describe it, of "luring the snakes out of the hole."[27] By early June, the spreading wave of student protests, worker strikes, and the collapse of agricultural collectives in the countryside convinced him that the party's influence and prestige had been seriously compromised. A June 8 editorial in the People's Daily unambiguously announced that the tide had turned. Warning that class struggle had not disappeared under socialism, it charged that certain people wanted to turn back the tide of history and overthrow the socialist system. The party immediately launched the Anti-Rightist Campaign to combat this threat. From the beginning, the brunt of the attack was directed against the Democratic League, especially its national leaders, Zhang Bojun (1895–1969) and Luo Longji (1896–1965). These two Western-trained intellectuals, long bitter rivals within the democratic parties, were accused of conspiring in an unholy alliance to undermine the socialist system. In retrospect, it is ironic that the opening salvo in the attack on these two was launched by the vice-mayor of Beijing and chairman of the city's Democratic League committee, the historian Wu Han (1909–69), who would himself become the first target of the Cultural Revolution less than ten years later.[28]

From the beginning of the Anti-Rightist Campaign, Ye Duyi was a prime target. His name was listed fourth in the *People's Daily* report of Wu Han's attack on his Democratic League colleagues. Duyi knew what he had to do and quickly began preparing his self-criticism. His major error was promoting the abolition of party organizations in the universities. He now acknowledged that this step could leave the party isolated from any base in the educated elite. His intent had been to remove a source of discontent and conflict, but now (quickly adopting Mao's language) he recognized that "class struggle, especially class struggle in the realm of thought, is inevitable and unavoidable." According to the *People's Daily*, his self-criticism was well received: "Ye Duyi acknowledged that among intellectuals born and raised in the old society, old, reactionary, capitalist thinking can emerge at any time. My [sic] erroneous thoughts and words illustrate this fully. The thought reform of intellectuals is a long and difficult process." But he was also careful to distance himself from Zhang Bojun and Luo Longji and their proposals for an expanded political role for the Democratic League.[29]

As editorials in the official press distinguished the majority of loyal Democratic League members from the small minority of "rightist careerist elements,"[30] Ye Duyi sought to associate himself with the former. He announced the League's official decision to launch the anti-rightist struggle in the organization and joined in exposing the history of errors committed by Luo Longji.[31] On July 15, the *People's Daily* devoted a half page to Duyi's denunciation of Luo's "anti-party and anti-socialist words and deeds" and his own self-criticism. He fully confessed to the erroneous thinking behind his earlier proposals but also noted that he had broken with Luo Longji in 1952. A careful reading of the entire self-criticism shows that it was artfully constructed. Duyi did not so much admit that his suggestions and criticisms were unwarranted as note the ways in which they had been deemed contrary to party policy, a judgment that he now accepted.

On each point, Duyi's self-criticism was careful to cite a party leader's speech or *People's Daily* editorial that revealed the error of his thinking—but, in most cases, the cited pronouncements came *after* his own suggestions. Thus, his proposal (in May) to abolish party committees in universities had aimed to eliminate unnecessary conflicts in the schools, but he learned in a July 13 *People's Daily* editorial that contradictions were natural and inevitable. Most notably, Ye Duyi stated that his erroneous thinking stemmed from his failure to understand the six criteria for criticism under socialism, especially the need to follow the socialist path and accept the leadership of the Communist Party.[32] As everyone knew, Mao's six criteria were the most important revision of his February speech "The Correct Handling of Contradictions among the People" and were added when the speech was published in China on June 19. This publication had been forced on the party by the *New York Times*'s June 13 publication of extended excerpts of the text obtained in Poland. Fearing that this text—with its exuberant encouragement of open criticism—would become known in China, the *People's Daily* published Mao's revised version on June 19, with the addition of the six criteria that would distinguish proper from "rightist" criticism.[33] Thus, the very structure of Ye Duyi's self-criticism contained the seeds of his self-defense. He never said that his criticisms were unwarranted or factually incorrect, and in later years, he would assert that he thought they *were* correct. The only problem was that after the party had invited him to make these criticisms, it had published new standards that made his views politically incorrect. He accepted that judgment and now wished to move on.

Unfortunately, moving on would not be so simple. From late June, the public criticism of leading rightists escalated to include the vague charge that their various public and private meetings amounted to forming an "amorphous organization" *(wuxing zuzhi)* to challenge the Chinese Communist Party. Zhang Bojun and Luo Longji were the alleged leaders of this "amorphous organization." By the end of August, as more and more accounts of the connections among the leading "rightists" emerged, Zhang and Luo were accused of leading "an anti-Communist group with organization, program, plans, and concrete activities." Now the "amorphous organization" was regularly appearing in quotation marks, implying that the informal contacts to which intellectuals had confessed had far more sinister purposes than their statements suggested.[34] Soon every conversation or visit to a friend's home came under suspicion. In mid-August, Luo Longji's common-law wife, a Communist Party member with whom he had been living for ten years, turned against him and also named Ye Duyi as a visitor to their home. Duyi was now identified as the liaison between Zhang Bojun and Luo Longji and was accused of trying to unite two men (whose rivalry and mutual disdain were well-known) in an anti-Communist plot. Pressed to confess further, he admitted to organizing small meetings on the pretext of "gathering friends for culture."[35]

In all the political campaigns of the Mao era, a critical issue was the relationship between one's behavior before and after 1949. Before 1949, intellectuals like Ye Duyi had all sorts of complicated relations as they interacted with each other and with the Nationalist government, Guomindang party members, Americans, colleagues who later went to Taiwan, or members of the Communist Party. In addition, most of them came from bourgeois or "feudal" landlord families—which were bad family backgrounds under the standards of the Communist regime. They could not escape these "historical problems," which were fully confessed and recorded in their dossiers during early reeducation movements and repeatedly dredged up in each successive campaign. Their task was to show their sincere efforts to break with the past, to reform themselves, and to accept the leadership of the Communist Party and serve the new People's Republic with unswerving loyalty. On the other side, the Communist Party's job in these campaigns was to link their adversaries to the dark past of Nationalist dictatorship and foreign imperialism and to show that these people had not changed but were intent on overthrowing the socialist regime and returning China to a discredited prerevolutionary system.

For Ye Duyi, the climax of this process was reported in a New China News Agency dispatch of November 2, 1957. The headline in the next day's *People's Daily* read, "Ye Duyi: Consistently Reactionary for 20 Years—Currying Favor with Japanese and American Imperialism, Staying Loyal to Many Anti-Communist Leaders." He was identified as the godson of Leighton Stuart, the president of Yenching University while Duyi was a student there and later the American ambassador to the Nationalist regime. Duyi was a student of the anti-Communist Zhang Dongsun (1886–1973), and when the war against Japan broke out, he briefly followed Zhang to Hankou to work for "Sino-Japanese peacemaking." Later he served as the Democratic League's English secretary, working with Americans and Nationalists and "resisting the Chinese Communists." Pro-American in his foreign policy views, he advocated a bourgeois democratic system for China.

Despite this unsavory past, the article went on, the party had been willing to forgive his errors and offer him a prominent position in the new regime. But he had continued to plot with Zhang Bojun and Luo Longji, becoming the liaison between them in 1956. He had opposed the party's leading position in China's schools, advocated a new party of intellectuals, and suggested that the People's Political Consultative Congress adopt a committee structure parallel to that of the People's Congress so that the two could serve as a bicameral legislature like those in capitalist countries. His previous confessions were deemed insufficient and insincere, and he was subjected to another round of criticism. Just six months earlier, the party had sought Ye Duyi's views for the reform of the new China. Now he stood accused of indelible links to Japanese and American imperialism and active plotting against the Communist Party.

Now officially labeled a "rightist," Ye Duyi was removed from all his official posts. The following year, he was sent to study at the Central Socialist Academy, where his fellow students included such famous intellectuals as the sociologist Pan Guangdan (1899–1967) and Fei Xiaotong (1910–2005), China's most eminent anthropologist and a classmate from Yenching. Both were also members of the Democratic League whose criticisms during the Hundred Flowers Movement had earned them rightist labels. Despite the eminent company, the mood was grim and humorless. They lived in dormitories near the National Minorities Institute in the western suburbs of Beijing, eating their meals in a cafeteria with a minimum of small talk. Every morning was devoted to "study," which meant reading the daily paper, identifying the political message, and then applying that message to their own experience, which usually entailed explaining how their bourgeois backgrounds and foreign training had led them to erroneous anti-socialist views. The regimen was not particularly intense. They were not required to do labor, and afternoons were free, so most of them did some form of physical activity—*taiji* exercises in Duyi's case. But the requirements of their schooling were clear: graduation would require complete confession of their rightist errors.

For Ye Duyi, the process came to an end on February 4, 1959, with the completion of a document entitled "My understanding of my crimes and ideas for future reform."[36] It is remarkable in many ways. Read fifty years after it was composed, large sections appear to be frank, sincere, and honest statements of his views. Beneath a rhetoric of Marxist platitudes about his bourgeois class standpoint and the party's objective truth, one can almost hear him saying, "This is what I believe. The party says it is incorrect and I accept that; but it is still what I believe." Thus, he describes his disappointment that in three years as a member of the National People's Congress, his role was only to listen to reports and never to debate policy. "The first sentence out of every mouth is always 'I completely support. . . . ' " He was a representative to the Congress but could not represent anyone. He then notes that this feeling of powerlessness was the result of his standing in opposition to the people, but he does not retract his criticism of the sterile quality of political debate in the PRC.

His comments on foreign policy are particularly interesting, for they are mostly a confession that his pro-American views made him suspicious of the Soviet Union. Thus, he records a farewell meeting with the American ambassador, Leighton Stuart, in 1949. Stuart warned that Communists could never be true patriots because their fatherland was always the Soviet Union, to which Ye Duyi replied, "I absolutely refuse to offer total obedience to the Soviet Union." He admits to longing for some form of détente with the United States but then cites the correct line according to Liu Shaoqi: "Either ally with the Soviet Union or ally with imperialism. It's one or the other. This is the line between patriots and traitors, between revolution and counter-revolution." Written in 1959, when relations with the Soviet Union were already becoming strained (and with a total break only a year away), Ye Duyi's self-criticism seems to be saying, "I warned you about the dangers of relying too much on the Soviet Union."

During the time he was studying at the Socialist Academy, Ye Duyi was sent with a small group to visit a village and witness the achievements of the new communes set up during the Great Leap Forward. This was during the height of leftist excess, when a "communist wind" blew through the countryside and led local cadres to make all sorts of extravagant claims for the achievements of the Great Leap. He listened in silence as an uneducated peasant leader described how the commune had produced an enormous 500-kilo hog by crossbreeding a pig and a cow and had bred a hen that could lay ten eggs per day. Elsewhere peasants were producing "satellite fields" with yields more than ten times the previous maximum. Duyi and the other intellectuals may have been poorly acquainted with rural life, but they knew that these stories were wild fabrications. To question them, however, would have betrayed "rightist" thinking, and they kept their mouths shut.[37]

In his self-criticism, Ye Duyi mentioned this trip to the countryside and recorded his erroneous reaction to the poverty of the countryside: "Is this what communism means? Their standard of living is not as high as mine. So that's all there is to communism?" Of course, he quickly noted that this questioning only betrayed his self-centered bourgeois perspective. To correct this error, he promised to adopt the perspective of the 600 million Chinese people. Quoting Liu Shaoqi again, he vowed that his thinking would "truly start from the 600 million people, and not from any particular group of people." Especially in the context of the disasters that the Great Leap was then inflicting on the Chinese people, this self-criticism could just as well have been a criticism of the "particular group of people" within the Communist Party who were charting China's course. If that was the subtext, however, it remained well below the surface. Ye Duyi concluded his self-criticism by promising to "conscientiously obey the party" in all his words and deeds.[38] And with that promise, he was released back into the bosom of his family.

The return was not easy. We recall that Duyi's relations with his wife had long been strained, and he had moved out to live in the Democratic League offices. Now dismissed from his job, he lost this housing as well. When he had come under criticism in the summer of 1957, his wife had joined in the accusations, which certainly did not improve marital harmony. Once he was forced to return home, she treated his homecoming as her victory and his surrender. Given the history of Duyi's marriage, these new tensions were no major change. With his children, however, the effect of his political troubles was more traumatic. His only son refused to talk to him and maintained his silence for three full years. This behavior was his way of heeding the party's call to "draw a clear line" between himself and rightist family members. Duyi's favorite daughter, Weizhen, had just been admitted to college when her father came under attack. With her father's rightist errors the subject of repeated newspaper stories, her bad family background was widely known, and she was pressured by the school's party secretary and teachers to break off relations with her father and join in exposing his crimes. Other students talked about her behind her back and in her hearing as well. Once she broke down crying in the middle of a math class. She was saved by a sympathetic department head, himself a member of the Democratic League, who sent her to a hospital, where she was diagnosed to be suffering from "hysteria" and granted a year of leave. This action was, in fact, an effort to protect her until the storm of criticism subsided. She returned to finish school once her father's self-criticism was complete. In 1960, Duyi's rightist label was removed, and he was finally able to reconcile with his son. The boy, then sixteen years old, approached his father and shook his hand. Duyi broke down in tears, soon joined by his beloved son.[39]

Because of his prominence in the national leadership of the Democratic League, Ye Duyi was an unusually prominent victim of the Anti-Rightist Campaign. Most other members of the family were less affected. In Tianjin, the eldest son, Duren, was always extremely circumspect. Indeed, he was so careful to follow the party's lead that it was precisely in 1957 that he was elevated to become secretary-general of the Tianjin branch of the Democratic League to supervise its "rectification." When Duyi was finished with his self-criticism and asked advice from his brother Ye Fang (then visiting Beijing from his party post in the Northeast), Ye Fang told him that his criticisms amounted to challenging the party. He should be less proud, and follow the example of the more obedient Duren, who as a member of the bourgeoisie had "surrendered to the proletariat and adhered to the party with all his heart."[40] As a party member, Ye Fang was himself relatively safe. The sisters of this generation and the fourth brother, Duxin, were divorced from politics. At the Academy of Sciences, Ye Duzheng was in one of the few academic units that was largely protected from the purges of the Anti-Rightist Campaign.[41]

Fang Shi, rising in the cadre ranks at the New China News Agency, became more caught up in the Anti-Rightist Campaign, but his role was more persecutor than victim. He had recently completed his training in Marxist philosophy and political economy at the Central Party School and served as one of four deputy directors in the domestic section of China's official news agency. His responsibility was politics and education, which put him in the thick of reporting on the Hundred Flowers Movement in the universities. In June and July 1957, however, he had an opportunity to travel abroad, as part of a delegation to East Germany, so he was away when the crackdown began. When the attacks escalated in August, he was back in Beijing and in charge of reporting on the Anti-Rightist Campaign. Thus, his section was responsible for the November 1957 New China News Agency attack on his elder brother Ye Duyi for being "Consistently Reactionary for 20 Years." He clearly understood that he could do nothing to protect his brother in this situation, and one wonders if perhaps he felt obliged to lean in the opposite direction. When Duyi visited him asking for advice, Fang Shi urged a thorough self-criticism, recognizing his primary obligation to be completely loyal to the party.[42]

Within his section, Fang Shi vigorously carried out his responsibility to uncover rightists. Like other cadres at schools and administrative units throughout China, he was expected—under guidelines that followed vague statements by Mao that only a small minority of intellectuals opposed socialism—to label roughly 5 percent of his subordinates rightists. Fang Shi exceeded his quota, finding roughly 7 percent.[43] He was proud of this achievement, convinced that he was doing his job well, obeying the party and supporting the socialist revolution. The most prominent "rightist" in his group was a young war reporter, Dai Huang, who had served heroically in the Civil War, Korea, and Vietnam. He had become disillusioned by the corruption and abuse of power he saw on a visit to his hometown, and after hearing the report of Khrushchev's criticism of Stalin, had dared to draft a letter criticizing bureaucratic rule in China and the rise of a new privileged class. Dai was a party member, so he was criticized only after the regime started rooting out rightist sympathizers in its own ranks. But he was targeted, labeled a rightist, divorced by his wife, and sent to labor in the bitter cold of the Northeast, where he was further persecuted. By the early 1960s, he was allowed to return to Beijing, and in early 1962, during a brief thaw in the political climate, he was encouraged to write about his mistreatment in the labor camp. Fang Shi read the account and sent it to his superiors for their reference. He hoped to foster sympathy for Dai Huang, for whose harsh fate he felt responsible. Unfortunately, the political climate had shifted (following a firm declaration by Mao that the party should never forget class struggle), and Dai Huang was condemned to another term of education through labor—a term that, with the Cultural Revolution, would last for fourteen years.[44]


The Ye brother who suffered the most from the Anti-Rightist Campaign was the agronomist Ye Duzhuang. His institutional home, the Chinese Academy of Agricultural Sciences, had been formally established in March 1957 out of the old North China Agricultural Institute. It was to serve as the national research center to bring the advances of socialist science to support the development of Chinese agriculture.[45] Headed by cadres trained in the Communists' rural bases, it was not a particularly progressive institution, either politically or academically. One objective of the Hundred Flowers Movement nationally was to liberate Chinese thinking from blind adherence to Soviet (especially Stalinist) models. In the biological sciences, this meant breaking free from the influence of Lysenko and his championing of Michurin's idea that acquired characteristics could be inherited. In 1953, James Watson and Francis Crick had proposed the double helix as the structural mechanism by which genetic DNA divided and reproduced itself. A revolution in genetic science followed from this discovery, but it required an abandonment of Michurin's ideas. This shift was already beginning with de-Stalinization in the Soviet Union, and in April 1956, Lysenko was removed as president of the Lenin Academy of Agricultural Science. In China, however, the Academy of Agricultural Sciences remained a bastion of Michurinism. In the fall of 1957, a scientist of the crop-breeding institute published an article in the academy's newsletter condemning those who, in the name of "reaching international standards," pursued "the most abstruse theoretical works in the world, like the currently popular DNA and RNA in the study of heredity."[46] As Western-trained scientists questioned the uncritical following of the Soviet Union, the newsletter published a spirited defense of Michurinism under the title "Smash the Rightist Conspiracy, Resolutely Study the Advanced Experience of Soviet Agriculture."[47] During the spring of 1957, the newsletter made no reference to the wave of intellectual criticism sweeping across China, unless the choice of graphics carried a veiled political message. Instead of the usual photos of abundant crops or helpful Soviet experts, the covers of the spring issues were filled with locusts, boll weevils, and fungus-damaged fruit.[48]

Ye Duzhuang had been severely criticized in the 1955 Campaign to Suppress Counter-Revolutionaries (the so-called Sufan campaign that followed the attacks on Hu Feng), and he was suffering from kidney problems. Feeling poorly as a result of his medical and political afflictions, he deliberately lay low during the spring, working at home on his translations of Darwin. The academy's party leadership visited him at home, flattering him with assurances that his views were always well respected. These overtures clearly reflected official policy encouraging members of the Democratic League to speak out. But these party leaders were precisely the ones whom he feared offending, with the inevitable consequences that would follow. Finally the Beijing leadership of the Democratic League, including Wu Han, also encouraged him, and the unprecedented chorus of criticisms appearing in the press convinced him that the party was serious about promoting open discussion of the problems encountered in building the new China. Thus, in late May, despite earlier troubles brought on by his outspoken nature, Duzhuang was persuaded to attend several forums assessing work at the academy.[49]

Viewed in their entirety, Duzhuang's comments were quite reasonable and commonplace for this period, but some of his language was characteristically blunt, and he certainly erred in criticizing two of the academy's leaders by name. His primary theme was that the directors should strive to better understand the academy's scientific mission. He echoed the common Hundred Flowers complaint that nonprofessional laymen *(waihang)* should not direct the work of experts and quoted a deputy director who had said that he did not understand the technical issues. Duzhuang's response: "If you don't understand, you should study!" and he pointedly suggested that such leaders might spend some time working as assistants to the academy's researchers.[50] Predictably, he thought the party leadership paid too much attention to politics, even seeking excuses to attack apolitical scientists as "backward." He complained of excessive meetings, endless trivial documents, and an old-style, *yamen*-like bureaucracy. He called for a greater role for the Democratic League, bemoaning the fact that "the League can only participate in the execution, not the formation of policy." He emphasized the need to pursue "long- term objectives and international standards" of research. In this respect, he found the academy's work falling short. In one statement that would come back to haunt him, he stated, "[The academy] has turned several somersaults [made abrupt changes in its research agenda] and had few accomplishments."[51]

On several occasions, he criticized two key leaders of the academy. The director, Chen Fengtong, lived directly upstairs from Duzhuang, and their personal relations were friendly. Nonetheless, at some point, Ye stated that Chen was "not a real agronomist."[52] His criticisms of the deputy director and party secretary Li Boyuan were even more pointed. At a Democratic League meeting at which Li was present, Ye expressed the common fear that people who criticized the party would suffer later: "In rectification, many old problems will be raised. But when these issues are raised, will they be solved? Or will people take revenge?" He cited an example from his experience. After the sharp attacks on Ye Duzhuang in the Sufan campaign, Li Boyuan had requested that Ye trade apartments with him because he wanted to be closer to director Chen's apartment for easy consultation and access to his private phone, though Li's current apartment was only about fifteen meters away. Ye was unwilling, saying that his family had lived there for some time, the children were used to the place, and he did not wish to disrupt the family. Soon after this refusal, the housing office took away the extra room Ye had been given in which to rest and recover from his tuberculosis. He got the message and moved out of the apartment.[53] Li, for his part, was unlikely to have forgotten this public airing of his abuse of power.

In June, when the tide turned and the Anti-Rightist Campaign began, Ye Duzhuang was hardly mentioned. The prime target at the academy was a young chemist, a pesticide specialist with an American Ph.D., who had become a committed advocate of birth control and published (with Duzhuang's assistance) ten thousand copies of a pamphlet putting forth his Malthusian views. Provocatively entitled "Throwing Bricks," the pamphlet argued that increases in agricultural productivity were not keeping up with population growth. "Where five people used to eat the food of three, now eight people have to eat food for four." Such negative thinking was unacceptable, and the academy was plastered with big-character posters attacking him for rightist thinking and anti-socialist views.[54]

Ye Duzhuang was only marginally affected, having helped arrange the publication of "Throwing Bricks." Only later was he seriously targeted as the academy sought to reach its 5 percent quota of rightists. With a problematic political history and long-standing relations with the Democratic League, he was a natural target. In addition, some of his criticisms had been reported in a *Guangming Daily* article about the academy just days before the crackdown, so the local party leadership had another reason to resent this troublemaker.[55] As a Democratic League member, he was first accused of serving with his brother Ye Duyi as a liaison between Zhang Bojun and Luo

Longji, but he was able to convince his accusers that he had never met with Zhang and Luo after 1949, and that charge evaporated. The focus then shifted to the public forum where he had commented on the leaders' lack of expertise in agronomy. Criticism sessions continued through the summer as he characteristically refused to admit his errors. Finally he confessed "I've gone right to the brink of being a rightist." The party secretary laughed and replied, "Just go one more step and we'll all be finished." By now, he was suspicious of the party's promise of lenience to those who confess, so he refused, and the secretary answered, "See you at the meeting. Somebody there will push you over!"[56] The final, climactic meeting in September was presided over by the party secretary. It had been carefully orchestrated. Party members and activists received a document titled "Thoroughly Repudiate the Reactionary Ideas of the Rightist Ye Duzhuang" that contained selected quotes from Duzhuang's talks and writings and suggestions for rebutting them. With this assistance, they were instructed to "prepare speeches for the mass meeting."[57] An unusually detailed account of the meeting shows the crude but remarkably effective rhetorical tools that the party used to disarm and humiliate its critics.[58]

At the heart of many intellectuals' criticisms during the Hundred Flowers Movement was the claim that the party was ignoring their advanced academic training and expertise. In this respect, the confrontation was a classic contest between "reds" in the party and "experts" in academia. To counter the criticism of such experts, the party sought to characterize their training as "bourgeois" and infected with the ideas of American and Japanese imperialists. But it also wanted to demonstrate in more specific ways that these experts were not really as smart or as well educated as they claimed to be. They needed to be stripped of their academic legitimacy and exposed to public ridicule and humiliation. This denigration would isolate them socially and intellectually, depriving them of potential supporters and forcing them, in the end, to submit to the will of the party. Such was the function of the struggle meetings against Ye Duzhuang. They were designed to demonstrate that this man who claimed by be a "senior researcher" was in fact no expert at all, but only a "cultural broker and political cheat who had sneaked into the world of agricultural science."

Ye Duzhuang had always been proud of his classical Chinese training, and the first step in the attack was to call his classical learning into question. Citing an unpublished essay entitled "Let's Also Speak of Reading Books" that he had submitted to People's Daily, his critics found one incorrectly written character in a classical quote and determined that he had relied on Japanese scholarship for his discussion of Chinese agricultural treatises. But these criticisms seemed rather trivial and desultory. Things began to heat up when the topic switched to the more relevant issue of his command of agricultural science. Duzhuang's most recent work had been in agricultural economics (a field that the academy had abolished), and his agronomy training in Japan was now twenty years behind him. Immediately, he found himself on uncertain ground. Already worn down by months of struggle sessions, he attempted to escape by simply admitting all errors. But his interrogators would not let him off easily.

QUESTION: *You said the North China [Agricultural] Institute turned somersaults over the last few years and accomplished very little? What was the basis for this?*
ANSWER: I was speaking nonsense. The North China Institute made great accomplishments.
Q: *What accomplishments?*
A: Lots of accomplishments! For example, they learned how to produce rinderpest vaccine, 666 [pesticide], learned how to cure sweet potato fungus, promoted the cultivation of early premium wheat.

The account then notes that the institute had 149 research accomplishments, but Ye could only list these four.

Q: *How do you cure sweet potato fungus, do you know?*
A: Probably you heat the sprouts in warm water. (The meeting erupts in laughter. Actually you should soak slices of potato.)
Q: *What are the characteristics of "early premium wheat?"*
A: High yields, early ripening. (Masses: Ai! Early premium wheat ripens early! Note: early premium wheat is a late ripening variety. Ye was just guessing based on the name.)
Q: *What kind of an expert are you? How can you not understand even the most basic things? How could you have been the editor of "Agricultural Sciences Newsletter"?*
A: I am a fool. I don't understand anything.[59]

His translation of Darwin and Michurin (whom he continued to support) were then dismissed as not the work of an expert but only the product of a "cultural broker" relying on the scholarship of others. Finally, the meeting turned to his most significant publication, his 1948 monograph on the economics of north China cotton cultivation. This well-regarded study relied extensively on careful Japanese surveys, but this Japanese scholarship, in the context of revolutionary China, was dismissed as "reactionary fallacies." Duzhuang made no attempt to defend this work:

Q: *Please explain some technical terms in your book. What is alluvial loess soil?*
A: I don't know. I copied it from others. What is loess soil? What is alluvial soil? I really cannot say.
Q: *Doesn't the book cover clearly say "Written by Ye Duzhuang"?*
A: These last few days I have come to recognize that, from head to foot, I am nothing but a cultural broker, a faker. The book is completely copied from others. I myself don't know anything.

Q: *You're still a grade IV researcher!*
A: I'm completely unqualified.
Q: *The contents are copied. Surely the preface is not copied!*
A: All copied. The preface was copied too. (The hall erupts in laughter. Copying someone else's preface is really utterly unheard of.)

Having stripped Ye Duzhuang of his academic legitimacy, the session finally turned to his politics, as determined by a tortuous reading of his monograph's preface. In discussing the problematic Japanese data on which his study was based, his preface refers to the "Japanese invasion and occupation of north China." His accusers determined that this phrasing ignored the popular resistance to that invasion, thus denying the existence of the Communist-led guerrilla struggle. His conclusion that "it is difficult to be satisfied with" the Japanese efforts to improve cotton cultivation was understood to be "taking pity on Japanese imperialism." Most critically, his accurate reporting that most north China peasants were owner-cultivators was interpreted as an attack on land reform, "aiming to suggest that the target of land reform was the owner-cultivator." The detailed surveys of the American agronomist John Lossing Buck had also shown that north China had few landlords, but the CCP vigorous rejected that view.[60] Now Ye Duzhuang was accused of being "a corrupt and rotten-to-the-core agricultural economist peddling Buck's viewpoint in service of the landlord class." So his scholarship was not only faked and wrong, it also served the interest of the old ruling class. Thus, it was clearly and deliberately anti-socialist and thereby part of a reactionary political agenda.

Following this final struggle meeting, Duzhuang was officially declared a rightist on September 31, 1957. Criticisms continued in small group meetings, loudspeaker broadcasts, and big-character posters plastered around the academy's walls. In the meetings, friends and colleagues rose to condemn him according to the script provided by the party. Some younger activists and opportunists were more aggressive, seeking advantage from the fall of a senior researcher. At this stage, the struggle shifted from his academic work to his personal history. His class background, which he had once listed as the relatively progressive "national bourgeois," was now labeled "bureaucratic capitalist," which put him among the enemies of the people.[61] His brief wartime service with the Communists' Eighth Route Army was said to have ended when he "abandoned the revolution." The party paid great attention to his continuing relations with Americans after the war, especially with Graham Peck, who had introduced him to the OSS. To associate with American allies in the war against Japan was one thing, but in the postwar era, when the United States was aiding the Chinese Nationalists in the Civil War, such friendships—especially with newsmen or people once associated with American intelligence activities— were viewed with much greater suspicion. Out of all the admitted complexities in Ye Duzhuang's background and character, the party sought to paint a simple and coherent picture: here was a man with a wealthy bourgeois background who was tied to the old official class; he had studied in Japan, abandoned the revolution after brief service in the army, served as an American spy in wartime and continued his association with his American handlers after the war, authored academic writings in defense of Japanese imperialism, entertained frustrated ambitions in the PRC, and finally engaged in wild and unjustified criticism of the Communist Party, betraying his reactionary and counter-revolutionary agenda.[62]

Hurtful as the process of public criticism was, the participants all realized that speaking in his defense would not be helpful, and he had no defenders. Old friends ignored him: one walked by without saying a word when Ye and his wife encountered him on the street in downtown Beijing.[63] Even his extended family provided little support. His brothers were aware of Duzhuang's troubles (the criticism sessions were reported in *People's Daily*), but could do nothing to help.[64] His social and political ostracization was complete.

Duzhuang's daughters were teased and harassed at school as children of a rightist. Teachers urged them to turn on their father and reveal his crimes. They resisted. His second daughter, then barely eight years old, stubbornly insisted, "My father is not a rightist!" and returned home to assure him, "Dad, you're not a rightist. You're a good man." He was deeply touched but also painfully aware of the suffering that he had brought upon his family. When the girls refused to break with their father, they paid a price at school. Before, they had been the teachers' favorites, both because of their good grades and because of their father's financial support of the school with income from his magazines. Now they were often scolded or criticized for being proud, as the sins of the father were visited on the children. The change was sudden, and though they understood that their altered fate was not their fault, there was no easy way to understand or accept it. Perhaps they could have gained some relief from their predicament by blaming their father, but they were unwilling to take that step. Duzhuang's wife was somewhat less forgiving, believing that many of his problems were brought on by his stubborn refusal to readily confess whatever was asked. The children sometimes heard their parents quarrel at night, which only increased their anxieties.[65]

Ye Duzhuang, meanwhile, waited at home for the final disposition of his case. He had received written notice that he had been labeled an "extreme rightist," and in February 1958, he had filled out an "application" for a sentence of "education through labor."[66] This would leave the family without his salary, and they all began to economize in preparation for hard times. A month later, he was demoted from fourth- to sixth-class researcher and then assigned to work in the library.[67] On the afternoon of June 28, 1958, he endured one final self-criticism session. The edited notes that survive in his personnel dossier are not a complete record of his confession, but the wide range of topics covered is interesting (and highly unusual). The theme that runs through them is his distress that people who had long served the revolution were in the end repudiated. He admitted his surprise at the 1953 purge of Gao Gang, an important founder of the revolution in the northwest. Gao's unceremonious ouster and suicide reminded him of the proverb about "the morning guest becoming the evening prisoner." He was similarly shocked by the recent criticism of Stalin, of whom he had heard only praise in the past. However, he believed that Stalin had insulted Mao in 1950 when he failed to greet Mao personally at the Moscow train station. Such comments on high politics appear nowhere else in Duzhuang's file and were perhaps selected to demonstrate that he was attentive to the most sensitive affairs of state. The rest of his comments are a routine confession of all his alleged transgressions, and he concludes with a classic promise to reform:

> Through the Anti-Rightist Campaign, I have come to a clear understanding. Although I am still far from [completing] a thorough transformation, I am a different person. From right to left is a 180-degree turn. [But] there can be a great leap forward, a breakthrough. Of course, for someone over 45 years old this takes effort. As a result of the Anti-Rightist Campaign, and now under the strict supervision of comrades working with me in the library I have returned to the ranks of the people. A change of heart is a long process. In the future, whenever there is a problem, I will correct it, and voluntarily accept education by the party.[68]

In the summer of 1958, he happened to run into the party secretary, who invited him to his home for tea and a smoke of expensive imported cigarettes. The secretary told Duzhuang that a decision on his case had been reached: he would not be assigned to hard labor, his family would not suffer financially, and he should consider his choice of work assignment. The secretary also hinted that his case had been considered by higher authorities, observing that his CCP contact in Beijing in the 1940s, Xu Bing (1903–72), now a prominent leader of the United Front Department, "is very saddened by your position." Duzhuang was so delighted by the news that he took his two daughters to a fancy Western restaurant and spent the exorbitant sum of twenty yuan on a meal of fried shrimp.[69]

One morning, while Duzhuang was working at his new job in the library, a cadre from the security department came to get his signature on a confession in which he had admitted to criticizing the excesses of the Sufan movement and opposing leadership by nonprofessionals. This form seemed quite trivial, and he readily signed. In his mind, the academy's leadership was simply meeting its quota of 5 percent rightists. At last, his troubles appeared to be coming to an end. Then on September 18, 1958, while he was doing *taiji* exercises in the library stacks during his morning break, a colleague called him to the phone, where he was told that the academy needed to send him to Nanjing. This was the height of the Great Leap Forward, and the press was reporting bumper harvests across the country. Foreign journalists were requesting historical data on past record harvests, and he was to go to Nanjing's Agricultural History Research Institute to collect the data. He had heard about this idea several weeks before, but now he was told he must hurry to catch a 2:00 P.M. train. He went to a nearby shop to buy a new pair of pants. His daughter helped him pack, interrupting the process at one point when she heard the knife sharpener outside and, pitying the man's paltry income, insisted that her father go have him sharpen the kitchen knife. His wife would not return until six that evening, so he left her a note. His daughter accompanied him to the gate, where he gave her a few coins to buy candy for herself and her sisters. As he got in the taxi, she waved good-bye and called out, "Dad, come back soon!"

At the gate, he was introduced to a young colleague, recently transferred from the army, who was to accompany him on the trip to Nanjing. Once on the train, his companion went to upgrade their tickets to sleeper class for the overnight trip. This seemed an unusual extravagance, but Duzhuang was told that the academy was concerned about his health and wished him to be comfortable. Soon a conductor came to tell him his ticket was ready, and he was led to the conductor's compartment. When the door opened, he was pushed inside and confronted by two men, one in a police uniform, one in plain clothes. Ordered to identify himself, he asked what was going on.

"You are under arrest," said the plain-clothed officer.

"For what?"

"You are a counter-revolutionary."

"How can that be?"

"Shut up!" replied the officer, who ordered him to sign the arrest warrant.

The three men detrained at the next station. The uniformed policeman walked ahead, as though not part of the group, and the plain-clothed officer carried Duzhuang's bag, acting like an aide. They climbed into a waiting Volga sedan and returned to Beijing. Duzhuang was ordered to keep his head down and not to look out until they reached Beijing's Caolanzi Detention Center.

His wife was never informed of this secret arrest, and she assumed he was doing his research in Nanjing. When days and then weeks went by with no letter from him, she began to worry and asked the academy administration if there was any problem. No, she was told; and from his associates in the Democratic League she got a similar reassuring message. Even if he had been detained, he had only said a few things wrong, and he should have no problem. Finally she approached a well-connected acquaintance, who called the minister of public security. The next day she was given his reply: there was no arrest warrant for Ye Duzhuang. This search went on for three months before she was finally informed of his imprisonment, and told to send a package of winter clothes, bedding, and soap.[70]

Even years later, after Ye Duzhuang was cleared of all charges, he and his family never learned the true reason for his abrupt arrest in the fall of 1958. His dossier contains a document from the Ministry of Agriculture dated August 8 stating that the United Front Department of the Communist Party had approved his demotion to sixth-class researcher. At the bottom of the page is a note by someone at the academy: "Ye Duzhuang was already arrested on September 18 by the municipal Public Security Bureau. Reason: counter-revolutionary."[71] The change in the verdict on his punishment came sometime between mid-August and mid-September—precisely the time when the Taiwan Straits crisis broke out, with Communist shelling of the offshore islands held by the Nationalists, U.S. naval support for its Taiwan ally, and air battles between the two sides in the Taiwan Straits. A wave of anti-American propaganda filled the media, and it is likely that in this context, Ye Duzhuang was swept up as a still-unresolved case with past connections to American intelligence. Thus did the high politics of the Cold War affect the lives of ordinary citizens.[72]

At the Caolanzi Detention Center, Duzhuang was given a meal of corn dumplings, water, and seaweed, and provided bedding, on which he quickly fell into an exhausted sleep. At midnight, he was awakened by a sharp bang on the cell door and a guard shouting "Interrogation!" Led into a room with a long table in the center, he faced an interrogator and secretary seated under a large portrait of Chairman Mao. He sat on the bench in front of the table and was sharply rebuked: "Who told you to sit down?" He stood until ordered to sit by the stone-faced interrogators. Then began the typical interrogation regimen:[73]

Q: *Do you understand why you were arrested?*
A: Don't you people say I am a counter-revolutionary?
Q: *(pounding the table): Don't give me that nonsense! Why do* you *think you were arrested?*
A: I don't know.
Q: *Your arrest was not the decision of one or two people. Don't harbor any false hopes. Tell us everything. Bow your head and admit your guilt! That is the only way out for you. . . . Lenience for those who confess their crimes, but severe punishment for those who stubbornly resist.*

The first interrogation lasted about an hour, and similar questioning took place over the next several days as he was forced to recite his entire history again and again. The focus was always on his service with the American military and OSS and on his relations with the American journalists Peck and Burke in the postwar years. After three months, his interrogators despaired of getting anything new and told him to write out his confession. He was to include no exculpatory details, such as approval from his Democratic League superiors to join the OSS. He was to make clear that in providing information to Peck and Burke, his purpose had not been to offer propaganda on behalf of the revolution but knowingly to provide information to U.S. agents. Though his handlers essentially dictated the confession, he was to write it in his own hand and swear that he was giving it voluntarily. When he finally finished to their satisfaction, he was promised that his revolutionary history "will not be forgotten." The slim hope that his ordeal might soon be over was dashed when, a few days later, he received the package of winter clothes, bedding, soap, and toothpaste from his wife. He realized that his stay would be a long one.[74]

At this point, Duzhuang was moved to a large cell, and the routine of prison life set in. Caolanzi was an old Guomindang prison. Indeed, the chief architect of the Anti-Rightist Campaign in Beijing, the municipal party secretary Peng Zhen (1902–97), had been imprisoned there in the 1930s. Old-style, one-story brick buildings had smaller cells for a couple of prisoners and large ones in which twenty or thirty were crowded, sleeping side by side on one enormous *kang*. The prisoners got two meals a day, each with two corn dumplings and a soup that consisted of little more than salty water with a few scraps of Chinese cabbage. Each cell had a pot on the floor to pee, and inmates were released once a day for ten minutes to shit. Despite these primitive sanitary conditions, the authorities paid attention to hygiene. Bedding was regularly aired and checked for lice, and a doctor visited every few days. Most of the waking hours were spent in group study of materials from the newspapers, discussion, and confession, with sessions in the morning, afternoon, and evening. Most were well accustomed to this routine of Chinese life, though in prison the sessions were more frequent and led by a "duty officer" who was a cellmate. Duzhuang was particularly upset that his cell's duty officer was a former Nationalist agent, the sort of person he was dedicated to removing from power. The other prisoners were a cross-section of the enemies of the Chinese state: a Muslim publisher, a Tsinghua physics professor, a leader of a proscribed religious sect (Yiguandao), a protestant minister, several former Guomindang functionaries, an ordinary bandit and kidnapper, a young technical school teacher who complained too much, an Overseas Chinese, several men who had tried to contact foreign embassies to leave China, and a middle school grad who had the bad judgment to prefer Spinoza to Marx.

This was not a good time to be in prison in China, though hundreds of thousands suffered that unjust fate as a result of the Anti-Rightist Campaign. The disastrous failures of the Great Leap Forward led to widespread famine in rural China and severe food shortages in the urban areas. Naturally, the prison population suffered more than most.[75] For a time, rations went down to three bowls of thin gruel twice a day but this fare left many too weak and dizzy to carry on. When the steamed dumplings were restored, they were of black flour, presumably barley, which left Duzhuang and many others severely constipated. Even the medicine they used could not loosen their bowels, and they had to stick their fingers up their own anuses to release the hardened feces.

Once he realized that he would be in prison for some time, Duzhuang thought to occupy his time by resuming his translation of Darwin. He requested a copy of Darwin's *The Descent of Man* and some related books in English and Japanese, plus an English-Chinese dictionary. When, to his surprise, they were delivered, the concession was a mixed blessing, for it was another sign that the authorities expected his stay to be a long one. Because prisoners were allowed paper only to write confessions, he inscribed his translation of Darwin between the lines of the Japanese version. He spent most of his spare time and evening hours on the translation and regarded it as his best work. Unfortunately, this draft, which he later managed to deliver to one of his brothers, was burned during the Cultural Revolution.[76]

In quiet moments, his thoughts naturally turned to home and family, and he recorded some of them in poems. Thinking of his wife, he wondered whether "the sweet and sour of their thirteen years together will ever be enjoyed again" and mourned their lost youth. Once, watching swallows swooping and diving for insects outside his window, he realized that his daughters could be watching a similar scene and imagined them "morning and evening, watching for father's return, / An ocean of feeling that cannot be parted. / A high wall rises to heaven."[77]

In the summer of 1961, he was transferred to another detention center for prisoners whose cases had been "wrapped up" following confession and then moved to a jail at the court. Conditions were better there, with a bathhouse, better food, access to cigarettes and a toilet, and movies every couple of weeks. In addition, for the first time, family visits were allowed, always preceded by a haircut and clothes washing. The rules were strict: no complaining, no asking for food. Meetings were held across a long wooden table, closely watched by a guard. On his wife's first visit, following a postcard from him, she came with Ye Duzheng, his younger brother from the Academy of Sciences. Duzhuang showed them his emaciated arms and openly asked for food—for which he was later sharply upbraided by the prison administrators. But he did begin receiving regular packages of dried foods.

The dawn of 1962 brought a brief window of hope. Chairman Mao's standing in the party hierarchy had been badly damaged by the economic collapse and widespread famine that followed the excesses of the Great Leap Forward. As Mao retired from direct involvement in day-to-day government affairs, a new pragmatic approach guided the top leadership. Rural reforms were instituted, allowing a greater role for free markets and weakening the communes and collective agriculture. In literature and the arts, there was a brief relaxation in party control that many compared to the thaw of 1956–57. Intellectuals were again encouraged to speak up, and many accused rightists were rehabilitated and had their rightist "hats" removed.[78]

In May 1962, Ye Duzhuang was summoned to the doctor's office. "What's bothering you?" he was asked. "I'm hungry," he replied. No examination followed, but he was transferred to the medical ward. A few days later, he was told to collect his belongings and go to the tuberculosis ward. He was mystified, but more experienced prisoners knew exactly what was happening: "You're getting out—for medical treatment!" Regulations did not permit medical release from an ordinary prison cell, and this prison followed regulations. He was given money from his account—earned in the menial prison labor he had done over the past few years—and taken to court, which announced a decision of medical parole: "If you don't do anything illegal on the outside, you won't be called back." On May 28, he was sent to wait for his wife and a taxi to take him home. Holding his hand tightly on the ride back, she said only "The children are all well."[79]

Back at home, Sun Song made him a cup of hot chocolate and offered some cookies. He emptied the whole jar, then ate a big bowl of noodles, the first noodles he had tasted in four years. His wife was so alarmed by his appetite that she rushed out to buy medicine to help his digestion. When the children returned from school, they hardly recognized the emaciated figure before them. One was so alarmed that she went directly to her room and fell sobbing on the bed. Slowly, they got used to each other, and one day they sought to relive old times with a family expedition to the Moscow Restaurant, but the outing proved a disappointment. There was no borsch, and the ice cream melted in the summer heat.

After Duzhuang's return home, his younger brother Fang Shi twice visited from the New China News Agency. The first time, the brothers were utterly circumspect and avoided talking of Duzhuang's plight. On the second visit, Duzhuang told him the whole story, and his brother offered to investigate. Back at the news agency, he spoke with his party superior, who told Fang Shi not to get involved; his superior would have someone else talk to the key people—especially the underground party leaders in Beijing after the war, who could attest to Duzhuang's cooperation with the party at that time.[80]

A few old friends came to visit, most notably a Democratic League leader who was a vice-chair of the People's Political Consultative Conference. Listening to Ye's story, he reacted strongly to the injustice and urged an immediate appeal. Duzhuang was reluctant. He had lost his characteristic will to fight. Feeling defeated and no longer eager to be a hero, he wished only to live in peace with his family. He knew the consequences of resisting the party's verdict. But his friend was insistent: such thoughts betrayed a lack of trust in the party. He returned several times, pressing for materials with which to present an appeal, finally angrily giving Duzhuang a deadline of early July.

On June 28, exactly one month after his release, Ye Duzhuang was rearrested, taken directly to the court, and sentenced to ten years for being an American spy. No new evidence was presented beyond his past confessions, and once again, at sentencing, the judge promised that his contribution to the revolution would not be forgotten. He was given one week to appeal, and he stayed up late at night to draft one, handing it in the next day. Older prisoners in his cell urged him to withdraw it immediately: an appeal signaled resistance to the decision of the state and would only bring harsher punishment. They pointed out that he had already served four of his ten years; he could be out in another six years. But he was not permitted to withdraw his appeal, and two month later his sentence was upheld, "after appeal."[81]

We may never know the reasons for Ye Duzhuang's release and rearrest in the summer of 1962, but two factors almost certainly played a role. First, as in the case of the journalist Dai Huang of the New China News Agency, a critical shift in party policy occurred in the middle of 1962. At an unusual party conference in January and February, which involved seven thousand cadres from the central, provincial, and local levels, the central leadership had been uncharacteristically forthright in · confessing and taking responsibility for the leftist errors of the Great Leap Forward. In the following months, thousands of cadres who had been punished and purged for rightist errors were rehabilitated. Duzhuang's release in May was clearly part of this process. Then gradually over the summer, Mao, in part emboldened by good summer harvests ending the disastrous famine of the previous years, moved to the left again, famously declaring in the August meetings at the beachside resort of Beidaihai that the party should never forget class struggle. In part, Duzhuang seems to have been caught up in this new lurch to the left.[82]

But there was also a more specific reason for his victimization. In the wake of the post-Leap disasters and signs of widespread popular discontent, Chiang Kai-shek in Taiwan had stepped up U-2 flights and covert operations to infiltrate agents into China in an attempt to stir up trouble, hoping for an opportunity to "recover the Mainland." The New China News Agency prepared a major report on these activities, urging the utmost vigilance against such "counter-revolutionary diehards" and on June 18 Chairman Mao ordered the report distributed to all party committees for discussion. Six days later, it was published in the People's Daily. For any career-conscious member of the public security system, such a report clearly suggested that releasing an accused American spy was not a good idea. Ye Duzhuang's rearrest on June 28 was in all likelihood tied to this turn of events. Once again, he fell victim to high politics that were in no way his own doing.[83]

When Ye Duzhuang was rearrested in 1962, his family was evicted from his apartment at the Chinese Academy of Agricultural Sciences. His wife and daughters were given a small one-room apartment at the Beijing Film Studio where Sun Song worked. Slowly, their living conditions at the film studio improved, until in 1964, the family was given a comfortable two-bedroom flat where the girls would spend their adolescence. For a time, Duzhuang was imprisoned in Beijing, and his wife visited him. Walking in the yard, he suggested that perhaps for the sake of the children, she should divorce him. This was the sort of ritual demonstration that the party appreciated—"drawing a clear line" between oneself and family members who ran afoul of the regime. But Ye Duzhuang had spent much of his life pursuing this high school sweetheart, even listing as an alias on his personnel forms "Heart set on [Sun] Song" (Xinsong), a nickname he had adopted while studying in Japan.[84] For him, suggesting divorce was intensely painful, and he kissed his wife gently on the cheek when she left. Several days later, a letter came agreeing to a divorce. For Sun Song, it was a purely procedural move, an act of convenience for the children's sake. She remained in touch with him, sent packages in the mail, and never remarried. Though he was the one who had suggested the move, Duzhuang was devastated, nearly fainting when he got the letter. The two never saw each other again.

# 13

# The Cultural Revolution

Late in 1960, the New China News Agency sent Fang Shi to lead a delegation of visiting reporters from Latin America and Eastern Europe to the capital of Anhui province. The group flew directly to Hefei from Beijing and was ushered immediately to the best hotel, carefully sheltered from any contact with the local population. The foreign journalists were given a series of official briefings on the progress of the Great Leap Forward, then taken to a tourist boat on a nearby lake. As they drifted about admiring the rural scenery, a group of brightly clad young girls collected lotus roots along the shore. Everything was carefully choreographed to support the idea, endlessly repeated in the PRC's domestic and international propaganda organs, that peasants across China were reaping "rich harvests" in the new people's communes of the Great Leap Forward.[1]

Fang Shi knew perfectly well that it was all a lie. Had the reporters traveled by train, they would have passed through northern Anhui where millions of peasants were dying from malnutrition. The famine was the worst in Chinese history: reliable estimates now put the death toll between twenty and thirty million people. Most tragically, it was largely a man-made disaster. Chairman Mao's utopian dreams of a communist paradise produced communal mess halls that ate up too much food. Enthusiastic cadres exaggerated the productive achievements of the new communes, leading to excessive state collection of grain. Vital labor power was diverted to backyard steel furnaces intended to lead China to outstrip Great Britain in steel production but in the end producing mostly useless iron scrap. By 1960, overworked and underfed peasants did not have the energy to collect all the grain they had planted, and millions died as a result.[2]

Fang Shi had a reasonable idea of just how bad conditions were because he had visited Guizhou province in May that year. Guizhou was a poor province, but it was not the hardest hit by the famine that would later be euphemistically called the "three hard years" (1959–61). He noticed that the faces of many of the peasants laboring in the fields were almost black, their skin shiny and puffed up. The local cadres quietly told him that many would soon die of malnutrition. But the New China News Agency wrote only of the peasants' enthusiasm for Mao's experiment in leaping straight into communism. In the summer of 1959, Chairman Mao had turned furiously on critics of the Great Leap Forward, purging the skeptics for "right opportunism." Soon afterward, seven provincial heads of the New China News Agency were replaced for less-than-enthusiastic reporting. The message was clear to all, and from that time forward, even the agency's secret background reports to the party center gave only the positive news.[3]

Within the party leadership, however, the failures of the Great Leap were becoming increasingly apparent. Food shortages in the cities forced humiliating grain purchases from abroad. A dearth of raw materials caused drastic declines in industrial production, forcing a 45 percent reduction in the labor force, sending many workers back to the countryside. In this atmosphere of economic crisis, Mao retired from the front line of day-to-day policy making to concentrate on broader strategic issues and the intensifying ideological conflict with the Soviet Union. In the political space opened by Mao's retreat, key lieutenants such as Liu Shaoqi, number two in the party hierarchy and now head of state, and Deng Xiaoping, head of the party secretariat, charted a more moderate course. Their pragmatic policies would later be summed up in a slogan attributed to Deng: "It doesn't matter if it's a black cat or a white cat, as long as it catches the mouse it's a good cat."[4] Empowered by such signals from the center, some provincial and local cadres began quiet experiments in dismantling the collective structures in agriculture, reopening rural markets, and restoring incentives that rewarded individual farming initiatives.

As a result of these reforms, the economy began to recover, but Mao was troubled by the abandonment of socialist ideals. The Chairman feared that China might follow the "revisionist" path traversed by the Soviet Union after the death of Stalin. His colleagues seemed inclined toward the "capitalist road." By 1962, Mao and his radical allies had begun to fight back against the party pragmatists. The threat to Mao was brought home in the fall of 1964, when the Soviet Union's Central Committee removed Nikita Khrushchev from power for his arbitrary and erratic decision making. The Chairman had no intention of suffering a similar fate, and soon he initiated a series of intricate plots to expose and purge his critics and rekindle the fires of revolutionary fervor. The result was the Great Proletarian Cultural Revolution.[5]

The Cultural Revolution began innocently enough with an article attacking a historical play by Wu Han, vice-mayor of Beijing and, ironically, the man who had led off the attacks on his Democratic League colleagues in the 1957 Anti-Rightist Campaign. At Mao's urging, the campaign expanded into a broader assault on various

bourgeois authorities in the academic field, and by the spring of 1966, a great explosion of confused debate about the nature and identity of the real "capitalist roaders" erupted in China's elite high schools and colleges. To shape and focus these
campus debates, the party set up leadership groups in the capital and the provinces,
sending in work teams of veteran cadres—a long-established and conventional
mechanism for managing mass campaigns. But Mao quickly judged these work
teams to be an unjustified interference in the revolutionary actions of the students
and ordered them withdrawn. The students, meanwhile, began organizing into the
groups that would become one of the classic manifestations of the Cultural Revolution: Red Guards.[6]

In the Northeast city of Shenyang, Ye Fang was party secretary in the Propaganda
Department of Liaoning province. In that capacity, he was appointed to the provincial leadership group for the Cultural Revolution and helped organize the work
teams in the schools. His middle three children were in middle and high school at
the time, and they eagerly joined the Red Guards. Like Red Guards everywhere,
they were unsure what the movement was all about, but once the press published
Mao's endorsement of the slogans "To rebel is justified!" and "Bombard the headquarters!" they recognized that this struggle was terribly important and poured their
hearts into it. All of their Red Guard comrades were from the revolutionary classes,
and most were the offspring of party cadres who filled the elite schools. Since childhood they had heard about the revolutionary feats of their parents' generation. Now
they too had an opportunity to participate in the revolution and prove their worth.
This mission seemed so much more important and rewarding than memorizing boring textbooks to get into college and contribute to socialist production. They soon
became fervent participants in the Great Proletarian Cultural Revolution.

As the child of a revolutionary cadre, Ye Fang's fifteen-year-old daughter was a
leader of the Red Guards in her school. One teacher had been particularly strict
with her, sometimes publicly scolding her when she secretly read novels behind her
textbook in class. But the teacher was from a "bad" bourgeois family, and this in-
ferior status gave the teenager an opportunity to attack her and get even. The situation was a classic reversal of authority relations and was repeated in thousands of
schools across the country. As she later recalled, the Cultural Revolution provided
an excuse to wreak revenge on a teacher who was "not nice" to her, while feeling
like a revolutionary hero.[7]

Much of the off-campus activity of these young Red Guards involved raiding the
homes of long-established targets of the revolution: landlords, capitalists, counter-
revolutionaries, and rightists. To a degree, this was an opportunity for party leaders to deflect the revolutionary ardor of youth from the "capitalist roaders" in the
party (who were Mao's primary concern) to the "class enemies" they had all been

taught to despise. The raids were carried out in the name of attacking the "four olds": old ideas, old culture, old customs, and old habits of the exploiting classes. Old books, translations of foreign literature, religious icons, artwork, photo albums, and jewelry were all subject to confiscation or destruction by the Red Guard bands. Neighborhood committees helped identify the targets, and then the youths moved in, usually striking late at night when their victims were home asleep and the teenage raiders were less likely to be recognized.

Because the "class enemies" who were the focus of the raids had been so frequently targeted in past campaigns, they usually possessed little of value to seize. Furthermore, once the raiding began, targeted families preemptively destroyed old photos and artwork, burned journals, and disposed of antiques. In Tianjin, Ye Duren's children persuaded their father to destroy the old photos and artwork that had been left to him as first son of the family.[8] Still, some families attempted to hide a few treasured pieces of jewelry or memorabilia, sewing them into quilts or secreting them within walls. When a few such instances were discovered (or rumored), the Red Guards became all the more persistent and destructive in their search for hidden treasure. Closets were emptied, chests broken apart, clothing shredded, furniture trashed. All confiscated items were supposed to be recorded and turned in to the authorities, but as the night raids became increasingly chaotic, Ye Fang's children noticed some of the Red Guards occasionally slipping a piece of jewelry or perhaps an interesting book into their pockets under cover of dark. The revolutionary assault on old culture was becoming an excuse for adolescent pilferage.[9]

In August 1966, Mao Zedong began a series of mass reviews of his Red Guard acolytes in Beijing's Tiananmen Square. Ye Fang's high school–age daughter and son learned of these massive ceremonies and, eager to express their unswerving loyalty to the Chairman and join in the youthful commotion, they hopped on a train to the capital. They had no tickets, but when the conductor asked for one, these confident children of the revolution simply demanded, "Will you prevent us from going to see Chairman Mao?" No humble ticket taker would be that bold, so like most of the revolutionary youth, they traveled to the capital free of charge. Amid the millions of other students, the Shenyang youths were so far from the podium that Chairman Mao and his colleagues were scarcely visible, but the experience nonetheless fired their revolutionary enthusiasm.

But there were limits. While in Beijing, they took the opportunity to visit their cousins, including the daughters of Ye Duzhuang, who were close to their own ages. Duzhuang, of course, had been in prison since his arrest in the Anti-Rightist Campaign and now stood convicted in the eyes of the state of being a counterrevolutionary and an agent of American imperialism. His children in no way accepted this verdict, but the revolutionary visitors from Shenyang were untroubled by their cousins' resistance to the party's standards of justice. As Ye Fang's daughter later explained, she had a youthful confidence that despite her revolutionary duty to attack bad people, "bad people could not come from my family. Family and friends could not be bad people."[10]

After the visits to Beijing to see Mao, many of the younger generation set out across the country as part of a great wave of revolutionary tourism, all at the expense of the state. Ye Fang's children, joined by their cousins from Ye Duzheng's family in the Academy of Sciences, traveled all the way to Canton on a train so packed with students that for four days they could scarcely move to eat or get to the bathroom. Once in Canton, they visited schools, read and copied wall posters, and exchanged revolutionary experiences with their contemporaries from southern China. Since nobody was checking the background of these youths, even the daughters of accused "rightist" Ye Duzhuang, who had been ostracized and excluded from Cultural Revolution activities in their own schools, took this opportunity to see the country—one joining a great horde of students climbing to the top of Jinggangshan, the mountain redoubt where Mao Zedong had launched his rural revolutionary movement in the 1920s. They left almost as soon as they got to the revered site, cleared out by authorities who were alarmed after an outbreak of deadly spinal meningitis.

By the winter of 1966, Ye Fang's daughter was beginning to get homesick and also cold as she returned to the north from tropical Canton with nothing more than her summer clothing. From Beijing, she called home, only to discover that the phone had been disconnected: her own house had become a target for Red Guard raids. The Cultural Revolution had reached a new stage, and even veteran party members like her father were becoming targets, in his case for having organized the work teams that were now judged to have "suppressed the student movement" in the summer of 1966.[11]

After the work teams were withdrawn in August of 1966, Ye Fang was forced to criticize his errors in meetings at the various schools in Shenyang, but he was allowed to stay at home as a party leader who had committed errors. By the winter of 1966, however, radical pressure on party leaders intensified, and he was taken into custody by one of the city's Red Guard units. Ye Fang had always been an extremely loyal and circumspect party member, but in the past he had quietly (within the party) expressed mild skepticism about the excesses of the Great Leap Forward and had been criticized on "suspicion of right opportunism." Now his lack of ideological fervor again made him a target, but he was also a hostage whom the Red Guards were using in hopes of extracting incriminating information about more important provincial leaders.[12]

The pubic struggle meetings against Ye Fang took a familiar form, one repeated again and again across China. He was hauled onto a stage with a large placard hung from his neck listing his name and alleged crimes, then forced to bow down in the "airplane position" with his arms pulled back and up above his head. Though the "airplane" was a painful and exhausting posture to maintain during the long struggle sessions, the abuse of Ye Fang was more psychological than physical. For a veteran of the revolution, the humiliation of bowing before mobs of young people screaming all sorts of accusations could be unbearable, and in Liaoning, as elsewhere in China, thousands were driven to suicide by the experience.

The inevitable logic of political campaigns in China required a search for deep historical roots of political error. The targets of Mao's Cultural Revolution were people taking the capitalist road, or "capitalist roaders." This label not only reflected the Chairman's growing tendency to interpret all political differences in class terms, but it also implied that the accused wished to reverse the achievements of China's socialist revolution. This put them on the same side as those whom the revolution had overthrown, most notably the Nationalist government that had ruled China from 1927 to 1949. How could long-time Communists like Ye Fang be working to restore the Nationalists, with whom they had fought for decades? The logic of the Cultural Revolution suggested that perhaps they were really Nationalist agents or sympathizers who had wormed their way into the party and gone along with the revolution until the time was ripe to oppose Chairman Mao. So the Red Guards and Mao's allies within the investigative arms of the party went to enormous length to uncover evidence and extract confessions linking the targets of the Cultural Revolution to the Guomindang.

The charges against Ye Fang were fairly typical of the contorted logic of these accusations, and also revealed young people's intractable ignorance of China's recent history. In 1935, Ye Fang had been an activist in the December 9th Movement (see chapter 9) protesting the Nationalist government's pusillanimous policy toward Japanese aggression. One tactic of that movement had been to petition Chiang Kai-shek to mobilize the country to resist Japan's advance in northern China. Thirty years later, in the context of the Cultural Revolution, petitioning Chiang Kai-shek implied that one thought the Nationalists might be persuaded to defend the nation. At best, the students must have had some faith in Chiang Kai-shek's patriotism; at worst, the petition meant that their real desire was to see the Nationalists, rather than the Communist Party, lead the War of Resistance against Japan. In the 1930s, everyone understood the December 9th Movement to be a patriotic (and generally leftist) student movement directed against the policies of Chiang Kai-shek's Nationalist government. Now, during the Cultural Revolution, the participants were accused of being Nationalist agents.

The charges were patently absurd, but by the end of 1966, the main target of Mao's Cultural Revolution was Liu Shaoqi, who had been the primary party operative working underground to organize radical student activists after the December 9th Movement. Moreover, the December 9th generation included some of the better-educated members of the party, who were Liu's natural allies. Indeed, the preliminary verdict on Ye Fang in 1973 was, "For seventeen years [1949–66] he carried out the reactionary bourgeois line of Liu Shaoqi." Most of the other activists from the student movement of the 1930s suffered the same fate, purged and persecuted in the 1960s.[13]

Another Red Guard tactic was to sully the reputations of party leaders' family members. As we have seen, Ye Fang's feisty spouse, Lin Ying, had been expelled from the party in 1950 for fleeing Shenyang during the Korean War. To that black mark was added the fact that she had been imprisoned by the Guomindang following the 1941 incident in which Chiang's troops had turned on and killed or captured most of the headquarters detachment of the Communists' New Fourth Army. Lin Ying was now accused of having had an affair with the Nationalist officer who had enabled her release from captivity—a charge presumably based upon the child she had borne before she met Ye Fang. All of these sordid accusations were enough to drive Lin Ying from Shenyang to seek refuge at her natal home in the south. Ye Fang, meanwhile, was left with another complicated history to explain.[14]

As the Cultural Revolution spread and escalated, all of Ye Fang's brothers suffered to one degree or another. Fang Shi was accused of being a "capitalist roader" at the New China News Agency. Posters attacking him were plastered around his Beijing compound, and he was repeatedly hauled before struggle sessions and forced to wear a tall hat with "black gang" written on it and to bow before his accusers in the airplane position. He was assigned to light physical labor, mostly demeaning jobs like cleaning toilets. Soon the focus shifted to his "historical problems." First, his accusers revived the issue of his arrest and release in Tianjin while a student, the same incident for which he had been confined in Yan'an during the rectification campaign of the 1940s. Then they focused on the fact that, as part of the United Front and under party orders, he had joined the Guomindang during the war in order to work in the political section of the Shanxi warlord Yan Xishan's army. His home was twice searched in an effort to uncover some enduring connection to the Nationalist Party, and all his photos, family journals, and books were taken and lost forever. Finally he was hauled off to another school and held in a fourth-floor classroom, from which many others fell to their deaths, either pushed or as suicides. There he was repeatedly beaten, despite his citation of Mao's injunction to struggle verbally and avoid violence. This punishment went on for three days, while he struggled to stay awake, fearing that he might be thrown out the window in his sleep. But he resisted any confession and was eventually returned to his family.[15]

At the Academy of Sciences, the campaign was less intense and far less violent. Ye Duzheng was initially targeted as an American-trained "scientific authority"—clearly an advocate of "bourgeois science." His "historical problems" had two aspects: first, before going abroad in the 1940s, he had been required to participate in a political training class at the end of which he was enrolled in the Nationalist Party. He could not remember anything about a party membership card, which only made his accusers more suspicious. Second, some of his meteorology research at the University of Chicago had been funded by the U.S. Navy, which brought him under suspicion of being an American spy, especially because he had left a better-paying U.S. job to return to China. His patriotic abandonment of a comfortable academic position in America was now being held against him. For the first time, he began to question the wisdom of his decision to return to China. But in general, his treatment was quite mild. Even the Red Guard who was assigned to watch him became his protector, passing messages to him and telling him of others' "confessions" so that he could harmlessly repeat the same thing. In 1969, he was released, to clean toilets for a month and then work in the cafeteria kitchen.[16]

Of the intellectuals among the Ye brothers, the rehabilitated Democratic League "rightist" Ye Duyi was subjected to the greatest attention, and he also left the most detailed record.[17] Since his downfall in the Anti-Rightist Campaign, he had lost his position in the Justice Ministry and was now working at an office that compiled historical reminiscences of members of the old elite, working alongside such figures as the last emperor of the Qing (and puppet emperor of Manchukuo under the Japanese), Puyi, who had just finished a famous memoir.[18] As the Cultural Revolution began, the head of the office came in for criticism. Duyi knew enough to sit quietly as his younger colleagues assailed the director for his bourgeois errors. The former emperor was less discreet—at one point jumping up to join in shouting "Down with all monsters and demons!" Duyi pulled him back to his seat, whispering that this was not their time to speak out.

His intellectual colleagues were even more discerning. At the Democratic League, as meetings were called to criticize Wu Han and his historical drama, Ye Duyi met often with the anthropologist Fei Xiaotong, his friend and classmate from Yenching. "It looks like another campaign is coming," Duyi suggested in one private moment. "It's going to be a big one," replied Fei Xiaotong. For a while, Ye Duyi joined Fei for Sunday meals to exchange views, but soon the renewed attention to his own background convinced him that he was about to become a target of the movement himself. He withdrew from the lunches with Fei to avoid endangering a friend. Fei Xiaotong sent him a brief note quoting a line from the Book of Changes (Yijing), but making a small change to one character, so that "Escape the world and all its worries; do not fear to stand alone," became "There is no escape from this world; [but] do not fear to stand alone."[19]

In August 1966, the Red Guards summoned Ye Duyi to a session in which he was especially criticized for his student years at Yenching University and his relations with Leighton Stuart, Yenching's American president who became ambassador to China in the late 1940s. Ye's home was searched, and he was compelled to make the usual confessions of suspicious relations with the American "spymaster." Then he was sent to labor in the countryside—which he found something of a relief after the incessant political campaigns of Beijing.

Late in 1967, he was back in Beijing, and the rebel faction of the Democratic League Red Guards resumed their investigation of every aspect of his relations with

Leighton Stuart. By early 1968, they had forced him to admit that his rightist ideas in 1957 demonstrated that he in effect was acting as a proxy for people like Leighton Stuart. Finally, one evening in early April, he was summoned for another interrogation, told that he was in detention, and forced to confess to their logic: Leighton Stuart was the chief American agent in China, Duyi had later acted as Leighton Stuart's proxy; therefore his relationship with Leighton Stuart was that of an American secret agent. Day and night for the next three days, he was pressed to supply the details of his secret agent activities. When he could come up with nothing, he was prompted with specific espionage activities that the interrogators claimed others had testified to. When he refused to admit to these activities, he was charged with refusing to make a full confession, doubting the authenticity of the state's evidence, protecting his fellow conspirators, and resisting the Cultural Revolution. Finally on April 26, he was formally arrested by several officers of the People's Liberation Army "based on the demands of the revolutionary masses."

Ye Duyi was taken to Qincheng, the penitentiary outside of Beijing reserved for China's most important political prisoners. There he was left to consider his fate for about three weeks, after which he was subjected to several days of intensive interrogations. At the beginning of each session, he was ordered to bow to the portrait of Chairman Mao hanging on the wall and loudly announce, "I am an American spy. I have committed serious crimes as a secret agent *(tewu)*. I confess and request punishment from Chairman Mao."[20] The interrogations would continue day and night for several days, stop for about a month, and then resume.

Unlike others held in Qincheng, Ye Duyi was not drugged, nor was he subjected to physical torture.[21] He was, however, forced to stand bowing for long periods, until he became dizzy and ready to collapse. He suffered most from the psychological stress of solitary confinement and from his arthritis, which was aggravated by the cold, dark, damp conditions in his cell. His warm clothes had been taken from him, and he was not even allowed to wrap himself in the thin blanket on his bed. Always subject to insomnia, Duyi suffered greatly from this condition in prison, where he was forced to sleep with a light on, in one position facing the door. His mouth was perpetually dry, the three bowls of water provided each day insufficient to quench his thirst. Prisoners were allowed out for fresh air and exercise only once a month, and in these conditions, his health steadily deteriorated.

After the first interrogations in April, the questioning periodically shifted from Duyi's relations with Leighton Stuart to his interactions with Xu Bing, the CCP representative in Beijing after the war. Xu Bing had since risen to become head of the party's United Front Department. As the man in charge of relations with the democratic parties and former members of the Guomindang, he was an inevitable target of the Cultural Revolution. In August, the interrogators came directly to the point and informed Ye Duyi that Xu Bing lay at the heart of his case. He was told to reveal the information Xu Bing had passed to him as an American spy. When he was unable to do so, they pulled out a copy of an alleged confession by Xu Bing, who (unbeknownst to Duyi) was being held separately in Qincheng. They read out Xu's supposed confession so that Ye Duyi could copy it down as his own. The statement included all manner of military intelligence from the Civil War period, which, since Ye Duyi had scarcely spoken to Xu, he could not possibly have known. In the end, to make the whole story fit, he had to confess to passing intelligence from Xu Bing to Leighton Stuart in Beijing—though the alleged transfer occurred at a time when Stuart was on leave in the United States. For a while, the interrogations came to an end.

Ye Duyi was not the only (or even the first) family member victimized by the party's effort to gather materials against Xu Bing. Ye Duzhuang had been in a prison labor camp since the brief reunion with his family in 1962. In the fall of 1966, as the Cultural Revolution was just getting under way, he was transferred to a labor farm in his ancestral province of Anhui—a large sprawling complex that held twenty to thirty thousand prisoners in dozens of cellblocks, each surrounded by a moat. Weakened by his kidney problems and years in jail, he was unable to do heavy labor and was assigned to collect night soil or work in the vegetable garden. As the Cultural Revolution heated up, the camp was frequently visited by teams of investigators digging for dirt on "capitalist roaders" in the party. Duzhuang was questioned several times by the team working on Xu Bing's case. In the immediate postwar years, Duzhuang's relations with Xu had in fact been much closer than his elder brother's, and Xu had approved and helped arrange his visit with Graham Peck to the Communist liberated areas. Now that Ye Duzhuang was a convicted U.S. agent, this connection was used to implicate Xu Bing in the alleged plot.

In March 1967, Duzhuang was summoned to his work brigade's headquarters, where two policemen told him to gather his effects to go to Beijing. For a moment, he thought that the Cultural Revolution investigations had somehow cleared him, but when the policemen put him in handcuffs for the train trip to the capital, he realized this was not the case. Like his brother Duyi, he was brought to Qincheng, but the two brothers did not learn until years later that they had been in the same jail at the same time. In Qincheng, Duzhuang found the food and the living conditions, with a sink and a flush toilet in his solitary cell, better than those of his previous confinement. The interrogations were another matter. Ye Duyi had not been subject to physical violence, but Duzhuang was a convicted American spy, and the PLA officers running the show were a good deal less restrained with him. In his initial interrogation, some thirty men were in the room, most in PLA uniforms, and when he refused to say that Xu Bing had done any spying for the Americans, he was forced into the airplane position and then pushed to the ground and repeatedly kicked by one leather-shoed officer. Subsequent interrogations brought the same treatment—by the same man. Eventually Duzhuang wrote out a vague confession that he was working under Xu Bing's direction and that their relationship was of a "counter-revolutionary" nature. This ended the process until October 1968, when, like Duyi, he was provided a prepared script of specific incidents in which Xu Bing supposedly imparted confidential information to pass to his American friends. He resisted confessing to these acts, was roughed up again, and finally wrote a confession according to the script, with one small change. He claimed that the information provided in 1947 was passed on to Graham Peck (not John Burke, as the script had it). Because Peck had returned to the United States by 1947, this detail made the whole fabrication impossible, but the confession satisfied his interrogators, and he was sent back to the Anhui labor farm.[22]

Ye Duyi stayed another four years in Qincheng. Conditions improved slightly after the end of 1968. He was allowed to read newspapers and gain some sense of political trends in the country. The published citation of a Mao speech against forced confessions gave him renewed hope, and as he adjusted to prison conditions, his health and spirits improved. But he had low moments as well, in particular a letter from home announcing that his children had all renounced any relations with him and urged him to confess his crimes to the authorities. This effort to break his spirit only backfired. Any cooperation he had offered in previous confessions had been partly motivated by concern for his family. If his family had already drawn a clear line to insulate itself from his problems, he saw no need for further cooperation with his persecutors. When interrogations resumed the next day, he confessed to the new crime of having falsified all his previous confessions. This statement started the process all over again, and eventually his interrogators composed another confession for him to copy. The early 1970s brought some relief, as the party dealt with its deepening internal divisions, until eventually on August 16, 1972, he was formally convicted of "committing secret agent crimes" but released to go home on account of his full confession and demonstrated remorse. His daughter went to greet him but hardly recognized the frail, white-haired man she found buying food in a nearby restaurant. When he saw her, he said apologetically, "I'm just buying a little something to eat." She burst into tears, then led him home—supporting his unsteady walk all the way.[23]


Ye Duyi and his brother Duzhuang ended up in Qincheng with China's most notorious political prisoners. But they were essentially collateral damage in Mao's Cultural Revolution. The Cultural Revolution was fundamentally about removing "capitalist roaders" from the party, not about persecuting the old intellectuals of the democratic parties. The Qincheng interrogators were not really interested in the Ye brothers' alleged crimes, only in fabricating a case against a more important target in the party, Xu Bing of the United Front Department. Back in Shenyang, Ye Fang was certainly not a man of Xu Bing's stature, but he was a senior member of the provincial leadership and the sort of loyal servant of the party organization who was likely to become a target of this great purge. In that respect, his family's experience was quite typical of what happened in many party members' households.

When Ye Fang was detained by the Red Guards of the Shenyang Rebel Alliance, his teenage children were also active in the Red Guards. Their initial reaction to the dramatic reversal of their family's fortune was not to question the Cultural Revolution—and certainly not to doubt the wisdom of Chairman Mao—but to blame the Red Guard group that had arrested their father. That group was surely misguided in targeting loyal revolutionaries; their group would make no such errors! Thus, in 1967, as hundreds and thousands of young revolutionaries made similar judgments, the Red Guards began to fragment into competing factions. Ye Fang's children gravitated to what would later be considered the conservative or royalist (baohuang) faction, which tended to be more sympathetic toward senior party members like their parents, while other factions were allied with the army. Eventually, the conflict between the factions in Shenyang and elsewhere degenerated into armed struggle, as the Red Guards went out to seize weapons from the arsenals of the local militia. In one such raid, fifteen-year-old Yangyang went along with his older brother in a truck commandeered from his school. He was toward the rear of the group, and in his haste to seize an old Japanese rifle and bayonet, he fell and cut a deep gash in his knee. He was overjoyed at his success in seizing the weapon, but his mother was alarmed by the wound and anxious about the escalating armed struggle. So she sent her son to Beijing to the relative safety of his seventh uncle's home in the Academy of Sciences. There he stayed for a few months until things settled down.[24]

The armed struggles of 1967 sufficiently alarmed the party leadership that Mao and his colleagues moved to rein in the movement and restore order. During the early stages of the Cultural Revolution, the Red Guards had been Mao's chosen instrument to prepare a new generation of revolutionary leaders. But the wave of factional fighting in 1967 had proven them unequal to the task, and Mao was forced to rely increasingly on the army, the only organization that had maintained a certain degree of institutional coherence. In 1968, the urban youths of the disbanded Red Guards were sent off to the countryside to absorb revolutionary virtue from the poor peasants. Ye Fang's teenage children joined this urban exodus, and soon the entire family was scattered. Ye Fang was sent to the countryside for reform through labor. His wife would soon flee to her ancestral home in Jiangsu. The oldest children were working, the middle children were in the countryside, and the three younger ones (then fourteen, twelve, and eight years old) were left to fend for themselves at home. They had only their father's dependents' allowance to live on and survived on cornmeal dumplings from the communal cafeteria and scavenged leftover vegetables. When factional violence broke out in the city, they hid in the air-raid shelters. (They sought the same refuge when a border dispute with the Soviet Union erupted into armed conflict in 1969 and threatened to spread south.) The youngest of the three attended primary school but received no real instruction.

The twelve-year-old felt stigmatized as the "little bastard" of an accused capitalist roader. The fourteen-year-old spent his time reading translated foreign literature—Tolstoy, Romain Rolland, Gogol—and the classics of Chinese history, often exactly the type of "old culture" that the Cultural Revolution was supposed to eradicate. Perhaps most importantly, the children acquired the street smarts to survive on their own in an increasingly unpredictable world. This experience brought skills that would serve them well in the years ahead.[25]

In rural China, the teenagers were acquiring useful skills of their own. Ye Boli was the oldest of this group, twenty years old by the time he went to the countryside in the fall of 1968. He had been a senior in high school when the Cultural Revolution broke out and had participated in the Red Guards from the earliest raids on "bad" family households to the mass rallies in Beijing and the armed struggles of 1967. In the countryside, his leadership skills were quickly recognized, and he rose to the position of production team leader in his village's agricultural collective. Indeed, he was so successful that several years later the county recommended him as part of its "worker-peasant-soldier" quota of students for college, and he later prospered in academia and then as a local government official.

Boli's next younger siblings, Yangyang and his sister Binbin, now in their late teens, managed to get assigned to the same state farm, about two hours by train from Shenyang. They set off with great enthusiasm, singing the "Anthem of the Pioneers." Their group of about 120 youths all came from the same school and were assigned their own fields to cultivate under the leadership of a local peasant cadre. They initially lived together in a cold tractor garage, then in brick dormitories that the local peasants helped them build. Conditions were primitive: the only drinking water came from a stagnant pond created by seepage through the dikes of the nearby Liao River. Binbin managed to avoid drinking from the pond for almost a week, surviving on water from a canteen she had brought from the city. But in time she joined the others in sweeping the bugs and debris from the surface and drinking it with her hands. Food was relatively plentiful; they ate the rice that they grew themselves along with Chinese cabbage and potatoes, all stewed in a great communal pot.

Within a few months, young Binbin became homesick. A classmate had already managed to get back to Shenyang, and Binbin had her send a telegram saying her mother was seriously ill. Binbin took the message to the PLA officer in charge of the farm, but he easily saw through the ruse and denied leave. So she sneaked off and hopped a train to Shenyang. There her mother insisted she bathe before entering the house. After a week of home cooking, she dutifully returned to the farm. A clever and well-tutored daughter of a party cadre, she knew exactly what to do. She went immediately to the political director of the team and confessed fully: "As soon as I got home, I regretted what I had done. I have disobeyed Chairman Mao's instructions to the youth of China to unite with the poor peasants. I have aided the class enemies of the revolution. I deserve the full punishment of the revolutionary masses and will accept it with pleasure." Pleased and impressed by her performance, the director only had her write a simple confession and make an oral apology to her classmates.[26]

It took only a few months of hard work in the countryside for the youthful enthusiasm of these privileged cadre children to fade. Steeling themselves through labor, appreciating the plight of the peasantry, and learning the simple virtues of the masses were one thing. Spending the rest of their lives tilling the fields was another. One by one their classmates sought ways to enlist in the army or finagle assignments to factory work. These were the only practical ways to escape agricultural labor, but the children of PLA officers got the first army slots, and the children of local cadres were favored for factory work. With Ye Fang still in political disgrace, his children had no ready means of escape, and the Cultural Revolution rhetoric of selfless sacrifice was beginning to sound hollow.[27]

Several of Ye Fang's children proved quite capable in the countryside. As we have seen, Boli became a successful team leader and eventually parlayed that success into an opportunity to enter college. He counseled his younger brother Xinxin to follow the same route. Eager to prove himself, Xinxin requested assignment to one of the poorest teams and quickly made it profitable. But his success owed much to a pragmatic mode of leadership that involved maneuvering around irrational state policies. At one point, the leftist leadership of Liaoning pressed the peasants to level their ancestors' graves and return the land to cultivation. But Northeast China had abundant arable land, and the policy only antagonized the peasants' sense of respect for their forebears. So Xinxin had his deputy level the tops of a few old graves, left town for a few days, and then returned to report that the job had been done. On another occasion, he managed to acquire extra chemical fertilizer. He brought it to the village, then left for town so that the villagers could use it on their private vegetable plots, where it would do more good than on the collective fields. The peasants were happy, production increased, and he could claim ignorance of exactly how the fertilizer was used. In such ways Ye Fang's children learned how to get things done, how to please their constituents, and how to avoid responsibility when contravening official policy. They were discovering how the socialist system worked in China and gaining survival and management skills that would serve them well in later life. But they were not exactly internalizing or practicing the ideals of the Cultural Revolution.[28]

In 1969, Ye Fang was transferred from labor reform to assignment in a desolate and isolated village in Chaoyang prefecture on the edge of the Inner Mongolian desert. Soon he was joined by his wife and three of his younger children. This was not the first time his children had seen their father during the Cultural Revolution. On one occasion, his thirteen-year-old son had visited him at the labor camp during winter and been struck by the image of his father wearing a simple cotton padded jacket tied at the waist with a rope of braided straw. On another visit in summer, the boy had carried a large watermelon almost six kilometers before finally hitching a ride on a horse cart. He ate the whole melon with his father and a roommate, about whom he was warned on arrival, "Be careful what you say. That guy is here to watch me."[29] His daughter had a similar experience, walking twenty kilometers to visit her gaunt, bearded father, whom she hardly recognized. Because she was a former Red Guard, and old enough for the responsibility, the leaders of the camp urged her to persuade her father to cooperate more with their interrogations. But she made only a pro forma attempt, and all of their conversations were attended by one of the camp authorities.[30]

In Chaoyang, the five family members lived in the same house with the sympathetic village head, all five sleeping together on one large, heated *kang*. Although they relished their time together, a political gulf was opening between the two generations. The children who had once eagerly joined the Red Guards and volunteered to work alongside the peasants in the countryside were now jaded and skeptical of the lofty ideals of the revolution. The dinner table became a forum for increasingly intense debate. Despite all his own troubles, Ye Fang maintained his unshakable loyalty to the party, and he repeatedly chastised his children for their doubts. "Do you want to become Soviet revisionists?" he asked. But they had seen the idealistic Red Guards degenerate into bitter factional rivals and had witnessed the children of army officers use their family connections to escape the rigors of rural labor. The lofty rhetoric of serving the people and pledging loyalty to Chairman Mao was no longer persuasive—and they could not understand their father's steadfast allegiance to a party organization that had condemned them to impoverished isolation in a desolate corner of China.[31]

Understandably, the older children's first concern was their own careers. Boli had already made his way to college. The next in line, his sister Binbin, sought to enter the army, traveling all the way to Jiangxi to seek a friend of their father for an introduction. But when she arrived, she saw posters calling on the masses to boil the fellow in oil. She realized that he too had come under attack and could offer no help. Her brother Yangyang seemed luckier. A local army officer recruited the tall boy to play basketball for the PLA. He was the only member of the family to succeed in this military road to advancement. After four years in the army, he applied to join the party as the route into the officer corps, but his mother's unresolved political problems prevented his admission to the party, and he soon left the PLA. His younger brother Xinxin suffered an even greater setback. A brilliant and creative lad, he had the misfortune to take the revived college entrance exams just when Mao Zedong's nephew, Mao Yuanxin (1941– ), was the dominant authority in Liaoning and was pursuing an extreme leftist line. When Xinxin failed to give the appropriate leftist answers to some leading questions after the first day of exams, he was denied the chance to continue the next day. The family was later told that Mao Yuanxin had tar-

FIGURE 20. Ye Fang's family, 1982. Top row, from left: Ye Xinxin, Ye Yangyang, Ye Boli, Ye Jiamu; middle row: Ye Lin, Ye Binbin, Ye Zi, Ye Bao, Ye Boli's wife; front row: Ye Boli's daughter, Lin Ying, Ye Lin's daughter, Ye Fang, Ye Lin's daughter. Family photo.

geted the boy because of his father's political problems. The same thing happened to his sister Binbin. On Mao's nephew's orders, Ye Fang's children were not to be admitted to college. Thus were the alleged sins of the father visited on his children.[32]

At the outset of the Cultural Revolution, Mao and his radical allies appealed to the youth of China—the students and Red Guards—to rekindle the flames of revolution. "Youth is the great army of the Great Proletarian Cultural Revolution!" Mao proclaimed. "It must be mobilized to the full."[33] If the older generation was in danger of lapsing into Soviet-style revisionism, their children could correct them, criticize them, and if necessary, break off relations with their misguided elders. All of the Ye children experienced this trauma. As their fathers came under attack, teachers pressured them to "draw a clear line" between themselves and their parents, as Ye Duyi's children were eventually forced to do in their letter to their father imprisoned in Qincheng. But only one Ye child really turned on her parents: a daughter of the eldest son (Duren) and an instructor at Beijing Normal University. She led a group of Red Guards from her school to attack her parents and her grandmother in Tianjin. The old lady was forced to kneel before the revolutionary youths, an experience so traumatic that she died soon thereafter. The rest of the family never forgave the daughter's transgression.[34]

Duren's daughter was the exception. One of the most striking lessons of this chaotic period was the resilience of the Chinese family. Parents devised a number of techniques to protect their children. The most elementary was to avoid any discussion of sensitive personal or political matters in their children's presence. They knew that children would be pressured to inform on their parents or their parents' associates, and there was always the possibility that the children would innocently mention some detail of parental conversations to their friends. The best defense was to ensure that the children knew as little as possible.[35] In addition, as exemplified most clearly by Ye Fang in the Northeast, parents went out of their way to urge their children to trust and obey the party—even when they themselves where among its victims. Ye Fang was actually a loyal party member, but less steadfast parents also urged their children to protect their future by politically correct behavior.

While families sought to protect their young, the logic of the Chinese communist system meant that family connections could also pose a great danger. On every personnel form, an employee was required to enter the names of his or her close relatives: parents, uncles, brothers and sisters. In great political campaigns like the Cultural Revolution, when every aspect of one's past came under scrutiny, the political status of these relatives inevitably became an issue. If one family member got into trouble, the others would surely be endangered. When the Cultural Revolution broke out, the agronomist Ye Duzhuang was already in a labor camp as a convicted American spy. His brother Fang Shi at the New China News Agency, doubting the charges, had briefly tried to have them investigated in 1962. Although he had quickly abandoned his efforts when the political winds changed, his request was enough to cast suspicion on his loyalty in 1966. When the party went after Xu Bing of the United Front Department in 1967, Ye Duzhuang was hauled off to Qincheng for aggressive interrogation. The effort yielded little, but the next year Ye Duyi was brought to Qincheng for questioning on the same case. Duyi's relations with Xu Bing were tangential at best, but his name had undoubtedly come up somewhere in the long interrogation of Duzhuang, and soon the elder brother was also forced into a series of false confessions.

The most common effect of family relationships in the Cultural Revolution was the discrimination against or privileging of children based on the political status of their parents. A common slogan of the early Cultural Revolution was "If the father is a hero, the son is a good fellow; if the father is reactionary, the son is a bastard." Although this so-called bloodline theory was later repudiated by Mao and his allies, the very simplicity of this standard of political correctness gave it enduring appeal throughout the Cultural Revolution.[36] The children of favored elites, particularly of army officers, benefited greatly from the "bloodline" theory, escaping exile to the countryside earlier than others and gaining favored access to the PLA.

But for members of the Ye family, it presented only disadvantage. The daughters of the imprisoned agronomist Ye Duzhuang were shunned at school and soon withdrew, and for years, their father's troubles prevented them from resuming their education. Most of their cousins had a similar experience. In the Northeast, the children of Ye Fang were blocked in their efforts to enlist or advance in the army or to join the party, and they were prevented from taking the examinations for college.

The rhetoric of the Cultural Revolution put great stress on the individual's capacity to earn merit and advance through correct political behavior.[37] Thus, children were urged to "draw a clear line" between themselves and parents accused of a transgression, rid themselves of the self-serving bourgeois habits of the older generation, and reform their thinking and adjust their behavior to serve the people and Chairman Mao. Those who did so were promised the opportunity to escape the crimes of their ancestors and to join the new socialist community. But the reality was quite different. At a time when anyone could be accused of serious political error, one had to have completely trustworthy allies, and none were more trustworthy than members of one's own family. This lesson was obvious in the behavior of the Cultural Revolution leadership. Chairman Mao turned to his wife, the former movie actress Jiang Qing (1914–91), to oversee the reform of theater and the arts, and soon she was a member of the all-powerful Cultural Revolution Small Group. Later in the Cultural Revolution, Mao brought his young nephew Mao Yuanxin back from the Northeast to serve as his liaison officer.[38] Mao's "closest comrade in arms," the PLA commander Lin Biao (1907–71), promoted his son in the air force, while his wife ran his office and served as intelligence agent to discover the intentions of Mao and other key actors.[39] Throughout the Cultural Revolution, party leaders used family members as conduits to Red Guard units and other mass organizations, and everyone could see the extent to which the leadership relied on close relatives to carry out the most sensitive political tasks.

It is not surprising, therefore, that ordinary people also fell back on family members as their most trusted friends and associates in this time of troubles. It was, however, the nuclear family that proved most resilient. Members of the elder generation understood that contact with their politically tainted brothers was too dangerous, so the sorts of gatherings of uncles and cousins that had characterized the 1950s largely ceased during the Cultural Revolution.[40] The small families, however, drew even more tightly together. Two of Ye Duzhuang's daughters spent long years in the countryside, one in the arid caves of northern Shaanxi and one in Inner Mongolia, but they kept in contact through letters and New Year visits home, and their elder sister in Beijing provided books and encouragement when the 1970s opened some hope that they would be able to resume their education.

Ye Fang's family in the Northeast provides one of the best examples of family solidarity, for in the early stages of the Cultural Revolution, it had been scattered: Ye Fang to labor reform, his wife to her family in Jiangsu, the elder children in different rural assignments, and the younger fending for themselves in Shenyang. But when Ye Fang was finally posted to Chaoyang, the family gathered again, and despite the intergenerational debates around the dinner table, parents and children had a genuine sense of family solidarity forged by the experience of surviving hard times together. Thus, for all the iconoclastic attacks on the "feudal" family system and the evils of Confucian patriarchy, and for all the pressure to distance oneself from miscreant family members, the actual result of the Cultural Revolution may have been a strengthening of family ties. At a time when even best friends could be forced to turn on each other and reveal secrets, one's immediate family members could be most trusted to stick together.

By the early 1970s, the most violent and chaotic phases of the Cultural Revolution were over. In the summer of 1967, a tense confrontation in Wuhan between Mao's most radical supporters and the PLA carried the real threat of civil war, and after this event, Mao turned increasingly to the PLA to restore stability. The army did so through a campaign to "cleanse the class ranks," which was in fact the bloodiest phase of the entire Cultural Revolution, as the new ruling group in many provinces wreaked revenge on its factional enemies. Mao's declared disappointment in the undisciplined Red Guards became widely known, and sixteen million young people—without employment in the stagnant urban economy—were sent to the countryside to labor in the fields and learn the revolutionary virtues of the poor peasants.[41] Revolutionary committees were established at all levels of administration, from province to city to county to school and factory. In theory, these committees were to be "three in one" combinations of experienced cadres, young (usually Red Guard) activists, and PLA representatives, but in fact the balance of power almost always tilted toward the PLA. When the Ninth Party Congress met in April 1969, the new Central Committee was dominated by the PLA; and the defense minister, Marshall Lin Biao, was officially declared Mao's chosen successor.

The triumph of Lin Biao and the PLA was short-lived. Tensions between Mao and Lin escalated over a number of issues. Meanwhile, border disputes with the Soviet Union exploded into major battles along the Amur River. As the Russians contemplated preemptive strikes against Chinese nuclear facilities, the Chinese conducted intense campaigns of war preparation—digging deep tunnels and storing grain, as the slogan of the day put it. Mao also embarked on a surprising strategic initiative, inviting President Richard Nixon to China in a move to counter the growing Soviet threat. As preparations for the Nixon visit advanced, the tensions between Mao and Lin spun out of control. Lin Biao, egged on by his wife and son, who were alarmed by Mao's growing suspicion of Lin and the PLA, got involved in a still-mysterious plot against Mao and the central leadership. When the plot was discovered in September 1971, Lin fled with his wife and son on an airplane that crashed on its way to the Soviet Union, killing all on board.[42]

News of the Lin Biao plot was closely held and only slowly released in carefully controlled forums, but the effect was electric. Mao's anointed successor and "closest comrade in arms" was suddenly revealed to be a traitor to the party. Because the logic of party discourse required uncovering deep historical roots for his traitorous behavior, this revelation meant that the recent Party Congress had chosen as its next leader a man who for decades had been a traitor to the revolution. How could Mao have trusted such a man? What did this incident say about Mao's judgment and the party's mechanism for choosing its leaders? For millions of young people, already disillusioned by the way in which they had been used as Red Guards and then discarded after the early stages of the Cultural Revolution, the Lin Biao affair marked the end of their unquestioning faith in the party.

The early 1970s witnessed a slow and frequently interrupted restoration of normalcy to life in the People's Republic of China. Old cadres had their cases cleared and their reputations restored, as Mao sought to check the power of the PLA and balance the influence of the leftist group that would become known as the Gang of Four: his wife and three party leaders from Shanghai. The Nixon visit was followed by a gradual and carefully controlled opening to the outside world, and Deng Xiaoping was brought back to assist the ailing Zhou Enlai's efforts to stimulate growth in the economy and bring discipline and efficiency to the administration of the state. The left still controlled the propaganda apparatus and had great influence in culture and education, but the most radical and disruptive period of the Cultural Revolution was at an end.[43]

Slowly a semblance of normalcy returned to the Ye family as well. In 1971, Fang Shi of the New China News Agency was digging wells in Shanxi as part of his labor duties at the May Seventh Cadre School to which he (like most cadres) had been sent for political reeducation. When he learned of the Lin Biao incident, he thought that perhaps the Cultural Revolution would soon end, but when Lin's crimes were described as "rightist," he knew that the left still held influence at the centers of power. In the following year, however, he was rehabilitated and ordered back to work at the domestic section of the news agency. Though he harbored serious doubts about the course the revolution had taken, he kept them to himself.[44]

The other party member among the Ye brothers, Ye Fang, was in the Northeast, where Mao Yuanxin, the Chairman's nephew, provided powerful support to the left. As a result, Ye Fang's rehabilitation was a much slower process. When his case was resolved in 1973, he was still accused of carrying out the "reactionary bourgeois line of Liu Shaoqi," though his errors were treated as a "contradiction among the people." As a result, he was left with a charge that leftists could revive if necessary, but he was returned to duty at the prefectural propaganda department. There he worked loyally and cautiously and avoided any hint of resentment or revenge seeking against the colleagues who had turned against him. His discretion earned him steady advancement in the bureaucracy, and eventually he was transferred back to Shenyang, the provincial capital, where he became head of the Liaoning Academy of Social Sciences. By this time, his children were mostly grown up, and he quietly called on his connections to help them get jobs or return to school.[45]

At the Academy of Sciences, Ye Duzheng resumed his meteorological research after the Nixon visit in 1972. The first cautious academic exchanges began as Chinese-American scientists visited China and asked to meet with their Chinese counterparts. One delegation included a meteorologist, so Ye Duzheng was included when the group had a ceremonial visit with Premier Zhou Enlai. His brothers saw his name in the paper and for the first time knew he was out of danger, and only from that point did they dare resume contact.[46]

When Ye Duyi was released from Qincheng prison in August 1972, the victims of the most egregious leftist excesses were being rehabilitated in large numbers. Still, even those who had clearly been wronged had to be cautious. Duyi had made a daily habit in prison of reciting a detailed record of his entire interrogation experience, but on his release, his family would not let him write anything down. His brothers in Beijing visited him and gave the same advice. His release had been conditional on the promise that he would make no appeal, and the act of recording the facts of his various forced confessions would have suggested an intent to seek redress. So he continued the daily recitation of his prison experience and finally wrote it down only after the death of Mao and the fall of the Gang of Four in 1976.[47]

Ye Duzhuang returned from Qincheng to the Anhui labor camp in 1968, and in September of that year, his ten-year prison sentence was complete, but he was not allowed to return to his family in Beijing. One of the cruel anomalies of the Chinese system of judicial punishment was that even when a prisoner had completed his sentence, he was not free. Unless his employer welcomed him back (and most did not want former political prisoners), the prisoner was usually left to labor in the countryside "under the supervision of the masses."[48] So Ye Duzhuang became an employee at the farm, receiving a minimal salary of eighteen yuan per month, nine of which he needed for food. The first month he sent five yuan to his mother in Tianjin, only to receive a letter back from a brother that she had passed away. Soon he was transferred to work at an agricultural extension station, where he could at last put his professional expertise to work. He helped make an insecticide called "920" and did some experiments on cotton and rapeseed, two of which would result in publications in the journals he had once edited in Beijing.

In December 1975, the party announced a general amnesty for all persons imprisoned as Nationalist county-level agents or division-level officers. This was part of an overall policy aimed at improving relations with Taiwan, which was still ruled by the Nationalist Party under Chiang Kai-shek's son, Chiang Ching-kuo. Ye

Duzhuang was surprised to find himself included in this amnesty, and on December 17, 1975, order no. 380 of the Anhui Public Security Bureau called for his release, at age sixty-two, and full restoration of citizenship rights. His first reaction was that this was some sort of cruel joke, for in his eyes, he had opposed the corrupt Nationalist regime for his entire life. He even considered refusing the amnesty to avoid any association with the Nationalists, but a fellow prisoner dissuaded him from this thought, arguing that once he was out, "the whole chessboard would be changed."[49]

Seven years had passed since Ye Duzhuang had completed his prison sentence, and now he was the beneficiary of a general amnesty and transferred to a fish hatchery in central Anhui, where work was light and he was able to do more useful research. His colleagues appreciated his contribution, and for the first time in years, he was treated with some respect and addressed as Mr. Ye. But rejoining his family in Beijing was still not assured. He needed a job there and a place to live, so someone was sent to see if his wife would take him back. Only then did he learn that she had died of cancer in 1973. He sent a telegram to the children and learned that they were all right. Soon the process of reintegrating with the family began. The first step was not auspicious. Over Chinese New Year in 1976, he went to see his sister in Shanghai. She and her husband were delighted with the fish he brought from Anhui, and he was impressed by their television set, the first he had seen; but on New Year's day, his brother-in-law took him out walking all day on the Bund in the old International Settlement. He thought this an unusual way to spend the holiday. Only later did he realize that his sister was keeping the inconvenient ex-convict visitor out of sight of friends and neighbors coming to offer the ritual New Year greetings.

In the spring of 1976, Ye Duzhuang finally saw his daughters. The eldest, Ye Liang, came first, carrying an easel to paint while on vacation from the Central Art Academy. He had not seen her since 1962, when she was still a middle school student, and reestablishing their relationship took some time. He was worried by her interest in events in Beijing. Premier Zhou Enlai's recent death had prompted an outpouring of grief from intellectuals and young people who regarded him as their only friend and protector in the top party leadership. Great crowds gathered in Tiananmen Square to leave wreaths and poems at a makeshift memorial. The mourning demonstrations soon took on a political tone, and sharp criticisms of Jiang Qing and the leftist group in the party began to appear among the poems, which provoked a sharp and bloody crackdown by the party leadership. Ye Liang listened closely to the broadcasts about the "counter-revolutionary" incident in Beijing, and her father feared that she might be involved. Not long after, the middle daughter came, crowding together with her sister on a small bed next to the pig pen, and in the summer, the youngest arrived.

The next several years would see more visits from his daughters, but only in 1979, eleven years after the completion of his prison sentence, did Ye Duzhuang finally return to Beijing. His old employer, the Chinese Academy of Agricultural Sciences, was still under the control of a leftist group, even after Mao's death and the fall of the Gang of Four in 1976. The academy had initiated the charges against Duzhuang in 1958, and its leaders were loath to admit error. Eventually, however, as Deng Xiaoping consolidated his position in the post-Mao leadership, the rehabilitation of wrongly accused cadres and intellectuals accelerated. The party's United Front Department and the Public Security Bureau ordered a review of his case, and the Beijing Superior Court determined that its earlier conviction on "counter-revolutionary crimes was inappropriate and should be corrected." The previous court orders were vacated, and the court now pronounced that "Ye Duzhuang is not guilty."[50] On New Year's day, 1979, he boarded an empty train for Beijing, arriving early the next morning to take a pedicab to Ye Liang's apartment, where he woke his three daughters. At the head of the same bed that he had painted years before sat a box with his wife's ashes, and his eyes filled with tears.

Epilogue

# After the Deluge

Shortly after midnight on September 9, 1976, Mao Zedong died. Three weeks later, his wife and her radical colleagues were arrested and branded a conspiratorial Gang of Four. The revolutionary era of Chinese history had come to an end, and the country would soon embark on a new stage of economic reform and opening to the outside world that would transform China as fundamentally as had the revolution. The socialist planned economy was replaced by market mechanisms, and export industries were developed to take advantage of China's abundant young, cheap, and well-disciplined labor force. By 2002, China had entered the World Trade Organization and established itself as a major global manufacturing center. Cities were transformed by soaring skyscrapers; high-speed trains raced across the landscape; new fashions replaced drab unisex Mao jackets; rock music and internet access transformed the cultural scene; and in 2008, the world witnessed the Beijing Olympics, whose spectacular venues are unlikely to be matched in the foreseeable future. For years, Mao Zedong had struggled against the "restoration of capitalism," but this was one battle the Chairman would lose. A vibrant, if often corrupt crony capitalism now drives the Chinese economy at a feverish pace, while the Chinese Communist Party preserves its monopoly of political power. New China has again assumed a new face.[1]

Although the transformation of post-Mao China has been fundamental, the process unfolded gradually, guided by an ever-secretive party core under the paramount leader Deng Xiaoping. Deng's method of "groping for stones to cross the river" left everyone uncertain about how far the economic and social transformation would go. First, the leftist holdovers from the Mao-era party leadership were sidelined. Then the agricultural sector was loosed from the shackles of the collective economy, and market incentives were restored. Rural collectives established factories (so-called township and village enterprises), which prospered in coastal and suburban communities. Special economic zones were opened along the coast to attract foreign investment and stimulate the production of cheap goods for export. New technologies were imported from the West and Japan, often with whole factories, steel mills, or refineries bought from abroad. Initially, most of these factories were large state enterprises, but over time, the private and rural collective sector outstripped the state enterprises and came to dominate the new economy.[2]

With economic development replacing proletarian revolution as the guiding force of the Communist Party, the new leadership sought to purge the system of the divisive poison of endless political campaigns and to restore a level of stability, administrative order, and respect for technical and practical expertise. In short order, hundreds of thousands of disgraced cadres and former "rightists" were rehabilitated. By this time, the senior Ye brothers were already entering their twilight years. Born in the 1910s, most were already in their sixties. They were, however, restored to their jobs, and many finished their careers in positions of some comfort and prominence.

Ye Duzheng's career at the Academy of Sciences was certainly the most outstanding. The Academy of Sciences had always been protected from the worst excesses of the Cultural Revolution, and in 1975, the rising reformer (and later general secretary of the party) Hu Yaobang (1915–89) was appointed its president. With renewed emphasis on advanced research and academic exchange with the international science community, Ye Duzheng's position in the academy became increasingly important. In 1978, he was appointed head of the Institute of Atmospheric Physics, with its 480 employees and over 300 researchers. He was active in international conferences, and the institute benefited from exchange agreements with the United States that made American satellite imagery available to Chinese researchers.[3] From 1981 to 1984, Duzheng was vice-president of the Academy of Sciences, and his scientific achievements received national and international recognition. Though he had committed his life to scientific research, the party-state was always eager (with the important exception of the Cultural Revolution era) to recruit famous scientists and intellectuals into the regime. Thus, Ye Duzheng was elected to the National People's Congress in 1964, and again from 1974 to 1989, serving on the Congress's standing committee from 1979 to 1989. In 1979, with his rise to administrative leadership in the Academy of Sciences, he joined the Communist Party. None of these appointments indicated any renewed interest in politics, and he certainly had no ambitions to political power, but they helped keep him informed of political developments, and such knowledge was useful if not essential to a career in the People's Republic. Ye Duzheng continued to be active at the

FIGURE 21. Ye Duzheng with President Hu Jintao, in receipt of 2006 Highest National Science and Technology Award.

Academy of Sciences long after his official retirement in the 1980s, and in January 2006, his lifetime of accomplishments was recognized in an elaborate ceremony at the Great Hall of the People (and a postage stamp issued in his honor), where President Hu Jintao presented the 2005 Highest National Science and Technology Award.[4]

Ye Duzheng's level of national recognition was clearly extraordinary in the family, but his brothers also made their marks in the post-Mao era. When Ye Duzhuang returned to the Chinese Academy of Agricultural Sciences, he was already sixty-five years old. Although the academy provided a comfortable apartment, back wages, and a basic salary, he knew he could never resume an active research career, so he devoted the rest of his life to the translation of Charles Darwin's works. His translation of *The Origin of Species* was published in 1982, and eventually, by the end of the century, a multi-volume translation of Darwin's collected works was published.[5] Duzhuang also resumed his work with the Democratic League, attending meetings in Beijing and often joining technical delegations advising the government on issues like desertification in China's arid northwest.

The two brothers in the Communist Party saw their careers flourish briefly in their golden years. Fang Shi continued to work at the New China News Agency and rose to become head of the domestic news department. In the Northeast, Ye Fang's full rehabilitation in the party was long delayed by the influence of Mao Zedong's nephew, Mao Yuanxin, but with the Chairman's death and the fall of the Gang of Four, that barrier was removed. Ye Fang was recruited to head the theory department in the Central Party School, for the first time joining his brothers in Beijing, where he would live out the remainder of his life. Ye Duyi also returned to a leadership position in the Democratic League, though his years in prison had made him even more cautious than before, and he sought a quiet retirement, which was only occasionally punctuated by meetings of the League, when the party went through periodic and largely formalistic rituals of asking for its advice. In 1993, he joined the Chinese Communist Party, explaining that he "accepted its gods, but not its temple"—its ideals, but not its organization.[6] By the end of the century, this generation now had four Communists (after many years with only two), though by this time party membership involved little commitment to Marxism-Leninism.

One telling measure of the more relaxed environment of the post-Mao years was the resumption of long-lost contact with the entertainer Ye Lizhong in Chongqing. His brothers had not heard from the young Lizhong since he left to join the Chinese army training in India during World War II. Since that force had suffered the highest casualties of any Chinese unit as its fought its way back through Burma, most of his brothers assumed that Lizhong had perished in battle. Instead, he had been making his career as a comedian in Sichuan, still hurt by his elder brother's banishment on account of his improper life on the stage and too embarrassed to contact his brothers in Beijing. By the 1980s, however, his comedic reputation was well established: two volumes of his comic routines had been published.[7] He noted occasional newspaper references to his siblings, especially to the prominent scientist Duzheng, and in 1984, he contacted them through a fellow entertainer in the capital. Soon the long-separated brothers were reunited in a series of warm and nostalgic dinner parties—though all sides agreed that the ebullient manner (easily stimulated by a few cups of liquor) and sometimes coarse humor of this long-lost brother still set him apart from his more restrained and intellectual siblings in Beijing.

With Ye Fang's transfer to the Central Party School, most of the family was now

FIGURE 22. Ye brothers in Beijing, 1984. The brothers, from left, are Ye Duzhuang, Ye Duyi, Ye Duzheng, Ye Fang, Ye Lizhong, and Fang Shi. The women in front are Yao Xiang (Durou's daughter), Li Yifan (Duyi's wife), Ye Chen (Duzheng's granddaughter), and Feng Hui (Duzheng's wife). Family photo.

in Beijing. With telephones in their homes and access to automobiles, they could get together more easily, free of the political concerns that had made them wary of overly frequent interaction in the past. Now brothers and cousins would gather for weekend, birthday, and holiday celebrations. A New Year party at Fang Shi's New China News Agency compound was a particularly important annual event attended by all the relatives. An ample banquet in a nearby restaurant was inevitably accompanied by toasts to recent accomplishments, new children or in-laws, and much reminiscing about times past. At these events more than ever, the survival of this family through all the trials of war and revolution was displayed and warmly celebrated.

Such family gatherings often provoked a good deal of thoughtful discussion of current conditions in China. The elder generation welcomed the more relaxed political environment and was proud of China's rise as a world power. The brothers condemned the follies of the Mao era and rued the time lost in disruptive political campaigns. Yet even those who had suffered in prison at Mao's hand credited the Chairman for having led China's rise, fighting the Americans to a stand-off in Korea, building an atom bomb, launching a satellite. They were also highly critical of the corruption of the party in the reform era, and when the student demonstrations supporting reforms to fight corruption and promote democracy swept the country in 1989, they were uniformly sympathetic. Many of their children joined the demonstrations, at least for the major marches, and all were shocked and disheartened by the bloody suppression of the students in Tiananmen on June 4. In the years after 1989, the Ye family, including the party members, had a far more complex relation to the Chinese state. The brothers were proud of China's accomplishments but disparaging of its leaders; supportive of the market reforms but wary of the corruption that accompanied them; critical of China's autocratic politics but defensive against foreign critics of human rights violations. Fang Shi's transformation was particularly notable, and he was an important leader of the editorial group in the magazine *Annals of the Yellow Emperor (Yanhuang Chunqiu)* whose articles on party history became a vehicle for liberal criticism by senior retired party stalwarts.[8] In his late years, this journal allowed him to speak with his own voice in ways that were impossible at the New China News Agency.

The most notable change in the post-Mao era was in the fortunes of the family's younger generation. With the exception of the eldest few, all of the younger cousins had been born in the 1950s or just before. They were in high school, junior high, or even primary school when the Cultural Revolution shut down the schools and interrupted their education. Most were sent to the countryside—to villages in the Northeast, the barren hills of Shanxi and Shaanxi, or the wide plains of Inner Mongolia. We have seen the experiences of Ye Fang's children in the Northeast, as well as their continuing trials seeking access to higher education when the universities opened again in the 1970s. Only in 1978, when the class background and political status of one's parents ceased to be a consideration for college admission, were they able to resume their academic careers.

Ye Fang's daughter Binbin is a good representative of this generation. Her father had long admired her observant nature and keen mind. He thought she would make an excellent journalist or pursue a career in government. But the Cultural Revolution left her repelled by the very thought of politics, and she knew that a journalist could be little more than a mouthpiece of the party. She was unwilling to play that role, but she still wanted a career that would serve the people. She fixed on medicine, which would allow her to help people under any political regime. She first took the college entrance exams in 1973 but was denied admission because of her father's unsettled political status. Only in 1978, after a year working as a hospital technician, was she admitted to the Shenyang branch of the Chinese Medical College. She received her medical degree in 1983, returned for further advanced training in pediatric radiology from 1986 to 1989, and then left for advanced study and research in Japan in the 1990s, specializing in the use of magnetic resonance imaging (MRI) for neurological disorders. By this time, her father was in Beijing at the Central Party School, and apparently aided by his connections, her hospital received approval for an expensive imported MRI machine. With her native intelligence, advanced training in Japan, single-minded dedication to her career, and now the requisite tools of her trade, she became one of China's most accomplished radiologists, heading the radiology section of her hospital, publishing many articles in Chinese medical journals, and serving as the elected chair of the pediatric radiology group in the Chinese Radiology Society. In 2002, she transferred to a better-equipped hospital at Sun Yat-sen University in Guangzhou (Canton), where she is now a professor.

The determined avoidance of politics was common to this generation. Their grandfather, apprehensive about the perilous turn of politics in the early republic, had abandoned the commitment to official service that had dominated his ancestors' lives for generations. After the 1911 Revolution, he turned to the safer (and profitable) world of business. His sons, coming of age in the 1930s, had been drawn back to politics in patriotic response to the threat of Japanese imperialism. By the Cultural Revolution, politics had become both perilous and unavoidable, and the entire family suffered to greater or lesser degrees in the shifting political winds. Not surprisingly, the new generation again sought refuge from the perils of political strife. Ye Duzheng's children naturally gravitated to scientific careers. The eldest, Ye Weijiang, finished college before the Cultural Revolution but was then assigned to work in a factory. His chance arrived when the Nobel laureate Yang Zhenning (C. N. Yang) came to recruit bright young Chinese physicists to study at the State University of New York at Stony Brook. Weijiang was selected, and he now chairs the physics department at the University of Idaho. His younger sister and brother had to wait until 1979 for their chance to enter college, and they both chose scientific careers in computer science and have also ended up in the United States. When Ye Duzhuang was finally released from detention and his three daughters returned from the countryside to resume their education, they too turned to academics, studying first in China and then earning Ph.D.s in archeology and economics and an MFA in art from universities in the United States. Fang Shi's eldest daughter, Ye Weili, also became an academic and studied abroad, earning her Ph.D. in history at Yale and now teaching at the University of Massachusetts at Boston.

The one notable exception to this avoidance of politics was Ye Fang's second son, Boli, who had proved so capable as a production team leader in the countryside. In the later stages of the Cultural Revolution, he was able to attend Liaoning University as a "worker-peasant-soldier" student—a fairly common way for the children of party cadres to escape the countryside and resume their schooling, though the education they received in the highly politicized 1970s was of questionable quality. Boli studied economics and then Marxism-Leninism, good preparation for a future cadre. After a brief and troubled first marriage, he transferred to the Dalian Institute of Economics, where he established a reputation for new economic thinking in the reform era. He attracted the attention of a Politburo member who had known his father as a cadre in the Northeast, and this man recommended him for a post in Hainan in 1987. This south China island province was then something of a model for economic experimentation, and Boli was appointed a county magistrate. A successful term there attracted the notice of his superiors, and he was transferred to the provincial level. Then, just as his career was taking off, he was killed in an automobile accident during an inspection trip with the governor. Thus, at the age of forty-four, this generation's one official had his political career come to a tragic end.[9]

Given the dramatic changes that have reshaped the Chinese economy and the enormous opportunities provided by the new market economy, it is remarkable that so few members of the younger Ye generation have been drawn to careers in business. A notable exception is one of Ye Fang's younger sons, whose still-evolving career provides an intriguing glimpse into the life of a young Chinese businessman. Born in 1956, Ye Bao was only ten years old when the Cultural Revolution began. With his father held in detention and his mother taking refuge at her home in Jiangsu, he lived alone with two of his brothers in Shenyang, surviving on discarded vegetables and cornmeal soup, but also acquiring a lot of basic survival skills. In 1969, when tensions along the Soviet border threatened war, his mother brought him and his younger brother to her natal home, where they lived with his uncle and helped him grind grain after school. In 1972, the family was reunited in the Northeast, his parents living in a poor commune while he boarded at a nearby middle school. Next came several years working in the countryside—terracing fields, growing vegetables, and finally (the easiest work) raising pigs. By his own admission, Ye Bao's education was rudimentary. He had just started primary school when the Cultural Revolution began, and the instruction he received in the countryside was less than inspiring. When he took the exams for college admission in 1978, his score was only 97 points, far short of the minimum requirement of 280 for college admission.

By this time, his father had been transferred to the Central Party School, and he was able to help Ye Bao get a technical position at his uncle's unit, the Chinese Academy of Agricultural Sciences. While working there, Ye Bao attended the Beijing College of Industry, a two-year technical school where he studied electronics. With this training, he joined a project at the agriculture academy to develop a system to input Chinese characters into a computer—still a challenging task for which there was no uniform code in the early 1980s. The project was successful, and in 1987, Bao's team received a First Class Award from the Ministry of Agriculture. The prize was worth ten thousand yuan, a substantial sum in those days, but each of the four people who worked on the project received only two hundred yuan, the remainder going to their administrative superiors in the academy and agriculture ministry. The experience so disheartened Ye Bao that he lost all interest in his job. From then on, his work day changed: he would arrive at work at 9:00 A.M.

for an 8:00 shift, prepare tea and read the paper until 10:00, then break for Ping-Pong with his friends, leave early for lunch at 11:00, return at 2:00 to finish the paper, and then chat and perhaps do a little work before leaving early at 4:00 to beat the traffic home.

In the 1980s, he lived with his parents at the Central Party School. The market economy was still developing, with some prices controlled and others not, producing significant regional price disparities. Other young cadre sons living at the party school often returned from the more open economic zones in south China with scarce goods to sell, and Ye Bao eagerly joined their rackets. One friend came back with a batch of cheap digital watches that he had bought for two yuan each; in Beijing they could be sold for five. Another managed to import some motorcycles in a special duty-free arrangement, which he sold at a profit of over a thousand yuan each. When another friend had a lot of pocket calculators that he could not unload in the saturated Beijing market, Ye Bao took them to his old home in Shenyang and sold four hundred at a profit of five yuan each. He quickly recognized that he had a gift for selling things and also had the essential access to opportunities for profit. His ambitions expanded accordingly.

Family connections helped. In 1988–89, he participated in several joint ventures with Hong Kong businessmen in the air-freight business. His brother Boli introduced him to business contacts and helped him get the necessary permits. For a while he was making a handsome salary of three thousand Hong Kong dollars per month, and he handled several big projects—including importing the MRI machine for his sister Binbin's hospital. But soon he suspected he was not getting his promised 20 percent of the profits. When his Hong Kong partner refused to open the books, he quit. His next venture—a Dalian branch of the Hainan South Asia Trust—was also enabled by Boli. He had to borrow half a million yuan from a friend of his father to establish the credit to register the company (the money was returned as soon as the registration was complete), and most of the big deals—importing chemicals from Australia, selling steel to the south—fell through at the last minute. By 1992, he was essentially broke, unable even to afford a pack of cigarettes.

In 1992, Ye Bao met Zhu Fengyang, the daughter of a senior PLA general and Long March veteran. (She was not related to Zhu De, the founder of the Red Army, but rumors of this relationship surely did not hurt her career.) She had joined the army during the Cultural Revolution, aided by her father's connections, then left in 1985 to go into business. Within a few years, she was managing a five-star hotel in Dalian. She and Ye Bao started working together in 1992; and two years later they married. By this time, the Chinese economy was growing at a furious pace, and they recognized the profits to be made in real estate. Their contacts in the army, among powerful cadres in the Northeast, and with potential sources of capital in Hong Kong proved invaluable. One of their first projects was an international trade center to be built on land controlled by the Dalian Garrison Command. After locating a Hong Kong partner willing to invest a million yuan, they established their credibility by renting a large seaside resort as their headquarters and buying an expensive new Mercedes. In the end, the army was denied authorization to develop the land for profit, and the project came to nothing, but Zhu and Ye Bao had already earned a handsome commission and moved on to their next deal. In this case, their partner was a well-connected Hainan cadre who felt responsible for Boli's death. Feeling guilty and wishing to make amends to the family, he first offered Ye Bao a stock tip, then flew to Dalian when Ye Bao mentioned a potential real estate deal. This time the deal (with a village head) went through, and Ye Bao and Zhu Fengyang made a handsome 260,000 yuan profit.

Further development projects in Dalian followed, and the couple made a good deal of money. Then in the mid-1990s, Zhu and Ye Bao start playing the stock market. Given the heavy role of the government and the constant threat of insider manipulation, this was a risky business. For a while, they did very well, and they took out a large bank loan to invest further. Then the market crashed. The Mercedes was sold to repay the loan. Ye Bao was so depressed that he spent much of the next year lying in bed watching pirated DVDs of foreign movies. But after a time, the market recovered, and the couple ended up with about the million yuan they had started with.

When I interviewed Ye Bao at length in 2001, he and his wife had spent a few years promoting Amway in China and were now dividing their time between an investment consulting group and an environmental protection business. Because foreign foundations and donor organizations preferred to work with nongovernment organizations (NGOs), he and Zhu had formed an NGO staffed by people hired from the state's Environmental Protection Bureau. His key associates were well connected to senior party and government officials ("Business all depends on connections," he explained.) And he was the picture of a successful Chinese businessman, driving a black Mercedes, dressed in a neatly pressed white shirt and slacks, wearing rimless glasses and a large Rolex watch, his thinning hair slicked back in perfectly combed and immobile lines. He was perfectly frank about his ambition to achieve the wealth and prominence of his grandfather—and proud to be the family's most successful businessman.

Since that time, fate has not been so kind to Ye Bao. His marriage to Zhu Fengyang fell apart, and following the divorce, his businesses started to go downhill. In the economic downturn of 2008 and 2009, he is certainly struggling. But this ambitious, well-connected, street-smart, charming, and ever-optimistic young man has had plenty of disappointments in life, and it is far too early to count him out. More than any other member of the Ye family, he learned to profit from China's free-wheeling market economy. As a well-connected hustler, he did very well at the end of the last century, and only time will tell how he does in the twenty-first.[10]

The other businessman in the family followed a very different route. Fang Shi's son Ye Weijia was in middle school when the Cultural Revolution broke out. With the rural banishment of the Red Guards, he went with his sister to the northern Shanxi countryside in 1968, working in the fields for the next six years. He managed to return to Beijing in 1974 to study electronics at a technical school as a "worker-peasant-soldier" student. After a few years at a research institute following graduation, he earned a scholarship to the University of Pittsburgh Graduate School of Public and International Affairs in 1984. His wife was also studying at Pittsburgh, and their son was born there in 1987. After passing his Ph.D. comprehensive exams, Weijia shifted his focus to engineering and business. He was admitted to the university's engineering school on a full scholarship and worked part-time in a software company with some of his professors. He soon discovered his talent for business, and by 1991, he had joined Pittsburgh Plate Glass, which was looking to develop manufacturing plants in China. He stayed with the company for fourteen years, first learning the business in U.S. factories, then locating Chinese partners and overseeing manufacturing in China, and eventually becoming responsible for the mechanical glass group in all of Asia. Working from an office in Hong Kong, he was able to join his wife and son in Beijing only on weekends and holidays. He now directs an NGO in Beijing, the Dao Institute for Environment and Development, which advises Chinese companies on environmentally sustainable business models. With his graduate education abroad and return to work in China, Ye Weijia's business career was obviously very different from Ye Bao's (though they both have ended up in environmental NGOs). His success may perhaps be attributed to the self-reliance engendered by the Cultural Revolution years, the technical training of the 1970s, and the foreign experience of the post-Mao years, all of which have contributed to his career—and to China's rise as a global manufacturing superpower.[11]

. . .

Looking back at this history of the Ye family, one is struck by its resilience through the tumultuous years of rebellion, war, and revolution. We began this story with the family's flight from its ancestral home when the Taiping rebels seized Anqing. In the years that followed, the family hid in the hills of Anhui, then sent the women and children to safety in Shaanxi while the men joined the fight against the rebels. When Ye Kunhou and his brothers were separated, they constantly exchanged letters and poems, and when peace was restored, much of the family reassembled in Kaifeng. In the twentieth century, the Japanese invasion again scattered the family, with each of the brothers following a distinct personal and political trajectory, but in the early years of the PRC, most were again together in Beijing. Finally, the Cultural Revolution sent parents to prison or political detention and children to long years of hard and hungry labor in the countryside; but once Mao passed from the scene, the family regrouped and returned to its new home in Beijing.

To say that the family endured, however, is not to say that it remained unchanged. All the clichés about the strength of the Chinese family must be qualified by the caveat that the nature and meaning of family were in constant flux, and never so much as in the modern era. The mobility and periodic scattering of the modern family was one key aspect of this change. For over four hundred years, the Ye family genealogy had recorded generation after generation of the Ye lineage in Anqing. But after the flight before the Taiping occupation, none of Ye Kunhou's descendants would make their home there again. The life of a Chinese official was inevitably peripatetic, but the norm in the imperial era saw an official and his family retire to his ancestral home. Even in the imperial era, there were many exceptions to that rule, but in the modern era, it simply did not apply. Kunhou's offspring scattered, and the branch we have followed abandoned the interior provinces for the coastal treaty port of Tianjin, while others stayed in Kaifeng or settled in Wuhan and elsewhere. The wars and revolution of the twentieth century brought another era of mobility and life-changing experiences, as the brothers traversed the country, many tasting life in China's interior and rural villages for the first time. While the establishment of the PRC brought most of these dispersed brothers to a new family base in Beijing, one remained in Tianjin, another in Chongqing, and a third in the Northeast. The sisters were even more scattered: one in Beijing, one in Shanghai, and one in Kunming in the distant Southwest. In this sense, the present scattering of the family—with many of the younger generation in the United States or Europe or seeking their fortune in Hainan or Guangzhou—is but an extension of the enhanced geographical mobility of urban families in modern China.

The most important change in family structure was the pronounced decline of the large extended family of the late imperial period, a family form that survived into the early republic in Ye Chongzhi's large household in Tianjin. In the mid-nineteenth century, Ye Boying continued to live with his father even after marrying and having children, and he assisted Kunhou's career into middle age. The Ye brothers of the twentieth century established their own households after the family division of the 1930s and lived independently from the time they were married—the sole exception being the eldest brother, who lived with his mother and his father's widow in Tianjin. These new nuclear families, with the exception of those of the three older brothers, were the product of love marriages, and although, as we have seen, several had their problems, the centrality of the conjugal bond between husband and wife was assumed. The younger generation is all nuclear families—though the shortage of housing, the large apartments of several of the senior generation, and the convenience of grandparent child care has at various times drawn several back to live with their parents in stem families. A notable development of this generation has been divorce, almost unknown in imperial China and strongly discouraged during the Mao era but now increasingly common. With the conjugal bond now central to the success of a marriage, when that bond is frayed, divorce is often the result, and there have been seven divorces among the twenty-five members of the younger generation.

The transformation in the status of women has been fundamental. The family genealogy reflected all the misanthropic prejudices of Confucian conservatism, insisting that women be confined to the inner quarters and blaming them for all manner of family discord. The sources on the nineteenth-century women of the family are all conventional and laudatory. They suggest a significant distaff role, with women overseeing their children's and supporting their husbands' studies and having some influence as quiet advocates of humane governance, but there is no suggestion of any role outside the household—nor even of the sort of literary activities pursued by some women of the lower Yangzi region.[12] Twentieth-century treaty-port life brought a new form of female sociability centered on mahjong, but even in the early republican era, Ye Chongzhi did not see fit to educate his daughters beyond basic literacy and embroidery, and only the youngest attended school, mostly after his death. When Chongzhi's younger sons had the opportunity to choose their wives, however, they married women with some education, and their wives all had jobs in the PRC—though none as prominent as their husbands'. The present generation has made further strides toward gender equality, notably in academic fields, where three of the four Ph.D.s were earned by women. Politics (Boli) and business (Ye Bao and Weijia) remain primarily male preserves, but Ye Binbin's achievements in radiology make her one of the most successful of the cousins in China.

A central thread of this story is the impact of the great events of modern Chinese history on several generations of a Chinese elite family. The family lived through three periods of great turmoil—the rebellions of the mid-nineteenth century, the war against Japan, and the revolutionary campaigns of the People's Republic. Each of these upheavals consumed the attention of family members and fundamentally affected their lives and careers, though the impact of the turmoil and the responses of family members were in each case radically different.

For fifteen years, from the 1853 Taiping attack that drove the family from Anqing to the final suppression of the Nian Rebellion in 1868, Ye Kunhou's extended family was consumed by the task of restoring order to the realm. When the family fled Anqing, it fled as a unit, hiding in the hills until the women and children could be sent to safety in Shaanxi. As an official, Ye Kunhou approached his job as a family undertaking, with Ye Boying and his uncles assisting—so that Boying was over thirty, married and with children before his own first appointment in Beijing. More importantly, Boying's rise in the bureaucracy came only after 1868, when the family was rewarded for its service in suppressing the Nian, just as his initial appointment in 1856 had followed his father's audience with the emperor. Merit, in this era, was a family matter; and it is not surprising that Ye Kunhou's poetry was noted for the dictum that "governing the people is like governing the family." The stability of state and family were inextricably linked, and the two were ordered along parallel principles of hierarchy, discipline, ritual propriety, and paternalistic duty. Although the late imperial state had a host of regulations to guard against nepotism, in its final years, the Qing was generous in dispensing honors to relatives of its loyal officials. Even Ye Chongzhi, the family's last Qing official, held an official degree acquired on the basis of inherited merit.[13]

When the Japanese invasion of 1937 drove most of the Ye brothers from Tianjin, the family had changed dramatically and their departure was a very different process from their ancestors' 1853 flight from Anqing. Part of this difference was purely accidental: their father had died relatively young, whereas Ye Kunhou had lived on as family patriarch to the age of eighty-seven. Far more importantly, the boys' experience boarding at Nankai Middle School and then away at college provided alternative centers of socialization and affinity that competed with the family compound behind the Anhui Guildhall. A century earlier, Ye Boying had also left home to take the civil service examinations, and we have noted his enjoyment of these times with friends and courtesans away from home. But the Confucian classics and histories he was studying for the exams were the same texts he had studied at home (often tutored by his uncles), and when the exams were over, he went right back to serving his father. There was no cultural gap separating life inside and outside the family. At Nankai, the Ye brothers studied science texts in English, learned about Japanese aggression in Manchuria, visited factories and prisons, and absorbed a nationalist educational curriculum quite different from what they had learned at home. By the 1930s, many were reading radical pamphlets from their leftist friends, and Ye Duzhuang wrote his essay on "Imperialism and the Chinese Capitalist Class." They also participated in sports, student government, drama groups, and Boy Scouts, and they did so as members of a new social category, youth (qingnian), imbued with a powerful sense of obligation to serve their country. The Chinese nation, their Nankai classmates, and their political commitments inspired new loyalties to compete with family obligations. When the Japanese invaded in 1937, the younger brothers went off to join the resistance, leaving not as a family group but each with his own friends and classmates from school. These friends were their new comrades, with whom they felt most comfortable and with whom they wished to pursue their patriotic mission.

The five brothers who left Tianjin for the interior during the war did so as young men in the prime of life, in their early twenties, still unmarried, each charting an independent course. The war prolonged their years of independent bachelor life and forced them to make crucial life decisions on their own. These were confusing years politically and socially, and most of the brothers at one time or another worked with Communists, Nationalists, independent warlords like Yan Xishan in Shanxi, and patriotic liberal intellectuals like those who would form the Democratic League.

During the war, each man made choices that would define the course of his life. Their choices reflected the diverse influences of school, politics, love, and friendship that characterized the republican era, and they were not always the product of careful political deliberation. Ye Duzheng left the leftist National Liberation Vanguard when his girlfriend, counseled by her party comrades, spurned him for a more politically correct mate. Thereafter, he devoted himself to a career in science. Two of his brothers joined the Communist Party, in each case led in part by affiliations they had formed during the student movement of 1935. Ye Duzhuang's path was the most tortuous, involving service in the Communist Eighth Route Army, a leftist group affiliated with Yan Xishan's army, the independent Chinese Industrial Cooperatives, the Nationalist government, the Democratic League, and finally the United States OSS. For this hot-headed young patriot, all of these activities were part of a single mission to defeat Japan and build a more progressive Chinese nation. But his activities and affiliations would have momentous consequences in the years to come.

All the brothers welcomed the Communist "liberation" of China and establishment of the People's Republic. Given the diversity of their experiences during the war, it is remarkable that none followed the Nationalists to Taiwan, but devotion to China's future kept them all on the mainland. Under the new regime, all found gainful employment and devoted themselves to building a new China. But the new regime brought unexpected rigidities to the social system, placing each individual into a particular class category: landlord or poor peasant, worker or capitalist. For the Ye brothers, the relevant categories were more political than social: revolutionary cadre, national bourgeoisie, Democratic League intellectual. The crosscutting loyalties and political searching of the republican era came to an end, and the categories became increasingly fixed and inflexible. These labels affected more than the individual who had chosen to join the party or the Democratic League; they affected whole families, for class and political status were inherited under the Communist regime. The traditional system had called for marriage between social equals, and the Qing-era Ye had intermarried with respectable gentry families. In the new China, political status was more important than social class, and we have seen that both Ye brothers in the Communist Party married party comrades with party approval. So spouses as well as children tended to carry the political label of the male family head.

The political campaigns of the PRC—the Anti-Rightist Campaign and then the Cultural Revolution—brought the third tumultuous era to sweep over the Ye family. Now the attacks came not from anti-Manchu rebels or Japanese invaders but from Chairman Mao and his allies in the Communist party-state. A family's fate in this era was largely determined by historical choices made years earlier: Ye Duzhuang and Ye Duyi in the Democratic League suffered the most; Ye Duzheng at the Academy of Sciences was persecuted as a "bourgeois" scientific authority, but he suffered less. Fang Shi and Ye Fang were both party members suspected of "capitalist roader" sympathies, but Ye Fang's greater involvement in the December 9th Movement, with its ties to Liu Shaoqi, made him the target of more prolonged struggle. A high degree of random coincidence and arbitrary decision making also determined one's fate at the hands of the new, powerful, and incredibly intrusive state. On two occasions, Ye Duzhuang seemed on the verge of being cleared to return to his family when renewed tensions with the U.S.-backed Nationalist regime in Taiwan caused someone in the security apparatus to block the release of this wartime employee of the OSS. The problems of Ye Fang and his family in the Northeast derived in part from the powerful role of Mao's leftist nephew, Mao Yuanxin, in the regional party apparatus. During these campaigns, the party took explicit aim at family loyalties, urging wives and children to "draw a clear line" between themselves and their accused husbands and fathers. In some cases, this edict surely succeeded in fracturing family bonds. But in general, and certainly in the Ye family, the fact that children were accused along with their fathers seemed, in the end, to draw the family together. Everyone was in the same boat, being painted with the same brush, and parents and children had only each other to rely upon.

Much like the War of Resistance against Japan, the Cultural Revolution scattered the Ye family across the map of China. Most of the younger generation was sent as "educated youth" to labor in the countryside. With a few exceptions, the children of this generation went separately, with classmates rather than siblings. Unlike their fathers, however, they were not politicized by the experience but were repelled by politics; and they did not want to end up as members of a political party that would determine their fate. The experience unquestionably engendered a certain independent spirit of self-reliance among this generation, and for some, a set of savvy, pragmatic, street-smart skills that would serve them well in the market economy and in the more competitive academic environment of the post-Mao era. Family ties still counted. Just as Ye Kunhou's brothers and sons were rewarded in 1868 with official positions for the family's service against the newly defeated Nian rebels, so did a few children of the Ye party members gain entrance to college as "worker-peasant-soldier" students in the early 1970s. Their less-fortunate cousins would have to wait for the full establishment of competitive examinations in 1978. Their lives in the post-Mao era were even more diverse than their parents', and they scattered even more widely across China and the globe. But they remain one family, now bound together by a web of electronic communications, the leaves and branches of this tree now sharing a virtual space whose future waits to be written.

# NOTES

## PREFACE

1. The family histories I have found most useful are Robert Forster, *Merchants, Landlords, Magistrates: The Depont Family in Eighteenth-Century France* (Baltimore: Johns Hopkins University Press, 1980), and *The House of Saulx-Tavanes: Versailles and Burgundy, 1700–1830* (Baltimore: Johns Hopkins University Press, 1971); and John Demos, *Past, Present, and Personal: The Family and the Life Course in American History* (New York: Oxford University Press, 1986). General histories of the European family abound and are useful in suggesting avenues of inquiry and points of attention. See, for example, Lawrence Stone, *The Family, Sex and Marriage in England, 1500–1800* (New York: Harper and Row, 1979); Beatrice Gottlieb, *The Family in the Western World from the Black Death to the Industrial Age* (New York: Oxford University Press, 1993); Michael Mitterauer and Reinhard Sieder, *The European Family: Patriarchy to Partnership from the Middle Ages to the Present,* trans. Karla Oosterveen and Manfred Hörzinger (Chicago: University of Chicago Press, 1982).

2. Frank Ching, *Ancestors, 900 Years in the Life of a Chinese Family* (New York: Fawcett Columbine, 1988); Johanna Menzel Meskill, *A Chinese Pioneer Family: The Lins of Wu-feng, Taiwan, 1729–1895* (Princeton, N.J.: Princeton University Press, 1979); and Susan Mann, *The Talented Women of the Zhang Family* (Berkeley: University of California Press, 2007) are notable family histories. Anthropologists have also made important contributions, especially Margery Wolf, *The House of Lim: A Study of a Chinese Farm Family* (New York: Appleton-Century-Crofts, 1968); Francesca Bray, *Technology and Gender: Fabrics of Power in Late Imperial China* (Berkeley: University of California Press, 1997); and essays in Patricia Buckley Ebrey and James L. Watson, eds., *Kinship Organization in Late Imperial China, 1000–1940* (Berkeley: University of California Press, 1986). The modern transformation of the family has been examined in some early but still useful works: Olga Lang, *Chinese Family and Society* (New Haven, Conn.: Yale University Press, 1946); Marion J. Levy, *The Family Revolu-*

*tion in Modern China* (Cambridge, Mass.: Harvard University Press, 1949); and in Susan L. Glosser, *Chinese Visions of Family and State, 1915–1953* (Berkeley: University of California Press, 2003). Finally, in Chinese, an excellent five-volume series on the Chinese family appeared as this manuscript was nearing completion: Zhang Guogan, ed., *Zhongguo jiating shi* [Chinese family history], 5 vols. (Guangzhou: Guangdong renmin chubanshe, 2007). The two volumes I use here are Yu Xinzhong, vol. 4, *Ming-Qing shiqi* [Ming-Qing period], and Zheng Quanhong, vol. 5, *Minguo shiqi* [Republican period]. Their extensive bibliographies are an excellent entrée into the Chinese sources on family history. I am indebted to Linda Grove for calling these volumes to my attention.

3. Notable examples of this genre are Jung Chang, *Wild Swans: Three Daughters of China* (New York: Simon and Schuster, 1991); Nien Cheng, *Life and Death in Shanghai* (New York: Grove Press, 1987); and Anchee Min, *Red Azalea* (New York: Berkley Books, 1999).

4. Ye Kunhou, *Jiangshang xiao Penglai yinhang shicun* [Surviving poems to recite while sailing by Little Penglai (Anqing) on the Yangzi] (Shaanxi: 1883), 1:11. Here and throughout the book, all translations from Chinese sources are my own.

### 1. FLEEING THE LONG HAIRS

1. Ye Kunhou, *Jiangshang xiao Penglai yinhang shicun* [Surviving poems to recite while sailing by Little Penglai (Anqing) on the Yangzi] (Shaanxi: 1883): 8:16–17, 20.

2. Xie Guoxing, *Zhongguo xiandaihua de quyu yanjiu: Anhui sheng (1860–1937)* [A regional study of China's modernization: Anhui province, 1860–1937] (Taipei: Academia Sinica, Institute of Modern History, 1991): 7.

3. John Shryock, *The Temples of Anking and Their Cults: A Study of Modern Chinese Religion* (Paris: Librarie Orientaliste Paul Geuthner, 1931; reprint, New York: AMS Press, 1973): 23–24; Sen-dou Chang, "The Morphology of Walled Capitals," in *The City in Late Imperial China*, ed. G. William Skinner (Stanford, Calif.: Stanford University Press, 1977): 91; G. William Skinner, "Regional Urbanization in Nineteenth-Century China," in ibid., 238.

4. Ping-ti Ho, *Studies on the Population of China, 1368–1953* (Cambridge, Mass.: Harvard University Press, 1959); Susan Mann Jones and Philip A. Kuhn, "Dynastic Decline and the Roots of Rebellion," in *The Cambridge History of China*, vol. 10, *Late Ch'ing, 1800–1911, Part 1*, ed. John K. Fairbank (Cambridge: Cambridge University Press, 1978), 107–62; Pierre-Etienne Will, *Bureaucracy and Famine in Eighteenth-Century China*, trans. Elborg Forster (Stanford, Calif.: Stanford University Press, 1990); Pierre-Etienne Will and R. Bin Wong, with James Lee, *Nourish the People: The State Civilian Granary System in China, 1650–1850* (Ann Arbor: University of Michigan Center for Chinese Studies, 1991).

5. Ye Kunhou, *Jiangshang shicun*, 2:35, also 3:8, 5:40.

6. Mark C. Elliott, *The Manchu Way: The Eight Banners and Ethnic Identity in Late Imperial China* (Stanford, Calif.: Stanford University Press, 2001); Pamela Kyle Crossley, *The Manchus* (Cambridge, Mass.: Blackwell Publishers, 1997), and *Orphan Warriors: Three Manchu Generations and the End of the Qing World* (Princeton, N.J.: Princeton University Press, 1990); Edward J. M. Rhoads, *Manchus & Han: Ethnic Relations and Political Power in Late Qing and*

*Early Republican China, 1861–1928* (Seattle: University of Washington Press, 2000); Evelyn Sakakida Rawski, *The Last Emperors: A Social History of Qing Imperial Institutions* (Berkeley: University of California Press, 1998); William T. Rowe, *China's Last Empire: The Great Qing* (Cambridge, Mass.: Harvard University Press, 2009).

7. Ye Kunhou, *Jiangshang shicun*, 3:25.

8. Peter Ward Fay, *The Opium War, 1840–1842: Barbarians in the Celestial Empire in the Early Part of the Nineteenth Century and the War by which They Forced Her Gates Ajar* (Chapel Hill: University of North Carolina Press, 1975); Hsin-Pao Chang, *Commissioner Lin and the Opium War* (Cambridge, Mass.: Harvard University Press, 1964); Arthur Waley, *The Opium War through Chinese Eyes* (Stanford, Calif.: Stanford University Press, 1995); James M. Polachek, *The Inner Opium War* (Cambridge, Mass.: Council on East Asian Studies, Harvard University, 1992).

9. The best and most recent treatment of the Taiping Rebellion is Jonathan D. Spence, *God's Chinese Son: The Taiping Heavenly Kingdom of Hong Xiuquan* (New York, W. W. Norton, 1996). For an older and sympathetic Chinese account, see Jen Yu-wen, *The Taiping Revolutionary Movement* (New Haven, Conn.: Yale University Press, 1973).

10. Ye Kunhou, *Jiangshang shicun*, 9:7.

11. Ye Boying, *Gengjing tang nianpu* [Chronological autobiography from the hall for cultivating the classics], undated ms in Beijing Library [pagination added], 22; *Ye-shi zupu* [Ye family genealogy] (n.p.: 1944), 1:39. By the 1944 edition used here, the genealogy had grown to twelve volumes *(juan).* The first volume is labeled *"shou"* (head) and is cited here as Preface; after ten numbered volumes, the final volume is labeled *"mo"* (end) and is here counted as volume 11. References are to volume and page or, where sections within volumes are separately paginated, in this format: volume number, [section title], page number(s).

12. Ye Kunhou, *Jiangshang shicun*, 8:53; 9:4, 8, 18, 23, 35, 46; 16:48–49.

13. Ibid., 10:29–30.

14. Ibid., 9:28–29.

15. Unless otherwise noted, the following account is based on Ye Boying's autobiography, *Nianpu*, 30–54, and Xiangjun zizhu Tongzhi liunian yiqian nianpu" [Ye Kunhou chronological autobiography to 1867] (hereafter cited as Ye Kunhou autobiography), *Ye-shi zupu*, 11:14–16.

16. Ye Kunhou, *Jiangshang shicun*, 9:28; 10:3, 5.

17. Ye Boying, *Nianpu*, 32.

18. Ye Kunhou, *Jiangshang shicun*, 9:17, 25.

19. Ibid., 10:8–9.

20. Ibid., 10:3–4.

21. Jen Yu-wen, *Taiping Revolutionary Movement*, 108–11; Spence, *God's Chinese Son*, 168–71; Xu Chuanyi, *Taiping tianguo Anhui sheng shigao* [Draft history of the Taiping Heavenly Kingdom in Anhui] (Hefei: Anhui People's Press, 1991), 26–29.

22. Xieshan jushi (Xia Xie), *Yuefen jishi* [Narrative of the Guangxi miasma] (1869; reprint, Taipei: Wenhai, 1966), 5–7 (123–27); Xu Chuanyi, *Taiping tianguo*, 29–31; Ye Kunhou, *Jiangshang shicun*, 10:4, 6.

23. Ye Kunhou, *Jiangshang shicun*, 10:5.

24. Ibid., 10:4–5, 9:29; Xu Chuanyi, *Taiping tianguo*, 54–55.

25. See Ye Yun's epilogue to Ye Kunhou's autobiography, *Ye-shi zupu*, 11:14.

26. Jen Yu-wen, *Taiping Revolutionary Movement*, 140–45, 200–203; Xu Chuanyi, *Taiping tianguo*, 56–61, 86–121; Xie Guoxing, *Zhongguo xiandaihua: Anhui*, 65–67.

27. Philip A. Kuhn, *Rebellion and Its Enemies in Late Imperial China: Militarization and Social Structure, 1796–1864* (Cambridge, Mass.: Harvard University Press, 1970); Kathryn Bernhardt, *Rents, Taxes, and Peasant Resistance: the Lower Yangzi Region, 1840–1950* (Stanford, Calif.: Stanford University Press, 1992), ch. 3.

28. Ye Kunhou, *Jiangshang shicun*, 9:32.

29. *Ye-shi zupu*, 9: *xingzhuang* [obituary], 12; 11: *jielüe* [précis], 39–40; Xu Chuanyi, *Taiping tianguo*, 94.

30. Ye Kunhou, "Duli" [Alone] in *Jiangshang shicun*, 9:29.

31. Ye Kunhou, "Zongyan" [Unrestrained Words], in *Jiangshang shicun*, 9:30.

32. On Wang Yangming, see Tu Wei-ming, *Neo-Confucian Thought in Action: Wang Yangming's Youth (1472–1509)* (Berkeley: University of California Press, 1976).

33. Ye Kunhou, *Jiangshang shicun*, 10:8–9.

34. Ibid., 9:36, 43, 44; 10:12, 14. Kunhou returned to these themes later while traveling in the hills of Henan: 11:38.

35. Ibid., 10:18; see also 9:34, 38.

36. Ibid., 10:16.

37. Ibid., 10:12.

38. Ibid., 10:40.

39. Ibid., 9:38, 39; 10:21; 11:1

40. Ibid., 10:20–21.

41. Ibid., 9:30–31.

42. Ye Kunhou, "Fenyan" [Angry Words], in *Jiangshang shicun*, 10:29–30

43. Ibid., 3:25 (a poem from the early 1840s).

44. James M. Polachek, *Inner Opium War*, ch. 4; Kuhn, *Rebellion and Its Enemies*; see Ye Kunhou, *Jiangshang shicun*, 16:5, for his understanding of militia in the Opium War.

45. *Ye-shi zupu*, 11: *ba* [postscript], 12.

46. Ye Boying, *Nianpu*, 45.

47. Ibid., 46. The more reliable account on which most of this narrative is based appears in Ye Yun's biography of Ye Lian in *Ye-shi zupu*, 11: "Daixu Shaoqing liunian dingmao yiqian jielüe" [A biographical summary of Ye Lian's life to 1867, written on his behalf] (hereafter: Ye Lian biography), 17–18.

48. Ye Kunhou reports that both his sons married at age sixteen (Ye Kunhou, *Jiangshang shicun*, 6:30–31), but here I accept Boying's account.

49. Ye Boying, *Nianpu*, 49; *Ye-shi zupu*, 11: *ba*, 12–13.

50. Ye Kunhou, *Jiangshang shicun*, 9:48; also 10:7, 32.

51. Ye Boying, *Nianpu*, 52. The dating here follows Ye Boying's detailed narrative in his autobiography, but the chronological arrangement of Ye Kunhou's poems suggests that this may have happened in 1854. See Ye Kunhou, *Jiangshang shicun*, 11:4–5, 10.

52. Jen Yu-wen, *Taiping Revolutionary Movement*, 403–30.

53. *Ye-shi zupu*, 11: *jielüe*, 40.

## 2. FAMILY ROOTS

1. Hilary J. Beattie, *Land and Lineage in China: A Study of T'ung-ch'eng County, Anhwei, in the Ming and Ch'ing Dynasties* (Cambridge: Cambridge University Press, 1979), 26–28; *Huaining xianzhi* [Huaining gazetteer] (1915; reprint, Taipei, 1983), 12:22.

2. William T. Rowe, "Success Stories: Lineage and Elite Status in Hanyang County, Hubei, c. 1368–1949," in *Chinese Local Elites and Patterns of Dominance*, ed. Joseph W. Esherick and Mary Backus Rankin (Berkeley: University of California Press, 1990), 56–57.

3. *Ye-shi zupu* [Ye family genealogy] (n.p.: 1944), Preface:1–2.

4. Ibid., Preface:4; 3:28.

5. Ye Kunhou, *Jiangshang xiao Penglai yinhang shicun* [Surviving poems to recite while sailing by Little Penglai (Anqing) on the Yangzi] (Shaanxi: 1883), 6:25–26.

6. Ibid., 3:14, 4:6, 7:30, 9:20.

7. On examination success rates, see Benjamin A. Elman, *A Cultural History of Civil Examinations in Late Imperial China* (Berkeley: University of California Press, 2000), 143–44, 157–58, 653, 661–65, 680. On the gentry, see Chung-li Chang, *The Chinese Gentry: Studies on Their Role in Nineteenth-Century Chinese Society* (Seattle: University of Washington Press, 1955).

8. *Ye-shi zupu*, 4:6–7.

9. Elman's *A Cultural History of Civil Examinations* can be read as an extended defense of the cultural and political contribution of the Chinese examination system. In this respect, it is an answer to the usual critical appraisal, represented in Chang, *The Chinese Gentry*, 165–209 (see part 3, "The Examination Life of the Gentry of Nineteenth-Century China").

10. *Ye-shi zupu*, Preface:7–8; 10: *zhongpu* [loyal servants], 1–2.

11. Ibid., 1: *gaofeng* [imperial titles], 1–13. Title translations from Charles O. Hucker, *A Dictionary of Official Titles in Imperial China* (Stanford, Calif.: Stanford University Press, 1985).

12. *Ye-shi zupu*, 10: *beiji* [steles], 2.

13. Beattie, *Land and Lineage*; Esherick and Rankin, *Chinese Local Elites*; and Patricia Buckley Ebrey and James L. Watson, eds., *Kinship Organization in Late Imperial China, 1000–1940* (Berkeley: University of California Press, 1986).

14. *Ye-shi zupu*, 8: *qiju* [contracts], 2–3; 10: *beiji*, 2.

15. Ibid., Preface:1–2, 14.

16. Ibid., Preface:32–34.

17. Ibid., 4:4, 5.

18. Ye Kunhou, *Jiangshang shicun*, 1:10–11.

19. *Ye-shi zupu*, 3: *shipai* [generation lines].

20. On family instructions, see Charlotte Furth, "The Patriarch's Legacy: Household Instructions and the Transmission of Orthodox Values," in *Orthodoxy in Late Imperial China*, ed. Kwang-Ching Liu (Berkeley: University of California Press, 1990), 187–211.

21. Ye Kunhou, *Jiangshang shicun*, 1:10.

22. Margery Wolf has written perceptively of this pattern in terms of the "uterine family" that women constructed within the patriline (*Women and the Family in Rural Taiwan* [Stanford, Calif.: Stanford University Press, 1972]). See also Pingchen Hsiung, *A Tender Voyage: Children and Childhood in Late Imperial China* (Stanford, Calif.: Stanford University Press, 2005), 129–35.

23. *Ye-shi zupu*, 2: *jiafan* [family regulations], 12. For a general analysis of this pattern, see Yu Xinzhong, *Zhongguo jiating shi* [Chinese family history], vol. 4, *Ming-Qing shiqi* [Ming-Qing period] (Guangzhou: Guangdong renmin chubanshe, 2007), 225–332.

24. *Ye-shi zupu*, 2: *jiafan*, 40–41. On women in the mid-Qing, see Susan Mann, *Precious Records: Women in China's Long Eighteenth Century* (Stanford, Calif.: Stanford University Press, 1997). Mann's discussion of regional variation in women's activities is notable: Tongcheng, just north of Anqing and the major center of local Confucian scholarship in this era, was a center of particularly conservative views. The Ye genealogy seems to fit this mold.

25. *Ye-shi zupu*, 2: *jiafan*, 19.

26. Timothy Brook, *The Confusions of Pleasure: Commerce and Culture in Ming China* (Berkeley: University of California Press, 1998).

27. Ye Kunhou, *Jiangshang shicun*, 8:43, cf. 8:46, 47–48.

28. Ibid., 16:27–28.

29. Ibid., 8:36.

30. Ibid., 16:29.

31. *Ye-shi zupu*, 2: *jiafan*, 20–21, 23, 25. On *yamen* clerks and runners, see Bradly W. Reed, *Talons and Teeth: County Clerks and Runners in the Qing Dynasty* (Stanford, Calif.: Stanford University Press, 2000).

32. *Ye-shi zupu*, 2: *jiafan*, 14–15.

33. Ibid., 10: *hezhuan* [collective biographies], 2, 3, 8.

34. Ibid., 2: *jiafan*, 17; 4: *zhuan* [biographies], 4, 7; 10: *beiji*, 3–4.

35. Ibid., 10: *beiji*, 2.

36. Ibid., 2: *jiafan*, 19.

37. Ibid., 5:22.

38. Ibid., 2: *jiafan*, 22–23.

39. The calculations here are based on 135 males born during the Qianlong reign (1735–95) for which both lifespan and children are recorded (ibid., *juan* 5–6). For a summary of demographic issues and comparative discussion of lifespan, mortality, and infanticide, see William Lavely and R. Bin Wong, "Revising the Malthusian Narrative: The Comparative Study of Population Dynamics in Late Imperial China," *Journal of Asian Studies* 57, no. 3 (August 1998): 714–48.

40. *Ye-shi zupu*, 9: *xingzhuang* [obituaries], 14. Family members' ages are from 6:23, 57.

41. *Ye-shi zupu*, 2: *jiafan*, 67–68.

42. Ibid., 10: *zhuan*, 7–13; *muzhi* [eulogies], 1.

43. Ibid., 10: *beiji*, 1, 2; Preface:19.

44. Ibid., 3: *yixing* [extraordinary behavior], 28.

45. Ibid., 10: *muzhi*, 2–3.

46. Ibid., 4:13.

47. Ibid., Preface:6; 10: *muzhi*, 4–5.

48. Dorothy Ko, *Teachers of the Inner Chambers: Women and Culture in Seventeenth-Century China* (Stanford, Calif.: Stanford University Press, 1994); Mann, *Precious Records*; Yu Xinzhong, 228–32. On footbinding, see Dorothy Ko, *Cinderella's Sisters: A Revisionist History of Footbinding* (Berkeley: University of California Press, 2005).

49. *Ye-shi zupu*, 4:4, 5, 41; 5:12, 14.

50. The best clues on such matters are the genealogy's records on the mothers of the children of elite members. We often see the youngest children born by concubines after the men were in their forties. See, for example, ibid., 6:22, 54, 56, 59.

51. Ye Kunhou, *Jiangshang shicun*, 13:33; cf. 3:6, 13:36, 14:20.

52. *Ye-shi zupu*, 9: *xingzhuang*, 3–4; cf. 2:4.

53. Ibid., 9: *nüzan* [eulogies of women]; see also 2: *gaofeng*, 7–8, 28.

54. The best studies of the position of women in the family in this era are Francesca Bray, *Technology and Gender: Fabrics of Power in Late Imperial China* (Berkeley: University of California Press, 1997) and Mann, *Precious Records*. In Chinese, see Yu Xinzhong, *Zhongguo jiating shi*, vol. 4, *Ming-Qing shiqi*, esp. 194–206, 292–324.

55. *Ye-shi zupu*, 9: *xingzhuang*, 4.

56. Pingchen Hsiung, *Tender Voyage*, 128–55.

57. Ye Kunhou, *Jiangshang shicun*, 12:28.

58. Ibid., 12:49, 15:25.

59. Ibid., 1:27.

60. Ibid., 15:50–51.

61. Ibid., 2:23.

62. *Ye-shi zupu*, 10: *muzhi*, 13; 2: *xinzeng jiagui* [new family regulations] (1906), 8.

63. Ibid., Preface:3, 6; 4:13; 10: *muzhi*, 1–3.

## 3. FATHER, SON, AND FAMILY

1. *Ye-shi zupu* [Ye family genealogy] (n.p.: 1944), 5:59, 11: Ye Kunhou autobiography, 1.

2. Ibid., 11: *xingshu* [obituaries], 4–5.

3. Ibid., 11: *xingshu*, 7–8; 11: Ye Kunhou autobiography, 6–7; Ye Kunhou, *Jiangshang xiao Penglai yinhang shicun* [Surviving poems to recite while sailing by Little Penglai (Anqing) on the Yangzi] (Shaanxi: 1883), 7:41, refers to Kunhou's cousin returning to Anqing in around 1849 to redeem some of the mortgaged (or pawned) ancestral land.

4. Ye Kunhou, *Jiangshang shicun*, 14:14.

5. *Ye-shi zupu*, 11: *xingshu*, 6, 7.

6. Ye Kunhou, *Jiangshang shicun*, 2:22; Ye Boying, *Gengjing tang nianpu* [Chronological autobiography from the hall for cultivating the classics], undated ms in Beijing Library [pagination added], 6, 19; *Ye-shi zupu*, 5:58–59; 6:20–24.

7. Ye Kunhou, *Jiangshang shicun*, 1:3.

8. *Ye-shi zupu*, 11: *xingshu*, 1.

9. Ibid., 11: Ye Kunhou autobiography, 2; 11: *xingshu*, 5, 10.

10. Ye Kunhou, *Jiangshang shicun*, 1:5, 17:28–29.

11. Ibid., 6:15.

12. *Ye-shi zupu*, 9: *xingzhuang*, 4–5.

13. Ye Kunhou, *Jiangshang shicun*, 1:4–5.

14. Ibid., 1:8. None of these poems are dated, but the arrangement is chronological, and many can be dated from internal evidence. The dating here is from evidence in surrounding poems.

15. Ibid., 1:9.

16. *Ye-shi zupu*, 11: Ye Kunhou autobiography, 2–3.

17. Ye Kunhou, *Jiangshang shicun*, 6:30–31.

18. Ibid., 2:14.

19. *Ye-shi zupu*, 9: *xingzhuang* [obituaries], 9.

20. Ye Kunhou, *Jiangshang shicun*, 1:17, 20, 23; 2:14, 19, 24; 4:19–20; 5:12.

21. *Ye-shi zupu*, 11: Ye Kunhou autobiography, 3–5; Ye Kunhou, *Jiangshang shicun*, 14:28.

22. Normally the *juren* examinations were held in the provincial capital, but Anhui was a new province, and the examinations remained in the old capital, Nanjing.

23. Ye Kunhou, *Jiangshang shicun*, 4:3; cf. 6:30.

24. Ibid., 16:13–14.

25. Ibid., 1:19–20.

26. Ibid., 5:35–36.

27. Ibid., 1:28–29.

28. Ibid., 7:45–46. On imperial audiences, see Philip Alden Kuhn, *Soulstealers: The Chinese Sorcery Scare of 1768* (Cambridge, Mass. Harvard University Press, 1990), 203–10.

29. *Ye-shi zupu*, 11: Ye Kunhou autobiography, 5–8, and *xingshu*, 10; 9: *xingzhuang*, 9.

30. Ye Kunhou, *Jiangshang shicun*, 1:19–20, 23, 27.

31. Ibid., 1:21.

32. Ibid., 8:22.

33. Ibid., 3:28.

34. Ibid., 8:49.

35. Ibid., 8:41.

36. Ye Boying, *Nianpu*, 11–16, has the most complete account of the flood but places it in 1842. See also Ye Kunhou's autobiography in *Ye-shi zupu*, 11:9–10, which puts the flood in 1840; and Ye Yun's postscript in ibid., 11: *ba*, 11; and Ye Kunhou, *Jiangshang shicun*, 2:15–17, which correctly dates the flood to 1841. (See Kaifeng shi difangzhi bianweihui, ed., *Kaifeng shizhi* [Zhengzhou: Zhongzhou guji chubanshe, 1996], vol. 1, 48.)

37. Ye Kunhou, *Jiangshang shicun*, 5:16–17.

38. Ibid., 2:16.

39. Ibid., 7:3–4.

40. Ibid., 3:8; cf. 2:15–17, 28.

41. Ibid., 3:47.

42. Chung-li Chang, *The Income of the Chinese Gentry* (Seattle: University of Washington Press, 1962), 7–34.

43. Ye Kunhou, *Jiangshang shicun*, 1:27, 2:14.

44. *Ye-shi zupu*, 9: *xingzhuang*, 9–10.

45. Ye Boying, *Nianpu*, 9.

46. Ibid., 9; *Ye-shi zupu*, 9: *xingzhuang*, 6.

47. Ye Kunhou, *Jiangshang shicun*, 16:29.

48. *Ye-shi zupu*, 9: *xingzhuang*, 4.

49. Ibid., 11: *xu* [narratives], 20.

50. Ibid., 9: *xingzhuang*, 5.

51. Ye Kunhou, *Jiangshang shicun*, 6:1.

52. Ibid., 5:43.

53. Ibid., 4:8.

54. *Ye-shi zupu,* 9: *xingzhuang,* 10.

55. On the ethical influence of Qing women, see also Susan Mann, *Precious Records: Women in China's Long Eighteenth Century* (Stanford, Calif.: Stanford University Press, 1997), 205–16; and *The Talented Women of the Zhang Family* (Berkeley: University of California Press, 2007), 47, 196–200.

56. David Wakefield, *Fenjia: Household Division and Inheritance in Qing and Republican China* (Honolulu: University of Hawaii Press, 1998).

57. *Ye-shi zupu,* 10: *muzhi* [eulogies], 2.

58. Ye Kunhou, *Jiangshang shicun,* 2:14–15, 13:35, 17:20–21, 18:17–18. Ye Lian's son also assisted his father in Shandong (ibid., 8:34).

59. Ibid., 1:9; 2:14–15, 22; 3:14; 4:48; 6:15.

60. *Ye-shi zupu,* 11: *xingshu,* 15–21. Ye Yun's education post was so minor that it was exempt from the prohibition on serving in one's native province.

61. Ye Boying, *Nianpu,* 12, 16.

62. Ye Kunhou, *Jiangshang shicun,* 7:12.

63. *Ye-shi zupu,* 1:39.

64. Ibid., 11: *xingshu,* 12.

65. Ye Boying, *Nianpu,* 20.

66. Ibid., 20; *Ye-shi zupu,* 11: Ye Kunhou autobiography, 12, and *xingshu,* 12, 20, 37; Ye Kunhou, *Jiangshang shicun,* 7:41–42

67. Ye Kunhou, *Jiangshang shicun,* 16:43, describing a grand-nephew's journey to the exams.

68. Ibid., 2:18.

69. Ibid., 1:24.

70. Ye Boying, *Nianpu,* 7, 10, 16–21.

71. Ye Kunhou, *Jiangshang shicun,* 5:42; cf. 1:18, 2:24, 3:33.

72. Lu Xun, "The True Story of Ah Q" (1921), in *Selected Works of Lu Hsun,* vol. 1, trans. Yang Xianyi and Gladys Yang (Beijing: Foreign Languages Press, 1964), 102–54.

73. Ye Kunhou, *Jiangshang shicun,* 2:18.

74. Ibid., 6:4.

75. Ibid., 5:29. The bamboo and pine references are conventional metaphors for elite virtues. In the case of bamboo, a pun is involved, for modesty *(xuxin)* is literally "empty heart," which also applies to the hollow bamboo.

76. Ibid., 7:44, 7:10–11.

77. Ibid., 7:27–28.

78. The following narrative is based on Ye Boying, *Nianpu,* 23–31; *Ye-shi zupu,* 11: Ye Kunhou autobiography, 13–14.

79. Ye Kunhou, *Jiangshang shicun,* 4:46.

80. T'ung-tsu Ch'ü, *Local Government in China under the Ch'ing* (Cambridge, Mass.: Harvard University Press, 1988).

81. *Ye-shi zupu,* 11: Ye Kunhou autobiography, 12–13; Ye Kunhou, *Jiangshang shicun,* 8:16–17.

82. Ye Kunhou, *Jiangshang shicun,* 8:20.

83. Ibid., 15:22.

84. Ye Boying, *Nianpu,* 23–31; *Ye-shi zupu,* 11: Ye Kunhou autobiography, 13–14.


4. REBELLION

1. Ssu-yu Teng and John K. Fairbank, *China's Response to the West: A Documentary Survey, 1839–1923* (Cambridge, Mass.: Harvard University Press, 1954). For a critique of Fairbank's "Response to the West" paradigm, see Paul A. Cohen, *Discovering History in China: American Historical Writing on the Recent Chinese Past* (New York: Columbia University Press, 1984). An excellent standard textbook treatment with further suggested readings is Jonathan D. Spence, *The Search for Modern China,* 2nd ed. (New York: W. W. Norton, 1999), 141–263.

2. On the southwest Muslim rebellion, see David G. Atwill, *The Chinese Sultanate: Islam, Ethnicity, and the Panthay Rebellion in Southwest China, 1856–1873* (Stanford, Calif.: Stanford University Press, 2005); on the northwest rebellion, see Hodong Kim, *Holy War in China: The Muslim Rebellion and State in Chinese Central Asia, 1864–1877* (Stanford, Calif.: Stanford University Press, 2004); and Chu Wen-djang, *The Moslem Rebellion in Northwest China, 1862–1878: A Study of Government Minority Policy* (The Hague: Mouton, 1966).

3. Ping-ti Ho, *The Ladder of Success in Imperial China: Aspects of Social Mobility, 1368–1911* (New York: Science Editions, 1964), 218.

4. Arthur W. Hummel, *Eminent Chinese of the Ch'ing Period (1644–1912)* (Washington, D.C.: U.S. Government Printing Office, 1943–44; reprint, Taipei: Literature House, 1964), 515–16, 526–28, 721–22, 742–46.

5. Ye Kunhou, *Jiangshang xiao Penglai yinhang shicun* [Surviving poems to recite while sailing by Little Penglai (Anqing) on the Yangzi] (Shaanxi: 1883), 14:16; see also 11:12, 19, 22; *Ye-shi zupu* [Ye family genealogy] (n.p.: 1944), 11: Ye Kunhou autobiography, 16–17.

6. Ye Kunhou, *Jiangshang shicun,* 11:36–37, 13:35–36, 14:35.

7. *Ye-shi zupu* 11: Ye Kunhou autobiography, 17–18.

8. Ye Boying, *Gengjing tang nianpu* [Chronological autobiography from the hall for cultivating the classics], undated ms in Beijing Library [pagination added]), 53–55.

9. "Doushu zixun Tongzhi liunian dingmao yiqian jielüe" [An autobiographical summary of Ye Yun's life to 1867], *Ye-shi zupu* 11: 25–26. "Yuqing zixu Minguo wuwu nian yiqian nianpu" [Chronological autobiography of Ye Shuliang to 1918], in Ye Shuliang, *Tui'an shigao* [Poems from a retirement cottage] (n.p.: 1918), 1–3. (Shuliang was Ye Yun's son.)

10. Ye Boying, *Nianpu,* 55; *Ye-shi zupu* 11: Ye Lian biography, 18; 6:22–23; Ye Kunhou, *Jiangshang shicun,* 17:11–12. The genealogy, which becomes somewhat unreliable on this branch of the family after the 1867 edition that Ye Boying edited, gets the date of Ye Lian's death wrong. Ye Kunhou's contemporary and firsthand record puts his death in 1871.

11. Ye Kunhou, *Jiangshang shicun,* 12:26.

12. Ibid., 13:12.

13. Ibid., 7:13; cf. 13:7, 12.

14. Ibid., 13:10; cf. 12:10, 11:34.

15. Elizabeth J. Perry, *Rebels and Revolutionaries in North China, 1845–1945* (Stanford, Calif.: Stanford University Press, 1980), 96–151, gives the best account of the Nian Rebellion. See also Siang-tseh Chiang, *The Nien Rebellion* (Seattle: University of Washington Press,

1954); and Ssu-yu Teng, *The Nien Army and Their Guerrilla Warfare, 1851–1868* (Paris: Mouton, 1961).

16. Ye Boying, *Nianpu,* 23–24; Ye Kunhou, *Jiangshang shicun,* 8:4–5.

17. Ye Kunhou, *Jiangshang shicun,* 13:12.

18. Philip A. Kuhn, *Rebellion and Its Enemies in Late Imperial China: Militarization and Social Structure, 1796–1864* (Cambridge, Mass.: Harvard University Press, 1970).

19. Ye Kunhou, *Jiangshang shicun,* 12:5.

20. Ibid., 12:9–10.

21. Ibid., 12:7.

22. Ye Boying, *Nianpu,* 1: 65.

23. Miao Quansun, *Xu Beizhuan ji* [Collection of tombstone biographies, continued] (1910; reprint, Taipei: Wenhai, 1973), 13:1–2; Cai Guanluo, *Qingdai qibai mingren zhuan* [Biographies of seven hundred famous men of the Qing] (reprint, Taipei: Wenhai, 1971), 411–12.

24. Ye Boying, *Nianpu,* 62; *Ye-shi zupu,* 11:25–26.

25. Ye Boying, *Nianpu,* 66–71. See also Kuhn, *Rebellion and Its Enemies,* 41–50; and Perry, *Rebels and Revolutionaries,* 122–27, on the *jianbi qingye* policy, whose earliest use was during the Eastern Han dynasty, in the second century C.E.

26. Ye Kunhou, *Jiangshang shicun,* 13:2–3.

27. On religious sectarianism in north China and its association with popular rebellion, see Susan Naquin, *Millenarian Rebellion in China: The Eight Trigrams Uprising of 1813* (New Haven, Conn.: Yale University Press, 1976); and *Shantung Rebellion: The Wang Lun Uprising of 1774* (New Haven, Conn.: Yale University Press, 1981); Daniel Overmyer, *Folk Buddhist Religion: Dissenting Sects in Late Traditional China* (Cambridge, Mass.: Harvard University Press, 1976); Joseph W. Esherick, *The Origins of the Boxer Uprising* (Berkeley: University of California Press, 1987), 38–67, 333–40; and (for a work that questions the label "White Lotus") B. J. ter Haar, *The White Lotus Teachings in Chinese Religious History* (Leiden: E. J. Brill, 1992).

28. Most other sources call it Golden Tower Stockade (or Fort), the characters for "tower" and "brazier" having very similar pronunciations. For Golden Tower, see Perry, *Rebels and Revolutionaries,* 150n; also, the biography of Mao Changxi in Cai Guanluo, *Qibai mingren,* 414.

29. Ye Boying, *Nianpu,* 74–78; *Ye-shi zupu,* 10: *muzhi* [eulogies], 2.

30. Ye Kunhou, *Jiangshang shicun,* 12:1.

31. Ibid., 12:4; cf. 12:1.

32. Ibid., 8:4–5.

33. William T. Rowe, *Crimson Rain: Seven Centuries of Violence in a Chinese County* (Stanford, Calif.: Stanford University Press, 2007), 205–9. Rowe describes *jianbi qingye* as a "scorched earth" policy.

34. Ye Kunhou, *Jiangshang shicun,* 12:1.

35. Ibid., 12:10.

36. Ibid., 13:22–23, 12:19–20.

37. Ibid., 12:4–5

38. Ibid., 14:4–5.

39. Ibid., 11:44.

40. Ibid., 11:12.

41. Ibid., 11:48.

42. Ibid., 11:9.

43. Ibid., 13:41.

44. Ibid., 11:6.

45. Ibid., 12:3–4.

46. Ibid., 12:21; cf. 12:19–20.

47. Ibid., 12:2. The reference to the strange attire of these braves likely indicates that they were wearing looted clothing. For twentieth-century accounts of the bizarre clothing of predatory bandits, see Phil Billingsley, *Bandits in Republican China* (Stanford, Calif.: Stanford University Press, 1988), 129–32.

48. Ye Kunhou, *Jiangshang shicun,* 12:2.

49. Ibid., 11:15.

50. For Ye Kunhou's career in these years, see *Ye-shi zupu,* 11: Ye Kunhou autobiography, 14–22.

51. Ye Kunhou, *Jiangshang shicun,* 14:1.

52. Ibid., 12:44.

53. Ibid., 13:3, 11, 12.

54. Susan B. Carter, Scott Sigmund Gartner, Michael R. Haines, and Alan L. Olmstead, eds. *Historical Statistics of the United States,* vol. 1, *Earliest Times to the Present,* Millennial Edition (Cambridge: Cambridge University Press, 2006), part A: "Population," 217.

55. Xie Guoxing, *Zhongguo xiandaihua de quyu yanjiu: Anhui sheng, 1860–1937* [A regional study of China's modernization: Anhui province, 1860–1937] (Taipei: Academia Sinica, Institute of Modern History, 1991), 471–75, 705; Anhui difangzhi bianzuan weiyuanhui, ed., *Anhui shengzhi, renkou zhi* [Anhui provincial gazetteer: population](Anhui renmin, 1996), 18–21, 37.

56. Stanley Spector, *Li Hung-chang and the Huai Army: A Study in Nineteenth-Century Chinese Regionalism* (Seattle: University of Washington Press), 1964; Samuel C. Chu and Kwang-Chin Liu, eds., *Li Hung-chang and China's Early Modernization* (Armonk, N.Y.: M. E. Sharpe, 1994).

57. Ye Kunhou, *Jiangshang shicun,* 16:3, 14–15; Ye Boying, *Nianpu,* 89–90.

58. Yeh-chien Wang, *Land Taxation in Imperial China, 1750–1911* (Cambridge, Mass.: Harvard University Press, 1973).

59. See Mary C. Wright, *The Last Stand of Chinese Conservatism: The T'ung-Chih Restoration, 1862–1874* (Stanford, Calif.: Stanford University Press, 1957).

60. Ye Kunhou, *Jiangshang shicun,* 15:43–44.

61. Ping-ti Ho, *Studies on the Population of China, 1368–1953* (Cambridge, Mass.: Harvard University Press, 1959), 236–48. Ho notes, "Anhwei, a most contested province, received the deepest wounds" (239).

## 5. OFFICIAL LIFE IN THE LATE QING

1. The classic study of this era is Mary C. Wright, *The Last Stand of Chinese Conservatism: The T'ung-Chih Restoration, 1862–1874* (Stanford, Calif.: Stanford University Press, 1957). See also Jonathan K. Ocko, *Bureaucratic Reform in Provincial China: Ting Jih-ch'ang in Restora-*

*tion Kiangsu, 1867–1870* (Cambridge, Mass.: Harvard University Press, 1983); Stanley Spector, *Li Hung-chang and the Huai Army: A Study in Nineteenth-Century Chinese Regionalism* (Seattle: University of Washington Press, 1964); Mary Backus Rankin, *Elite Activism and Political Transformation in China: Zhejiang Province, 1865–1911* (Stanford, Calif.: Stanford University Press, 1986), ch. 5.

2. *Ye-shi zupu* [Ye family genealogy] (n.p.: 1944), 10: *muzhi,* 6 (eulogy of Ye Kunhou by Fang Changhan).

3. Ye Kunhou, *Jiangshang xiao Penglai yinhang shicun* [Surviving poems to recite while sailing by Little Penglai (Anqing) on the Yangzi] (Shaanxi: 1883), 17:21–22, 38–39.

4. Ibid., 11:41; cf. 16:2

5. Ibid., 17:41.

6. Ibid., 1:11, 4:44–45, 18:47

7. Ibid., 18:24.

8. Ibid., 4:44–46, 11:22, 18:24.

9. Ibid., 4:46, 5:5, 16:26–27, 16:26–27.

10. Ibid., 4:44.

11. Ibid., 15:22.

12. Ibid., 14:13.

13. Ibid., 13:33, 13:34.

14. Ibid., 15:22.

15. Ibid., 15:3.

16. Ibid., 14:31, 32–34.

17. Ibid., 18:23; cf 18:5.

18. Ibid., 18:5.

19. Ibid., 12:25, 27; 18:25.

20. Ibid., 18:5.

21. Ibid., 18:4–5.

22. T'ung-tsu Ch'ü, *Local Government in China under the Ch'ing* (Cambridge, Mass.: Council on East Asian Studies, Harvard University, 1988); John R. Watt, *The District Magistrate in Late Imperial China* (New York: Columbia University Press, 1972).

23. Ye Kunhou, *Jiangshang shicun,* 15:18, 26.

24. Ibid., 13:18, 15:1.

25. Ibid., 13:16–17.

26. Ibid., 7:10–11, 15.

27. Ibid., 11:37.

28. Ibid., 7:14–15, 31.

29. Ibid., 13:20–21.

30. Ibid., supplement *(yu),* part 1: 28.

31. Ibid., 15:26.

32. Ibid., 15:35.

33. Ibid., 4:5; cf. 7:5.

34. Ibid., 7:14, 7:33.

35. Ibid., 7:15. The Gurkhas' visit was around 1848.

36. Ibid., 6:13; 14:16–18, 25–26; 15:20, 37–38.

37. Ibid., 6:20.

38. Ibid., 15:28.

39. Ibid., 16:13–14.

40. Ibid., 14:30.

41. Ibid., 15:32.

42. Ibid., 14:14; cf. 7:10, 14:30.

43. Ibid., 12:34; 13:38; 14:24–26; 18:49, 52–53.

44. Ibid., 15:29.

45. *Ye-shi zupu*, 11: Ye Kunhou autobiography, 18–21; 3:8–9.

46. Ye Kunhou, *Jiangshang shicun*, 16:34, 18:23.

47. Ibid., 15:30–32.

48. Su Tingkai (Yellow River Commissioner), in 1867 preface to *Ye-shi zupu*, Preface:35.

49. *Ye-shi zupu*, 11: Ye Kunhou autobiography, 22–23; Ye Boying, *Gengjing tang nianpu* [Chronological autobiography from the hall for cultivating the classics], undated ms in Beijing Library [pagination added]), 177–78; letters from Ye Dujing (great-great-grandson of Kunhou) to Ye Duzhuang, 25 December [1987?] and 29 March 1995.

50. Ye Kunhou, *Jiangshang shicun*, 15:41, 42.

51. Ye Shuliang, *Tui'an shigao* [Poems from a retirement cottage] (n.p.: 1918), 3. The poem was by Shuliang's mother.

52. Ye Kunhou, *Jiangshang shicun*, 11:32–33, 46; 12:28, 40; 14:43–44, 46–47; 15:1, 17:16.

53. Ibid., 13:33.

54. Ibid., 14:26, 16:13.

55. Ibid., 15:25, 27, 29; 18:14–15, 44.

56. Ibid., 18:32.

57. Ibid., 13:36, 15:21.

58. *Ye-shi zupu*, 6:22–22, 56–57; 11: Ye Kunhou autobiography, 21–22; Ye Dujing to Ye Duzhuang, 25 December [1987?].

59. Ye Boying, *Nianpu*, 56–57.

60. The term that Ye Boying uses here is *jingji*, but he clearly does not have the modern meaning, "economics," in mind.

61. Ye Boying, *Nianpu*, 56–61.

62. Ibid., 62; *Ye-shi zhupu*, 11:25–26.

63. James L. Hevia, *English Lessons: The Pedagogy of Imperialism in Nineteenth-Century China* (Durham, N.C.: Duke University Press, 2003), 46–118.

64. Ye Boying, *Nianpu*, 80–84.

65. Ye Kunhou, *Jiangshang shicun*, 15:28, 39.

66. Ye Boying, *Nianpu*, 84–87; *Ye-shi zupu*, Woren preface (1867), Preface: 37–38. The biographical entries from this edition of the genealogy provide much of the information available on the family up to 1867. Unfortunately, the next edition of the genealogy did not update these biographies to include the post-1867 period, so our information becomes a good deal less complete.

67. *Ye-shi zupu*, 3: *xiuci ji* [lineage hall], 1–6.

68. Ye Boying, *Nianpu*, 71, 79.

69. Ibid., 88–90; Ye Kunhou, *Jiangshang shicun*, 16:3, 14–15; 18:19–20, 56.

70. On Zeng Guofan, see Arthur W. Hummel, *Eminent Chinese of the Ch'ing Period (1644–1912)* (Washington, D.C.: U.S. Government Printing Office, 1943–44; reprint, Taipei: Literature House, 1964), 751–55; on Tongzhi governance, Wright, *Last Stand;* Ocko, *Bureaucratic Reform.*

71. Ye Kunhou, *Jiangshang shicun*, 12:39–40.

72. Ye Boying, *Nianpu*, 96.

73. Ye Kunhou, *Jiangshang shicun*, 15:41.

74. Ibid., 16:3–5.

75. Ye Boying, *Nianpu*, 91–94.

76. Ibid., 166–67.

77. Ibid., 157–59.

78. Ibid., 126–27.

79. Mark Elvin, "Female Virtue and the State in China," *Past & Present* 104 (August 1984): 111–52; Matthew H. Sommer, *Sex, Law and Society in Late Imperial China* (Stanford, Calif.: Stanford University Press: 2000), 166–209; Janet M. Thiess, *Disgraceful Matters: The Politics of Chastity in Eighteenth-Century China* (Berkeley: University of California Press, 2004).

80. Ye Boying, *Nianpu*, 113, 123–24. Cf. Rankin, *Elite Activism.*

81. Ye Kunhou, *Jiangshang shicun*, 1:11.

82. Ye Boying, *Nianpu*, 128–30; Ye Kunhou, *Jiangshang shicun*, 15:40, also speaks of the officials' responsibility to care for vagrants.

83. See Pierre-Etienne Will, *Bureaucracy and Famine in Eighteenth-Century China*, trans. Elborg Forster (Stanford, Calif.: Stanford University Press, 1990). On the 1877–78 famine, see Kathryn Edgerton-Tarpley, *Tears from Iron: Cultural Responses to Famine in Nineteenth-Century China* (Berkeley: University of California Press, 2008).

84. Ye Boying, *Nianpu*, 132–34.

85. Ibid., 166.

86. Lillian M. Li, *Fighting Famine in North China: State, Market, and Environmental Decline, 1690s–1990s* (Stanford, Calif.: Stanford University Press, 2007), 38–73.

87. Ye Kunhou, *Jiangshang shicun*, 18:9–10.

88. *Da-Qing shilu (Tongzhi)* [Veritable records of the Qing Tongzhi reign], Tongzhi 13/2/14 (31 March 1874), 363: 7. Perhaps unsurprisingly, Ye Boying's autobiography makes no mention of this impeachment.

89. Zuo Zongtang was the critic of Li Hongzhang and Ye Boying's water-control work. The issues were extremely complex, but one aspect of the problem was Zuo's proposed solutions based on ancient geographic texts, on which he had become something of an expert. Part of Ye Boying's task was to demonstrate that the nineteenth-century rivers had quite different courses from those named in the ancient texts. On the incident, see Ye Boying, *Nianpu*, 164–65; *Ye-shi zupu*, 10: *muzhi*, 6; also Hummel, *Eminent Chinese*, 764–67; on Kunhou's warning, see Ye Boying, *Nianpu*, 103–4.

90. Ye Boying, *Nianpu*, 151. On Ye Boying and water control in general, see 99–102, 103–7, 108–11, 113–23, 124–27, 130–32, 133, 162–65; also *Ye-shi zupu*, 10: *muzhi*, 3–6. On an intendant's salary, see Chung-li Chang, *Income of the Chinese Gentry* (Seattle: University of Washington Press, 1962), 12–14.

91. Ye Boying, *Nianpu*, 2:135–36, 146. On pettifoggers in the Qing, see Melissa A. Macauley, *Social Power and Legal Culture: Litigation Masters in Late Imperial China* (Stanford, Calif.: Stanford University Press, 1998).

92. Ye Boying, *Nianpu*, 136–38.

93. Ibid., 136.

94. Ibid., 143–46

95. Ibid., 144–45, 157.

96. Ibid., 147–51.

97. Ibid., 170–72.

98. Ye Kunhou, *Jiangshang shicun*, 16:43.

99. Ibid., 17:1–2.

100. Ye Boying, *Nianpu*, 172–74.

101. Ibid., 146–47, 3:159–60.

102. Ibid., 174–79.

103. *Ye-shi zupu*, 6:55–56; 11: *zhuan* [biographies], 33–35; Ye Boying, *Nianpu*, 1:56, 3:214–17.

104. *Xu Shaanxi tongzhi* [Shaanxi provincial gazetteer, continued] (reprint, Taipei, 1969), 128:14–15; Ye Boying memorial, Guangxu 12/11/18 (13 December 1885) in *Shi'er chao donghualu: Guangxu chao* [Donghua records of the twelve (Qing) reigns], ed. Zhu Shoupeng [hereafter DHL] (reprint, Taipei, n.d.), 2161.

105. Guangxu 9/10/6 (5 November 1883), DHL, 1579–82, contains the Feng impeachment document, as well as that of the former lieutenant governor, and a mismanaged legal case from Shaanxi.

106. Ye Boying, *Nianpu*, 179.

107. Ibid., 180–81, 202–3; *Xu Shaanxi tongzhi*, 128:14; numerous Ye Boying memorials in the Gongzhongdang archives of the First Historical Archives [hereafter GZD], Beijing, esp. Guangxu 13/2/29, 13/8/19, 14/2/10.

108. Ye Boying, *Nianpu*, 184–85.

109. Ibid., 185–86; Ye Boying memorials, Guangxu 12/11/18, DHL, 24:2161; undated, *Huangchao Dao-Xian-Tong-Guang zouyi* [Memorials from the Daoguang, Xianfeng, Tongzhi, and Guangxu reigns] (reprint, Taipei, n.d.): 1459–60.

110. Ye Boying memorial, Guangxu 13/3/16, GZD.

111. Ibid., 13/run 4/15, GZD.

112. Ye Boying memorial, Guangxu 13/9/15, DHL, 24: 2316–18; cf. Guangxu 13/9/6 memorial, ibid., 2310–12. In the cases submitted for review and preserved in GZD, Ye Boying consistently asked for the most severe penalty, even where a contemporary reader would see substantial mitigating circumstances.

113. Ye Boying memorials in GZD, such as Guangxu 14/5/17 and 14/6/24 and numerous undated addenda. For a complaint from the court against such provincial autonomy, see the edict of Guangxu 12/12/6 (30 December 1886), DHL, 2169. On the appointment process, see Watt, *District Magistrate*, 45–58.

114. The most complete listing of Ye Boying's memorials, not all of which survive, is in the *Suishou dengji* records, First Historical Archives, microfilm reels 125–31 (Guangxu 11–14).

115. See William T. Rowe, *Saving the World: Chen Hongmou and Elite Consciousness in Eighteenth-Century China* (Stanford, Calif.: Stanford University Press, 2001), 242, for a contrary view; see Liu Ts'ui-jung, *Trade on the Han River and Its Impact on Economic Development, c. 1800–1911* (Nankang: Academia Sinica, 1980), 116–26, for similar proposals and their problems.

116. Ye Boying memorial, Guangxu 12/11/18 (13 December 1885), DHL 24:2161–63.

117. Ye Boying, *Nianpu*, 183, 189–90, 196, 197–99, 200–202, 217–18.

118. Ye Kunhou, *Jiangshang shicun*, 5:43.

119. Ibid., 1:10.

120. Benjamin A. Elman, *A Cultural History of Civil Examinations in Late Imperial China* (Berkeley: University of California Press, 2000), 190, 425–27.

121. Confucius, *Analects*, 6:4.

122. *Shaanxi weimo, Guangxu shisi nian* [Shaanxi examination essays, 1888] (n.p.: Hengjiantang, [1888?]).

## 6. A TIME OF TRANSITIONS

1. Ye Shuliang, *Tui'an shigao* [Poems from a retirement cottage] (n.p.: 1918), 5. Shuliang states that Kunhou's wife (Mme. Xu) was also brought back at this time; but as we have seen from Boying's account (ch. 5), she had been buried in 1867, shortly after her death. She was then reburied in 1891, together with her husband.

2. See the charts in *Ye-shi zupu* [Ye family genealogy] (n.p.: 1944), *juan* 4–7. Ye Kunhou's original name was Ye Fa, a single-character given name parallel to those of his brothers, Yun and Lian. The "Ji" in his son Jiquan's name was a different character from the "Ji" used by others of this generation.

3. Ye Kunhou, *Jiangshang xiao Penglai yinhang shicun* [Surviving poems to recite while sailing by Little Penglai (Anqing) on the Yangzi] (Shaanxi: 1883), 5:46.

4. Interviews with Ye Cuizhang and other members of the family in Anqing, February 1995.

5. *Ye-shi zupu*, 10: Yuanqi *muzhi* [eulogies], 1.

6. Ye Shuliang, *Tui'an shigao*, 3–6; Ye Kunhou, *Jiangshang shicun*, 18:56.

7. *Ye-shi zupu*, 6:89; 10: Yuanqi *muzhi*, 1–2. On the increase in "irregular" appointments of non–degree holders in the late nineteenth century, see Chung-li Chang, *The Chinese Gentry: Studies on Their Role in Nineteenth-Century Chinese Society* (Seattle: University of Washington Press, 1955), 29–32, 188.

8. This is the lineage described in Hilary Beattie's *Land and Lineage in China: A Study of T'ung-ch'eng County, Anhwei, in the Ming and Ch'ing Dynasties* (Cambridge: Cambridge University Press, 1979).

9. *Ye-shi zupu*, 6:89; 10: Yuanqi *muzhi*, 2–3. Years of search have yielded no trace of this title, *Quanqiu jiyao*.

10. On the Sino-Japanese War, see S. C. M. Paine, *The Sino-Japanese War of 1894–1895: Perceptions, Power, and Primacy* (Cambridge: Cambridge University Press, 2003); John L. Rawlinson, *China's Struggle for Naval Development, 1839–1895* (Cambridge, Mass.: Harvard

University Press, 1967); Allen Fung, "Testing the Self-Strengthening: The Chinese Army in the Sino-Japanese War of 1894–1895," *Modern Asian Studies* 30, no. 4 (1996): 1007–31.

11. Douglas R. Reynolds, *China, 1898–1912: The Xinzheng Revolution and Japan* (Cambridge, Mass: Council on East Asian Studies, Harvard University, 1993).

12. *Ye-shi zupu,* 10: Yuanqi *muzhi,* 3.

13. Luke S. K. Kwong, *A Mosaic of the Hundred Days: Personalities, Politics and Ideas of 1898* (Cambridge, Mass.: Council on East Asian Studies, Harvard University, 1984); Rebecca E. Karl and Peter Zarrow, *Rethinking the 1898 Reform Period: Political and Cultural Change in Late Qing China* (Cambridge, Mass.: Harvard University Asia Center, 2002).

14. Joseph W. Esherick, *The Origins of the Boxer Uprising* (Berkeley: University of California Press, 1987); Paul A. Cohen, *History in Three Keys: The Boxers as Event, Experience, and Myth* (New York: Columbia University Press, 1997); Lanxin Xiang, *The Origins of the Boxer War: A Multinational Study* (London: RoutledgeCurzon, 2003).

15. *Ye-shi zupu,* 10: Yuanqi *muzhi,* 2–5; Yuan Shikai memorial, Guangxu 28/7/6 (9 August 1902), ibid., 10: *zougao* [memorials], 1–2.

16. The school was the Lotus Pond (Lianchi) Academy. On its history and late Qing instruction, see Xing Zanting, "Lianchi shuyuan huiyilu" [Memoir of the Lotus Pond Academy], *Hebei wenshi ziliao xuanji,* no. 1 (1980): 222–29.

17. Ye Duzhuang, 1991 ms (untitled), 2.

18. See Albert Feuerwerker, "Economic Trends in the Late Ch'ing Empire, 1870–1911," in *The Cambridge History of China,* vol. 11, *Late Ch'ing 1800–1911, Part 2,* ed. John K. Fairbank and Kwang-ching Liu (Cambridge: Cambridge University Press, 1980), 1–69, figures from 33, 35, 54.

19. On the late Qing reforms, see Mary C. Wright, ed., *China in Revolution: The First Phase* (New Haven, Conn.: Yale University Press, 1968); Reynolds, *China, 1898–1912;* Stephen MacKinnon, *Power and Politics in Late Imperial China: Yuan Shi-kai in Beijing and Tianjin, 1901–1908* (Berkeley: University of California Press, 1980); Joseph W. Esherick, *Reform and Revolution in China: The 1911 Revolution in Hunan and Hubei* (Berkeley: University of California Press, 1976); Ralph L. Powell, *The Rise of Chinese Military Power, 1895–1912* (Princeton, N.J.: Princeton University Press, 1955).

20. Joseph W. Esherick, ed., *Remaking the Chinese City: Modernity and National Identity, 1900–1950* (Honolulu: University of Hawaii Press, 1999); Kristin Stapleton, *Civilizing Chengdu: Chinese Urban Reform, 1895–1937* (Cambridge, Mass.: Harvard University Asia Center, 2000); Joan Judge, *Print and Politics: 'Shibao' and the Culture of Reform in Late Qing China* (Stanford, Calif.: Stanford University Press, 1996); Barbara Mittler, *A Newspaper for China?: Power, Identity, and Change in Shanghai's News Media, 1872–1912* (Cambridge, Mass.: Harvard University Asia Center, 2004).

21. *Ye-shi zupu,* Ye Shanrong preface, Preface: 52–54.

22. Ibid.

23. *Ye-shi zupu,* 3: *xinzeng jiagui* [new regulations], 1–4. Ye Shanrong may not have represented all the lineage with these rules, for another set of distinctly less radical "new family regulations" soon followed.

24. Michael Gasster, *Chinese Intellectuals and the Revolution of 1911: The Birth of Modern Chinese Radicalism* (Seattle: University of Washington Press, 1969); Xiaobing Tang, *Global*

*Space and the Nationalist Discourse of Modernity: The Historical Thinking of Liang Qichao* (Stanford, Calif.: Stanford University Press, 1996), 80–162.

25. On Sun Yat-sen and the revolutionary movement, see Harold Z. Schiffrin, *Sun Yat-sen and the Origins of the Chinese Revolution* (Berkeley: University of California Press, 1968), and *Sun Yat-sen, Reluctant Revolutionary* (Boston: Little, Brown, 1980); Marius B. Jansen, *The Japanese and Sun Yat-sen* (Cambridge, Mass.: Harvard University Press, 1954); K. S. Liew, *Struggle for Democracy: Sung Chiao-jen and the 1911 Chinese Revolution* (Berkeley: University of California Press, 1971).

26. Edward J. M. Rhoads, *Manchus & Han: Ethnic Relations and Political Power in Late Qing and Early Republican China, 1861–1928* (Seattle: University of Washington Press, 2000), 121–72.

27. *Ye-shi zupu*, 11: *shilüe* [accounts], 4–4. His dismissal was on Xuantong [hereafter: XT] 3/4/3 (3 May 1911): see *Suishou dengji* archives 3:338 in First Historical Archives, Beijing.

28. Wang Zhiyuan, "Qingmo Zhili sheng de jingcha jiguan" [Police organization of Zhili in the late Qing], *Hebei difangzhi* [Hebei gazetteer] 1988.6: 29–30; Wang Shouxun, *Tianjin zhengsu yange ji* [A record of reforms in Tianjin administration and customs], 14:7–10. In English, see MacKinnon, *Power and Politics*. Chongzhi's appointment was on XT 3/6/13 (8 July 1911) (*Zhengzhi guanbao* [Political gazette], XT 3/6/14 [9 July 1911], vol. 46, 218). For an example of rules against political activities by students and soldiers, see *Minxingbao* [Popular revival news], XT 3/4/22 (20 May 1911).

29. See Esherick, *Reform and Revolution*, 177–215.

30. Ye Duzhuang, 1991 ms, 21–22; the official report of Chongzhi's dismissal gives no reason: edict of XT 3/10/11 (1 December 1911), in *Neige guanbao* [National cabinet gazette], vol. 51 (XT 3/10), 51.

31. Ernest P. Young, *The Presidency of Yuan Shih-k'ai: Liberalism and Dictatorship in Early Republican China* (Ann Arbor: University of Michigan Press, 1977).

32. *Aiguo baihua bao* [Patriotic vernacular news], nos. 1 (30 July 1913), 2 (31 July 1913), 3 (1 August 1913), 6 (4 August 1913), 17 (15 August 1913), 42 (9 September 1913).

33. *Ye-shi zupu*, 11: *shilüe*, 5–6; *Quanqiang bao* [Strength of the masses], no. 472, 25 September 1913; *Aiguo baihua bao*, 25 September 1913.

34. *Ye-shi zupu*, 11: *shilüe*, 2.

## 7. DOING BUSINESS IN TIANJIN

1. On the coast (littoral) and interior (hinterland) in modern China, see Paul A. Cohen, *Between Tradition and Modernity: Wang T'ao and Reform in Late Ch'ing China* (Cambridge, Mass.: Harvard University Press, 1974), 241–76.

2. The literature on twentieth-century Shanghai is enormous. Among the most useful volumes are Leo Ou-fan Lee, *Shanghai Modern: The Flowering of a New Urban Culture in China, 1930–1945* (Cambridge, Mass.: Harvard University Press, 1999); Hanchao Lu, *Beyond the Neon Lights: Everyday Shanghai in the Early Twentieth Century* (Berkeley: University of California Press, 1999); Frederic E. Wakeman, Jr., *Policing Shanghai, 1927–37* (Berkeley: University of California Press, 1995); Wen-hsin Yeh, *Shanghai Splendor: Economic Sentiments and the Making of Modern China, 1843–1949* (Berkeley: University of California Press, 2007);

and Nicholas R. Clifford, *Spoilt Children of Empire: Westerners in Shanghai and the Chinese Revolution of the 1920s* (Hanover, Vt.: Middlebury College Press, 1991).

3. Kwan Man Bun, *The Salt Merchants of Tianjin: State-Making and Civil Society in Late Imperial China* (Honolulu: University of Hawaii, Press, 2001).

4. Tenshin chiikishi kenkyūkai, *Tenshinshi—saisei suru toshi no toporoji* [The topology of a multifaceted city] (Tokyo: Tōhō shoten, 1999), is the best available history of Tianjin. In Chinese, see Liu Haiyan, *Kongjian yu shehui: jindai Tianjin chengshi de yanbian* [Space and society: the urban transformation of modern Tianjin] (Tianjin: Tianjin shehui kexue-yuan, 2003). For a history of the concessions from the imperialist perspective, see O. D. Rasmussen, *Tientsin: An Illustrated Outline History* (Tianjin: Tientsin Press, 1925); for an anti-imperialist Chinese perspective, see Tianjin shi zhengxie wenshi ziliao yanjiu weiyuan-hui, *Tianjin zujie* [The Tianjin concessions] (Tianjin: Tianjin renmin chubanshe, 1986). Useful English studies include Kwan, *Salt Merchants*; Gail Hershatter, *The Workers of Tianjin, 1900–1949* (Stanford, Calif.: Stanford University Press, 1986); Ruth Rogaski, *Hygienic Modernity: Meanings of Health and Disease in Treaty-Port China* (Berkeley: University of California Press, 2004); and Brett Sheehan, *Trust in Troubled Times: Money, Banks, and State-Society Relations in Republican Tianjin* (Cambridge, Mass.: Harvard University Press, 2003).

5. Rasmussen, *Tientsin*, 263, gives a figure of 1549 "foreigners" (and 1,200 Japanese) in 1901; but there were only 88 Japanese in 1900. (Tōa dobunkai, *Shina Shōbetsu zenshi* [China provincial gazetteers], vol. 18, *Chokurei sho* [Zhili province] [Tokyo: Tōa dobunkai, 1920], 47.)

6. Zhang Tao, *Jinmen zaji* [Miscellaneous jottings on Tianjin] (n.p. 1884), 2: 41–43.

7. *Tianjin baihua bao* [Tianjin vernacular news], 13 January 1910, 2.

8. Ibid., 23 June 1911, 4.

9. Tenshin kenkyūkai, *Tenshinshi*, 18–19; Rasmussen, *Tientsin*, 221–30; Ruth Rogaski, "Hygienic Modernity in Tianjin," in *Remaking the Chinese City: Modernity and National Identity, 1900–1950*, ed. Joseph W. Esherick (Honolulu: University of Hawaii Press, 2000), 34–41.

10. Shi Xiaochuan, *Tianjin zhinan* [Guide to Tianjin] (n.p.: 1911), 1:1–2. See also Lai Xinxia, ed. *Tianjin jindai shi* [History of modern Tianjin] (Tianjin: Nankai University Press, 1987), 206–28.

11. On *huiguan*, see Bryna Goodman, *Native Place, City, and Nation: Regional Networks and Identities in Shanghai, 1853–1937* (Berkeley: University of California Press, 1995).

12. Interview with Ye Duzheng, September 1994.

13. The Chinese for these mottos was *shou Tian zhiyou, yugu weixin* and *zhai zhuang, zhong zheng*.

14. This chapter's account of family life is based on Ye Duzhuang's untitled 1991 manu-script and interviews with his brothers.

15. Ye Duzhuang, 1991 ms, 39–41, 80.

16. Howard L. Boorman and Richard C. Howard, *Biographical Dictionary of Republican China*, vol. 1 (New York: Columbia University Press, 1967), 409–13; "Zhou Zhi'an xiansheng zishu nianpu" [Zhou Xuexi chronological autobiography], in *Zhou Xuexi zhuanji huibian* [Collected materials on Zhou Xuexi's biography], ed. Zhou Xiaojuan (Lanzhou: Gansu Wen-

hua chubanshe, 1997), 1–81; Hao Qingyuan, *Zhou Xuexi zhuan* [Biography of Zhou Xuexi] (Tianjin: Tianjin People's Press, 1991); Chunfu (pseudonym), "Zhou Xuexi yu Beiyang shiye" [Zhou Xuexi and Beiyang industry], in *Tianjin wenshi ziliao xuanji* 1966.1: 1–27; Lai Xinxia, *Tianjin jindai shi*, 203–6.

17. Lai Xinxia, *Tianjin jindai shi*, 209–13, 260–69; Gail Hershatter, *The Workers of Tianjin, 1900–1949* (Stanford, Calif.: Stanford University Press, 1986), 28–35; Marie-Claire Bergère, *The Golden Age of the Chinese Bourgeoisie, 1911–1937*, trans. Janet Lloyd (Cambridge: Cambridge University Press, 1989), esp. 63–75, 174–84.

18. Zhou Shutao and Li Mianzhi, "Qixin yanghui gongsi de chuqi ziben he zifang de paixi maodun" [The Qixin Cement company's early capital and clique conflict among the owners], *Wenshi ziliao zhuanji*, 53:11; Albert Feuerwerker, "Industrial Enterprise in Twentieth-Century China: The Case of the Chee Hsin Cement Co., " in *Approaches to Modern Chinese History*, ed. Albert Feuerwerker, Rhoads Murphy, and Mary C. Wright (Berkeley: University of California Press, 1967); on the Tianjin business and banking elite, see Sheehan, *Trust in Troubled Times*, 20–26, 45–53, 60–64.

19. Ye Duzhuang, 1991 ms, 26–28; *Ye-shi zupu*, 11: *shilüe* [accounts], Ye Chongzhi biography, 2–3.

20. On factionalism in Beijing politics, see Andrew J. Nathan, *Peking Politics, 1918–1923: Factionalism and the Failure of Constitutionalism* (Berkeley: University of California Press, 1976).

21. Zhou Shutao and Li Mianzhi, "Qixin yanghui gongsi," 24; Ye Duzhuang, 1991 ms, 28, 31–33, 39, 42.

22. Bergère, *Golden Age*, 63–98.

23. Ernest P. Young, *The Presidency of Yuan Shih-k'ai: Liberalism and Dictatorship in Early Republican China* (Ann Arbor: University of Michigan Press, 1977).

24. Arthur Waldron, *From War to Nationalism: China's Turning Point, 1924–1925* (Cambridge: Cambridge University Press, 1995).

25. See the Anhui *huiguan* meeting minutes for 1927 in Tianjin Municipal Archives 134 *quanzong: juan* 2–3, 23, 45.

26. Ye Duzhuang, 1991 ms, 55–61.

## 8. GROWING UP IN TIANJIN

1. Confucius, *Analects*, 2:4.

2. The limited sources are ably used in Ping-chen Hsiung, *A Tender Voyage: Children and Childhood in Late Imperial China* (Stanford, Calif.: Stanford University Press, 2005).

3. Jon L. Saari, *Legacies of Childhood: Growing up Chinese in a Time of Crisis, 1890–1920* (Cambridge, Mass.: Council on East Asian Studies, Harvard University, 1990); Catherine Pease, "Remembering the Taste of Melons: Modern Chinese Stories of Childhood," in *Chinese Views of Childhood*, ed. Anne Behnke Kinney (Honolulu: University of Hawaii Press, 1995), 279–320.

4. Interviews with Ye Duyi, 1995.

5. Ye Duzhuang, 1991ms (untitled), 103–4; interview with Yuan Fu, 21 July 1997.

6. Ye Duzhuang, 1991 ms, 70.

7. Interview with Ye Durou, March 1995.

8. Ibid.

9. On the status of wives and concubines, see Patricia Ebrey, *The Inner Quarters: Marriage and the Lives of Chinese Women in the Sung Dynasty* (Berkeley: University of California Press, 1993), 152–71, 217–34.

10. Ye Duzhuang, 1991 ms, 81–83; *Ye-shi zupu* [Ye family genealogy] (n.p.: 1944), 6:90, 7:18.

11. Stevan Harrell, "The Rich Get Children: Segmentation, Stratification, and Population in Three Chekiang Lineages, 1550–1850," in *Family and Population in East Asian History*, ed. Susan B. Hanley and Arthur P. Wolf (Stanford, Calif.: Stanford University Press, 1985), 81–109; Ebrey, *Inner Quarters*, 179; Ping-chen Hsiung, *Tender Voyage*, 74–99.

12. Interview with Ye Duzheng, 9 September 1994.

13. Ye Duzhuang, 1991 ms, 73.

14. Ye Duzhuang, "Guoyan yunyan" [Mist and clouds before my eyes], 1992 ms, 8.

15. Interview with Ye Duzheng, 18 May 1995; Ye Duzhuang, 1991 ms, 50.

16. Interviews with Fang Shi, 1995.

17. Ibid.

18. Ye Duzhuang, 1991 ms, 162–63.

19. Ibid., 70–74.

20. Surprisingly, in a March 1995 interview, the youngest girl (Durou) said that playing war was her favorite game.

21. Ye Duzhuang, 1991 ms, 133–52.

22. Interview with Ye Duzhuang, 24 November 1994.

23. Ye Duzhuang, 1991 ms, 120–27; "Guoyan," 13–22; 25 November 1994 interview.

24. Interview with Ye Durou, 2 March 1995. On women and education in this period, see Paul J. Bailey, *Gender and Education in China: Gender Discourses and Women's Schooling in the Early Twentieth Century* (New York: Routledge, 2007); Joan Judge, "Citizens or Mothers of Citizens? Gender and the Meaning of Modern Chinese Citizenship," in *Changing Meanings of Citizenship in Modern China*, ed. Merle Goldman and Elizabeth J. Perry (Cambridge, Mass.: Harvard University Press, 2002), 23–43.

25. Ye Duzhuang, 1991 ms, 128–33. On citizenship in republican China, see Henrietta Harrison, *The Making of the Republican Citizen: Political Ceremonies and Symbols in China, 1911–1929* (Oxford: Oxford University Press, 2000); Robert Culp, *Articulating Citizenship: Civic Education and Student Politics in Southeastern China, 1912–1940* (Cambridge, Mass.: Harvard University Asia Center, 2007); on physical education, see Andrew D. Morris, *Marrow of the Nation: A History of Sport and Physical Culture in Republican China* (Berkeley: University of California Press, 2004).

26. Interview with Ye Durou, March 1995.

27. Ye Duzhuang, 1991 ms, 110.

28. Interview with Ye Duyi, January 1995; Ye Duzhuang, 1991 ms, 36, 73, 137.

29. Ye Duzhuang, 1991 ms, 36, 40.

30. Chow Tse-tsung. *The May Fourth Movement: Intellectual Revolution in Modern China* (Cambridge, Mass.: Harvard University Press, 1960); Vera Schwarcz, *The Chinese En-*

*lightenment: Intellectuals and the Legacy of the May Fourth Movement of 1919* (Berkeley: University of California Press, 1986).

31. Frank Dikötter, *Sex, Culture, and Modernity in China: Medical Science and the Construction of Sexual Identities in the Early Republican Period* (Honolulu: University of Hawaii Press, 1995).

32. Allen S. Whiting, *Soviet Policies in China, 1917–1924* (New York: Columbia University Press, 1954); Alexander Pantsov, *The Bolsheviks and the Chinese Revolution, 1919–1927* (Honolulu: University of Hawaii Press, 2000).

33. Hans J. Van de Ven, *From Friend to Comrade: The Founding of the Chinese Communist Party, 1920–1927* (Berkeley: University of California Press, 1991); Arif Dirlik, *The Origins of Chinese Communism* (Oxford: Oxford University Press, 1989); and an older classic, Benjamin Schwartz, *Chinese Communism and the Rise of Mao* (Cambridge, Mass.: Harvard University Press, 1961).

34. Tony Saich, *The Origins of the First United Front in China: The Role of Sneevliet (Alias Maring)* (Leiden: E. J. Brill, 1991); C. Martin Wilbur and Julie Lien-ying How, *Missionaries of Revolution: Soviet Advisers and Nationalist China, 1920–1927* (Cambridge, Mass.: Harvard University Press, 1989).

35. C. Martin Wilbur, *The Nationalist Revolution in China, 1923–1928* (Cambridge: Cambridge University Press, 1984); Donald Jordan, *The Northern Expedition: China's National Revolution of 1926–1928* (Honolulu: University of Hawaii Press, 1976); Harold Isaacs, *The Tragedy of the Chinese Revolution* (Stanford, Calif.: Stanford University Press, 1961); Jay Taylor, *The Generalissimo, Chiang Kai-shek and the Struggle for Modern China* (Cambridge, Mass: Harvard University Press, 2009), 49–96.

36. Ye Duzhuang, "Guoyan yunyan," 26–27.

37. *North China Standard,* Beiping, Spring 1930.

38. Ye Duzhuang, 1991 ms, 43–49.

39. Ibid., 80–81.

## 9. STUDENT LIFE IN THE 1930S

1. Liang Jisheng, *Nankai yishi* [Memories of Nankai] (Shenyang: Liaohai chubanshe, 1998), 291–92. On sports in the national imaginary, see Andrew D. Morris, *Marrow of the Nation: A History of Sport and Physical Culture in Republican China* (Berkeley: University of California Press, 2004).

2. See the detailed plan for a 1931 reform of this course, "Shehui shicha xueke gaige cao'an" [Draft reforms of the social investigation curriculum], in *Nankai shuangzhou* 7.1 and 7.2 (1931).

3. On Nankai, see Liang Jisheng, *Zhang Boling jiaoyu sixiang yanjiu* [A study of Zhang Boling's educational thought] (Shenyang: Liaoning jiaoyu chubanshe, 1994); and *Nankai yishi*. Prominent alumni and teachers' biographies are in Wang Renjun, ed., *Nankai renwuzhi* [Nankai biographies] (Tianjin: Nankai University Press, 1994). In English, see Howard L. Boorman and Richard C. Howard, *Biographical Dictionary of Republican China*, vol. 1 (New York: Columbia University Press, 1967), 100–105; E-tu Zen Sun, "The Growth of the Academic

Community, 1912–1949," in *The Cambridge History of China*, vol. 13, *Republican China, 1912–1949, Part 2*, ed. John K. Fairbank and Albert Feuerwerker (Cambridge: Cambridge University Press, 1986), 372–74; on completion rates, see Ye Duzhuang, 1991 ms (untitled), 38.

4. *Qinghua zhoukan fukan* [Supplement to *Tsinghua Weekly*] 44, no. 5 (3 May 1936): 33.

5. Parks M. Coble, *Facing Japan: Chinese Politics and Japanese Imperialism, 1931–1937* (Cambridge, Mass.: Council on East Asian Studies, Harvard University, 1991); Rana Mitter, *The Manchurian Myth: Nationalism, Resistance, and Collaboration in Modern China* (Berkeley: University of California Press, 2000).

6. On the "plain-clothed corps" incident, see Tenshin chiikishi kenkyūkai, *Tenshinshi—saisei suru toshi no toporojī* [The topology of a multifaceted city] (Tokyo: Tōhō shoten, 1999), 200–202; Ye Duzhuang, "Guoyan yunyan" [Mist and clouds before my eyes], 1992 ms, 44–47.

7. See *Nankai nüzhong xiaokan* [Journal of Nankai Girls' School], 1933.5: 1.

8. On Ma Zhanshan, see Mitter, *The Manchurian Myth*, 1–5, 131–222.

9. Liang Jisheng, *Zhang Boling jiaoyu sixiang*, 261–69, 392.

10. Wang Xugong, "Zai 'wujiu' shuo de hua" [Talk on May 9], *Nankai shuangzhou* 7 [Nankai biweekly], no. 4 (May 1931): 2.

11. Ye Duzhuang, "Guoyan," 44–46.

12. On Zhang's "foppish playboy" reputation, see Hsiao Kung-ch'üan, "Nankai, Northeast and Yenching," from *Critical Reflections on My Pursuit of Learning*, trans. William A. Wycoff, in *Chinese Studies in History* 13, no. 4 (Summer 1980): 28.

13. On the student movement, see John Israel, *Student Nationalism in China, 1927–1937* (Stanford, Calif.: Stanford University Press, 1966); Jeffrey N. Wasserstrom, *Student Protests in Twentieth-Century China: The View from Shanghai* (Stanford, Calif.: Stanford University Press, 1991).

14. Liang Jisheng, *Zhang Boling jiaoyu sixiang*, 267–69; Bai Wenzhi, "Yier.jiu shiqi Nankai zhongxue dang zuzhi de chongjian" [The reestablishment of the party organization at Nankai Middle School at the time of December 9th], in Zhonggong Tianjin shiwei dangshi ziliao zhengji weiyuanhui, ed., *Yier.jiu yundong zai Tianjin* [The December 9th Movement in Tianjin] (Tianjin: Nankai University Press, 1985), 332.

15. "Zhuma zhuang wulang" [Ye Duzhuang], "Diguo zhuyi yu Zhongguo zichan jieji" [Imperialism and the Chinese capitalist class], *Nankai shuangzhou*, 1932. A slightly different version appears in *Nanzhong xuesheng* under Ye Duzhuang's own (undisguised) name and the title "Diguo zhuyi yu Zhongguo ziben zhuyi" [Imperialism and Chinese capitalism].

16. Arif Dirlik, *Revolution and History: The Origins of Marxist Historiography in China, 1919–1937* (Berkeley: University of California Press, 1978).

17. Frank J. Sulloway, *Born to Rebel: Birth Order, Family Dynamics, and Creative Lives* (New York: Vintage Books, 1997).

18. Ye Duzhuang, 1991 ms, 84–90; interviews with Duyi, Duzheng, and Fang Shi, 1995.

19. Olga Lang, *Chinese Family and Society* (New Haven, Conn.: Yale University Press, 1946), 122–25, 215–17.

20. Ye Duzhuang, 1991 ms, 93–96.

21. Philip West, *Yenching University and Sino-Western Relations, 1916–1952* (Cambridge, Mass.: Harvard University Press, 1976); Wen-hsin Yeh, *The Alienated Academy: Culture and Politics in Republican China, 1919–1937* (Cambridge. Mass.: Council on East Asian Stud-

ies, Harvard University, 1990), 207–10. Quoted passage from John Israel and Donald W. Klein, *Rebels and Bureaucrats: China's December 9ers* (Berkeley: University of California Press, 1976), 22.

22. Yeh Tu Yi, "The Development of International Organization" (thesis, Department of Political Science and the College of Public Affairs, Yenching University, May 1934), quotations from pp. 83–84, 149.

23. Prasenjit Duara, "Knowledge and Power in the Discourse of Modernity: The Campaigns Against Popular Religion in Early Twentieth-Century China," *Journal of Asian Studies* 50, no. 1 (February 1991): 67–83; Rebecca Nedostup, *Superstitious Regimes: Religion and the Politics of Chinese Modernity* (Cambridge, Mass.: Harvard University Asia Center, 2009).

24. Olga Lang, *Chinese Family and Society,* 227–29, 275–76.

25. Ye Duzhuang 1991 ms, 91–93; interviews with Ye Duyi, 1995.

26. Ye Duzhuang 1991 ms, 106–7.

27. Ibid., 107–10; interviews with Ye Durou, 1995.

28. Ye Duzhuang, 1991 ms, 110–12; interviews with Ye Durou (with interjections by Ye Duzhuang), 1995.

29. David Wakefield, *Fenjia: Household Division and Inheritance in Qing and Republican China* (Honolulu: University of Hawaii Press, 1998).

30. Interview with Ye Yun, August 2001.

31. Israel and Klein, *Rebels and Bureaucrats,* 52.

32. Ye Duzhuang, "Guoyan," 4; interviews with Ye Duzheng, September 1994.

33. Charles W. Hayford, *To the People: James Yen and Village China* (New York: Columbia University Press, 1990); Guy S. Alitto, *The Last Confucian: Liang Shu-ming and the Chinese Dilemma of Modernity* (Berkeley: University of California Press, 1979); Sidney D. Gamble, *Ting Hsien: A North China Rural Community* (Stanford, Calif.: Stanford University Press, 1968); R. David Arkush, *Fei Xiaotong and Sociology in Revolutionary China* (Cambridge, Mass.: Council on East Asian Studies, Harvard University, 1981).

34. Randall E. Stross, *The Stubborn Earth: American Agriculturalists on Chinese Soil, 1898–1937* (Berkeley: University of California Press, 1986).

35. Ye Duzhuang, "Guoyan," 127–33; interview with Ye Feng, spring 1995.

36. Sanetō Keishū. *Chūgokujin Nihon ryūgaku shi* [History of Chinese students in Japan] (Tokyo: Kuroshio, 1960), 128–35.

37. *Kōnōkai kaiho* [Bulletin of the Agriculture School Association], no. 157 (March 1936): 51.

38. Hubert Freyn, *Prelude to War: The Chinese Student Rebellion of 1935–1936* (Shanghai: China Journal Pub. Co., 1939), 4–5.

39. Yeh, *Alienated Academy,* 207–10, 213–15; *Guoli Qinghua daxue yilan* (Beiping: 1935) is Tsinghua's school catalogue describing (with photographs) the school, its history, curriculum, and regulations.

40. K. Huang, "On Freshman-Toss" (in English), *Qinghua zhoukan* [Tsinghua weekly] 34, no. 2 (October 1930); interviews with Ye Fang, 1995.

41. In the list of 1934 entrants, his name is listed 23rd (two after the famous historian He Bingdi [Ping-ti Ho]) out of 317. *Qinghua daxue shiliao xuanbian,* 4.2 (Beijing: 1991), 864.

42. Coble, *Facing Japan,* 182–282, Israel, *Student Nationalism,* 104–12; James B. Crow-

ley, *Japan's Quest for Autonomy: National Security and Foreign Policy, 1930–1938* (Princeton, N.J.: Princeton University Press, 1966).

43. Coble, *Facing Japan;* Israel, *Student Nationalism,* 111–12.

44. Yeh, *Alienated Academy,* 231.

45. Hu Sheng, then a senior in philosophy at Beijing University, cited in ibid., 243; cf. Israel, *Student Nationalism,* 109–10.

46. See *Qinghua zhoukan fukan* 42, no. 5 (19 November 1934): 12.

47. Freyn, who roomed with students at Yenching in 1935–36, wrote in *Prelude to War,* "A philosophy of pessimism makes no appeal to them" (5). This suggests that the pessimism and alienation perceived by Yeh Wen-hsin was, in part, the artifact of leftist rhetoric designed to stir students to greater activism.

48. *Qinghua daxue yilan* (1935), "History Department," 8.

49. Israel and Klein, *Rebels and Bureaucrats,* 25.

50. Freyn, *Prelude to War,* and Helen F. Snow (Nym Wales), *Notes on the Chinese Student Movement, 1935–1936* (Stanford, Calif.: Hoover Institution, 1959), are invaluable firsthand accounts of the December 9th Movement. Israel, *Student Nationalism,* 111–56, and Israel and Klein, *Rebels and Bureaucrats,* 1–136, are key secondary studies. Qinghua daxue xuesheng zizhihui jiuguo weiyuanhui [National Salvation Committee of the Tsinghua University Independent Student Union], *Jiuwang yundong baogaoshu* [Report on the Salvation Movement] (Beiping: 1936) is a critical leftist document from mid-1936. It and Hua Daoyi (pseud.), "Yierjiu yundong yinianlai zhi shi de jiantao" [A reflection on the year since December 9], *Qinghua zhoukan* 45, no. 7 (16 December 1936): 8–15 and 45, no. 8 (23 December 1936): 14–22 (also reprinted in *Qinghua daxue shiliao xuanbian* 2, no. 2: 947–74) provide excellent contemporary accounts from the leftist students' perspective.

51. On the Tianjin protests, see Zhonggong Tianjin shiwei dangshi ziliao zhengji weiyuanhui [Party history materials compilation committee of the Tianjin party committee of the Chinese Communist Party], ed., *Yier.jiu yundong zai Tianjin* [The December 9th Movement in Tianjin] (Tianjin: Nankai University Press, 1985), esp. 202–9, 331–40 (on Nankai Middle School).

52. Freyn, *Prelude to War,* 33–51, provides a compelling firsthand account of the student "pilgrimage" to the countryside. Quotes are from 49–50.

53. Quoted in ibid., 54.

54. Interview with Ye Duzheng, September 1994. On the February 29 incident, see Freyn, *Prelude to War,* 66–70; *Jiuwang yundong baogao shu,* 33–36.

55. Interview with Ye Fang, spring 1995.

56. "Chaozong" [Facing my ancestors—pseud.], "Yongqi jiuguo lun" [Saving the nation with courage], *Qinghua zhoukan* 44, no. 8 (3 June 1936): 26.

57. "Zaijie zaili de xuesheng yundong" [Carrying on the student movement], *Qinghua zhoukan* 44, no. 8 (3 June 1936): 3–4.

58. Ye Duyi, "Yi Tianjin Zhishi Shudian," [Remembering the Tianjin Knowledge Bookstore], in *Kangzhan jishi* [Accounts of the War of Resistance], ed. Bing Xin and Ba Jin (Beijing: China Friendship Press, 1989), 16–17; Ye Duzhuang, "Guoyan," 159, 164–65.

59. Snow, *Notes on the Chinese Student Movement,* 50.

60. Ye Duzhuang, "Wo zui nanwang de Song Erlian" [I cannot forget Song Erlian], *Qunyan* 9 (1995): 19.

61. Freyn, *Prelude to War,* 91–105, quote on 95; *Qinghua zhoukan* 45, no. 8: 17, 21.

62. Jay Taylor, *The Generalissimo, Chiang Kai-shek and the Struggle for Modern China* (Cambridge, Mass: Harvard University Press, 2009), 114–37.

63. On Yan Xishan and the Sacrifice League, see David S. G. Goodman, *Social and Political Change in Revolutionary China: The Taihang Base Area in the War of Resistance to Japan, 1937–1945* (Lanham, Md.: Rowman & Littlefield, 2000), 45–50.

64. Kiang Wen-lan (a YMCA secretary), cited in Israel, *Student Nationalism,* 179.

## 10. WAR

1. On the War of Resistance, see Akira Iriye, "Japanese Aggression and China's International Position, 1931–1949," and Lloyd Eastman, "Nationalist China during the Sino-Japanese War, 1937–1945," both in *The Cambridge History of China,* vol. 13, *Republican China, 1912–1949, Part 2,* ed. John K. Fairbank and Albert Feuerwerker (Cambridge: Cambridge University Press, 1986), 492–608; Jay Taylor, *The Generalissimo, Chiang Kai-shek and the Struggle for Modern China* (Cambridge, Mass.: Harvard University Press, 2009), 141–335; Lloyd E. Eastman, *Seeds of Destruction: Nationalist China in War and Revolution, 1937–1949* (Stanford, Calif.: Stanford University Press, 1984).

2. On Nationalist achievements during the Nanjing decade (1927–37), see William C. Kirby, *Germany and Republican China* (Stanford, Calif.: Stanford University Press, 1984); Thomas G. Rawski, *Economic Growth in Prewar China* (Berkeley: University of California Press, 1989); "Reappraising Republican China," special issue, *China Quarterly,* no. 150 (June 1997).

3. Chang-tai Hung, *War and Popular Culture: Resistance in Modern China, 1937–1945* (Berkeley: University of California Press, 1994).

4. On the wartime United Front and its demise, see Lyman P. Van Slyke, *Enemies and Friends: The United Front in Chinese Communist History* (Stanford, Calif.: Stanford University Press, 1967); Tetsuya Kataoka, *Resistance and Revolution in China: The Communists and the Second United Front* (Berkeley: University of California Press, 1974); Gregor Benton, *New Fourth Army: Communist Resistance along the Yangtze and the Huai, 1938–1941* (Berkeley: University of California Press, 1999).

5. On the Communist Party's rise during the war, see Chalmers A. Johnson, *Peasant Nationalism and Communist Power: The Emergence of Revolutionary China, 1937–1945* (Stanford, Calif.: Stanford University Press, 1962); Mark Selden, *China in Revolution: The Yenan Way Revisited* (Armonk, N.Y.: M. E. Sharpe, 1995); Yung-fa Chen, *Making Revolution: The Communist Movement in Eastern and Central China, 1937–1945* (Berkeley: University of California Press, 1986); Odoric Y. K. Wou, *Mobilizing the Masses: Building Revolution in Henan* (Stanford, Calif.: Stanford University Press, 1994).

6. Ye Duzhuang, 1991 ms (untitled), 93–94.

7. Interviews with Fang Shi, 1995. Later, in 1938, Duyi went to Hankou with another third-party leader, seeking a way to participate in the resistance to Japan. There he met Ye

Fang, who urged his return to Beiping. Ye Duyi, *Sui jiusi qi you weihui—bashi huiyi* [Despite nine deaths, I still have no regrets: memoirs at age eighty] (Beijing: Qunyan, 1994), 7.

8. Interview with Ye Weiquan, 2001.

9. On modern Chinese theater, see Joshua Goldstein, *Drama Kings: Players and Publics in the Re-creation of Peking Opera, 1870–1937* (Berkeley: University of California Press, 2007); Colin Mackerras, *The Chinese Theatre in Modern Times: From 1840 to the Present Day* (London: Thames and Hudson, 1975).

10. See John Israel, *Lianda: A Chinese University in War and Revolution* (Stanford, Calif.: Stanford University Press, 1998).

11. On Japan's precedent-setting attacks on civilian populations, see John W. Dower, *War Without Mercy: Race and Power in the Pacific War* (New York: Pantheon, 1986), 38–41.

12. On the spirited Shanghai resistance, see Taylor, *The Generalissimo*, 147–51.

13. On Duzhuang's work with the Eighth Route Army, see his "Guoyan yunyan" [Mist and clouds before my eyes], 1992 ms, 170–85.

14. Ye Duzhuang, 1937 diary, 2, 10–12, 20, and 30 November.

15. Ibid., 13–14 November.

16. Howard L. Boorman and Richard C. Howard, *Biographical Dictionary of Republican China*, vol. 1 (New York: Columbia University Press, 1967), 190–92.

17. "Ye Li" [Ye Duzhuang], "Yierjiu shi de guanghui zhanji" [The glorious military record of the 129th Division], *Xin Zhonghua bao* 5, 10, and 15 January 1938 (nos. 411, 412, 413). See also Ye Duzhuang, 1937 diary, 17, 25, and 30 November. On the Communist movement in this area, see David S. G. Goodman, *Social and Political Change in Revolutionary China: The Taihang Base Area in the War of Resistance to Japan, 1937–1945* (Lanham, Md.: Rowman & Littlefield, 2000).

18. Ye Duzhuang, 1937 diary, "Cash Notes" section, 179–74 *[sic]*.

19. On Chongqing at war, see Theodore White and Analee Jacoby, *Thunder out of China* (New York: William Sloan Associates, 1946), 3–18.

20. Joseph W. Esherick, "The Chinese Industrial Cooperatives Movement" (B.A. thesis, Harvard College, 1964).

21. Interview with Mao Zedong by John S. Service, August 23, 1944, in *Lost Chance in China: The World War II Despatches of John S. Service*, ed. Joseph W. Esherick (New York: Random House, 1974), 303. On Stilwell and American wartime policy toward China, see Herbert Feis, *The China Tangle: The American Effort in China from Pearl Harbor to the Marshall Mission* (Princeton, N.J.: Princeton University Press, 1953); Barbara W. Tuchman, *Stilwell and the American Experience in China, 1911–45* (New York: Macmillan, 1971); Tang Tsou, *America's Failure in China, 1941–50* (Chicago: University of Chicago Press, 1963 ); Charles F. Romanus and Riley Sunderland, *Stilwell's Mission to China* (Washington, D.C.: Office of the Chief of Military History, Department of the Army, 1953); Taylor, *The Generalissimo*, 188–295.

22. On the GBT team, see Yu Maochun, *The OSS in China: Prelude to Cold War* (New Haven, Conn.: Yale University Press, 1996), 203–8. Duzhuang and Ho Chi Minh were recruited by the same man, Charles Fenn. See Fenn's *Ho Chi-Minh: A Biographical Introduction* (London: Studio Vista, 1973).

23. AGAS in China was part of a worldwide secret intelligence service, called MIS-X,

devoted to rescuing downed airmen and prisoners of war. On MIS-X in China, see Lt. Col. A. R Wichtrich, *MIS-X: Top Secret* (Raleigh, N.C.: Pentland Press, 1997).

24. Ye Duzhuang, "Guoyan," 185–256; also "Jiefang yihou" [After liberation], 1991 ms, 25–26; "Yuzhong ji" [In prison], 1993 ms, 38–41. See also Graham Peck, *Two Kinds of Time* (Boston: Houghton Mifflin, 1950), 704.

25. On Wuhan in 1938, see Stephen R. Mackinnon, *Wuhan, 1938: War, Refugees, and the Making of Modern China* (Berkeley: University of California Press, 2008).

26. On the underground CCP in wartime Guilin, see *Guilin wenshi ziliao* 4 (1983).

27. See Frederic Wakeman, Jr., *Spymaster: Dai Li and the Chinese Secret Service* (Berkeley: University of California Press, 2003), esp. ch. 24.

28. On the New Fourth Army, see Benton, *New Fourth Army*; and Yung-fa Ch'en, *Making Revolution*.

29. The daughter, Ye Lin, was later considered Ye Fang's child, though she had her doubts, and the dates of her birth and of Ye Fang's meeting her mother make his biological paternity impossible (interview with Ye Lin, July 1997). Lin Ying's memoir, *Kanke de daolu* [Bumpy road] (Beijing: Dongfang wenhua guan, n.d. [1994 preface]), makes no mention of this child. This book, written in great anger late in her unhappy life, is regarded as unreliable by her children, who dismiss her tales of revolutionary deeds as "crazy." But some aspects of the book are probably reliable, with the silences as important as anything.

30. Interviews with Ye Fang, spring 1995; Lin Ying, *Kanke de daolu*, 83–102. Ding Ning, "Fang Ye-shi wu xiongdi" [Interviews with five Ye brothers], *Huanghe* 84, no. 2 (2000): 61. On the early struggle in the Northeast, see Harold M. Tanner, "Guerrilla, Mobile, and Base Warfare in Communist Military Operations in Manchuria, 1945–1947," *Journal of Military History* 67 (October 2003): 1177–1222.

31. Interviews with Fang Shi, 1995; "Tongxin qing shizhen—jinian wo he Bai Tian jiehun 50 zhounian" [With hearts united, our feelings are true—celebrating fifty years of marriage to Bai Tian], published in an internal Xinhua newsletter in 1989; Ding Ning, "Fang Ye-shi wu xiongdi," 55–58.

32. On the Rectification Campaign, see Boyd Compton, *Mao's China: Party Reform Documents, 1942–44* (Seattle: University of Washington Press, 1952); David E. Apter and Tony Saich, *Revolutionary Discourse in Mao's Republic* (Cambridge, Mass.: Harvard University Press, 1994); and in Chinese, Chen Yongfa, *Yan'an de yinying* [Yenan's shadow] (Taipei: Academia Sinica, 1990); and Gao Hua, *Hong taiyang shi zenyang shengqi de: Yan'an zhengfeng yundong de lailong qumai* [How the Red Star rose: the full story of the Yan'an rectification movement] (Hong Kong: Zhongwen daxue chubanshe, 2000).

33. Interviews with Fang Shi, 1995; Fang Shi, "Jinzhang de gongzuo, yan'ge de xunlian—Xibaipo bianji shenghuo huiyi" [Stressful work, rigorous training—a memoir of editorial life at Xibaipo], in *Xinhua she huiyilu* [Memoirs from the New China News Agency] ed. Xinhuashe xinwen yanjiusuo, (Beijing: Xinhua, 1986), 221–29; "Buke momie de jiyi—jinian Mao Zedong danchen 100 zhounian" [An ineradicable memory—celebrating the 100th anniversary of Mao Zedong's birth], *Laonian shenghuo* (Xinhua retired cadres internal newsletter), 26 December 1993: 1–8. On party journalism, see Timothy Cheek, *Propaganda and Culture in Mao's China: Deng Tuo and the Intelligentsia* (Oxford: Oxford University Press, 1997).

34. Sun Song, "Wenyi riji" [Literary diary], 18 July 1938. On declining her teaching job, see the 3 September 1938 entry and letter draft, n.d. (101–3).

35. Ibid., 30 July 1938, 2 January 1939.

36. Her skillful painting is noted in Shen Roujian, "Xinsijun zhandi fuwutuan huihuazu jishi" [A record of the New Fourth Army battlefield service team painting group], www.jswyw .com/gb/ylcq/fenghuosuiyue/094050556.shtml (accessed 16 May 2006).

37. Ye Duzhuang, "Guoyan," 95–96.

38. Sun Song, "Wenyi riji," 17 October 1942.

39. Ibid., 12 October 1941.

40. Ibid., 22 February 1942.

41. Ibid., esp. 159–65, 174–75; 50–51 (Zheng); "Suixiang" [Random thoughts], diary ms, from 1944–45 on Cheng Ji.

42. Sun Song, "Wenyi riji," 4, 8, and 19 March 1944.

43. Christopher Rand to Barbara Stephens, 20 December 1945, cited in Peter Rand, *China Hands: The Adventures and Ordeals of the American Journalists Who Joined Forces with the Great Chinese Revolution* (New York: Simon and Schuster, 1995), 276.

44. Sun Song, "Suixiang," n.d., n.p. (quote is from the last draft of the letter).

45. John Hersey met Ye Duzhuang again in 1981 and wrote a series of *New Yorker* articles on their visits and reminiscences (*New Yorker,* 10, 17, 24, and 31 May 1982; esp. 24 May, 61–62).

46. Barbara Stephens to Christopher Rand, 6 April 1946, cited in Rand, *China Hands,* 281.

47. Ye Duzhuang, *Huabei mianhua ji qi zengchan wenti* [Cotton in north China and the problem of increasing output] (Nanjing: National Resources Commission, 1948). On saving Japanese agricultural records, see Peck, *Two Kinds of Time,* 716.

48. Peck, *Two Kinds of Time,* 724. Peck ends his book with this incident: liberal intellectuals going over to the CCP.

49. *Hu lianhe wanbao* [Shanghai evening news], 25 June 1946, quoted in *Renmin ribao* [People's daily], 6 July 1946; see also 1 and 5 July 1946.

50. See Stuart's memoir: *Fifty Years in China: the Memoirs of John Leighton Stuart, Missionary and Ambassador* (New York: Random House, 1954), 160–212.

51. On the Civil War, see Suzanne Pepper, *Civil War in China: The Political Struggle, 1945– 1949* (Berkeley: University of California Press, 1978); Odd Arne Westad, *Decisive Encounters: The Chinese Civil War, 1946–1950* (Stanford, Calif.: Stanford University Press, 2003) .

52. Ye Duyi, *Sui jiusi,* 6–58.

53. Interviews with Ye Duzheng, September 1994, May 1995, June 1997; Zhou Jiabin and Pu Yifen, *Qiuzhen qiushi deng gaofeng—Ye Duzheng* [Ascending the heights seeking truth and facts—Ye Duzheng] (Beijing: Xinhua chubanshe, 2008), 14–29.


11. FAMILY LIFE IN NEW CHINA

1. Mao Zedong, "Preserve the Style of Plain Living and Hard Struggle," speech of 5 March 1949, cited in Kenneth G. Lieberthal, *Revolution and Tradition in Tientsin, 1949–1952* (Stanford, Calif.: Stanford University Press, 1980), 10.

2. Mao Zedong, "On the People's Democratic Dictatorship," 30 June 1949, in *Selected Readings from the Works of Mao Tsetung* (Beijing: Foreign Languages Press, 1971), 371–88.

3. Lieberthal, *Revolution and Tradition*, 42–51; Ye Duyi, *Sui jiu si qi you weihui—bashi huiyi* [Despite nine deaths, I still have no regrets: memoirs at age eighty] (Beijing: Qunyan, 1994), 60–61.

4. Interview with Ye Yun, 2001. On Liu's visit to Tianjin, see Lieberthal, *Revolution and Tradition*, 42–51.

5. A. Doak Barnett, *Communist China: The Early Years, 1949–55* (New York: Praeger, 1964), 5.

6. William C. Kirby, "Continuity and Change in Modern China: Economic Planning in the Mainland and on Taiwan, 1943–1958," *Australian Journal of Chinese Affairs* 24 (July 1990): 125–32.

7. On Sino-Soviet relations in this period, see Chen Jian, *Mao's China and the Cold War* (Chapel Hill: University of North Carolina Press, 2001); Sergei Goncharov, John W. Lewis, and Xue Litai, *Uncertain Partners: Stalin, Mao, and the Korean War* (Stanford, Calif.: Stanford University Press, 1993); and in Chinese, Yang Kuisong, *Mao Zedong yu Mosike de enen yuanyuan* [Mao Zedong's debt to and grievances with Moscow] (Nanchang: Jiangxi renmin, 1999).

8. Ye Duyi, *Sui jiu si*, 55–56.

9. Interviews with Ye Duzheng, September 1994, May 1995; Zhou Jiabin and Pu Yifen, *Qiuzhen qiushi deng gaofeng—Ye Duzheng* [Ascending the heights seeking truth and facts—Ye Duzheng] (Beijing: Xinhua chubanshe, 2008), 26–29.

10. Ye Duyi, *Sui jiu si*, 61; for the composition of the Political Consultative Conference, see *Renmin ribao* [People's daily], 22 September 1949.

11. On the committee and its responsibilities, see *Zhongguo gongchandang lishi da cidian: shehui zhuyi shiqi* [Historical dictionary of the Chinese Communist Party: socialist period] (Beijing: Zhongguo zhongyang dangxiao, 1991), 4; *Renmin ribao* lists the members in the 22 October 1949 edition and the officers in the 16 September 1950 edition.

12. Ye Duyi, *Sui jiu si*, 69.

13. Frederick C. Teiwes, "Establishment and Consolidation of the New Regime," in *The Cambridge History of China*, vol. 14, *The People's Republic of China, Part I: The Emergence of Revolutionary China, 1949–1965*, ed. Roderick MacFarquhar and John K. Fairbank (Cambridge: Cambridge University Press, 1987), 77.

14. *Renmin ribao*, 14 March 1951.

15. Ibid., 13 October 1951.

16. Ye Duzhuang, "Jiefang yihou" [After liberation], 1991 ms, 1–8; *Renmin ribao*, 12 and 26 July 1950. On Lysenko and Michurin, see David Joravsky, *The Lysenko Affair* (Cambridge, Mass., Harvard University Press, 1970); Valery N. Soyfer, *Lysenko and the Tragedy of Soviet Science*, trans. Leo Gruliow and Rebecca Gruliow (New Brunswick, N.J.: Rutgers University Press, 1994). On Lysenko's influence in China, see Laurence Schneider, ed., *Lysenkoism in China: Proceedings of the 1956 Qingdao Genetics Symposium* (Armonk, N.Y.: M. E. Sharpe, 1987; Lawrence Schneider, *Biology and Revolution in Twentieth-Century China* (Lanham, Md.: Rowman & Littlefield, 2003), 117–85.

17. Interviews with Ye Yun, August 2001; and Ye Duyi, January 1995. Yu Duzhuang, 1991 ms (untitled), 88–90.

18. Ye Duzhuang, 1991 ms, 94–96.

19. Interview with Ye Lizhong, February 1995.

20. Hong Yung Lee, *From Revolutionary Cadres to Party Technocrats in Socialist China* (Berkeley: University of California Press, 1991), 35, 49.

21. Interviews with Ye Fang, spring 1995.

22. Ye Duzhuang, 1991 ms, 107–16; interview with Ye Durou, March 1995.

23. Interview with Chen Cheng, February 1995.

24. For a vivid picture of the privileged life in these compounds, see Jung Chang, *Wild Swans: Three Daughters of China* (New York: Anchor Books, 1992), 242–55.

25. Interviews with Ye Fang, 1995; Ye Xinxin, July 1997; Ye Lin, July 1997; Ye Bao, August 2001; Ye Binbin, August 2001; and Ye Yangyang, August 2001.

26. Sun Song, "Meishu riji" [Art diary], 1955, 8–11, 25–28, 54, 80. Some entries give these amounts in ten thousands of yuan, which was the official unit of currency, the much-inflated values of the 1940s having continued into the mid-1950s until the *wan* (ten thousand) multiplier was simply dropped.

27. Ye Duzhuang, "Guoyan yunyan" [Mist and clouds before my eyes], 1992 ms, 103–17; interview with Ye Liang, July 2002.

28. Ye Weili and Ma Xiaodong, *Growing Up in the People's Republic: Conversations between Two Daughters of China's Revolution* (New York: Palgrave Macmillan, 2005), 29.

29. Interview with Fang Shi, September 2001.

30. Ibid., 1995.

31. On the changing position of women in modern China, see Wang Zheng, *Women in the Chinese Enlightenment: Oral and Textual Histories* (Berkeley: University of California Press, 1999); Elisabeth Croll, *Changing Identities of Chinese Women: Rhetoric, Experience, and Self-Perception in the Twentieth Century* (Hong Kong: Hong Kong University Press, 1995); Kay Ann Johnson, *Women, the Family, and Peasant Revolution in China* (Chicago: University of Chicago Press, 1983); Margery Wolf, *Revolution Postponed: Women in Revolutionary China* (Stanford, Calif.: Stanford University Press, 1985); Neil J. Diamant, *Revolutionizing the Family: Politics, Love, and Divorce in Urban and Rural China, 1949–1968* (Berkeley: University of California Press, 2000).

32. Interviews with Fang Shi, 1995.

33. Ye Duzhuang, "Guoyan," 108–10, 112–13.

34. Interview with Ye Binbin, August 2001. Lin Ying's complaints are unveiled at length in her book, *Kanke de daolu* [Bumpy road] (Beijing: Dongfang wenhua guan, n.d.).

35. *Renmin ribao,* 15 January 1950, 28 February 1950.

36. Interview with Ye Duyi, January 1995.

37. Ye Duyi, *Sui jiu si,* 63–64.

38. Ye Duyi, *Sui jiu si,* 70–72; *Renmin ribao,* 12 November 1950.

39. Sheldon H. Harris, *Factories of Death: Japanese Biological Warfare, 1932–45, and the American Cover-up* (New York: Routledge, 2002); Hal Gold, *Unit 731: Testimony* (Tokyo: Yenbooks, 1996).

40. Resolution of the Presidium of the USSR Council of Ministers about Letters to the Ambassador of the USSR in the PRC, V. V. Kuznetsov, 2 May 1953, *Cold War International History Project Bulletin* 11. On the veracity of the charges, see Katherine Weatherby, "Deceiving the Deceivers: Moscow, Beijing, Pyongyang, and the Allegations of Bacteriological Weapons Use in Korea," *Cold War International History Project Bulletin* 11: 176–84; and Mil-

ton Leitenberg, "New Russian Evidence on the Korean War Biological Warfare Allegations: Background and Analysis," *Cold War International History Project Bulletin* 11: 185–99. For an interesting essay on the origins and implications of the Chinese germ-warfare experience, see Ruth Rogaski, "Nature, Annihilation, and Modernity: China's Korean War Germ-Warfare Experience Reconsidered," *Journal of Asian Studies* 61, no. 2 (May 2002): 381–415.

41. Interviews with Fang Shi, 1995, September 2001. *Renmin ribao*, 17 May 1952, carries the New China News Agency account. See also reproductions of written confessions by the two airmen, dated 8 and 14 April 1952, published in *Renmin ribao*, 6 May 1952.

42. Interviews with Fang Shi, 1995, September 2001.

43. Personnel document dated 6 July 1949; "Sixiang zizhuan" [Intellectual autobiography] and "Lishi zizhuan" [Historical autobiography], n.d. (1951?); "Ye Duzhuang zai da xuexi zhong buchong cailiao zhi er" [Ye Duzhuang's second group of supplementary materials for big study], September 1951, all from the Ye Duzhuang dossier in the Chinese Academy of Agricultural Sciences archives. This 135-page dossier appears remarkably complete up to the time of Ye Duzhuang's arrest in 1958. After that time, Public Security presumably handled his file and may have lost or removed some portions, because some pages are missing.

44. *Renmin ribao*, 12 November 1950.

45. Quotations from an undated fragment in the cadre appraisal section of the Ye Duzhuang dossier. The dossier lists the "corrupt" funds in the old inflated currency, yielding the impressive sum of 456,500 yuan.

46. Merle Goldman, "Hu Feng's Conflict with the Communist Literary Authorities," *China Quarterly* 12 (October–December 1962), 102–37; Andrew Endrey, "Hu Feng: Return of the Counter-Revolutionary," *Australian Journal of Chinese Affairs* 5 (January 1981): 73–90.

47. *Renmin ribao*, 17 June 1955.

48. The agent was Charles Fenn. See Ye Duzhuang memoirs, "Jiefang yihou," 26, "Yuzhong ji" [In prison], 1993 ms, 38–41; Yu Maochun, *The OSS in China: Prelude to Cold War* (New Haven, Conn.: Yale University Press, 1996), 207–8.

49. Ye Duzhuang, "Jiefang yihou," 24, 36–49; "Yuzhong ji," 37.

## 12. HUNDRED FLOWERS AND POISONOUS WEEDS

1. *Guangming ribao* [Guangming daily], 6 June 1957. This was the third and clearest statement of Ye Duyi's argument. See also 8 May 1957, on the original Tsinghua meeting, and 17 May 1957.

2. Ibid., 8 May 1957.

3. Ye Duyi, *Sui jiusi qi you weihui—bashi huiyi* [Despite nine deaths, I still have no regrets: memoirs at age eighty] (Beijing: Qunyan, 1994), 86.

4. *Guangming ribao*, 8 May 1957 [emphasis added].

5. Ye Duyi, *Sui jiusi*, 80, citing a "Central Work Summary" from Democratic League archives. In later publications of Mao's speech, his language is more circumspect: "Now it seems that the system of party committees in schools is perhaps inappropriate. It should be somewhat modified." Cited in Roderick MacFarquhar, Timothy Cheek, and Eugene Wu, eds., *The Secret Speeches of Chairman Mao: From the Hundred Flowers to the Great Leap Forward* (Cambridge, Mass.: Council on East Asian Studies, Harvard University, 1989), 367. This lat-

ter version may have been altered to make Mao's pronouncement more ambiguous, but Ye Duyi was certainly basing his suggestion on the version he heard on May 5. Shen Zhihua has argued that Mao's speech was earlier in the day in a meeting at Zhongnanhai. (Shen Zhihua, *Sikao yu xuanze: cong zhizhifenzi huiyi dao fanyou yundong* [English title: Reflections and Choice: The Consciousness of the Chinese Intellectuals and the Anti-Rightist Campaign (1956-1957)] [Hong Kong: Chinese University of Hong Kong Press, 2009], 521n).

6. On the Hundred Flowers Movement, see Roderick MacFarquhar, *The Origins of the Cultural Revolution*, vol. 1, *Contradictions among the People, 1956-1957* (New York: Columbia University Press, 1974), and *The Hundred Flowers Campaign and the Chinese Intellectuals* (New York: Praeger, 1960); for an authoritative recent Chinese study, see Shen Zhihua, *Sikao yu xuanze*. For Mao's speech, see Mao Zedong, "On the Correct Handling of Contradictions among the People (Speaking Notes)," 27 February 1957, translated in MacFarquhar, Cheek, and Wu, *Secret Speeches*, 131-89.

7. MacFarquhar, *Origins*, vol. 1, 169-76. Quote is from a Mao speech of November 1956, cited on 171.

8. Mao Zedong, "On the Correct Handling of Contradictions," in MacFarquhar, Cheek and Wu, *Secret Speeches*, 178.

9. Ibid., 134.

10. Ibid., 143.

11. Ibid., 141-44.

12. Ibid., 162.

13. Ibid., 170-71, 173, 175.

14. MacFarquhar, *Origins*, vol. 1, 186-87; Shen Zhihua, *Sikao yu xuanze*, 483-85.

15. *Guangming ribao*, 8 May 1957.

16. Ye Duyi, *Sui jiusi*, 73; Dai Huang, *Jiusi yishen: wo de "youpai" licheng* [Nine deaths, one life: my experience as a "rightist"] (Beijing: Zhongyang bianyi chubanshe, 1998), 1-2.

17. Xu Yiguan, *Guangming ribao*, 6 June 1957, in MacFarquhar, *Hundred Flowers*, 68.

18. MacFarquhar, *Origins*, vol. 1, 200. The phrase belonged to Fei Xiaotong, the American-trained anthropologist. Fei's article was published in *Renmin ribao* [People's daily], 24 March 1957.

19. Ye Duyi, *Sui jiusi*, 75-76.

20. *Renmin ribao*, 17 May 1957.

21. Ibid., 17 May 1957; *Guangming ribao*, 17 May 1957.

22. *Guangming ribao*, 23 May 1957.

23. MacFarquhar's *Hundred Flowers* provides a useful collection of these criticisms.

24. Cited and translated in MacFarquhar, *Hundred Flowers*, 87-88. On the movement on the campuses, see Rene Goldman, "The Rectification Campaign at Peking University: May-June 1957," *China Quarterly* 12 (October-December 1962):138-53; and MacFarquhar, *Hundred Flowers*, 77-114, 174-94.

25. On worker activism in 1957, see Elizabeth J. Perry, "Shanghai's Strike Wave of 1957," *China Quarterly* (March 1994): 1-27.

26. Min Ganghou in *Renmin ribao*, 4 July 1957, provides the fullest account of this meeting. Also translated in MacFarquhar, *Hundred Flowers*, 167-70.

27. Shen Zhihua, *Sikao yu xuanze*, 551–62; Li Shenzhi, "Mao zhuxi shi shenme shihou jueding yinshe chudong de" [When did Mao decide to lure the snake out of the hole?], in *Liuyue xue: jiyizhong de fanyou yundong* [Snow in June: memories of the Anti-Rightist Campaign], ed. Niu Han and Deng Jiuping (Beijing: Jingji ribao chubanshe, 1998), 114.

28. MacFarquhar, *Hundred Flowers*, 261–65; Shen Zhihua, *Sikao yu xuanze*, 563–628; *Guangming ribao*, 9 June 1957.

29. *Renmin ribao*, 14 June 1957; cf. *Guangming ribao*, 14 June 1957.

30. *Guangming ribao*, editorial, 14 June 1957.

31. *Renmin ribao*, 16 and 19 June 1957; *Guangming ribao*, 27 June 1957.

32. *Renmin ribao*, 15 July 1957.

33. MacFarquhar, *Origins*, vol. 1, 262–69.

34. *Renmin ribao*, 27 June 1957, 11 and 17 July 1957, 12 August 1957, 3 September 1957. Quote is from Shi Liang accusation in 28 August 1957.

35. Ibid., 28 August 1957. For Pu Xixiu's (Luo's partner's) accusations, see *Renmin ribao*, 13 August 1957. For more on Pu Xixiu's role, see Hu Ping, *Chanji—1957: Kunan de jitan* [Zen spell—1957: an altar of bitterness], vol. 1 (Guangzhou: Guangdong lüyou chubanshe, 2000), 390–96.

36. The entire document is reproduced in Ye Duiyi, *Sui jiusi*, 97–112.

37. Interview with Ye Duyi, January 1995.

38. Ye Duyi, *Sui jiusi*, quotes from 110–12.

39. Ibid., 97; interviews with Ye Duyi, January 1995; and Ye Weizhen, August 2001.

40. Ye Duyi, *Sui jiusi*, 112; interview with Ye Yun, August 2001.

41. Shuping Yao, "Chinese Intellectuals and Science History at the Chinese Academy of Sciences," *Science in Context* 3, no. 2 (Autumn 1989): 455–56.

42. Interviews with Fang Shi, summer 1995, September 2001.

43. Seven percent is the figure Fang Shi recalled, but he also said that some fifteen to eighteen were labeled rightists out of a total of over two hundred. Dai Huang, one of his victims, says that 20 percent of the employees in the domestic bureau were accused (Dai Huang, *Jiusi yisheng*, 83).

44. Dai Huang, *Jiusi yisheng*, 76–90, 272–303; Hu Ping, *Chanji*, vol. 1, 419–24; interviews with Fang Shi, September 2001.

45. *Nongye kexue tongxun* (Newsletter of Agricultural Science), 1957.4.

46. Chen Gengtao, " 'Xueshu ziyou' he 'ganshang guoji shuiping' " ["Academic freedom" and "reaching international standards"], *Nongye kexue tongxun*, 1957.11: 623–24. On Lysenko in China, see Laurence Schneider, *Biology and Revolution in Twentieth-Century China* (Lanham, Md.: Rowman & Littlefield, 2003), 117–211.

47. Zu Deming, "Fensui youpai yinmou, jianding de xuexi Sulian nongye kexue xianjin jingyan" [Smash the rightist conspiracy, resolutely study the advanced experience of Soviet agriculture], *Nongye kexue tongxun*, 1957.11: 605–6.

48. See the covers for *Nongye kexue tongxun* 1957.4, 1957.6, and 1957.7.

49. "Ye Duzhuang diyici jiaodai" [Ye Duzhuang's first confession], 14 August [1957], Ye Duzhuang dossier. Section 5 of Ye Duzhuang's dossier in the Chinese Academy of Agricultural Sciences archives, "Zhengzhi lishi qingkuang de shencha cailiao" [Investigation mate-

rials on political history], is devoted to this period. It includes records of his forum talks, materials organized for criticism of his case, confessions, and judgments on punishments. All of the archival sources for this narrative come from that section of the dossier.

50. Ye Duzhuang, "Wo dui dang xian tichu wuge wenti—wei shenme Huabei suo xueshu kongqi shifen baoruo?" [I have five questions for the party: why is the academic environment at the North China Institute so feeble?] n.d. [1957], Ye Duzhuang dossier.

51. Gao Huimin (Chinese Academy of Agricultural Sciences, Soil and Fertilizer Institute), "Shishi sheng yu xiongbian" [Facts speak louder than words], *Nongye kexue tongxun*, 1957.11: 624–25; Ye Duzhuang dossier, section 5.

52. Gao Huimin, "Shishi," 625.

53. "Minmeng Huabei nongyansuo zhibu zuotanhui zhaiyao" [Summary of the Democratic League forum of the North China Agricultural Research Institute branch], n.d. [May 1957?], Ye Duzhuang dossier.

54. *Nongye kexue tongxun*, 1957.11: 476–77; Ye Duzhuang, "Yuzhong ji" [In prison], 1993 ms, 2–5.

55. *Guangming ribao*, 4 June 1957. The documents in his dossier repeatedly mention this article, suggesting the party's irritation at his comments. Document no. 5–3, untitled and undated, stamped *jimi* (secret), and the following untitled document in Ye Duzhuang dossier.

56. Ye Duzhuang, "Yuzhong ji," 11–12.

57. "Chedi quanmian bodao youpai fenzi Ye Duzhuang de fandong yanlun" [Thoroughly repudiate the reactionary ideas of the rightist Ye Duzhuang], Ye Duzhuang dossier.

58. " 'Neihang' waiyi bei bodiao, yupai fenzi Ye Duzhuang dangzhong chuchou" [His "expert" cloak removed, the rightist Ye Duzhuang makes a fool of himself in public], *Nongye kexue tongxun*, 1957.11: 630–31.

59. Ibid.

60. John Lossing Buck, *Land Utilization in China* (Shanghai: University of Nanking, 1937), and *Land Utilization in China: Statistics* (Shanghai: University of Nanking, 1937). For an analysis of these and other sources on land tenure, see Joseph W. Esherick, "Number Games: A Note on Land Distribution in Prerevolutionary China," *Modern China* 7, no. 4 (October 1981): 387–411.

61. "Renshi dang'an biao" [Personnel registry], 27 July 1949, Ye Duzhuang dossier. Document no. 5–3, untitled and undated, Ye Duzhuang dossier.

62. Ibid.; "Chedi quanmian bodao youpai fenzi Ye Duzhuang de fandong yanlun," Ye Duzhuang dossier.

63. This was Xin Zhichao, a party member whom Duzhuang had long listed as a reference on his past history. See "Ye Duzhuang suo jiaodai de zuijin de pengyou youpai fenzi [Li] Huangwu yu Zhang Yunchuan" [Recent friends confessed by Ye Duzhuang: rightists Li Huangwu and Zhang Yunchuan], 21 August 1957, Ye Duzhuang dossier.

64. *Renmin ribao*, 4 December 1957.

65. Ye Duzhuang, "Jiefang yihou" [After liberation], 1991 ms, 55–56; interview with Ye Liang, July 2002.

66. "Shenqing laodong jiaoyang chengpi biao" [Education through labor application form], 5 February 1958, Ye Duzhuang dossier.

67. Ministry of Agriculture order, 30 March 1958, Ye Duzhuang dossier.

68. Untitled notes on Ye Duzhuang's confession at forum of 28 June 1958, Ye Duzhuang dossier.

69. Ye Duzhuang, "Jiefang yihou," 60–62; "Yuzhong ji," 17–18.

70. Ye Duzhuang, "Jiefang yihou," 62–69, "Yuzhong ji," 19–28.

71. Order from the Ministry of Agriculture Rectification Group, 8 August 1958, Ye Duzhuang dossier.

72. On the Taiwan Straits crisis, see Chen Jian, *Mao's China and the Cold War* (Chapel Hill: University of North Carolina Press, 2001), ch. 7.

73. For other accounts of the Chinese interrogation regimen at the Caolanzi Detention Center, see Allyn Rickett and Adele Rickett, *Prisoners of Liberation* (New York: Cameron Associates, 1957); and Bao Ruo-Wang (Jean Pasqualini) and Rudolph Chelminski, *Prisoner of Mao* (New York: Coward, McCann and Geoghegan, 1973).

74. Ye Duzhuang, "Jiefang yihou," 72–81; "Yuzhong ji," 30–34, 38–54. The focus on his postwar contacts with the Americans is clear throughout Ye Duzhuang's dossier.

75. Harry Wu and Carolyn Wakeman, *Bitter Winds: A Memoir of My Years in China's Gulag* (New York: John Wiley, 1994), 62–130; Bao Ruo-Wang and Chelminski, *Prisoner of Mao*, 208–58.

76. Ye Duzhuang, "Jiefang yihou," 92–95, "Yuzhong ji," 91. He would redo this translation in the 1970s, and it was published in 1982: *Renlei de youlai ji xingxuanze* [The Descent of Man, and Selection in Relation to Sex] by Charles Darwin, trans. Ye Duzhuang and Yang Xizhi (Beijing: Xinhua shudian, 1982).

77. Ye Duzhuang, "Yuzhong ji," 93.

78. Roderick MacFarquhar, *The Origins of the Cultural Revolution*, vol. 3, *The Coming of the Cataclysm, 1961–1966* (New York: Columbia University Press, 1997), 23–120; Merle Goldman, *China's Intellectuals: Advise and Dissent* (Cambridge, Mass.: Harvard University Press, 1981), 18–60; Dali Yang, *Calamity and Reform in China: State, Rural Society, and Institutional Change Since the Great Leap Famine* (Stanford, Calif.: Stanford University Press, 1996), 21–94.

79. Ye Duzhuang, "Yuzhong ji," 136–38.

80. Interviews with Fang Shi, 1995, 2001.

81. Ye Duzhuang, "Yuzhong ji," 139–53.

82. This is the view of his well-informed brother Fang Shi (1995 interview). On the politics of this period, see MacFarquhar, *Origins*, vol. 3, 137–283.

83. On American-supported Nationalist military provocations, see Qi Jianmin, *Guoshi jishi benmo (1949–1999)*, vol 4, *Shehui zhuyi tansuo shiqi (xia)* [A complete narrative history of the PRC (1949–1979), vol. 4, part 2: the socialist experiment] (Shenyang: Liaoning renmin chubanshe, 2003), 150–55. On the New China News Agency report, see Mao Zedong, *Jianguo yilai Mao Zedong wengao* [Mao Zedong's writings since the founding of the PRC] (Beijing: Zhongyang wenxian chubanshe, 1996), vol. 10, 101–3.

84. "Renshi dang'an biao" [Personnel form], 27 September 1949, Ye Duzhuang dossier.

## 13. THE CULTURAL REVOLUTION

1. Interview with Fang Shi, September 2001; *Peking Review*, 1960.

2. Jasper Becker, *Hungry Ghosts: Mao's Secret Famine* (New York: Free Press, 1996); Ralph

A. Thaxton, Jr., *Catastrophe and Contention in Rural China: Mao's Great Leap Forward Famine and the Origins of Righteous Resistance in Da Fo Village* (Cambridge: Cambridge University Press, 2008).

3. Interview with Fang Shi, September 2001.

4. See Roderick MacFarquhar and Michael Schoenhals, *Mao's Last Revolution* (Cambridge, Mass.: Harvard University Press, 2006), 69, where they note that Deng was probably not the original source of this slogan.

5. By far the best study of the origins of the Cultural Revolution is Roderick MacFarquhar, *The Origins of the Cultural Revolution*, vol. 3: *The Coming of the Cataclysm, 1961–66* (New York: Columbia University Press, 1997).

6. Among the wealth of memoirs and scholarly studies of the Red Guards, the most notable are Gordon A. Bennett and Ronald N. Montaperto, *Red Guard: The Political Biography of Dai Hsiao-ai* (Garden City, N.Y.: Doubleday, 1971); Gao Yuan, *Born Red: A Chronicle of the Cultural Revolution* (Stanford, Calif.: Stanford University Press, 1987); Liang Heng and Judith Shapiro, *Son of the Revolution* (New York: Knopf, 1983); Hong Yung Lee, *The Politics of the Chinese Cultural Revolution: A Case Study* (Berkeley: University of California Press, 1980); Anita Chan, Stanley Rosen, and Jonathan Unger, "Students and Class Warfare: The Social Roots of the Red Guard Conflict in Guangzhou (Canton)," *China Quarterly* 83 (September 1980): 397–446; Stanley Rosen, *Red Guard Factionalism and the Cultural Revolution in Guangzhou (Canton)* (Boulder: Westview Press, 1982); Andrew G. Walder, *Fractured Rebellion: The Beijing Red Guard Movement* (Cambridge, Mass.: Harvard University Press, 2009).

7. Interview with Ye Binbin, August 2001.

8. Interview with Ye Yun, August 2001.

9. Interviews with Ye Binbin, August 2001; and Ye Yangyang, August 2001.

10. Interview with Ye Binbin, August 2001.

11. Ibid.

12. Ibid. The fact that Ye Fang was seized by the Liaoning Rebel Alliance (Liaolian), which is usually regarded as the Red Guard unit affiliated with the civilian party leaders like Ye Fang is puzzling. (Fang Zhang, "Mao Zedong dui Zhou Enlai—gonghe juezhan" [Mao Zedong vs. Zhou Enlai, the final battle of the PRC], Huaxia wenzhai zengkan: wenge bowuguan tongxun (China News Digest, Cultural Revolution newsletter), supplement no. 473, 2006.1.3, www.cnd .org/HXWZ/ZKO6/zk473.gb.html (viewed on 1 September 2006). However, a Red Guard publication sympathetic to the PLA and the left, *Erwen mudu* [What we have heard and seen], no. 1–47 (Liaoning: 1967), shows the extent to which the Rebel Alliance had splintered by this time. (My thanks to Michael Schoenhals for providing a copy of this source.)

13. John Israel and Donald W. Klein, *Rebels and Bureaucrats: China's December 9ers* (Berkeley: University of California Press, 1976), 268–82.

14. Lin Ying, *Kanke de daolu* [Bumpy road] (Beijing: Dongfang wenhua guan, n.d. [1994 preface], 51–58, 119–24.

15. Interview with Fang Shi, 1995.

16. Interviews with Ye Duzheng, May 1995.

17. Ye Duyi, *Sui jiusi qi you weihui—bashi huiyi* [Despite nine deaths, I still have no regrets: memoirs at age eighty] (Beijing: Qunyan, 1994), 114–69. During his lengthy imprisonment with neither watch nor calendar, Ye Duyi made a daily habit of reciting to himself an

account of his prison experience, a practice he continued until Mao Zedong's death and the arrest of the Gang of Four. Then he wrote down the account on which this section is based.

18. Puyi, *From Emperor to Citizen: The Autobiography of Aisin-Gioro Pu Yi*, trans. W. J. F. Jenner (Oxford: Oxford University Press, 1987). The Chinese original was published in 1964.

19. Ye Duyi, *Sui jiusi*, 114, 119–20.

20. Ibid., 130.

21. On conditions in Qincheng, see MacFarquhar and Schoenhals, *Mao's Last Revolution*, 342–45; for a first-person prisoner's account, see Sidney Rittenberg, Sr., and Amanda Bennett, *The Man Who Stayed Behind* (Durham, N.C.: Duke University Press, 2001), 387–432.

22. Ye Duzhuang, "Yuzhong ji" [In prison], 1993 ms, 188–208.

23. Interview with Ye Weizhen, August 2001.

24. Interviews with Ye Yangyang, August 2001; and Ye Binbin, August 2001.

25. Interviews with Ye Bao, August 2001; and Ye Xinxin, August 2001.

26. Interview with Ye Binbin, August 2001.

27. Interview with Ye Yangyang, August 2001.

28. Interview with Ye Xinxin, August 2001.

29. Ibid., July 1997.

30. Interview with Ye Binbin, August 2001.

31. Ibid.

32. Ibid.; interview with Ye Xinxin, July 1997; Lin Ying, *Kanke de daolu*, 140–41.

33. "Talk to the Leaders of the Center," 21 July 1966, in *Chairman Mao Talks to the People: Talks and Letters, 1956–1971*, ed. Stuart Schram (New York: Pantheon, 1974), 253.

34. Ye Duzhuang, "Yuzhong ji," 77–78.

35. Interview with Ye Duzheng, June 1997.

36. Yan Jiaqi and Gao Gao, *Turbulent Decade: A History of the Cultural Revolution*, trans. and ed. D. W. Y. Kwok (Honolulu: University of Hawaii Press, 1996), 101–8.

37. Richard Curt Kraus, *Class Conflict in Chinese Socialism* (New York: Columbia University Press, 1981), 89–114.

38. MacFarquhar and Schoenhals, *Mao's Last Revolution*, 385.

39. Frederick C. Tiewes and Warren Sun, *The Tragedy of Lin Biao: Riding the Tiger during the Cultural Revolution, 1966–1971* (Honolulu: University of Hawaii Press, 1996); Jin Qiu, *The Culture of Power: The Lin Biao Incident in the Cultural Revolution* (Stanford, Calif.: Stanford University Press, 1999), 137 ff.

40. Interviews with Ye Duzheng, June 1997.

41. On the rustification of urban youth, see Thomas P. Bernstein, *Up to the Mountains and Down to the Villages: The Transfer of Youth from Urban to Rural China* (New Haven, Conn.: Yale University Press, 1977).

42. On the Lin Biao incident, see Tiewes and Sun, *The Tragedy of Lin Biao;* Jin Qiu, *The Culture of Power.*

43. On the late stages of the Cultural Revolution, see MacFarquhar and Schoenhals, *Mao's Last Revolution*, 253 ff.; Yan and Gao, *Turbulent Decade*, 337 ff.

44. Interviews with Fang Shi, 1995.

45. Interviews with Ye Binbin, August 2001; Ye Yangyang, August 2001; and Ye Xinxin, July 1997.

46. Interviews with Ye Duzheng, September 1994, June 1997.

47. Ye Duyi, *Sui jiusi,* 168.

48. Harry Wu and Carolyn Wakeman, *Bitter Winds: A Memoir of My Years in China's Gulag* (New York: John Wiley, 1994), 236–38.

49. The release order is reproduced in Ye Duzhuang, "Yuzhong ji," 231–32.

50. Ibid., 241–43.

## EPILOGUE: AFTER THE DELUGE

1. See Richard Baum, *Burying Mao: Chinese Politics in the Age of Deng Xiaoping* (Princeton, N.J.: Princeton University Press, 1994); Randall Peerenboom, *China Modernizes: Threat to the West or Model for the Rest?* (Oxford: Oxford University Press, 2007); Yasheng Huang, *Capitalism with Chinese Characteristics: Entrepreneurship and the State* (Cambridge: Cambridge University Press, 2008).

2. Barry Naughton, *Growing Out of the Plan: Chinese Economic Reform, 1978–1993* (Cambridge: Cambridge University Press, 1995); and *The Chinese Economy: Transitions and Growth* (Cambridge, Mass.: MIT Press, 2007).

3. See the English-language volume he edited and contributed to: Duzheng Ye, Congbin Fu, Jiping Chao, and M. Yoshino, eds., *The Climate of China and Global Climate* (Beijing: China Ocean Press, 1987).

4. Zhou Jianbin and Pu Yifen, *Qiuzhen qiushi deng gaofeng—Ye Duzheng* [Ascending the heights seeking truth and facts—Ye Duzheng] (Beijing: Xinhua chubanshe, 2008).

5. *Daerwen jinhualun quanji* [Darwin's Complete Works on Evolution], 13 vols. (Beijing: Kexue chubanshe, 1994–96).

6. Ye Duyi, *Sui jiu si qi you weihui—bashi huiyi* [Despite nine deaths, I still have no regrets: memoirs at age eighty] (Beijing: Qunyan, 1994), 179.

7. Ye Lizhong with Zhang Jilou, *Wai jiaoshu: chuantong xiangsheng ji* [Crooked teaching: a collection of traditional comic dialogues] (Chengdu: Sichuan renmin chubanshe, 1980); and *Guaibing guaizhi: chuantong xiangsheng ji* [Strange cures for strange ills: a collection of traditional comic dialogues] (Chengdu: Sichuan renmin chubanshe, 1984).

8. On *Yanhuang chunqiu,* see http://en.wordpress.com/tag/yanhuang-chunqiu/ (accessed 28 August 2009)

9. Interviews with Ye Binbin, August 2001.

10. Interviews with Ye Bao, August 2001.

11. Interview with Ye Weijia, September 2009.

12. For example, there is no evidence among these Ye women of poetry writing such as that described by Susan Mann in *The Talented Women of the Zhang Family* (Berkeley: University of California Press, 2007).

13. *Ye-shi zupu* [Ye family genealogy] (n.p.: 1944), 7:16b.

# GLOSSARY

ba　跋

Bai Tian　白天

*baohuang*　保皇

*baojia*　保甲

*beiji*　碑記

*caoshou*　操守

Chen Fengtong　陳鳳桐

*daotai*　道台

*duli*　獨立

Fang Shi　方實

*fengshui*　風水

*fenyan*　憤言

*fulanshimen*　腐爛尸們

*fumu guan*　父母官

*gaofeng*　誥封

*geji*　歌姬

*gongsheng*　貢生

*guojia zhuyi de minzu*　國家主義的民族

*hezhuan*　合傳

*huiguan*　會館

Ji (generation name)　積

*jiafan*　家範

*jianbi qingye*　堅壁清野

*jiansheng*　監生

*jielüe*　節略

*jinshi*　進士

*juan*　卷

Juanshu ju　捐輸局

Junxu zongju　軍需總局

*juren*　舉人

*kang*　炕

Li Boyuan　李博元

Liang Siyi　梁思懿

*liche meng*　笠車盟

*likin* [*lijin*]　釐金

Lin Ying　林鶯

Liu Hongsheng　劉鴻生

*luanren*　亂人

Ma Zhanshan　馬占山

*mantou*　饅頭

Mao Changxi　毛昶熙

*minzu chaoliu*　民族潮流

357

| | | | |
|---|---|---|---|
| *mo* 末 | | *yanjiuyuan* 研究員 | |
| *mu* 畝 | | Yao Zengyi 姚曾廙 | |
| *neican* 內參 | | Ye Bao 葉寶 | |
| *nianpu* 年譜 | | Ye Binbin 葉濱濱 | |
| *nüzan* 女贊 | | Ye Boli 葉勃力 | |
| *pailou* 牌樓 | | Ye Boying 葉伯英 | |
| *qiju* 契據 | | Ye Chongju 葉崇榘 | |
| *qinggao sixiang* 清高思想 | | Ye Chongshi 葉崇實 | |
| *qingnian* 青年 | | Ye Chongzhi 葉崇質 | |
| *sange* 三哥 | | Ye Cuizhang 葉萃章 | |
| *sangou* 三狗 | | Ye Ducheng 葉篤成 | |
| *sanye* 三爺 | | Ye Dulian 葉篤廉 | |
| *shafumo* 殺父魔 | | Ye Duquan 葉篤全 | |
| *shaobing* 燒餅 | | Ye Duren 葉篤仁 | |
| *shengyuan* 生員 | | Ye Durou 葉篤柔 | |
| *shentong* 神童 | | Ye Dushen 葉篤慎 | |
| *shipai* 世派 | | Ye Dushi 葉篤詩 | |
| *shou* 首 | | Ye Dusong 葉篤頌 | |
| *shou Tian zhiyou, yugu weixin* 受天之佑, | | Ye Duxin 葉篤信 | |
| 與古為新 | | Ye Duya 葉篤雅 | |
| *sidang* 死黨 | | Ye Duyi 葉篤義 | |
| Sun Song 孫竦 | | Ye Duzhi 葉篤智 | |
| *tewu* 特務 | | Ye Duzheng 葉篤正 | |
| *tongnian* 同年 | | Ye Duzhuang 葉篤莊 | |
| *waihang* 外行 | | Ye Fang 葉方 | |
| Wang Ruolan 王若蘭 | | Ye Hua 葉華 | |
| *wuxing zuzhi* 無形組織 | | Ye Jingchang 葉景昌 | |
| *xiaojie* 小姐 | | Ye Kunhou 葉坤厚 | |
| *xingshu* 行述 | | Ye Lian 葉蓮 | |
| *xingzhuang* 行狀 | | Ye Shanrong 葉善鎔 | |
| *xinzeng jiagui* 新增家規 | | Ye Sheng'er 葉盛二 | |
| *xu* 序 | | Ye Shuliang 葉叔亮 | |
| Xu Bing 徐冰 | | Ye Weijia 葉維佳 | |
| Xu Shichang 徐世昌 | | Ye Weijiang 葉維江 | |
| *yamen* 衙門 | | Ye Weili 葉維麗 | |

Ye Xinxin    葉新新

Ye Yangyang    葉楊楊

Ye Yuanqi    葉元琦

Ye Yun    葉運

Ye Yuting    葉玉廷

Yiguandao    一貫道

*yixing*    逸行

*youtiao*    油條

*zhai zhuang zhong zheng*    齋莊中正

Zhang Boling    張伯苓

Zhang Xiluan    張錫鑾

Zhao (generation name)    兆

Zhengzhi falü weiyuanhui    政治法律委員會

*zhongpu*    忠僕

Zhou Fu    周馥

Zhou Xuexi    周學熙

Zhu Fengyang    朱鳳陽

*zhuan*    傳

*zongyan*    縱言

*zuotan hui*    座談會

# SELECTED YE FAMILY BIBLIOGRAPHY

General secondary works are fully cited in the notes. The sources here relate specifically related to the Ye family.

Ding Ning丁宁. "Fang Ye-shi wu xiongdi" 访叶氏五兄弟 [Interviews with five Ye brothers]. *Huanghe* 黄河 84, no. 2 (2000): 55–58.

Fang Shi 方实. "Bu ke momie de jiyi—jinian Mao Zedong danchen 100 zhounian" 不可磨灭的记忆—纪念毛泽东诞辰100周年 [An ineradicable memory—celebrating the 100th anniversary of Mao Zedong's birth]. *Laonian shenghuo* 老年生活 26 December 1993: 1–8.

———. "Jinzhang de gongzuo, yan'ge de xunlian—Xibaipo bianji shenghuo huiyi" 紧张的工作，严格的训练—西柏坡编辑生活回忆 [Stressful work, rigorous training—a memoir of editorial life at Xibaipo]. In *Xinhua she huiyilu* 新华社回忆录, ed. Xinhuashe xinwen yanjiusuo, 221–229. Beijing: Xinhua, 1986.

———. "Tongxin qing shizhen—jinian wo he Bai Tian jiehun 50 zhounian" 同心情始真—纪念我和白天结婚50周年 [With hearts united, our feelings are true—celebrating fifty years of marriage to Bai Tian]. Xinhua internal newsletter, 1989.

Lin Ying 林莺, *Kanke de daolu* 坎坷的道路 [Bumpy road]. Beijing: Dongfang wenhua guan, n.d. [1994 preface].

*Shaanxi weimo, Guangxu shisi nian* 陕西闱墨,光绪十四年 [Shaanxi examination essays, 1888]. N.p.: Hengjiantang, [1888?].

Sun Song 孙竦. "Meishu riji" 美术日记 [Art diary]. Fragment, ms, 1955.

———. "Suixiang" 隨想 [Random thoughts]. Ms, 1944–45.

———. "Wenyi riji" 文藝日記 [Literary diary]. Ms, 1938–39, 1941–45.

Ye Boying 葉伯英. *Gengjing tang nianpu* 耕經堂年譜 [Chronological autobiography from the hall for cultivating the classics]. Undated ms in Beijing Library.

Ye Duyi 叶笃义. *Sui jiusi qi you weihui—bashi huiyi* 虽九死其犹未悔—八十回忆 [Despite nine deaths, I still have no regrets: memoirs at age eighty]. Beijing: Qunyan, 1994.

Ye Duzhuang 叶笃庄. 1937 Diary, 1937. Ms.

———. "Guoyan yunyan" 过眼云烟 [Mist and clouds before my eyes], 1992. Ms.

———. *Huabei mianhua ji qi zengchan wenti* 華北棉花及其增產問題 [Cotton in north China and the problem of increasing output]. Nanjing: National Resources Commission, 1948.

———. "Jiefang yihou" 解放以后 [After liberation], 1991. Ms.

———. Personnel dossier. Chinese Academy of Agricultural Sciences archives, Beijing.

———. Untitled manuscript on the family in Tianjin, 1991.

———. "Yuzhong ji" 狱中纪 [In prison], 1993. Ms.

Ye Kunhou 葉坤厚. *Jiangshang xiao Penglai yinhang shicun* 江上小蓬萊吟航詩存 [Surviving poems to recite while sailing by Little Penglai (Anqing) on the Yangzi]. Shaanxi: privately published by Ye Boying, 1883.

*Ye-shi zupu* 葉氏族譜 [Ye family genealogy]. N.p.: 1944.

Ye Shuliang 葉叔亮. *Tui'an shigao* 退庵詩稿 [Poems from a retirement cottage]. N.p.: 1918.

Ye Weili and Ma Xiaodong. *Growing Up in the People's Republic: Conversations between Two Daughters of China's Revolution.* New York: Palgrave Macmillan, 2005.

Yeh Tu Yi (Ye Duyi). "The Development of International Organization." Thesis, Department of Political Science and the College of Public Affairs, Yenching University, May 1934.

Zhou Jiabin 周家斌 and Pu Yifen 浦一芬. *Qiuzhen qiushi deng gaofeng—Ye Duzheng* 求真求实登高峰—叶笃正 [Ascending the heights seeking truth and facts—Ye Duzheng]. Beijing: Xinhua chubanshe, 2008.

# INDEX

abortion, 236

agriculture: under Communism, 225, 228–29, 256, 261, 265, 278–79, 290, 301–2; imperial officials' attention to, 42, 57, 68, 71, 81, 86, 89, 96, 117; in economy of China, 37, 42, 61–62, 85, 166; modernization of, 108, 166–67, 169; rebellions' effects on, 67, 93; in war effort, 204; Ye Duzhuang and, 213–14, 229; as Ye family livelihood, 18, 28, 29–31, 37, 40

Anhui province: guildhall, 121, 125, 158; origin of, 3; damage to, from rebellions, 66–67, 79; in Nian Rebellion, 55–56, 60, 62–63; in PRC, 278; in Taiping Rebellion, 15, 18; Ye family residents in, 3, 15, 18, 66, 79, 87, 124, 133–34

Anqing: damage to, from rebellions, 10, 67, 79; political and cultural significance, 3–4; in Taiping rebellion, 4–5, 8, 10–11, 14, 17; Ye family residents in, 3–5, 17, 18, 21, 28, 29, 31, 36, 99–100

antiques. *See* elite: lifestyle

Anti-Rightist Campaign (1957), 257–63, 273, 279

Ba Jin, 161

Bai Tian, 203–8, 240

Baoding, 82, 84, 85, 86, 92, 105, 106, 135

*baojia* (household registration system), 87, 93, 96

Beijing (or Beiping): anti-Japanese student movement in, 173, 175; in anti-Japanese war, 171–72, 179; in Boxer rebellion, 105; move of national government from (1927), 137; Ye family residents in, 146, 159, 163, 186, 209, 211, 215, 218, 226, 231, 238, 285, 289, 298, 304, 305, 311

Beiyang College, 163

birth order, 29, 37, 129, 132, 134, 150, 157–58, 232

Bo Yibo, 181

*Book of Changes (Yijing)*, 38, 79, 96, 285

bourgeois(ie): "national," 268; as negative term in PRC, 239, 247, 259, 260, 261, 262, 266, 280, 283, 285, 295; status under Communism, 224, 226, 253, 259, 260, 262, 268, 280, 315; peasants as, 253

Boxer Uprising, 104–6, 111, 120, 123, 154, 169, 170–71, 180

Boy Scouts, 145, 150, 314

broadcasting, 132, 140–41, 187, 208

brothers: differences among, 146, 150, 158, 166, 218, 262; relations among, 23, 37, 38, 47–48, 158, 218, 238–39, 275, 294, 298, 304, 309. *See also* birth order

Buck, John Lossing, 268

bureaucracy, 51–52: clerks, 51–52, 59, 71, 87; inefficiency, 90, 251, 264; infighting among, 44. *See also* officials

burial, 26, 27, 29, 31, 79, 85, 99, 101, 121, 146, 291

Burke, James, 213, 248, 272

TEXT

10/12.5 Minion Pro

DISPLAY

Minion Pro

COMPOSITOR

Integrated Composition Systems

CARTOGRAPHER

Bill Nelson

PRINTER AND BINDER

Sheridan Books, Inc.